LITIGATING HEALTH RIGHTS

LITIGATING HEALTH RIGHTS

Can Courts Bring More Justice to Health?

Edited by Alicia Ely Yamin and Siri Gloppen

Human Rights Program Series
Harvard Law School

Harvard University Press

The International Human Rights Clinic at Harvard Law School's Human Rights Program publishes a "Human Rights Program Series" of books with Harvard University Press. Books in this series are designed to further interdisciplinary scholarship and practical understanding of leading human rights issues.

International Human Rights Clinic
Human Rights Program
Harvard Law School
1563 Massachusetts Avenue
Pound Hall 401
Cambridge, MA 02138
United States of America

hrp@law.harvard.edu
www.hup.harvard.edu

Printed in the United States of America

ISBN: 978-0-979-63955-5

Library of Congress Cataloging-in-Publication Data

Litigating health rights : can courts bring more justice to health / edited by Alicia Ely Yamin and Siri Gloppen.
p. cm. — (Human rights practice series)
Includes bibliographical references and index.
ISBN 978-0-9796395-5-5
1. Medical care—Law and legislation. 2. Right to health. 3. Health services accessibility. 4. Medical policy. 5. Right to health—Cross-cultural studies. 6. Health services accessibility—Cross-cultural studies. I. Yamin, Alicia Ely. II. Gloppen, Siri.
K3601.L57 2011
344.03'21—dc23 2011017921

Printed by Signature Book Printing, www.sbpbooks.com

CONTENTS

Acknowledgments

This book would not have happened but for the contributions of individuals and institutions in many parts of the globe. First, we thank the Norwegian Research Council for generously funding this project through a grant from its programs for global health research (GLOBVAC) and development research (FRIMUF); this funding permitted both empirical investigations and critical opportunities to come together and share ideas. We extend special thanks to Bruce M. Wilson and Ole Frithjof Norheim for their initial ideas and contributions to the research proposal. The institutions of several of the book's contributors also provided support, including Harvard Law School, Warwick University Law School, San Andrés Law School, the Universidad Torcuato di Tella, the University of Bergen, and the project's host institution, the Chr. Michelsen Institute (CMI).

This volume was developed through fieldwork-based research and discussions from a series of workshops and panels in Bergen, Norway; Buenos Aires, Argentina; Cambridge, Massachusetts; and Chicago, Illinois. A number of people helped us develop and refine ideas by commenting on drafts at workshops and conferences or by serving as reviewers. Special thanks are due to Helena Alviar, Eduardo Appio, Daniel Brinks, Mary Clark, Christian Courtis, Javier Couso, Norman Daniels, Jackie Dugard, Leonardo Filippini, Varun Gauri, Gines González García, Aeyal Gross, Kathryn Hochstetler, Sara Hossain, Malcolm Langford, Sigrid Morales, Gustavo Ríos, Olman Rodríguez, Cesar Rodríguez Garavito, Julieta Rossi, Michelle Taylor-Robinson, Alejandro Uslenghi, Carlos Vassallo, Kurt Weyland, and our anonymous reviewers. In addition, we benefited early on from the insights of Mark Goodale, Peter Houtzager, Helena Nygren-Krug, and Kristin Sandvik.

We are also grateful to participants of The Right to Health in Resource Constrained Settings, a course at the 2010 Bergen Summer Research School on Global Development Challenges that Siri Gloppen, Alicia Ely Yamin, and Ole Frithjof Norheim jointly taught and to which other participants of this project contributed.

Thanks are also due to those who assisted behind the scenes, including arranging the workshops. In Cambridge, we would like to thank Adriana Benedict and Kaitlyn Hennigan; in Buenos Aires, we thank Lucas Arrimada and Ignacio César; and in Bergen at CMI, we thank Ingvild Hestad and Kristi Staveland-Sæther.

We deeply appreciate the tireless efforts of those who helped us prepare the manuscript for publication—most of all, our diligent and ever-efficient copy-editor, Morgan Stoffregen, who assumed responsibilities far above and beyond what could be expected. We also want to thank Catlin Rockman for her excellent work on the layout; Ståle Almenning for the cover design; AFP/Noah Seelam for the photo; Susan Holman for proofreading; Lisa Kleinholz for indexing; and of course Cara Solomon, Communications Director at the Harvard Human Rights Program, for shepherding the book through the process.

As editors, we have found this project immensely rewarding for the insights that it has provided and for the opportunity to learn from coauthors and other academics who have generously shared their time and ideas. Equally important has been the opportunity to interact with practitioners, including those dedicated judges who, aware of the potential pitfalls, nevertheless struggle to navigate the complexities of health rights litigation in ways that bring justice to health, and who are eager to learn what can be gleaned from this volume regarding how best to do so.

Alicia Ely Yamin and Siri Gloppen
August 2011
Cambridge, MA, and Bergen

INTRODUCTION

Chapter 1

Introduction: Can Litigation Bring Justice to Health?

Siri Gloppen and Mindy Jane Roseman

This book sets out to explore the phenomenon of health rights litigation and its consequences. Globally, court cases regarding the right to health are on the rise, and views diverge sharply on whether this trend toward judicialization is positive or negative for the advancement of the right to health and whether it can bring more justice to health care.

In Brazil, for example, patients are turning to the courts in increasing numbers to claim medication and treatment that is not provided by the public health-care system—but to which, they argue, their constitutional right to health entitles them—and judges more often than not support the claims. Some welcome this as a positive development that protects the constitutional right to health and strengthens the public health-care system. Others fear that as more patients are encouraged to follow suit, this "epidemic of litigation" will lead health-care costs to spiral out of control and will undermine attempts to strengthen the public health-care system through health plans and rational priority setting (Ferraz in this volume). The situation in Brazil is not unique—nor is it the most dramatic. Colombia and Costa Rica were the first countries in the region to experience large numbers of individuals going to court to claim their right to health, starting in the early 1990s after constitutional reforms eased access to the courts[1] and growing exponentially since the turn of the century. In 2008, Colombian courts heard more than 140,000 health rights cases and, in a landmark judgment, the Constitutional Court ordered a radical restructuring of the health system. This has placed the Court at the center of a contentious policy process over health-care reform, the outcome of which is still to be seen (Yamin et al. in this volume). In Costa Rica, politicians, health administrators, and analysts express divergent

---

The authors would like to thank Alicia Ely Yamin, Paola Bergallo, Amy Senier, Sarah Sorscher, and Baker Woods for their contributions.

views on whether the role of the Constitutional Chamber of the Supreme Court, known as the "Sala IV," is positive or negative; but all agree that it has become a—if not *the*—main shaper of health policy (Wilson in this volume). Health rights litigation has also become a significant avenue for health-care demands in other parts of the region, such as Argentina, for example, where individual, collective, and structural cases are making their mark on the country's fragmented health system (Bergallo in this volume).

While the number of cases has grown most exponentially in Latin America, where it is higher than in any other region, this increase appears to be part of a global trend that, as we shall see, may be having similar impacts elsewhere. Courts are asked to act to protect and fulfill the right to health in domestic and international courts of the global North, as well as in more resource-constrained countries of the global South, which are the focus of this book. Areas where litigation has played an important role include the struggle for antiretroviral treatment for HIV/AIDS; the protection of prisoners' right to health-care services; access to affordable generic drugs; battles over reproductive rights; and efforts to secure underlying preconditions of health, such as water, food, and the right to live in a healthy environment. Developments in India and South Africa are notable in this regard. The South African Constitutional Court, in a celebrated judgment, ordered a recalcitrant government to roll out treatment to prevent HIV-positive mothers from passing the virus to their babies, a decision with wide-ranging implications, as we shall see in later chapters (in this volume, Cooper; Norheim and Gloppen). In both South Africa and India, courts have ordered their governments to institute policies to protect basic preconditions of health, including shelter for vulnerable groups; and Indian courts have also issued a number of rulings protecting the right to a healthy environment (Parmar and Wahi in this volume).

What drives this phenomenon of health rights litigation, and what are the consequences? Should people who care about the right to health applaud and encourage this development? Is litigation a vehicle for advancing the right to health in society? Does it serve to hold governments accountable for their commitments toward vulnerable groups whose right to health is at risk? Or rather does it increase inequalities in health by providing a tool for privileged groups to access expensive treatments and an unfair share of health-care spending?

These questions—and the fact that the preliminary evidence points in very different directions—motivated an interdisciplinary and international group of researchers to join efforts to investigate the phenomenon of health rights litigation across three continents in a research project entitled "Right to Health through Litigation? Can Court-Enforced Health Rights Improve Health Policy?"[2] This book is an outcome of these efforts.

Research Question and Aim

Simply stated, our aim in this book is to explore under which circumstances health rights litigation is a good thing—and for whom. Given that the "litigation epidemic" is likely to be around for a while, and likely to grow, understanding this phenomenon is not only academically interesting but also politically and socially important. We hope that a more nuanced understanding of the dynamics of health rights litigation and its impacts can help practitioners (judges, lawyers, activists, policy makers, health administrators, and doctors) deal with the health litigation phenomenon in ways that cultivate its constructive potential and minimize aspects that are problematic from the perspective of the overall right to health in society.

As a preliminary matter, we should state clearly that our concept of "right-to-health litigation" does not include all litigation affecting health. Health rights litigation may be motivated by various concerns (e.g., common good or personal needs), but in order for it to be the basis for a lawsuit, the case must be framed in terms of a violation of a legal rule or *right*, especially to health. Most commonly, a right to health is articulated in a nation's constitution or through national health legislation and/or insurance. The right to health is also a recognized international human right. Understanding how the international right to health is framed informs our definition and criteria for case inclusion.

Internationally, this right is most firmly anchored in article 12 of the International Covenant on Economic, Social and Cultural Rights, which obliges states that have ratified the Covenant to "recognize the right of everyone to the enjoyment of the highest attainable standard of physical and mental health."[3] The United Nations Committee on Economic, Social and Cultural Rights has further interpreted the right to health, noting that it is not a right to be healthy but rather a set of freedoms and entitlements, among which is "the right to a system of health protection which provides equality of opportunity for people to enjoy the highest attainable level of health."[4]

Realizing the right to health also requires the realization of a range of other rights—to food; housing; work; education; human dignity; life; nondiscrimination; equality; freedom from torture; privacy; access to information; and freedom of association, assembly, and movement (see Commission on Social Determinants of Health 2008). States' obligations in this regard are progressive, understood to require resources that may be constrained. However, states do have an immediate obligation to take "deliberate, concrete and targeted" steps toward full realization and to do so in a nondiscriminatory manner. They also have a "core obligation to ensure the satisfaction of, at the very least, minimum essential levels of each of the rights . . . including essential primary health care."[5]

For the purposes of the current study, we follow the conception of the right to health given by the Committee on Economic, Social and Cultural Rights in General Comment 14, but include only the immediate preconditions of health (rights to food, water, sanitation, safe and healthy working conditions, and a healthy environment) and not the broader social determinants (education and housing). Thus, we limit ourselves to the rights most relevant for our research question concerning the impact of litigation on health systems and health policy. We believe that this limited focus is necessary to facilitate a deeper analysis of litigation in the context of particular health systems and political environments. The right to health narrowly conceived differs from other social rights in ways that are important for understanding the dynamics that drive litigation, as well as its effects. Due to the inherently expansive nature of the right to health,[6] the ethically sensitive and technical nature of the field,[7] and the enormous economic interests involved, asymmetries of knowledge and power are particularly great when it comes to health and health litigation. The analysis must take these asymmetries into account and explore their implications, considering especially, for example, who benefits and how international actors (such as pharmaceutical companies, donors, and nongovernmental organizations) influence litigation processes. Our universe of health rights litigation thus include cases that

- make claims based on a constitutional right to health (or related right) or an internationally recognized human right to health;
- concern access to health facilities, goods, and services (including medication); or
- concern the underlying preconditions for health.

While this operational definition of the right to health operates reasonably fairly across the cases discussed here, it is not without problems. The nature of the right-to-health claim differs between countries. Some nations articulate a right to health in their constitutions or national health-care and insurance laws, and others articulate it by ratifying an international legal treaty that contains health rights (and taking the necessary measures to give the treaty national effect). Brazil and South Africa explicitly recognize health rights as justiciable rights in their constitutions, while judges in Argentina, Colombia, Costa Rica, and India have constructed a justiciable right to health from other constitutional rights—such as the rights to life and life with dignity—while also relying on international human rights instruments (which are incorporated into domestic law to varying degrees). These differences will have an effect on where and how a right-to-health claim is pleaded.

In some legal systems (Colombia, Costa Rica, and India), basic rights violations claims—such as those regarding the rights to life or health—are granted easy access to courts and are used to vindicate a wide range of health-related concerns. Elsewhere, constitutional challenges are cumbersome and expensive, and litigants are likely to cast similar concerns in a legal language not involving constitutional rights, such as medical malpractice, in order to have access to a court. Artful though the distinction may be, such cases are excluded from our analysis unless they are framed as a rights violation by a public entity.[8] This means that there is not full symmetry in the cases included in the various country studies. For example, cases regarding denial of treatments that are included in health-care plans are considered only when they are litigated as a breach of constitutional rights (as in Argentina and Colombia, where such claims constitute a large share of the cases). When such cases are directed toward administrative bodies or framed as civil claims against private providers, they are excluded.

State of the Research

Several growing bodies of literature help provide some tentative answers to the questions that have shaped this book. While some of this literature relates to the right to health and health litigation specifically, most concerns social rights more broadly. These existing works provide not only an important foundation for the current study but also points of disagreement and engagement. In this section, we briefly outline some of the leading debates and contributions to the field, emphasizing where this volume contributes to the discourse and—in our view—takes it forward.

Research on health litigation and its impacts is part of a broader debate on legal enforcement of economic, social, and cultural rights, which has recently shifted from focusing on judgments—with court victory as the criterion of success—to also considering the implementation of judgments, including relationships between litigation and broader social mobilization. This builds on an established (predominantly North American) body of literature examining strategic litigation more generally and its (lack of) social effects (see, e.g., Scheingold 2004; Galanter 1974; Rosenberg 1991; Bakan and Schneiderman 1992; McCann 1994; Schultz 1998; Bell 2004).[9] However, until recently, empirically based work investigating the effects of social rights litigation generally and health rights litigation in particular has been rare.[10]

We wish to situate and distinguish *Litigating Health Rights* from some of the more recent scholarship on social rights.[11]

We begin with reference to *Courts and Social Transformation in New Democracies: An Institutional Voice for the Poor?*, edited by Roberto Gargarella, Pilar Domingo, and Theunis Roux (2006). Two members of the team behind the current volume (Gloppen and Gargarella) also played central roles in the *Courts and Social Transformation* project, which provides a theoretical and methodological point of departure for this book. *Courts and Social Transformation* identifies two trends as coinciding: an increase in democratically elected governments and new rights-rich constitutions after 1990, and an increase in social rights litigation. Its editors and contributing authors seek to flesh out the relationship between the two, theoretically and through comparative studies. Do democratic constitutions and recourse to courts for social and economic objectives mean that courts are sites for meaningful social transformation (Gargarella et al. 2006, 1)? To answer that question, *Courts and Social Transformation* explores theoretical and historical constraints to court-generated social policy making and informs those discussions through a series of empirical and country-based studies. These case studies utilize an analytic template developed by Gloppen to elaborate how courts can be relevant to the concerns of poor and marginalized individuals and communities. This framework is further developed in the current volume.

In a nutshell, *Courts and Social Transformation* finds that judiciaries—liberated from authoritarian constraints and overcoming unease with democratic division-of-powers concerns—have been enabled to act with relative autonomy within the realm of the new constitutional parameters. In responding to petitions, the courts in Hungary, for example, sought to preserve the social rights architecture inherited from state socialism, which was being challenged by newer free-market policies. Conversely, in South Africa, this autonomy meant that the courts, and the Constitutional Court in particular, could assist in transforming the architecture inherited from the apartheid system. Courts in India and Latin America have demonstrated a similar receptiveness to entreaties to preserve or provide access to social constitutional entitlements, such as education, housing, and health.

Litigating Health Rights differs from and goes beyond *Courts and Social Transformation* in important respects. While *Courts and Social Transformation* looks broadly at all social rights litigation (e.g., housing, education, land, and environment) *Litigating Health Rights*, as discussed above, focuses more narrowly on the right to health, thus enabling a deeper and more systematic exploration and description of the litigation process and how it plays out in different contexts.

Another study, *Social Rights Jurisprudence: Emerging Trends in International and Comparative Law*, edited by Malcolm Langford (2008), provides a good overview of the recognition of the entire range of social rights by national, regional, and international jurisdictions. The book demonstrates the variety of social rights that have been litigated and shows that courts are competent to address breaches of these rights and establish accountability for the promotion and protection of, among other rights, health, education, and housing. We appreciate the value of *Social Rights Jurisprudence* in offering a descriptive and comprehensive compendium of court cases that recognize the justiciability and enforceability of social and economic rights. However, the book does not analyze the dynamics that bring the cases to court, nor does it address the enforcement and impact of the court decisions. Rather, it focuses simply on the fact that courts have rendered decisions. Here, we attempt to take the analysis further. Courts may well be appropriate fora for settling legal disputes over social rights entitlements—but why is this so, what enables and encourages the litigation and adjudication of health rights, and what are the effects of these decisions? Are they enforced? Do they lead to transformations in judicial output? Do they have normative impact and change governments' (or other actors') behavior? Do they transfer health resources away from the "haves" to the "have-nots"? These are some of the questions our volume addresses.

Courts and the Legal Enforcement of Economic, Social and Cultural Rights: Comparative Experiences of Justiciability, written by Christian Courtis for the International Commission of Jurists (2008b), brings to the fore rich comparative material on economic, social, and cultural rights cases, with a broader perspective on the circumstances under which such litigation is likely to succeed in terms of implementation. However, it explores neither the dynamics of the litigation process nor the broader *impact* of such litigation in terms of social outcomes and the protection of social rights within the population.[12]

The literature that explores the impact of litigation specifically is limited. One published study suggests that social rights litigation can measurably improve the quality of the lives of vulnerable and marginalized members of society and may contribute to social transformation in particularized settings (Pieterse 2006a). There is also a small body of literature on individual lawsuits that may have public consequences in the course of seeking private relief.[13]

The most ambitious attempt yet to analyze the impact of health rights litigation is *Courting Social Justice: Judicial Enforcement of Social and Economic Rights in the Developing World*, edited by Varun Gauri and Daniel Brinks (2008). This is a comparative study of litigation on health and education in five countries: Brazil, India, Indonesia, Nigeria, and South Africa. The study moves beyond legal analysis and normative discussion (whether social rights are justiciable and whether they should be) to focus on the impacts of litigation. As we do in the present volume, Gauri and Brinks analyze the dynamics of litigation, identifying the legal opportunity structures and factors that enable social rights litigation; they track the impact of court decisions to see if and how social and economic resources are redistributed as a result of litigation; and finally, they offer an opinion on the relative ethics of using courts to address questions of social and economic injustice.[14]

Gauri and Brinks rely on an impressive database of cases and a metric of their own design to estimate the number of persons who directly and indirectly benefit from judicial decisions, both within each country and comparatively. To identify a comparable measure of the impact of litigation, they (i) calculate the number of cases in each country where the courts have enforced these rights (controlled for population size) and (ii) estimate the degree to which the decisions have been implemented. They add a standard multiplier for cases that aim to change policy—such as test cases with precedent-setting effect, which are typical of common-law countries—as it makes little sense to compare these cases directly with typical civil-law system cases, which focus narrowly on individual remedies.[15] *Courting Social Justice* thus draws attention to the importance of systemic enforcement of social rights. Enforcement resulting in policy change—if implemented—can easily outweigh the impact of thousands of individual cases where courts enforce individual rights but refrain from generalizing the remedy. To take one example, in its famous judgment on vehicle pollution in Delhi, the Indian Supreme Court demanded a shift toward cleaner fuel in Delhi's public transport system, affecting millions of people and advancing their right to live in a healthy environment.

In contrast with the well-known position of Upendra Baxi (1988), who finds that social rights litigation offers little transformative benefit to the underclass and that Indian public interest litigation is driven by elites (lawyers detached from social movements) for their own aggrandizement, Gauri and Brinks (2008, 303) conclude that, on balance, the effects of social rights litigation are positive. Social goods, they argue, are redistributed to those who need them; the poor are at least as likely to benefit as the better-off; the privileged are neither monopolizing the issues nor capturing the revenues of the state; and the courts are not undermining democracy or separation of powers. However, their analysis shows that while those who use the courts and benefit from their judgments are, in general, not the elites (who need not rely on public services), they are also not the most vulnerable and excluded (who, by definition, do not access public services); rather, the beneficiaries are the relatively enfranchised middle and lower-middle classes. We question their conclusion that litigation has a favorable social justice effect when lower-middle classes have improved access to health services, particularly in light of the inequality and massive poverty within these societies. Still, Gauri and Brinks's findings in *Courting Social Justice* are interesting. Their quantitative analysis corrects for the normative overreach of some courts' rhetoric, showing instead more modest direct and indirect effects of court decisions (325). They find that court decisions have not (yet) had demonstrable macroeconomic consequences (344), but worry that there will be a backlash as costs mount (319–20).

The analytical approach and empirical descriptions in *Courting Social Justice* have provided important input for the present study. We seek to build on Gauri and Brinks's work and take their analysis of litigation dynamics and impacts even further. While *Courting Social Justice* looks at litigants' opportunity structures, it does not consider how litigation responds to problems and opportunities in the health system. Nor does it systematically consider the political dynamics of litigation. To address these concerns, *Litigating Health Rights* develops a new taxonomy regarding the analysis of the adjudication process, distinguishing, among other things, between how courts deal with the legal basis for the claims and what factual arguments are presented. And while *Courting Social Justice* tells us something about *how many* people are influenced by court decisions, and tries to analyze *who* the litigants and beneficiaries are, it does not tell us *how* (or how much) they are affected or how litigation affects the overall right to health (or education) in society. In this volume, we address these aspects of impact and add to their analysis by exploring not just how many people, and whom, (certain forms of) health litigation affects—but how. In our analysis of the litigation process, we also examine how differences in health systems and policies influence litigation patterns and the social effects of litigation. Furthermore, *Litigating Health Rights* includes more recent developments and analyzes other countries that have witnessed important health rights litigation (Argentina, Colombia, and Costa Rica). These examples, we believe, reveal dynamics different from those analyzed in *Courting Social Justice.*

Beyond the literature on social rights litigation, scholarship on legal opportunity structures deeply informs our discussion in this volume. Cases are litigated because they can be litigated and because other avenues are closed or comparatively more difficult or costly—or more effective when combined with litigation.[16] In his influential study of the "rights revolution" in the United States (1961–75), Charles Epp argues that the revolution's success was contingent on the advocacy of well-organized rights actors (1998). Other scholars have pointed to a range of factors that coalesce to make social rights litigation possible: adequately funded rights advocates (or cause lawyers) (Sarat and Scheingold 1998; Scheingold and Sarat 2004), constitution-centered litigation, judicial willingness, liberal standing rules, and/or waivers of the legal representation requirement (Byrne 2007; Centre on Housing Rights and Evictions 2003; Hogerzeil et al. 2006). Yet others have pointed to the importance of rights consciousness for transforming the felt needs of individuals or groups into rights violations that can form the basis of a legal claim.[17]

Litigating Health Rights addresses a set of questions concerning courts' effectiveness and legitimacy in making social policy. These questions have both normative and empirical dimensions. Normative questions concern, most centrally, the role of courts in a democratic society and courts' accountability to the tax-paying public, which is affected by decisions on social expenditures. There is a substantial normative literature in political theory concerned with courts' relationship to social justice (Abramovich 2009; Ackerman 1991; Bork 1979, 1990; Dworkin 1996; Ely 1980; Fabre 2000; Fiss 2003; Gargarella 2005, 2006a, 2006b; Holmes 1993; Nino 1996; Sunstein 2004; Tushnet 2008b; Waldron 1994, 2009). Mark Tushnet, for example, in his book *Weak Courts, Strong Rights: Judicial Review and Social Welfare Rights in Comparative Constitutional Law* (2008b), finds that courts do not "overstep" their normative roles but that there are a number of factors that influence the extent to which judicial decisions have impact. He uses a comparative legal approach to show that "weaker forms" of judicial review—especially where courts have few enforcement powers—allow for the articulation of robust social rights by the executive and legislative branches. Roberto Gargarella's chapter in this volume engages this literature and uses a conception of deliberative democracy to defend courts' legitimacy in taking on social rights questions, provided they do so in a dialogic manner.

The empirical questions relate to courts' institutional capacity to decide social rights cases and bring about significant social change. It is often argued that courts lack expertise on complex socioeconomic (or medical) issues and that the casuistic nature of court decisions makes it difficult for judges to take the overall distributive considerations into account when they make decisions with budgetary implications. This concern aside, there is still the question of whether litigation is an effective strategy for social change. As indicated earlier, we face a paucity of information on this front; very few studies exist that explore litigation's actual social and economic effects—or that explore whether, in the absence of litigation, society would be inflicted with even more health disparities. Our review of the scant existing empirical literature on the impact of health litigation turns up mixed results. Some studies, while suggesting the potential of health rights litigation to redistribute social public goods to the disadvantaged, point out that court decisions seldom set (or interrupt) a policy agenda—rather, litigation injects the language of rights into political discussions and courts serve as another forum for debate (Gauri and Brinks 2008, 304). Other studies, referring to litigation more generally, have pointed out the limits of litigation alone, claiming that it succeeds in effecting social change only when teamed up with additional efforts, such as demonstrations, boycotts, media pressure, and political campaigns (Coleman et al. 2005).

Some scholars, notably Gerald Rosenberg (1991), take an even dimmer view. In *The Hollow Hope: Can Courts Bring About Social Change?*, he suggests that legal victories mask social and political inequality and thwart the potential for mass movement:

> Courts can seldom produce significant social reform. Yet if groups advocating such reform continue to look to the courts for aid, and spend precious resources in litigation, then the courts also limit change by deflecting claims from substantive political battles, where success is possible, to harmless legal ones where it is not. Even when major cases are won, the achievement is often more symbolic than real. Thus, courts may serve an ideological function of luring movements for social reform to an institution that is structurally constrained from serving their needs, providing only an illusion of change.[18] (427)

While Rosenberg's pessimism may seem out of proportion to his empirical findings, his book reminds advocates and scholars that courts alone do not change deeply entrenched social norms. Our volume recognizes the value of Rosenberg's warning about the limits of litigation in effecting profound and structural social change. If health rights litigation does not remedy (or in fact upholds or exacerbates) the structural problems of a flawed health system, localized benefits should not be overrated. At the same time, our analysis suggests that health rights cases can, under some circumstances, have transformative value and reduce social injustice. Landmark judgments may also spur litigation on other issues and in other places, leading to effects beyond the individual case.

The Structure of this Book

The following chapters are organized to lead the reader into a series of specific case examples and then consider, through analysis of cross-cutting themes, what these cases may teach us. Chapter 2 establishes the groundwork for discussion by presenting the reasoning behind our selection of cases, a comparative look at the social and economic conditions within the countries studied, and an outline of the analytical framework for the book.

Chapters 3 through 8 present the six case studies, organized alphabetically by country. The authors for Argentina (Bergallo), Brazil (Ferraz), Colombia (Yamin, Parra-Vera, and Gianella), Costa Rica (Wilson), India (Parmar and Wahi), and South Africa (Cooper) tell the stories of health rights litigation in each of the countries. These country studies provide insights into the driving forces behind litigation—the sociopolitical and legal factors that make litigation possible and attractive (at least for certain potential litigants)—and the type of claimants and the type of cases filed. The authors explain how the courts deal with the cases brought before them and seek to assess to what extent compliance actually follows in successful cases, to the benefit of claimants. They also address the cases' broader impacts in terms of changes in policies and practices, including effects on jurisprudence and on decision-making and participation processes. Such impacts are not reserved for "successful" cases, however; instances where court cases were lost or settled in the shadow of threatened litigation may be equally relevant. While the investigation of each country case follows a common framework (outlined in chapter 2), the country chapters differ in structure and emphasis to best reflect the particularities of each context.

The second part of the book consists of comparative thematic chapters investigating different aspects of health litigation in order to highlight and understand trends across countries and regions. Chapter 9 (Gargarella) explores whether social rights adjudication is something that judges ought to do and outlines a theory of when and how courts should enforce the right to health specifically and social rights more broadly. This chapter's central argument is that by dealing with cases in a dialogic manner—as is sometimes done—courts can enforce social rights at the same time that they respect and strengthen the democratic process by broadening and deepening participation. Chapter 10 (Roseman and Gloppen) raises questions about what drives litigation, including the role of international actors in the litigation wave. Chapter 11 (Mæstad, Rakner, and Ferraz) addresses the important "so what" question: what are the on-the-ground consequences of the health litigation wave? This chapter suggests various ways in which impact can be assessed and draws on findings from the country chapters to explore how the social and political impacts of litigation differ depending on the legal and political context. Chapter 12 (Norheim and Gloppen) takes the analysis a step further, examining how litigation regarding medication affects priority setting and justice in health. The book's conclusion (Yamin) collects insights from the case studies and thematic chapters, formulating tentative conclusions to the central question motivating this study: under what circumstances does health rights litigation advance the right to health in society and make health-care systems more just?

NOTES

1. The reforms establishing the *Sala Constitucional* in Costa Rica took place in 1989, while the constitutional reforms that established the Constitutional Court in Colombia took place in 1991 (for details on how these reforms increased access to the courts, see the respective chapters in this volume).
2. The Research Council of Norway provided the core research grant for the "Right to Health through Litigation?" project, which is a collaborative effort between the Chr. Michelsen Institute (Bergen, Norway), the University of Bergen Faculty of Medicine (Norway), Harvard Law School (United States), the Centre for Applied Legal Studies (South Africa), and individual researchers from the countries included in the study. Research support has also been provided by the participating researchers' home institutions.
3. International Covenant on Economic, Social and Cultural Rights, G.A. Res. 2200A (XXI), 21 U.N. GAOR Supp. (No. 16) at 49, U.N. Doc. A/6316 (1966), 993 U.N.T.S. 3, entered into force January 3, 1976. Similar formulations can be found in other declarations and treaties. See article 25 of the Universal Declaration of Human Rights, G.A. Res. 217A (III), U.N. Doc A/810 at 71 (1948); articles 11 and 12 of the Convention on the Elimination of All Forms of Discrimination against Women, G.A. Res. 34/180, 34 U.N. GAOR Supp. (No. 46) at 193, U.N. Doc. A/34/46 (1979), entered into force September 3, 1981; article 5(e)(iv) of the International Convention on the Elimination of All Forms of Racial Discrimination, G.A. Res. 2106 (XX), Annex, 20 U.N. GAOR Supp. (No. 14) at 47, U.N. Doc. A/6014 (1966), 660 U.N.T.S. 195, entered into force January 4, 1969; article 24 of the Convention on the Rights of the Child, G.A. Res. 44/25, Annex, 44 U.N. GAOR Supp. (No. 49) at 167, U.N. Doc. A/44/49 (1989), entered into force September 2, 1990; article 11 of the European Social Charter, 529 U.N.T.S. 89, entered into force February 26, 1965; article 16 of the African (Banjul) Charter on Human and Peoples' Rights, adopted June 27, 1981, OAU Doc. CAB/LEG/67/3 rev. 5, 21 I.L.M. 58 (1982), entered into force October 21, 1986; article 10 of the Additional Protocol to the American Convention on Human Rights in the Area of Economic, Social and Cultural Rights, "Protocol of San Salvador," O.A.S. Treaty Series No. 69 (1988), entered into force November 16, 1999, reprinted in Basic Documents Pertaining to Human Rights in the Inter-American System, OEA/Ser.L.V/II.82 doc.6 rev.1 at 67 (1992); and article 25 of the International Convention on the Protection and Promotion of the Rights and Dignity of Persons with Disabilities, G.A. Res. 61/106, Annex I, U.N. GAOR, 61st Sess., Supp. No. 49, at 65, U.N. Doc. A/61/49 (2006), entered into force May 3, 2008.
4. United Nations Committee on Economic, Social and Cultural Rights, General Comment 14, U.N. Doc. E/C.12/2000/4 (2000), para. 8.
5. Ibid., para. 43. This includes access to health facilities, goods, and services on a nondiscriminatory basis; access to the minimum essential food that is nutritionally adequate and safe; access to basic shelter, sanitation, and an adequate supply of safe and potable water; access to essential drugs; equitable distribution of health facilities, goods, and services; and implementation of a national public health strategy and plan of action.
6. Health rights are inherently expansive since needs depend closely on what is possible to treat, the frontiers of which are ever expanding. Hence, the potential financial implications of granting health rights are enormous, placing increased pressure on budgets to an extent that is generally not the case for other social rights.

7. That the right to health concerns life and death in very direct ways makes it a particularly difficult ethical and moral terrain to navigate. The knowledge asymmetries and the need to rely on (often contested) expert knowledge are also greater than in most other fields.
8. There are many other domains of law—tort and administrative, for example—that have a bearing on health; there are also other human rights (e.g., the rights to privacy and to information) that directly and indirectly relate to health. However, literature on litigating the rights of patients regarding their medical providers and institutions, malpractice, informed consent, confidentiality, access to medical records, and complaint mechanisms for protecting these rights are excluded. Also excluded is any literature concerning administrative regulations for health facilities or pharmaceuticals, unless the right to health is explicitly in focus.
9. For the policy impact of judicial decisions more generally, see, for example, Canon and Johnson (1998), Feeley and Rubin (2000), and Hertogh and Halliday (2004). Recent works on the dangers of "juristocracy" displacing democracy to the advantage of the privileged include Hirschl (2004) and Silverstein (2009).
10. For activists' efforts to document the effects of social rights litigation, see the International Network for Economic, Social and Cultural Rights at www.escr-net.org.
11. We are quite selective in this short literature review; there is an abundance of publications and we do not purport to write a review essay of all social rights, or even right-to-health, publications. For example, early works by Leary (1994) and Toebes (1999) lay out the legal dimensions of the right to health internationally and conceptually but do not concern themselves with jurisprudence. A more recent and very substantial compendium edited by Clapham and Robinson (2009) focuses on how international institutions, partnerships, and nongovernmental organizations have engaged the right to health. The book makes the case for the existence of an international right-to-health movement; it does not engage health rights jurisprudence. Similarly, the volume edited by Baderin and McCorquodale (2007) focuses broadly on social rights obligations but does not examine national-level jurisprudence per se.
12. On the shortcomings in this regard, see Gloppen (2009).
13. Vernick et al. (2007) note that although private lawsuits against the tobacco industry, which began in the United States in the 1950s, were not successful until 2006—when *Engle v. Liggett* (Florida Supreme Court, United States) awarded US$12.7 million but vacated punitive damages—collective public lawsuits filed in the 1990s by attorneys general of all fifty states did reform the industry somewhat. The authors contend that *Engle* will encourage other attorneys to bring suits and will pose a "substantial future threat to the industry and a corresponding potential benefit for the public's health," as it will increase the cost of doing business, pass off costs to smokers, and place tobacco out of the reach of young people (88–89).
14. In some cases, their definition of the universe of litigation includes negligence and other tort claims. They also focus on education and health, while we restrict our cases to those claiming a human right to health.
15. The multiplier used is 100, which they (rightly) see as a conservative measure. The summary we offer here presents only a simplified sketch of their methodology; a more detailed account can be found in the concluding chapter of *Courting Social Justice*.
16. Studies of political mobilization have adapted the concept of opportunity structure from the sociology of cultural deviance (focusing on how subcultures provide parallel

opportunity structures that serve as routes to delinquency). Successes of social movements are often explained in terms of their political opportunity structure (see, e.g., McCann 1994; Meyer 2004, 125–45). Litigation is likely where the legal opportunity structure (the barriers and opportunities that a particular legal system presents to people with health concerns) is more favorable than other avenues for remedying the problem (such as complaint mechanisms in the health system, political mobilization, media pressure, or ombuds offices). For more on legal opportunity structure, see Wilson and Rodríguez (2006) and Andersen (2005).

17. Development of rights consciousness changes the identity of the individual or nongovernmental organization into that of a rights bearer, whose rights can be vindicated in the courts (Vanhala 2006). For example, UK-based disability rights organizations initially thought of themselves as service organizations, not rights vindicators. However, as litigation around nondiscrimination norms mounted, with little opposition from politicians, disability "rights" groups began to file lawsuits that reframed nonaccommodation not as bad manners but as unequal treatment. In turn, this ratcheted up the costs for noncompliance by countries subject to various European conventions and laws, making litigation an effective strategy, at least at the normative level (Vanhala 2006, 559–60).
18. Meydani and Mizrahi (2006) argue along similar lines.

Chapter 2

Litigating Health Rights: Framing the Analysis

Siri Gloppen

To understand the phenomenon of health rights litigation, its driving forces, and its impacts on health policy and resource allocation requires a multidisciplinary and comparative approach that combines knowledge of the law and legal processes with knowledge of health systems, health policies, and political and economic contexts. This chapter presents the reasoning behind our case selection, provides a comparative context against which the individual case studies should be understood, and lays out the analytical framework underlying this book.

Methodology and Case Selection

The researchers behind this book are experts in law, political science, economics, medicine, public health, medical ethics, political theory, and priority setting. There are clear benefits of a multidisciplinary analytical prism: it provides a fuller understanding of health litigation by bringing out different facets of this complex phenomenon. At the same time, a multidisciplinary approach presents challenges, some of which we have only partially succeeded in overcoming. It takes considerable time and effort to understand and integrate different theoretical perspectives in a coherent manner. It also takes time to extend approaches developed for a particular context to new and unfamiliar empirical settings. This brings us to the other main principle—namely, the comparative nature—of our approach.

The author would like to thank Erla Katrine Løvseth for research assistance and Mindy Jane Roseman, Alicia Ely Yamin, and Paola Bergallo for valuable comments. Thanks are also due to all who contributed to earlier versions, including the editors and reviewers at *Health and Human Rights*. The theoretical framework presented in this chapter is adapted from Gloppen (2008a).

Case studies are necessary to understand the interactions between various actors in the litigation process, as well as the dynamics that drive litigation and determine its impact on the right to health in society and on the allocation of resources.[1] Effective analysis of case studies requires not only interdisciplinary understanding but also deep knowledge of the specific context. At the same time, there are limits to what can be learned from a particular case. Careful comparative analysis is required for understanding the particular dynamics of health rights litigation and discerning more general patterns. Our approach is thus based on comparing structured and focused descriptions of country case studies that exhibit significant health rights litigation. A common analytical framework, outlined below, facilitates rigorous comparison, while a qualitative analysis takes into account the rich context and specific legal-political dynamics of each country. The research team for the case studies comprises experts with deep empirical knowledge of the countries included in the study, and each of the case studies is based on extensive fieldwork collecting data from a range of sources and through different methodologies. Due to differences between the cases, the data collected differ somewhat; but in general, they include court registers, judgments, and other information on court cases; public statistical data and reports; survey data; interviews with politicians and public officials responsible for health policy; interviews with judges and judicial officials; and interviews with lawyers, civil society activists, and litigants.

Litigating Health Rights is an empirical study aiming to uncover the dynamics of litigation and litigation's effects on policy processes and the distribution of health. However, the analysis of litigation's impact also relies, in part, on counterfactual reasoning—seeking to establish what would have happened in the absence of litigation. This involves problems of attribution: in complex real-world settings, it is difficult to know what can reasonably be ascribed to litigation as opposed to other factors. There are also normative aspects to the analysis. While we do not argue from the ideal, we look at litigation's impact in terms of justice in health—whether litigation benefits disadvantaged sections of society or instead widens social inequalities by benefiting those already advantaged (in terms of health care or other resources), and whether it leads to a prioritization of drugs and treatments that runs counter to what would be regarded as reasonable based on established criteria for priority setting. This involves conceptions of justice and fairness that inevitably are contested.

Our study is explorative rather than aiming to test prior theories. However, given that we seek to investigate how and why the dynamics and effects of health litigation differ between countries, our selection of country cases should take into account variables that are most likely to be of importance.

Based on existing knowledge, our hypothesis was that the dynamics of health rights litigation, both in terms of driving forces and effects, vary according to the nature of a country's health and legal systems. With regard to a country's health system, we assumed that the nature and volume of litigation is influenced by how the system is organized, particularly whether there is a reasonably well-functioning universal public health-care system (in principle open to the whole population) or a more fragmented and competitive system of predominantly privately financed and/or provided health care. Many countries undertook health-care reforms in the 1990s, often as part of wide-ranging economic reforms and structural adjustment packages. In most cases, these reforms led to more privatized (more private providers and/or insurers) or commercialized (co-payment- and incentive-based financing) health systems; in other cases, they led countries to adopt more universal public health care. We assumed that both the design and functioning of health-care systems and the direction of health-care reforms influence litigation patterns.

There is also considerable divergence between legal systems; in some systems, cases normally have an *erga omnes* effect (in the sense that individual cases set precedence for others similarly situated), while in others, each individual claim in principle is settled on its own terms without creating precedence. We assumed that these differences would influence the volume and nature of cases. We also assumed that the threshold of access to the courts for different types of litigants is important. Country cases were selected to allow a comparison across these three dimensions.

The six country cases that form the basis for this book are Argentina, Brazil, Colombia, Costa Rica, India, and South Africa—all middle- or low-income countries with significant health rights litigation. On the private versus public health-care dimension, they represent examples across the continuum. Costa Rica is a good example of a well-functioning public health system (with a relatively small section of the most affluent relying on private health insurance). Brazil and South Africa also have unified health-care systems that in principle are open to the whole population (but in practice the middle and upper classes rely overwhelmingly on private health insurance). At the other end of the spectrum, India's health-care system is overwhelmingly privatized, both in financing and provision. In between, we find Argentina and Colombia, with fragmented and semi-privatized health-care systems—union-based in Argentina and insurance-based managed competition in Colombia. For our purposes, we regard these as privatized health systems. The categorization on the private/public dimension is not unproblematic, however. All six countries have a mixture of private and public health provision, and if we look solely at how health care is financed, we find that the country where the government shoulders the largest share of total health expenditure is Colombia (84%), ahead of Costa Rica (77%). The lowest, by far, is India (28%), with Argentina (50%), Brazil (44%), and South Africa (40%) in the middle range (World Health Organization 2010a; see also table 2.2 below).

Within the public health-care group, we find countries with different legal traditions (Glenn 2000). Costa Rica and Brazil have civil-law systems (in which court decisions generally do not create precedent), while South Africa has a common-law system (in which decisions create binding precedent for all similar cases). We find a similar mix in the private health-care group, with Colombia and Argentina's civil-law systems and India's common-law system.

The threshold of access to the courts determines how difficult it is for individuals and organizations to file a health rights case. This is a function of cost as well as legal and procedural barriers, including the status of the right, rules of standing (such as whether cases can be brought in the public interest or only by those with a direct interest), appeal procedures, and possibilities for direct access to superior courts. Among the countries with public health care, access to the courts is easiest for people in Costa Rica, where litigants can easily access the Constitutional Chamber directly and do not need to hire a lawyer or pay fees. Access is most difficult in South Africa, where the legal procedure is quite rigid and legal aid is scarce. Brazil falls somewhere in between. Among the countries with more privatized health care, access to the courts is very easy in Colombia, where the *tutela* mechanism enables people to file cases before any local court, without a lawyer, and receive a quick decision. Access is somewhat more difficult in Argentina and India, where lawyers are needed. Within the civil-law countries, access to the courts is easier in Colombia and Costa Rica than in Argentina and Brazil. Among the common-law countries, India has easier access to the highest court in public interest cases than does South Africa, where direct access is rarely granted.

Figure 2.1 illustrates these various dimensions for case selection and the placement of the country cases. The figure shows that among our country cases, the legal systems without formal precedence (civil-law systems) are also the systems with easiest access to the courts.

Context: Health Challenges and Resources

With regard to health challenges and the resources available to meet them, the six selected countries display both similarities and differences.

One striking difference is that of size. As shown in table 2.1, Costa Rica, with 4.5 million inhabitants, is about one-tenth the size of Argentina (40 million), Colombia (45 million), and South Africa (49 million). Brazil, with 192 million people, is larger than these four combined, while India eclipses the rest. With 1.14 *billion* inhabitants, India is six times the size of Brazil, twenty-four times the size of South Africa, and more than two hundred fifty times the size of Costa Rica (or Norway, which, together with the United States, is included in the table for comparison purposes).[2] The differences in size are important to keep in mind because they say something

Figure 2.1. Case selection matrix

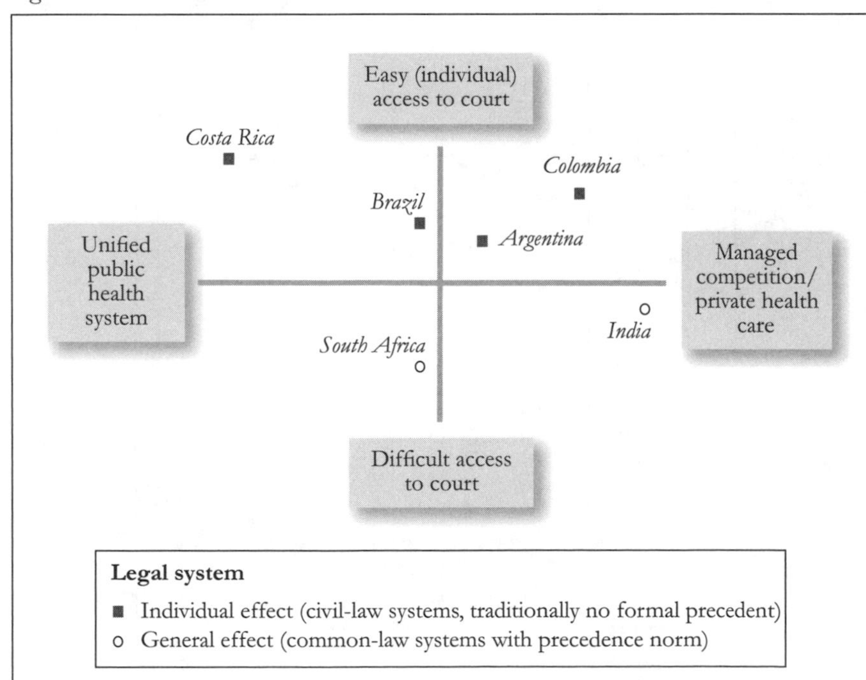

Table 2.1. Basic conditions: Similarities and differences between country cases

Country	Population (2008)	HDI[a] rank (2009)	GDP per capita (PPP[b] US$) (2008)	Gini index (newest)	Gini-health (2008)[c]	Life expectancy at birth (2008)	Healthy life expectancy at birth (2007)	HIV prevalence % adults 15–49 years (2007)	Under-5 mortality per 1,000 live births (2007)
Argentina	39,882,980	49	13,220	48.81	12	76	67	.5	16
Brazil	191,971,506	75	9,520	55.00	14	73	64	.6	22
Colombia	45,012,096	77	8,130	58.49	13	76	66	.6	20
Costa Rica	4,519,126	54	10,370	48.91	11	78	69	.4	11
India	1,139,964,932	129	2,720	36.80	19	64	56	.3	72
South Africa	48,687,000	134	9,340	57.77	26	54	48	18.1	59
Norway	4,768,212	1	49,420	25.79	09	81	73	.1	4
United States	304,060,000	13	42,810	40.81	11	78	70	.6	8

Note: The HDI ranking is from the United Nations Development Programme's Human Development Report 2010. Population, GDP per capita, the Gini index, and HIV prevalence are from the World Bank's World Development Indicators (http://data.worldbank.org/indicator). Gini-health is calculated by Ole Frithjof Norheim on the basis of data from the World Health Organization's 2008 life tables (see chapter 12 in this volume). The data on life expectancy, healthy life years, and under-five child mortality are from the World Health Organization's Global Health Observatory (http://apps.who.int/ghodata).

[a] Human Development Index.
[b] Purchasing power parity.
[c] Gini-health shows inequality in the population with regard to health (life years).

about the complexity of the challenges that governments face in developing health policies. Larger countries are also more likely to be federal in structure. In our selected countries, Costa Rica and Colombia are the only unitary countries; the other six have a federal structure (though with different degrees of autonomy for states or provinces, including autonomy in health policy).

The Latin American countries included in this study all have medium or high levels of human development according to the United Nations' Human Development Index (HDI), but with conditions in Argentina and Costa Rica markedly better than in Brazil and Colombia. South Africa and India rank somewhat lower on the HDI scale.

Figure 2.2 shows how, with the exception of South Africa, the HDI score improves for all of these countries over time, and most markedly in India.

India is the only low-income country among the six. Its gross domestic product (GDP) per capita is less than a third of that of the other countries, which are all in the middle-income range, with Argentina as the most well-off and Colombia as the poorest. It is important to note, however, that GDP per capita is an average measure without regard for the distribution of resources.

A striking feature of most of these countries is their inequality. Colombia,

Figure 2.2. Human Development Index

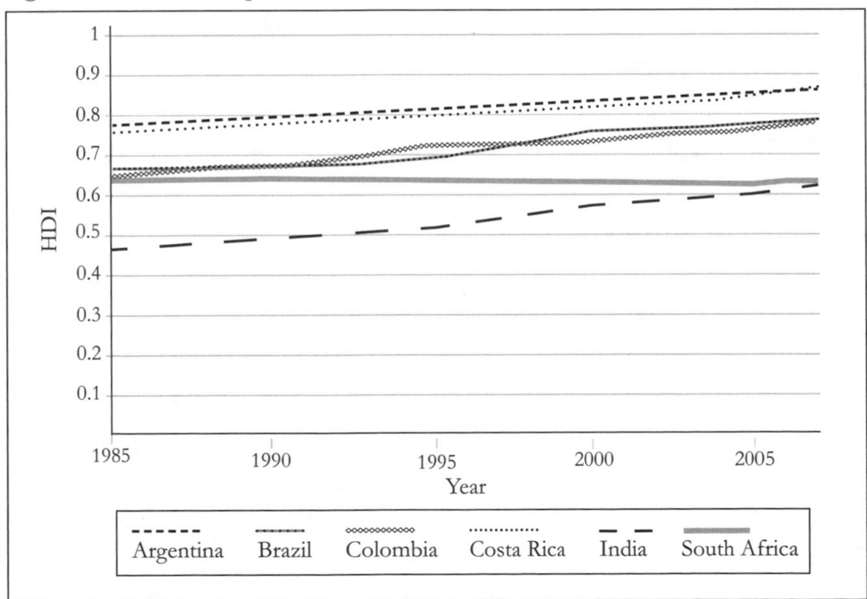

Source: United Nations Development Programme (2009, table G).

South Africa, and Brazil are among the most unequal countries in the world. Colombia is most unequal, with a Gini index of 58.5, closely followed by South Africa (57.8) and Brazil (55.0).[3] It is interesting to note that, according to these data, Colombia has replaced Brazil as the most unequal country in Latin America (see figure 2.3). While inequalities have gradually decreased in Brazil, this has not happened in Colombia despite years of economic growth. Argentina (48.8) and Costa Rica (48.9) are somewhat less unequal than the other two Latin American countries, but still considerably more unequal than India (36.8)—or the United States (40.8). For comparison, Norway, one of the most equal societies in the world, has a Gini index of 25.8. These disparities are reflected in the fragmented nature of their health systems (with the partial exception of Costa Rica). To roll out unified health systems including the whole population on terms that would satisfy the health-care demands of the wealthy elite is a huge challenge, politically and financially.

From our perspective, it is interesting to look at how the differences in per capita income and inequality are reflected in health indicators such as life

Figure 2.3. Development of social inequality: Gini index

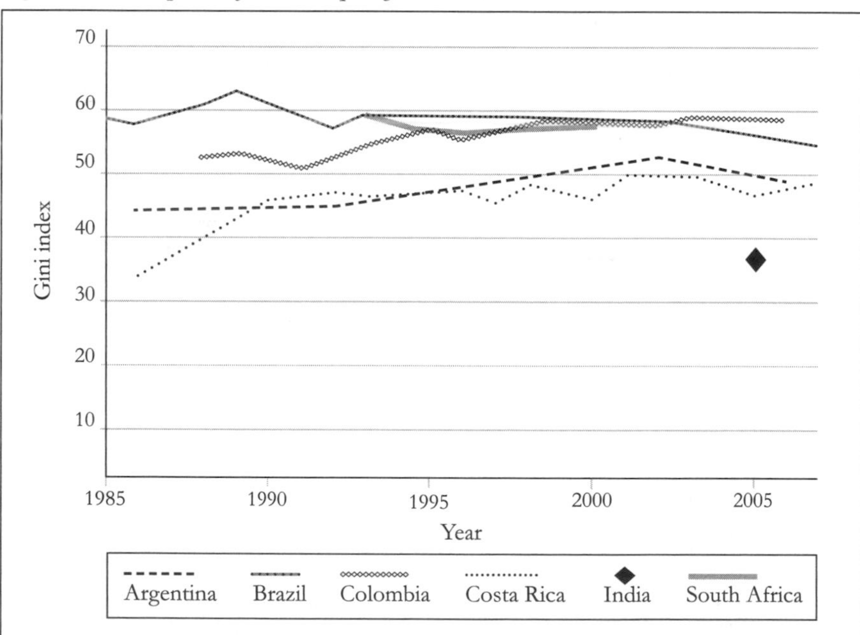

Source: World Bank (2009).
Note: Data are not available for all years for all countries, and are particularly limited for India (only 2005) and South Africa (only 1993, 1995, and 2000).

expectancy and healthy life expectancy. Chapter 12 looks more closely into inequalities in health specifically, but the Gini-health measure included in table 2.1 shows that the Latin American countries have a much more equal distribution of life years in the population than do India and South Africa, where far more people die young.

If we compare life expectancy at birth between the Latin American countries, Costa Rica seems to convert its resources into health more effectively than the others. In fact, compared to the United States, Costa Rica—with just a quarter of the economic resources and higher levels of social inequality—has the same life expectancy and only marginally lower healthy life expectancy. Life expectancy is somewhat lower in the other Latin American countries (including the more affluent Argentina), with Brazil furthest behind. Estimates of healthy life expectancy (or quality-adjusted life years) show the same ranking but with slightly less difference between the countries. From a global perspective, all of the Latin American countries studied here are doing reasonably well on these measures.

Life expectancy in India is considerably lower than in the Latin American countries, trailing behind Brazil by about nine years. The most striking difference in life expectancy, however, is between South Africa and the other countries. While South Africa has about the same levels of economic resources and inequality as Brazil and Colombia, its life expectancy lags twenty years behind—in 2007, South Africa's life expectancy was fifty-four

Table 2.2. Health expenditure (2008)

Country	Total expenditure on health (THE) as % of GDP	Government expenditure on health as % of THE	Private expenditure on health as % of THE	Government expenditure on health as % of general government expenditure	Government expenditure on health per capita (PPP[a] US$)
Argentina	9.6	49.8	50.2	14.3	690
Brazil	8.4	44.0	56.0	6.0	398
Colombia	5.9	83.9	16.1	18.8	435
Costa Rica	8.2	76.9	23.1	26.2	720
India	4.0	28.0	72.0	4.1	33
South Africa	8.3	40.3	59.7	10.2	333
Norway	8.6	84.2	15.8	18.0	4,201
United States	16.0	46.5	53.5	19.2	3,506

Source: World Health Organization (2010a).
[a] Purchasing power parity.

years. India, with GDP per capita at less than a third of South Africa's, has a higher life expectancy by ten years. Looking at figure 2.4, we see that while life expectancy has increased steadily in the other countries, it has dropped dramatically in South Africa.

What explains this? The answer is HIV/AIDS. As figure 2.5 vividly demonstrates, the HIV/AIDS pandemic emerged in South Africa in the 1990s and is a problem on a much higher magnitude than in the other countries. While the other countries have HIV/AIDS prevalence well below 1% (ranging from 0.3% for India and 0.6% for Brazil and Colombia), HIV/AIDS prevalence among adult South Africans is a devastating 18.1%. In real terms, this means that there are far more HIV-infected people in South Africa than in all the other countries combined. This is important to keep in mind when we look at the role of health litigation in South Africa, where litigation regarding HIV/AIDS treatment has been very central. The potential implications of such litigation in terms of health gains and costs are radically different in countries where it is a matter of scarce clusters of people than in those where it concerns large sectors of the population.

If we turn from basic indicators on economic resources and health challenges to indicators on what governments actually *do* in terms of health, we see a striking difference in health spending.

Measured in terms of standardized dollars (purchasing power parity), India spent only US$33 per capita on health in 2008. This is just one tenth of what South Africa spent on health (US$333 per capita), which, in turn, is much lower than in the Latin American countries. Costa Rica (US$720) and Argentina (US$690) both spend two times more per capita than South Africa and twenty times more than India.

In India, only 4.1% of total government spending is spent on health. Costa Rica, in comparison, allocates 26.2% of its total spending to health. Percentages in the other countries range from 6% (Brazil) to 18.8% (Colombia) (see table 2.2). Figure 2.6 shows that in Colombia, the share of government expenditure devoted to health rose sharply in the mid-1990s but started to drop again after 1998. In 2001, it leveled off at below the 1994 level—which is still higher than most other countries in the region. The exception is Costa Rica, where the share of government spending devoted to health was relatively stable at a high level until 2005, after which it started to rise sharply until 2008, when it was the highest in the region by far. Brazil saw a marked decrease in the share of government expenditure on health from 1995 until 2000, when it stabilized at a level lower than other countries in the region. In

Figure 2.4. Life expectancy

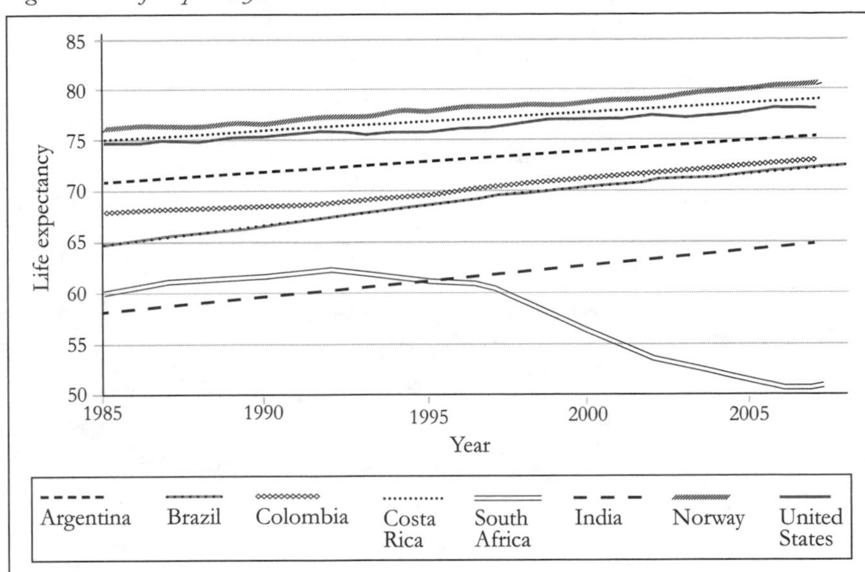

Source: World Bank (2009).

Figure 2.5. HIV/AIDS prevalence in adult population 15–49 years

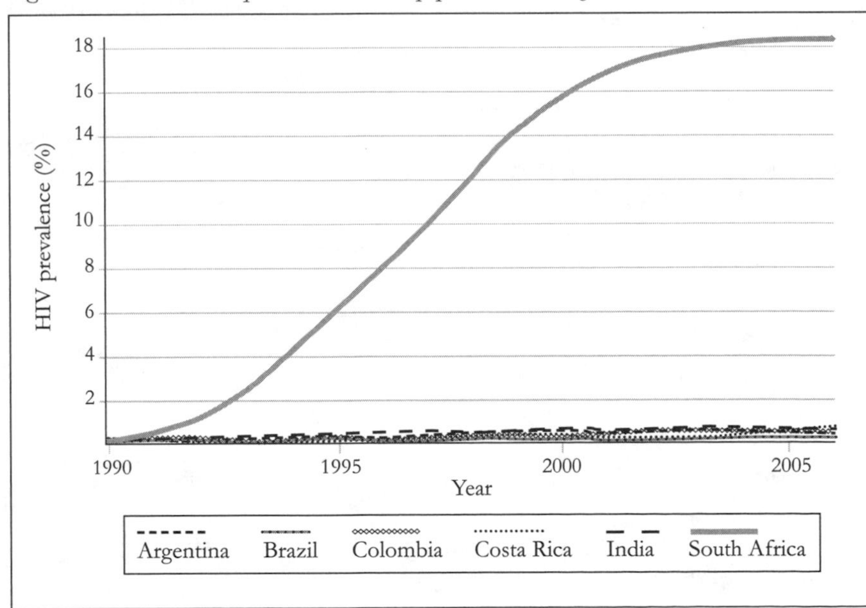

Source: World Bank (2009).

Figure 2.6. Government expenditure on health as % of general government expenditure

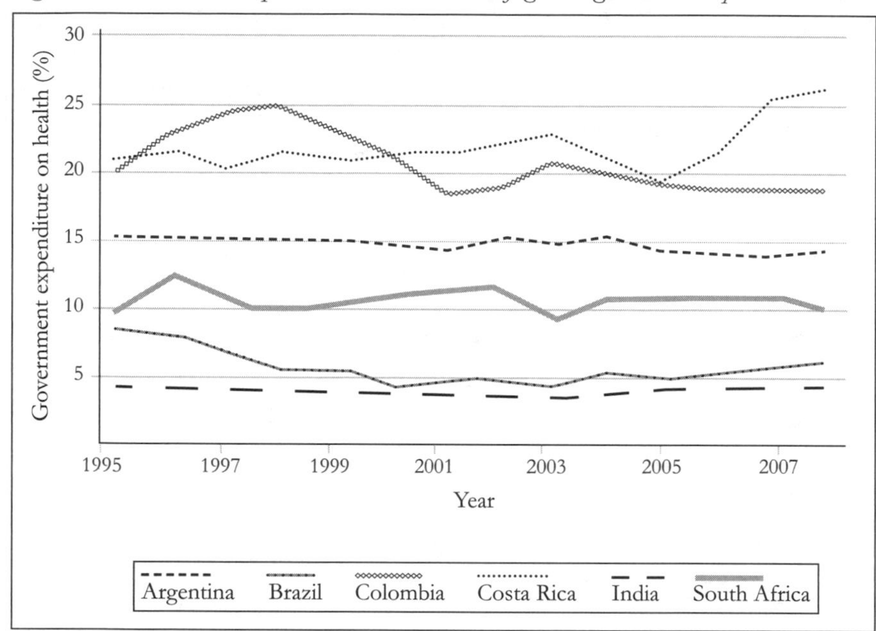

Source: World Health Organization (2010a).

Figure 2.7. Total expenditure on health as % of GDP

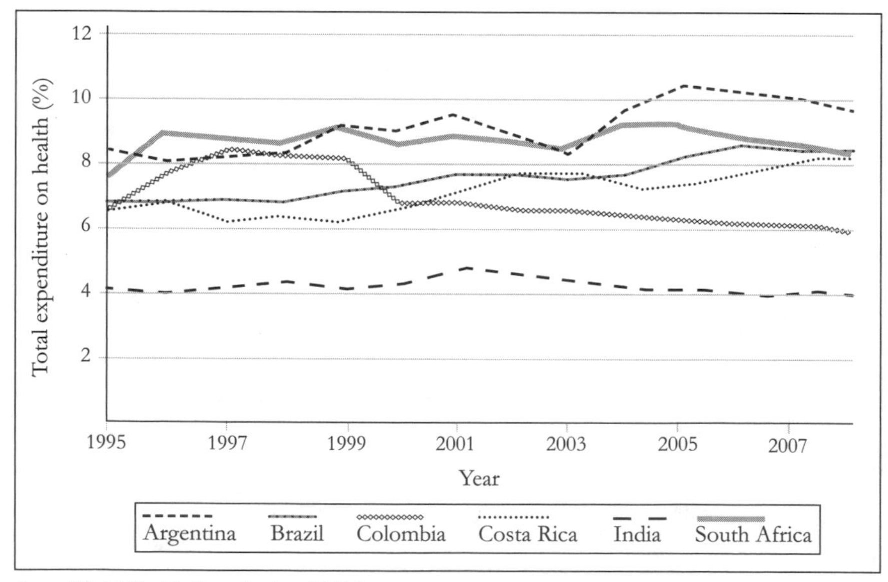

Source: World Health Organization (2010a).

Argentina and South Africa, government expenditure on health as a share of general government expenditure was relatively stable throughout this period.

Indians cover a far higher share of health-care costs privately than do citizens of the other countries analyzed here (72% compared to 16% in Colombia, 23% in Costa Rica, and 50–60% in Argentina, Brazil, and South Africa). But even taking private spending into account, India spends far less on health, both in real terms and as a percentage of GDP (4% compared to 5.9% for Colombia and 8.2–9.6% for the other countries) (see figure 2.7).[4]

To sum up, the cases represent a group of highly unequal middle-income countries—with the exception of India, which is poorer and less unequal. South Africa stands apart due to the special challenges posed by the HIV/AIDS pandemic. Spending on health—and government spending on health in particular—differs widely. It is against this backdrop that we must consider the recent rise in health litigation in these countries, and the associated consequences.

Analytical Framework

The analytical framework guiding the case studies and informing the analysis identifies a range of factors that may influence the ways that health litigation plays out in different social and political contexts and is prone to affect health policy and the allocation of resources for health.

As illustrated in figure 2.8, we disaggregate the processes of health rights litigation into different stages: claims formation, adjudication, implementation, and social outcomes.[5] These stages are shared by all cases but may take different forms and involve different actors. Stages may also be repeated—for example, when cases are appealed or when implementation is subject to judicial oversight or follow-up litigation.

Our analytical framework seeks to isolate and specify factors that are important for the outcome of each part of the health litigation process. While the nature of these factors and their relative importance varies, the framework identifies generic questions to be asked of each case that are critical for understanding what drives litigation, what its implications are, and who stands to benefit.

The Claims-Formation Stage

The first stage of the litigation process concerns the formation of claims. The key actors in focus here are the litigants. Who are they? And what motivates

Figure 2.8. The litigation process from health claim to outcome

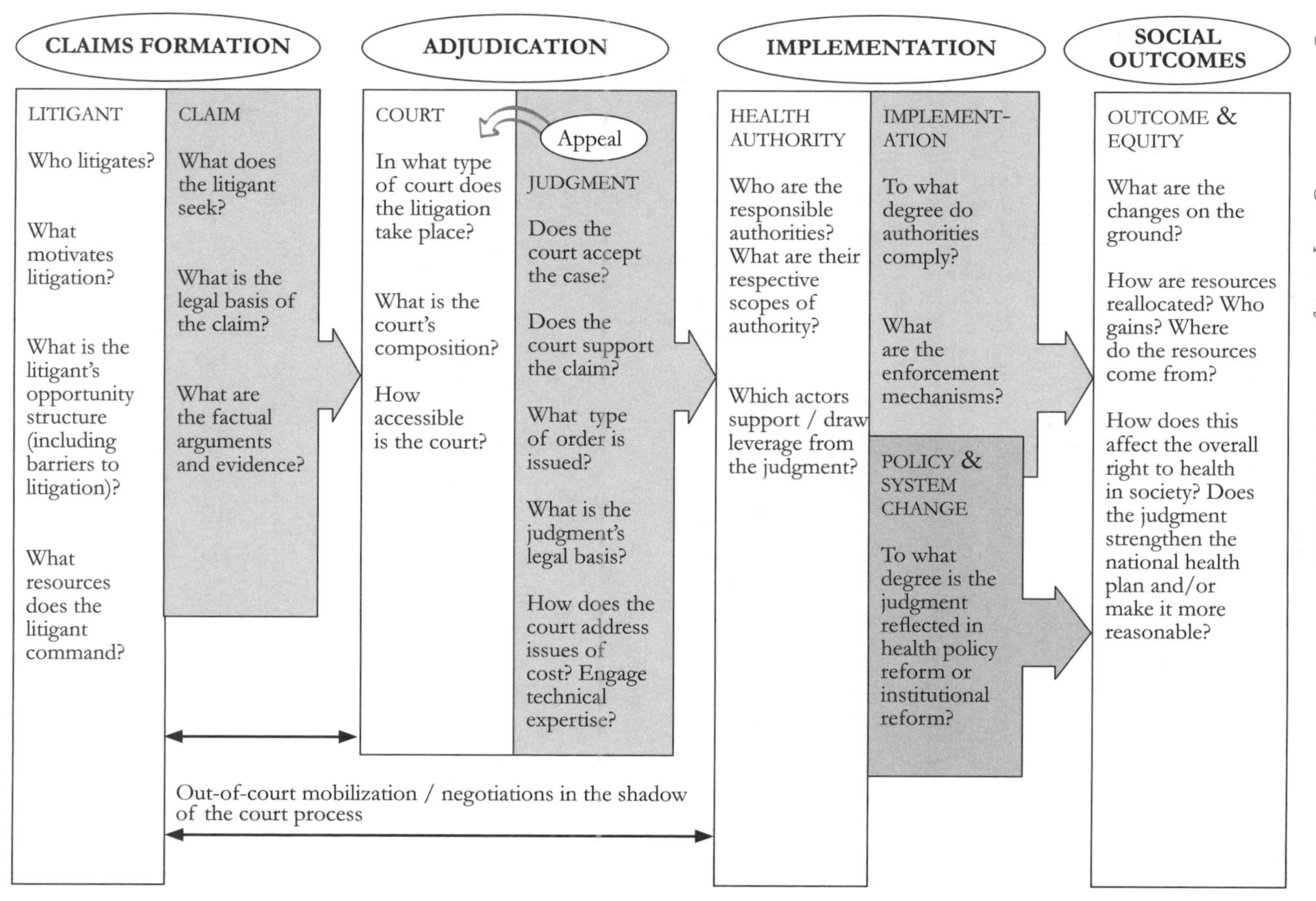

their decision to litigate? In some countries, health claims are overwhelmingly brought by individuals or groups of patients seeking specific interventions to address their own health concerns. In other countries, cases are more often brought by organizations litigating on behalf of others or seeking to change policies in the public interest. In some cases, claims are brought by corporate actors. What are the litigants' health concerns? What is their social and economic background? What do they expect to gain from going to court? Our main focus is on those who actually litigate, but it is also interesting to examine potential litigants—those who might consider litigation and decide against it.

Whether or not litigation is perceived as a worthwhile effort is related to *the litigants' opportunity structure.* It depends, firstly, on how the litigants expect to benefit (the prospective gain). This, in turn, depends on the social, economic, and political context—and especially the perceived capacity of the state to provide (which is related to the nature of the health system) and the possibility of activating this capacity through litigation (which is related to the nature of the legal system and decision makers' respect for court rulings). Whether going to court is a worthwhile strategy also depends on what is required in terms of time and resources (the barriers and costs involved), and whether these requirements are within the litigants' possibility set. And it depends on whether litigation is perceived as the best option given the alternatives. Other possible routes by which prospective litigants may get what they need and desire in terms of health services and treatments is, again, context dependent.

An important aspect of litigants' opportunity structure is *which resources they command* that aid them in the process of formulating claims and bringing them to court. This may be litigants' capabilities as individuals and groups (financial resources, legal skills, relevant information, and/or organizational capacity) or it may be external resources, ranging from local to global, that they can mobilize and link to (legal service organizations, activist networks, social movements, patient organizations, medical companies, media, political decision makers, and/or donors). It is important to recognize that these external "support structures" are agents with their own agendas that may not always coincide with those of the litigants and that may themselves be drivers of litigation (see Gloppen 2008b).

The data required for a full socio-legal analysis of litigants and their opportunity structure may be hard to find, at least on an aggregate level. The case studies presented here use different methodologies to obtain information that can begin to answer these questions; and while there is still quite a way to go before we have a complete picture, the case studies provide some indications and a basis for further investigations.

The central output from the claims-formation stage is *the claim* placed before the court (although this may not necessarily be at the center of litigants' efforts, as litigation may be just one piece of a broader strategy). The nature of claims varies between and within countries, but in the framework guiding the present analysis, we assess the claims along five general dimensions: (i) the substantive focus (what they ask for in terms of health interventions); (ii) their scope (individual, collective, or public interest); (iii) their aim (whether they address policy gaps or implementation gaps); (iv) their legal basis; and (v) their factual basis. The first three dimensions regard *what litigants seek* in terms of the right to health. Is the substantial focus of the claim an expensive new drug or operation, or is it a public health measure? Does it seek something that the health system covers in principle but not in practice or not in a timely and adequate manner (an implementation gap)? Or is it something that goes beyond what the health system is designed to cover (a policy or regulatory gap)? And if the latter, does the claim ask for structural or policy changes that would be applicable to everyone with a particular health-related concern or for an ad hoc remedy for a specific patient? The last two dimensions regard the way that litigants back their claims: *what is the legal basis*? Are they based on an existing right to health in the constitution or domestic legislation, are they derived from other constitutional rights (to life, dignity, and nondiscrimination), or are they based on international law? And, finally, what *factual arguments* are presented to back up the claims? Do the litigants provide information to prove the medical need and effectiveness of the intervention, and if so, what kind of information and from what source (e.g., their physician or scientific findings)?

The Adjudication Stage

The second stage of the litigation process that we identify in our analytical framework is the adjudication stage, or, in other words, what takes place in court. Analytically, this comprises three different phases: the first concerns *access* (whether or not the court agrees to hear the case); the second is the *presentation of arguments* in the case; and the third is the actual *adjudication* process (where the judges deliberate, decide on remedies, and hand down judgment). We simplify this by considering arguments presented in the case as part of the claim and belonging to the claims-formation stage, together with any out-of-court mobilization in support of (or against) the case. Likewise, if a deal is negotiated "in the shadow" of the court process, this is seen in relation to the litigant's opportunity structure and the decision of whether or not to (continue to) litigate. While these processes might seem somewhat marginal, they should not be underestimated. Court processes and threatened litigation may give litigants privileged access to decision makers—particularly where litigation involves considerable economic and political costs on the part of the authorities—and are central to understanding litigation's political and social impacts.

During the adjudication stage, the court is the central actor. Our analysis for this stage seeks to identify characteristics of courts that may affect whether and which health rights cases come before them—and the destiny of the cases that do. We examine the *types of courts* in which health litigation takes place. In some countries (such as Costa Rica), all cases involving constitutional rights, including the right to health, go straight to a constitutional court or chamber, which then serves as the court of first and last instance. In the other countries, cases pass though the lower tiers of the court system before (potentially) reaching a constitutional court (as in Colombia and South Africa) or an ordinary supreme court of appeal (as in Argentina, Brazil, and India). Cases regarding the right to health may also go to regional courts (such the Inter-American Court of Human Rights) and before quasi-judicial bodies (such as the Inter-American Commission on Human Rights). Courts differ in their *composition*, and it may make a difference whether cases are decided by a single judge or by a broad bench, as well as who the judges are (how they are selected and their professional, personal, and ideological backgrounds). Finally, and perhaps most importantly, it matters how *accessible* the courts are. In some countries where health rights litigation is a significant phenomenon (Colombia, Costa Rica, and India), the courts have increased access by simplifying procedures, relaxing requirements regarding standing or who is allowed to bring a case, and reducing or completely abolishing the need for professional assistance (in Costa Rica, for example, the Constitutional Chamber employs its own lawyers who prepare the cases for litigants). This reduces costs for potential litigants and broadens the group of people able to bring cases. While some courts can select the cases they want to hear, others must accept all cases that come before them. Together, these variables influence both the number and type of health rights claims that courts can expect to receive.

The output of the adjudication stage is the *judgment*, which is the traditional focus of legal analysis. The nature and form of judgments vary from court to court and sometimes from judge to judge. Some decisions are short, presenting little underlying reasoning, while others consist of several hundred pages. Some allow individual judges to give their own dissenting or concurring judgments, while others speak in one voice. Yet there are certain dimensions that run across judgments and help us understand the phenomenon of health litigation and the conditions under which it is likely to bring more justice to health.

First, we need to establish to what extent—and in what form—the court *accepts right-to-health cases* within its jurisdiction. Where the court decides such cases on their merits, to what extent does it *support right-to-health claims* placed before them? This is less straightforward to assess than it may seem. Courts often support part of a claim while rejecting other parts, and sometimes courts redefine the issue or introduce new elements. Hence, a broader contextual analysis is necessary to determine to what extent the litigant(s) won the case in actual terms.

Secondly, we are interested in *the legal basis of the judgment*, or how the judges conceptualize the right to health. This should be seen in context, taking into account a country's law, constitution, and international treaty obligations—as well how the various legal sources are interpreted. Thus, the formalization of a right to health is neither a necessary nor sufficient condition for an active or expansive jurisprudence on the right to health. While a constitution explicitly providing for a justiciable right to health may encourage health rights litigation and jurisprudence, it also constrains, particularly if the right is expressly subject to progressive realization within available resources (as in South Africa). Conversely, in countries where there is no explicit justiciable right to health written into the constitution (Costa Rica, India, and, to some extent, Colombia), courts may construct or expand the right to health based on constitutional rights to life, dignity, and nondiscrimination and establish a "minimum core content" standard that is consonant with international legal norms. In this context, it is interesting to consider which international social rights instruments countries have ratified and how they are used.[6]

We are interested not only in how the courts conceptualize the legal norms involved but also in how they treat the facts of the case. Cases regarding the right to health often involve difficult medical evidence, and it is important to understand how the courts relate to this—particularly *whether and how the courts engage technical expertise* on the matter. On which sources (e.g., physicians, scientific findings, and national or international boards of experts or authorizing agencies) do courts rely for authority regarding the effectiveness and suitability of the treatment or intervention? To what extent does the court bring in evidence beyond what the parties themselves have brought to the case? How does the court deal with the issue of *costs* (resource constraints or the cost-effectiveness of the interventions)?

Finally, we consider the orders given and the *remedies* provided. Do claimants get an immediate and concrete entitlement to particular health services or does the order "only" establish a duty on the part of the authorities to address a health need in terms of general policy? If the former, is the decision ad hoc in the sense that it is limited to the particular claimant, or does it establish a precedent securing the same for everyone in a similar position? Does the order apply only to the state or also to private actors? And if the court requires a policy change, does it issue simply a declaratory ("soft") order stating that the current situation is in violation of the right to health (or a related right), leaving the government to decide what to do about it and when? Or does it issue a mandatory ("hard") judgment specifying particular remedies? Does it give a structural judgment specifying particular processes and criteria for broader reform, and if so, does this include requirements for public participation? Does the court take on a supervisory role, retaining authority over the case and setting time limits for authorities to report back on implementation? Does it keep the case open for other litigants to join at a later stage? These factors are important for evaluating the broader impact of health rights litigation.

The Implementation Stage

The impact of a strong judgment in support of health rights claims—on both litigants and society—depends on whether the decision is complied with and how it is implemented. As discussed earlier, analyses of social rights litigation often stop with the judgment, without assessing whether and how court victories (and losses) are reflected on the ground. There are many reasons for this. It is not always obvious what should be regarded as compliance with or implementation of a judgment, especially one requiring policy change; the time from court decision to expected implementation may be long or disputed; and data may be difficult to find. Our framework helps us get a better picture by outlining a set of considerations for assessing implementation processes.

Firstly, *the authorities responsible* for the remedies specified in the judgment must be identified. Sometimes these parties are clearly stated in the judgment; but in other cases, particularly when a judgment requires a change of policy, identifying the actors and agencies that should be held accountable for implementation requires a contextual knowledge of how the health system works, who has authority over what, and how policies are made.

The next step is to assess to what extent authorities *comply with the judgment.* Compliance may range from blatant disregard to full implementation of the judgment. If a ruling concerns only one patient or a limited group of patients, assessing compliance is, in theory at least, relatively straightforward; but if the judgment has an *erga omnes* effect on all similar cases, the assessment is more complex—and even more so if the judgment orders a policy change, when interpretations may differ as to what constitutes compliance. In these more complex cases, official statistics and reports from public agencies (such as human rights commissions) or civil society organizations may be useful in assessing the form and extent of compliance and implementation. Often, however, the available information is limited or biased, and the best way to get an impression is through key informant interviews. We are also interested in *what the enforcement mechanisms are.* Sometimes oversight bodies are established or existing bodies are tasked with monitoring implementation. Courts may also build other enforcement mechanisms into their judgment, setting report-back timelines and charging officials with contempt of court if they refuse to cooperate. Litigants or other interested parties can instigate (or threaten) follow-up litigation or engage in street protests, lobbying, or shaming activities. While the latter are not formal enforcement mechanisms, they nevertheless often serve the same purpose and are important to consider.

Even where a judgment does not require (or even intend) concrete policy changes or generalization of the right to all similarly situated, it may provide impetus and serve as leverage for health policy reform or institutional changes to the health system. In these cases of indirect policy impact, problems of *attribution* become more acute. While it is usually difficult to determine to what extent the actions we regard as compliance or implementation are in fact caused (solely) by the litigation process/court order, or would have occurred independently, attribution problems increase when the judgment itself does not provide a yardstick. Such problems may be reduced by considering other factors that might have influenced the policy process and by tracing how the judgment and the broader litigation process play into the social and political dynamics. Who supports or draws legitimacy from the judgment? Which political and social actors use it to mobilize support—or are mobilized by the judgment to support a particular reform? When assessing indirect policy impacts of litigation, we should also keep in mind that judgments can acquire a broader influence by setting precedence, both formally or informally, for how other cases are decided (sometimes even in other policy areas and other countries).

Social Outcomes and Equity

The last stage of our analytical framework addresses the impact of health litigation. This brings us back to the overall aim of the book, which is to understand how health litigation affects the right to health in society. Does litigation contribute toward better and more just health systems, more inclusive and participatory procedures, and more equitable spending on health services? Or does it draw resources in the opposite direction? We are interested not only in whether particular health services or goods are delivered (i.e., instrumental effects) but also in whether a judgment changes procedures and decision-making processes and the ways in which particular health-related issues are conceived and debated (i.e., symbolic effects), which, in turn, may influence future reforms (Rodríguez Garavito 2010).

These questions are both complex and normative. Answering them requires (i) an understanding of the long-term, direct, and indirect changes on the ground—how litigation affects budgetary allocations, decision-making procedures, and provision of health services, as well as who benefits and who (if anyone) loses—and (ii) establishing standards for evaluating what constitutes positive changes in terms of the right to health. Both are fraught with difficulties.

Assessing the long-term impact of litigation presents conceptual as well as practical challenges. Conceptually, there is, in addition to the problems of attribution discussed above, the question of what would have happened without litigation (*counterfactuals*). There is also the question of on *whom* impact should be measured (e.g., litigants, other beneficiaries, and the general public) and in terms of *what* (e.g., costs, healthy life years, democratic participation, and accountability).[7] At the practical level, the greatest challenge is finding appropriate and reliable data. Statistical data are often of poor quality, incomplete, scattered, and hard to access. And the data that can be found are often not sufficiently disaggregated to provide information for the categories needed in the analysis.

Establishing criteria for what constitutes a "positive" effect of litigation in terms of the right to health is inescapably linked to the question of what constitutes a good health system, which, of course, is highly normative and political. Still, it is possible to rely on criteria that have relatively wide support.

One point of departure in this regard could be a country's national health plan. Does litigation contribute to health spending and practices more in line with the plan? If not, does litigation undermine the health plan? Or does it make the health plan more reasonable by forcing authorities to include services and treatments that should be prioritized from the perspective of the overall right to health in the society, taking into account the needs of the less advantaged? Such assessments may be based on common priority-setting criteria, such as the seriousness of the medical condition and the effectiveness and cost-effectiveness of the treatment, and may also consider the effects on inequality in health (see Norheim and Gloppen in this volume).

Conclusion

With this outline of our methodological approach and theoretical framework guiding the studies, and a comparative overview of some basic conditions relevant for understanding the state of health and health care in the countries under study, this chapter sets the stage for an empirical scrutiny of health rights litigation in the six countries. As we will see, each of these countries has significant experience with the phenomenon, but in quite dissimilar ways and with different consequences for their health systems.

NOTES

1. On the merits and limits of case studies, see King et al. (1994), Gerring (2004), and George and Bennett (2005).
2. The two countries are among those highest ranked by the United Nations' Human Development Index (in the 2010 report, Norway is number 1 and the United States is number 13), and they represent two different health-system models. Norway has an overwhelmingly public health-care system while the United States is the paradigmatic case of a private health-care system.
3. The Gini index lies between 0 and 100. A value of 0 represents absolute equality, while 100 is absolute inequality (World Bank 2010).
4. Let us compare health spending in these countries to Norway and the United States: in Norway, spending on health as percentage of GDP (8.6%) is similar to Brazil, Costa Rica, and South Africa (the countries with the highest spending among our cases), while in the United States, it is almost twice as high (16%). In real terms, Norway and the United States spend at least ten times more per capita (PPP) on health than any of the

countries analyzed in this book (with the United States spending much more per capita than Norway once private spending is taken into account). In this context, it is interesting to note that the high spending on health in the United States is not reflected in the country's health indicators, which, as table 2.1 shows, are very similar to those of Costa Rica.

5. The figure is adapted from Gloppen (2008a), which provides an in-depth presentation of the theoretical framework informing this study. The framework builds on Gloppen (2006, 2008b), as well as on an established socio-legal literature analyzing strategic litigation and its (lack of) effect, some of which is reviewed in this volume's introductory chapter. See, e.g., Scheingold (2004); Galanter (1974); Rosenberg (1991); McCann (1994); Epp (1998); Feeley and Rubin (2000); Hertogh and Halliday (2004); Hirschl (2004).
6. For example, South Africa has not ratified the International Covenant on Economic, Social and Cultural Rights, G.A. Res. 2200A (XXI), 21 U.N. GAOR Supp. (No. 16) at 49, U.N. Doc. A/6316 (1966), 993 U.N.T.S. 3, entered into force January 3, 1976. In the *Grootboom* case, the country's Constitutional Court rejected the minimum core approach adopted by the United Nations Committee on Economic, Social and Cultural Rights in favor of its own reasonableness approach, which does not establish an individual right to a particular good but rather aims to secure a reasonable and participatory process for realizing the right. See Liebenberg (2010); Cooper (this volume).
7. For a more detailed discussion, see Mæstad et al. (this volume) and Norheim and Gloppen (this volume).

CASE STUDIES

Chapter 3

Argentina

Courts and the Right to Health: Achieving Fairness Despite "Routinization" in Individual Coverage Cases?

Paola Bergallo

In Argentina, the judicialization of health has emerged against the backdrop of changed legal contexts—most notably, the 1994 reform of the Constitution and the incorporation of a handful of human rights treaties and procedural innovations that citizens and lawyers have been trying to enforce ever since (Centro de Estudios Legales y Sociales 2008). Drawing from that context, this chapter explores the contours and potential effects of a particular segment of the judicialization of health that remains largely unexamined from an empirical perspective: the routinization—or sustained accumulation and clustering of cases around certain demands—of right-to-health claims filed by individuals seeking coverage of a variety of health services or drugs.

In this chapter, I begin with a description of the broader legal and institutional context of the transformed role of courts. After an overview of right-to-health cases in Argentina, the discussion then focuses on cases that claim coverage of services or drugs sometimes included in and sometimes absent from the *Plan Médico Obligatorio* (Obligatory Medical Plan, or PMO), Argentina's basic health plan by which all health-care insurers must abide.

Legal discussions of right-to-health litigation in the country have tended to celebrate individual cases for their successes as test cases or for

---

This chapter was written using data and parts of chapters from the author's dissertation. The author is thankful for the research assistance of Laura Roth, Agustina Michel, Sonia Ariza, and Sabrina Cartabia, and for the financial assistance of the Chr. Michelsen Institute (Bergen, Norway) and the Norwegian Research Council. I also want to thank Deborah Hensler, Siri Gloppen, Alicia Ely Yamin, Daniel Brinks, Marcelo Alegre, Octavio L. Motta Ferraz, and Karen Engle for their comments on earlier drafts.

their legal merits in granting access to the right to health (Courtis 2008a; Damsky 2006). However, after exploring the accumulation and persistence of such litigation over time—as demonstrated by the cycles of routinization, discussed below—I caution against such isolated and static assessments. This may especially be the case given that a majority of the claims surveyed in this chapter sought very individualized solutions for different types of regulatory and implementation gaps in the PMO's coverage, even though such gaps can be attributed largely to flaws in the design of the health system, the lack of state governance capacities (both legislative and executive), and long-standing political blockages for broad health reform.

Indeed, as Octavio L. Motta Ferraz discusses in his chapter on Brazil, data suggest that—in spite of motives for praising the growing justiciability of the right to health—the predominance of a traditional private-law style of litigation that fails to address inequities and structural governance constraints in health policy, coupled with the aggregated effects of accumulated cases, may ultimately reinforce inequalities. In other words, judicialization may be exacerbating problems rather than remedying them.

Legal Enabling Factors for Litigation

As Catalina Smulovitz (2010) has illustrated for other areas of judicialization in Argentina, a variety of enabling legal conditions foster intervention by the courts in social policy. Certain traits of Argentina's legal culture and legal institutional histories set the scene for courts' increasing participation in protecting human rights. Regarding the judicialization of health in particular, courts' increased involvement can be connected to new substantive and procedural legal developments, an increased perception of courts as independent bodies for ensuring government accountability, and the evolution of legal support structures with various degrees of specialization.

The Substantive Basis for Right-to-Health Claims

Argentina has a federal system of government, and health is regulated at the national and provincial levels. Although social rights were not included in Argentina's first Constitution, written in 1853, they acquired a strong constitutional presence during the first half of the following century through the introduction of the ideals of social constitutionalism.[1] In 1957, after the short life of the 1949 Constitution, the corporativist labor rights version of social constitutionalism entered the current text through article 14 (bis). The new section offered, among other things, grounds for the consolidation of a social security system that included a state-run pension system and a contributory health system for workers.

In 1994, a new constitutional convention, originally summoned to remove the barriers for presidential re-election, introduced new institutions, rights, and principles that would reshape the textual protections of social rights, particularly the right to health. The new text contained several references to social justice and equality, modeling an *Estado Social de Derecho* (Abramovich 2009). The granting of constitutional status to a handful of human rights treaties in article 75.22 was one of its main innovations. This incorporation gave rise to a process of internalization of human rights norms that deeply transformed the original specification of rights in the constitutional text and that continues to evolve today.

The current constitutional protection of the right to health stems from several references scattered throughout the text and from human rights treaties. The Constitution protects the collective right to "a healthy and balanced environment fit for human development" (art. 41) and consumers' rights "to the protection of their health, safety, and economic interests" (art. 43). Moreover, article 75 delineating Congress's mandate creates a responsibility to legislate in keeping with a social justice agenda[2] and to provide certain specific health protections on the basis of equality.[3] The right is further defined by several references in the human rights treaties included under article 75.22.[4] Also, at the federal level, a set of statutes establishes the legal framework for the provision of the right to health.[5] This regulatory framework is supplemented and additionally developed by the twenty-four provincial constitutions and provincial health regulations. The twelve provincial constitutions amended since 1984 expressly recognize a right to health[6] and often detail principles and rules governing local health systems.

These textual innovations set the principles and standards for the development of several lines of precedents by which federal and state courts have defined fragments of the right to health. A comprehensive description of the multiplicity of doctrines and their evolution exceeds the scope of this chapter; however, several studies have analyzed and classified the main holdings of right-to-health claims decided by the Supreme Court in the last decade (Abramovich and Pautassi 2008; Courtis 2008a). In a majority of the cases surveyed by scholars, the Court has acknowledged the constitutional status of the right to health as a result of its protection in human rights treaties incorporated into the Constitution.[7] The Court has also held that the right creates negative and positive duties and has enforced it horizontally across contributory insurers. For example, negative duties have included protection against unilateral termination of health services by different health insurers,[8] and positive duties have encompassed the state's obligation to guarantee access to treatment.[9] Moreover, in various cases against public (provincial) and contributory insurers, the Court has stressed the federal government's role as subsidiary guarantor.[10] Human rights treaties have often been cited in support of the different doctrines, and the Court has repeatedly asserted the government's international responsibility under the treaties signed. Human rights norms have also been found to ground the positive duties of contributory insurers, regardless of contractual provisions.[11] Lastly, in other cases, the Court has defined segments of the right to health of vulnerable groups, such as children,[12] people with disabilities,[13] people with severe diseases,[14] and marginalized indigenous communities.[15]

Procedural Reforms

Procedural tools and expanded standing rules have also offered a framework for the increased use of courts for right-to-health demands. Summary proceedings for constitutional rights protections, such as the *amparo* and the recently created *amparo colectivo* (protection writ and collective protection writ, respectively), have provided enabling procedural tools for different styles of legal mobilization on the right to health (Maurino et al. 2005). A majority of the individual cases brought before Argentine courts have used *amparo* proceedings to address disputes regarding insurance contracts and coverage through constitutional arguments. In certain collective cases, groups of individuals or nongovernmental organizations have resorted to the *amparo colectivo*, created in 1994, which the courts have positively received.

In addition, the procedural availability of preliminary injunctions, for which the courts have loosened requirements, has been an important tool for the judicialization of health. A majority of the individual cases described below obtained preliminary injunctions. The relatively easy access to preliminary measures has greatly shaped the substance of the disputes in court proceedings.

Courts, Accountability, and Support Structures

The presence of legal texts, precedents, and procedures is a necessary but not sufficient enabling condition for judicialization. The availability of what Varun Gauri and Daniel Brinks (2008) term "logistical variables" is another requirement. In effect, a functioning court system with clearly established jurisdiction over the relevant rights claims is another key structural precondition for the judicialization of health. In Argentina, it was not until the late 1990s—a decade after the return to democratic rule—that courts across the country began to accept their role in the justiciability of social rights (Abramovich 2009). Since then, the existence of several barriers to accessing the judicial system (see, e.g., Scioscioli 2005) do not seem to have deterred people from turning to the courts for the enforcement of the right to health.

Moreover, researchers have argued that various factors may have played a role in increasing the accountability function of courts, their independence, and public perception of their independence. These factors include the 1994 constitutional reform of procedures for judicial appointments, the establishment in 2003 of new standards for nominating Supreme Court and federal judges, and the subsequent appointment of four prestigious Supreme Court judges after the impeachment of two of their predecessors (Smulovitz 2010). Also, public confidence in the judiciary has varied greatly, reaching a low point during the 2001–2 economic and political crisis. Since then, available data on trust in the judiciary produced annually by the School of Law of the Universidad Torcuato Di Tella show a moderate increase in public confidence.[16] Furthermore, confidence in the courts as a site for rights claims may have also improved as a result of courts' recent role in providing forums for seeking justice for massive human rights violations of the 1970s (Centro de Estudios Legales y Sociales 2008).

Finally, the existence and strength of support structures—that is, human rights lawyers and organizations as well as financial resources—are important factors in determining potential litigants' capacity to bring rights claims to courts (Epp 1998). According to Smulovitz (2010), an overall transformation of support structures occurred over the last two decades, with roots that can be traced to lawyers in the human rights and labor rights movements. The existence of new legal advocacy organizations seems to have been an enabling condition for the judicialization of health, as demonstrated by the involvement of some of Argentina's growing legal advocacy groups (such as Centro de Estudios Legales y Sociales and Asociación por los Derechos Civiles) in the litigation of multiple right-to-health claims. Yet litigants have also used four other types of legal representation in right-to-health cases: private lawyers, public defenders, ombudspersons, and consumer rights lawyers.

The structure of litigation costs has also been an important factor for enabling right-to-health litigation. In particular, the availability of the *beneficio de litigar sin gastos*, which provides a waiver for plaintiffs in case of the claim's failure, has been an incentive for private lawyers to work for free in cases of uncertain results. Indeed, lawyers have acknowledged that through the reduction of cost risks for both claimants and lawyers, the *beneficio de litigar sin gastos* helped them file Argentina's early right-to-health cases when uncertainty about their result was high. However, this tool was not prominently used in the right-to-health litigation explored in this chapter.

The Health System

Before focusing on the actual cases, it is necessary to understand at least superficially the complexity of Argentina's institutional framework for the judicialization of health—namely, the health system and its multiple fragmentary actors. The origins of today's health system can be traced to the mid-twentieth century, when Argentina began to redefine the system's structure. Under the Peronist government and in consonance with the principles endorsed by the short-lived 1949 Constitution, the system evolved from a model based on the private supply of medical services and scattered facilities to a centrally organized and planned system. However, in the following decades, the system was decentralized (Katz 1993).

The structure that emerged from the first and the second presidencies of Juan Domingo Perón (1945–55) and the process of decentralization that followed resulted in a national health system and twenty-four provincial health systems, each of which comprises a public sector and a contributory sector. The contributory sector is, in turn, divided into a large variety of work-centered social security insurers known as *Obras Sociales* (OSSs),[17] run by unions, and a web of private insurers known as *Empresas de Medicina Privada* (EMPs). OSSs are of compulsory affiliation for workers, and since their expansion in the 1970s, they have contracted out their services to help develop a private-sector system. As a result, today they function primarily like U.S. health maintenance organizations (McGuire 2010).

Over the decades since the health system's inception, vertical and horizontal fragmentation has increased significantly. Proposals to universalize the system and centralize its governance, put forward in 1974 and in 1984, failed;[18] they contributed only to the introduction of piecemeal reforms that fostered more decentralization, including those that were undertaken in the 1990s under the auspices of the World Bank and the Washington Consensus (Belmartino 2005). While the above-mentioned references to the right to health were being incorporated into the Constitution in the 1990s, the public health system and semi-public, or social, health system were subject to a set of structural neoliberal reforms guided by fiscal and efficiency concerns contradicting what at the time seemed only aspirational provisions (Yamin 2000).[19]

Figure 3.1 provides a simplified description of the different subsectors of the Argentine health system.

From a vertical point of view, the Argentine health system today is composed of a national health system, provincial health systems, and a myriad of municipal systems. Each of these, in turn, is horizontally fragmented, with three subsectors: the public; private; and semi-public, or social health, systems. Table 3.1 offers an aggregated picture of the percentages of the total population covered by each of these subsectors. Such percentages vary greatly over time, depending on Argentina's employment rate, and also vary within each of the provincial health systems, where, in some cases, the public health sector represents 70% of health services (Báscolo 2008).

Figure 3.1. The Argentine health system

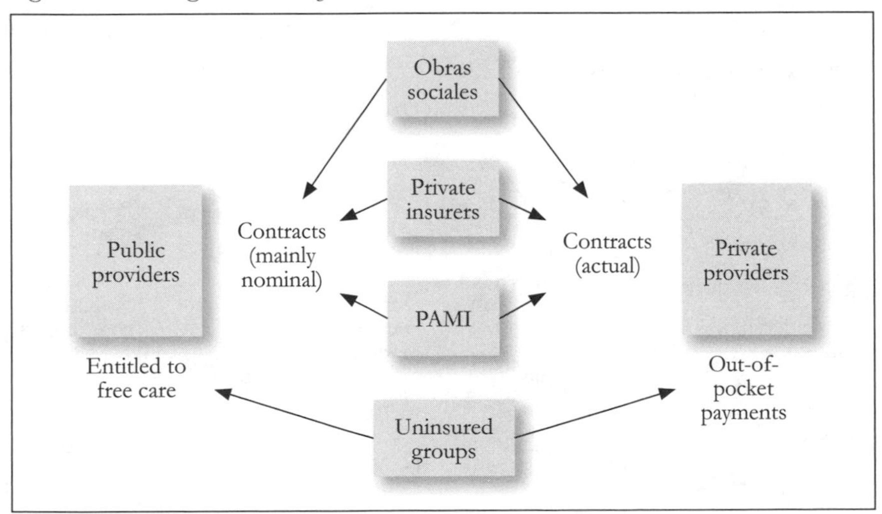

Source: Lloyd-Sherlock (2005).

The national and provincial public health sectors operate under the principle of universal access. In practice, people lacking access to the private or social health subsectors are the primary users of public health care. However, as a result of the universal guarantee, people insured by other sectors may voluntarily choose public care for certain services, depending on the services and the coverage offered by the sector to which they are subscribed.

Argentina's public health expenditure amounts to 27% of total health expenditure; of that number, 16% is spent by the national government while 71% is spent by provincial governments (Báscolo 2008). Also, though the social security subsector covers approximately 74.3% of the population, its expenditure contributes only 38% of total health expenditure (McGuire 2010). Households contribute a considerable 36% of the country's total health expenditure.

Regulation and Governance of the Health System

The health system is regulated by national and provincial health departments and an intricate web of public institutions at the national, provincial, and municipal levels. The National Health Department retains stewardship of the system.

The creation of a basic health plan with a minimum package of benefits, known as the PMO, was one of the reforms promoted by the World Bank in the 1990s.[20] The PMO functions as the mechanism that sets the alleged minimum content of medical services provided by contributory insurers in order to satisfy the right to health (Lloyd-Sherlock 2005).[21] As a result, the PMO is the key institutional arrangement for the allocation of resources and priority-setting decisions. The federal government regulates the content and procedures for the determination of the PMO. Additionally,

Table 3.1. Populations covered by the health system's three subsectors

	Public sector	Social sector			Private sector
		National OSSs	PAMI	Provincial OSSs	
Type of population covered	Everyone	Workers, family members, and retirees	Retirees, pensioners, and families	Provincial public employees and family retirees	Voluntary contributors
Number of people covered	39,745,613	18,336,500	3,985,409	5,508,733	3,636,000
% of population	100	46.1	13.8	14.4	10

Source: Báscolo and Blejer (2009).

the federal government controls national OSSs' compliance with the PMO through the *Superintendencia de Servicios de Salud* (SSSalud), the national agency charged with supervising OSSs. Due to the lack of a regulatory agency with the power to supervise EMPs, the monitoring of EMPs' compliance with the PMO is dispersed among an array of institutions functioning as receivers of claims filed by individuals using either the public or private health sector. These other institutions include ombudsperson offices and consumer-protection agencies.

As demonstrated in the following sections, PMO definition and monitoring is at the core of a substantial number of right-to-health claims. It is therefore important to bear in mind that unlike in other countries, Argentina does not have a well-equipped, particularized agency devoted to designing, reforming, and adjusting PMO rules and content.

Courts and the Right to Health

Although courts in Argentina over the last twenty years have provided a forum for individuals and civil society to seek the enforcement of the right to health, little is known about the contours of such litigation or courts' performance. Official, systematized data on the phenomenon have not been produced by any of the three branches of government. Against this backdrop of a lack of information, this section offers a preliminary profile of litigants and their claims.

Information was extracted from five databases and from discussion of preliminary database findings with ten interviewees in the city of Buenos Aires who were involved in right-to-health litigation—five lawyers, three court officers, and two judges. The first database, Database Legal Reporters (Database LR), compiles all court decisions published in (i) the two leading legal reporting publications of Argentina (*La Ley* and *Jurisprudencia Argentina*) from January 1, 1983, to December 31, 2007, and (ii) the online database of Argentina's Supreme Court, which contains cases from 1996 onward. The second database, Database Federal Cases (Database FC), contains data from January 1, 1997, to December 31, 2007, on all cases filed with the Federal Civil and Commercial Courts (located in the city of Buenos Aires). The third, Database Provincial Cases (Database PC), includes the numbers of all cases on the right to health reported by three provincial courts for 2006, 2007, and 2008. The fourth, Database Files 2001/2008 (Database F01/08), contains the complete records of sixty dockets selected from Database FC, including ten cases randomly selected for each of the years 2001, 2002, and 2005–8. And finally, the fifth, Database Files 2008 (Database F08), features forty randomly selected cases filed in 2008 from Database FC. Although the information retrieved from these databases should not be regarded as representative of all right-to-health litigation in either the city of Buenos Aires or the country, each of the databases does provide valuable information for understanding the judicialization of health in Argentina.

Figures 3.2 and 3.3 depict the quantitative evolution of right-to-health claims. Figure 3.2 draws on data from published cases to suggest the growth of right-to-health claims in Argentina from 1983 to 2007. The graph shows a rise from one case in 1987 to eighty-one and seventy-five in 2006 and 2007, respectively.[22] Similarly, figure 3.3 reflects the total number of *amparos* against the three health subsectors brought to one of the main courts in the city of Buenos Aires with jurisdiction over health claims: the Federal Civil and Commercial Courts.[23] This figure shows a consistent growth in health claims, with the number almost tripling after ten years, growing from 449 health cases filed in 1998 to 1,159 cases filed in 2007.[24]

Right-to-health litigation has also been an increasing phenomenon in some provinces. Even if the lack of systemic information precludes an evaluation of the structure and prevalence of such litigation at the provincial level as a whole, table 3.2 provides a preliminary look by showing the number of right-to-health *amparos* filed with courts in three provincial districts.[25]

Finally, a study of court decisions in Databases LR and F01/08 shows that litigation has been characterized by plaintiffs' high rate of success in obtaining their demands: litigants have an 80% success rate for the cases in Database LR and a 90% success rate for the cases in Database F01/08.

Table 3.2. Health amparos filed before courts located in the provinces of Buenos Aires, Mendoza, and Tucumán

Province	Number of cases		
	2006	2007	2008
Buenos Aires (1 tribunal)	2	19	32
Mendoza (1 of 3 jurisdictions)	787	162	180
Tucumán (1 jurisdiction)	31	. . .	48

Source: Database PC.

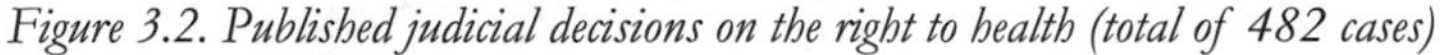

Figure 3.2. Published judicial decisions on the right to health (total of 482 cases)

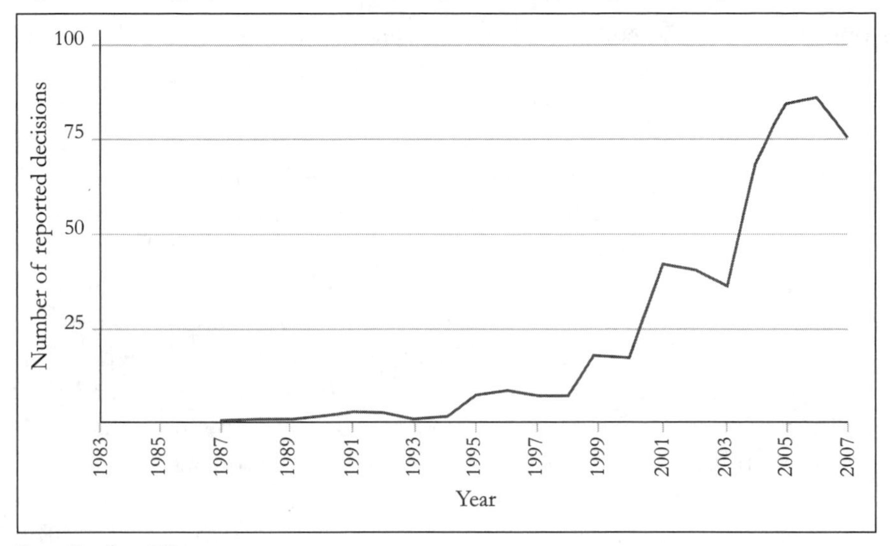

Source: Database LR.

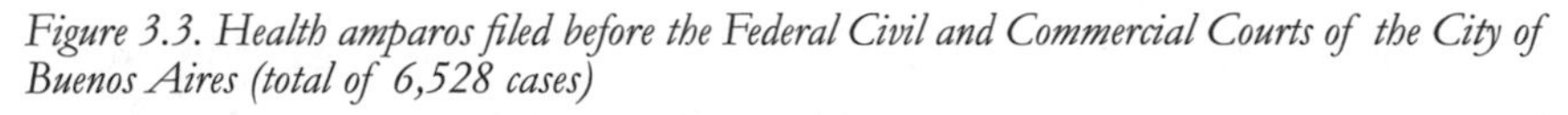
Figure 3.3. Health amparos filed before the Federal Civil and Commercial Courts of the City of Buenos Aires (total of 6,528 cases)

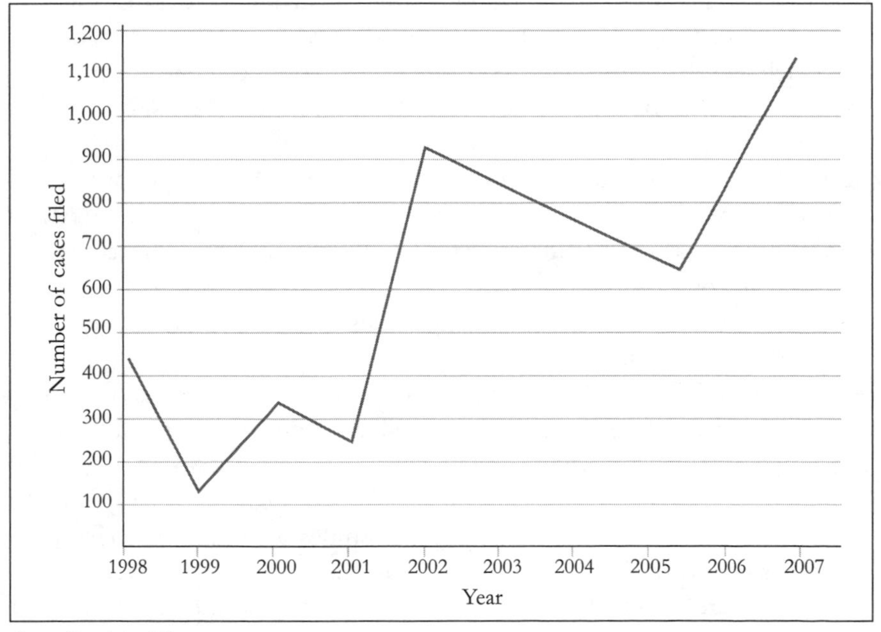

Source: Database FC.

Litigants

Both individual and collective litigants have used the courts to seek the realization of their right to health. Collective actors have included ombudspersons and organized civil society—namely, human rights and consumer rights organizations, professional associations of physicians, and patient groups. Health-care insurers and providers, insurers' associations, and pharmaceutical companies have mostly been on the side of defendants but have occasionally used the courts to claim protection of the right to health.[26]

The data collected reveal that most cases were filed by individual, and not collective, plaintiffs. In federal courts, individual litigants accounted for almost all cases. For example, in Database FC, 98.5% of the plaintiffs were individuals. Of the 6,528 health cases filed with the Federal Civil and Commercial Courts from 1998 to 2007, collective plaintiffs filed only 75 cases. In provincial courts, individual litigants represented 100% of the cases. Finally, in Database LR, where complex decisions can be overrepresented in the legal reporters due to publisher interest in the diffusion of high-profile precedents, individual claimants still accounted for 91% of the cases.

The fledgling nature of Argentine civil society mobilization around health issues might be one contributing factor in the dearth of collective cases. With the exception of the *Mendoza*[27] case seeking decontamination of the Riachuelo River, the databases do not offer much evidence of a significant development or coordination of civil society organizations, at either the national or provincial levels, around structural health-care issues or a public health agenda. As in other countries across the world, an important exception in this regard is collective mobilization in the context of HIV/AIDS; nongovernmental organizations were the first to resort to the courts on this issue in collective right-to-health cases during the 1990s. With regard to other health issues, a few smaller organizations have filed claims on behalf of rather narrowly defined categories of patients.

Though the available information does not allow us to assess the socioeconomic profile of individual plaintiffs, table 3.3 offers an exploratory exercise conducted on the basis of the domicile declared in the sixty court files of Database F01/08 and the forty court files of Database F08. Table 3.3 shows that most litigants came from communities where the average family income is relatively high. The data also show that either none or very few of the claims were filed by litigants domiciled in the southern region, where the average family income is much lower. Though this finding is preliminary, it advances the possibility that litigation is not necessarily being used by those most in need. This hypothesis is also confirmed by the prevalence of litigants from the contributory system, indicating that they are employed or able to contract private insurance.

Defendants included actors in the public, social, and private health-care sectors, as well as public health authorities at the state and national levels. Most prevalent among these were social health insurers, which proves the frequency of the horizontal imposition of right-to-health duties on private actors within the contributory health sector. In 54% of the cases surveyed in Database LR, defendants were OSSs, and in the remaining 46%, half were public providers and the other half were EMPs. In the other four databases, an average of 70% of the defendants were OSSs, while EMPs and governmental organizations accounted for the remaining 30%. In addition, in many cases, plaintiffs sued more than one defendant (e.g., the federal and provincial governments) in search of the subsidiary guarantee.

Table 3.3. Number of cases filed and average family income per community per region in the city of Buenos Aires (CABA)

Region and its population	Commune	Average income per family (AR$)[a]	Number of cases, Database F01/08	Number of cases, Database F08
Buenos Aires Province	...	...	19	16
CABA East Region 643,081 inhabitants	C1	1,380	13	8
	C3	1,008	...	...
	C4	676	6	1
CABA West Region 937,858 inhabitants	C5	1,061	1	...
	C6	1,200	2	2
	C10	881	4	3
	C11	850	...	0
	C15	957	4	3
CABA North Region 890,912 inhabitants	C2	1,851	...	1
	C12	993	2	...
	C13	1,552	4	4
	C14	1,542	2	2
CABA South Region 562,128 inhabitants	C7	942	1	...
	C8	511	1	...
	C9	754	...	...

Source: Databases F01/08 and F08; Argentine Ministry of Health (2008).
[a] Figures rounded to the nearest peso.

With regard to legal representation, evidence from Database F01/08 shows that none of the plaintiffs used the free public defense system. Only one of the litigants requested a *beneficio de litigar sin gastos*, exempting her from court and lawyers' fees. According to the other databases, when information regarding legal representation was available, private lawyers represented litigants in a significant proportion of the individual cases. *Defensores del Pueblo*, or ombudspersons, also defended a small group of collective cases (three, according to Database LR).

Types of Claims

The decisions in Database LR suggest that right-to-health cases focus mainly on (i) claims for access to medical services, treatments, and medicines (72%); (ii) claims requesting basic reforms in public health policies and facilities (11%); (iii) judicial authorizations for certain health services related to autonomy and sexual and reproductive rights (12%); and (iv) other claims, such as those regarding basic preconditions for health (5%).

Claims in the largest category—access to services, treatments, and medicines—sought a variety of health-care goods. Firstly, plaintiffs sought access to a range of drugs, from HIV/AIDS medicines to asthma and diabetes medicines to medicines for rare diseases. Some claims requested inexpensive medicines, while others sought extremely costly drugs requiring importation. Secondly, plaintiffs sued OSSs or EMPs to obtain an extension in their health insurance coverage contracts. Among other things, these claims included requests for the renewal of OSS coverage after loss of employment, disputes over pre-existing conditions, requests for extension of coverage to partners, requests for the protection of seniors excluded on the basis of age, and requests for reimbursement of services paid in advance for urgent treatments outside contractual provisions. Thirdly, claims sought a diverse array of medical services, including oncology; rehabilitation; psychological or psychiatric services; gerontology; treatment for drug addiction; in vitro fertilization (IVF); bariatric surgery; and expensive clinical tests. Such treatments ranged from inexpensive to extremely costly. In a few of the claims, plaintiffs requested expensive treatments provided only outside of Argentina; and in the case of provincial litigants, transportation to the country's capital for complex treatments was often demanded. In a smaller number of cases, plaintiffs disputed the quality of a provider's service and asked for a treatment (for which coverage was undisputed) to be performed in a more expensive facility or abroad. Fourthly, some plaintiffs requested goods such as wheelchairs, hearing aids, glasses, prostheses, and pacemakers. Lastly, cases included a significant number of petitions for the provision of special goods for people with disabilities.

Figure 3.4 shows the rapid growth in this category of cases—those demanding individual curative treatments in the form of medical services and drugs.

During the first years of the increase in right-to-health litigation, from the mid-1990s until the onset of the 2001–2 crisis, litigation was concentrated around treatment for people with disabilities or certain diseases (such as HIV/AIDS), or around high-cost, low-impact treatments (such as those

Figure 3.4. Evolution by type of case

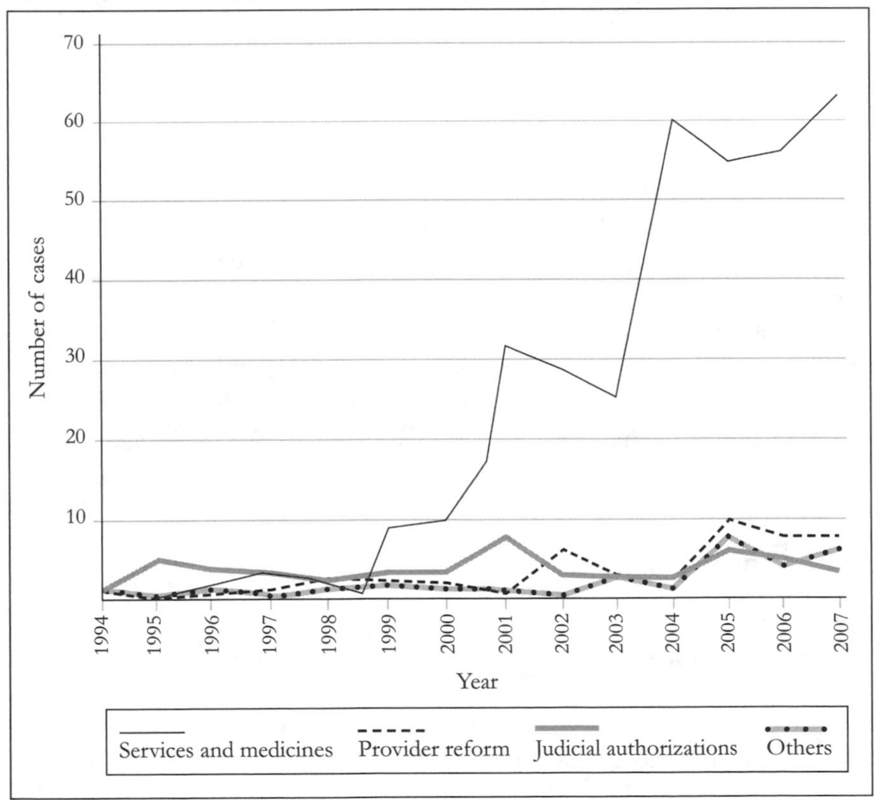

Source: Database LR.

for multiple sclerosis). The litigation of less expensive drugs and medical services intensified significantly between 2001 and 2002, given the critical economic and social situation of the country and the health system. Finally, as Argentina's economic situation started to improve in 2003, claims for provisions of basic urgent health-care services decreased, and claims seeking expensive treatments and treatments for the needs of certain special groups of patients began to grow. Also, more recently, of particular relevance has been the increasing demand for the supply of services needed by people with disabilities, ranging from therapeutic escorts to special schooling. In particular, after the Supreme Court decision in *Cambiaso Péres de Nealón*,[28] these services have come to be regarded as mandatory medical supplies to be covered by all insurers. In Database F01/08, such claims accounted for sixteen of the sixty cases surveyed. In contrast, claims centering on HIV/AIDS treatment—noticeably present during the early years of right-to-health litigation—have significantly decreased since 2006.

Claims Regarding PMO Implementation, Regulatory, and Policy Gaps

As the set of rules and procedures establishing the basic health plan, the PMO is the key regulatory priority-setting device used by Congress and the executive branch to define coverage requirements for contributory insurers. In fact, many of the cases examined here are ultimately disputes over the scope of the mandatory coverage rules enshrined in the PMO or the scope of the subsidiary and universal guarantees of the public health system. Even if court decisions do not always clearly articulate whether or not the medical services sought by plaintiffs were covered under PMO rules, most individual claims and judgments can be read as types of PMO coverage disputes. A review of the sixty complete dockets of Database F01/08 and forty cases of Database F08 shows that PMO coverage was clearly at stake in 50% of the cases.

Therefore, a deeper classification of PMO-related cases would be useful for understanding the cycles of such litigation and their effects with regard to priority setting and health policies. To this end, I have distinguished three varieties of right-to-health cases regarding the PMO: (i) those seeking to close *PMO implementation or enforcement gaps*; (ii) those addressing *PMO regulatory gaps*; (iii) and those searching to bridge *PMO policy gaps*.

Based on Siri Gloppen's classification (2009), I identify *PMO implementation-gap* cases as those where the parties ask the courts to intervene and order compliance with an existing and valid PMO coverage rule. Of the sixty files reviewed in Database F01/08, twelve corresponded to *PMO implementation-gap* cases. In these cases, there was a clear rule mandating coverage; however, as an implicit rationing device, OSSs or EMPs failed to comply with what they should have provided by law.

A second group of PMO cases arises out of *regulatory gaps*. These are cases where there is no rule or where the existing rule does not clearly set out what is covered and what is excluded. In eighteen of the sixty cases in Database F01/08, plaintiffs were litigating *PMO regulatory gaps* demanding the provision of a new medical service or drug that was either not expressly included in the PMO, was of a higher quality (for instance, a type of wheelchair or prosthesis with certain quality attributes), or was not specified in detail in the general coverage rule (as in the case of certain medical supplies for people with disabilities). In addition, *PMO regulatory-gap* cases arose when certain drugs or treatments included under the PMO were allegedly due by provincial or governmentally related OSSs that refused to voluntarily adhere to PMO rules and thus argued their subsequent lack of duties regarding PMO coverage. In these *PMO regulatory-gap* cases, insofar as the courts' expansion of PMO rules constituted a judicial precedent that often was subsequently followed by other courts, court decisions effectively defined what can be termed a "judicial PMO."

A third type of case, generally absent in the surveyed cases but prevalent in other countries, comprises litigation seeking to bridge *PMO policy gaps*, by which I mean problems in PMO policies. PMO policies are understood as (i) a set of proceedings and conditions for establishing the priority-setting rules that determine PMO content, and (ii) the set of monitoring mechanisms that control compliance with allegedly already-valid PMO coverage rules. Actually, this type of case would be more prevalent if courts were to address coverage-denial conflicts with a procedural approach, by first assessing whether PMO rules and procedural mechanisms satisfy any standard of reasonableness, and then by evaluating the constitutionality of procedural resources, their actual operation, and their substantive results. As we shall see below, the fact that this type of argument has not been present in most right-to-health litigation does not mean that it has no place under Argentine law. It will require, however, that the courts apply a more sophisticated approach to evaluating coverage decisions and the state capacities causing them. Whether such an approach will ultimately have fairer effects than the existing cases remains, however, an open question.

The Routinization of PMO Regulatory- and Implementation-Gap Cases

Looking at the individual cases of the five databases from a diachronic perspective, we find evidence of another interesting phenomenon, one that Victor Abramovich has described as routinization (2009). Routinization is the result of the accumulation of cases clustering around certain demands. Clusters of PMO implementation- and regulatory-gap cases may emerge around disputes over coverage for a particular illness or a particular group of patients. For instance, routinization was present in the early HIV/AIDS cases and was later observed regarding other needs, such as multiple sclerosis or the demands of people with disabilities, obese persons, or infertile couples. In Database F01/08, it is possible to trace the sustained accumulation of disability claims and, more recently, IVF claims, which represented only one case in 2006 and climbed to three out of ten in 2008; these cases represented seven out of forty cases in Database F08. Moreover, clusters of cases might form around particular insurer defendants, regardless of the medical service demanded, due to problems faced by the insurer in complying with PMO coverage standards. This is shown in the different databases for cases against PAMI (the functional equivalent to Medicare) and IOMA (the social health insurer for public employees of the province of Buenos Aires) that predominated during the 2001–2 crisis. More recently, a pattern of increased cases can also be observed against private insurers.

The formation of clusters of cases and the ensuing routinization proposed here illuminate a process that has different stages and that can lead, in certain situations, to its confrontation by relevant institutional actors. However, the stages at which identification of and/or reaction to the routinization may occur are not always reached. Therefore, the aggregate effects of the individual cases may not always be tackled. In fact, health authorities' widespread complaints about the judicialization of health do not necessarily indicate that authorities have attempted to diminish such litigation.

Figure 3.5 captures the three phases through which clusters of PMO implementation- and regulatory-gap cases could evolve. To better understand the various steps within these phases, let us follow recent cases regarding coverage demands for gastric bypass surgery and IVF treatments.

As the figure shows, the process moves through an initial phase that begins at *T1*, when the first individual cases filed are won and reported to be won, thus establishing a precedent for other courts to follow or reject.[29] For gastric bypass claims, this occurred in 2006, when the first successful cases were reported in legal periodicals and the media.[30] With regard to IVF, the first reported cases where coverage was granted were decided in 2007.[31]

Through either a change in existing precedents or the setting of new precedents, *T1* marks the beginning or intensification of a process recognizing the right to health and its judicial enforceability. In the specific cases here, it also marked the commencement of the judicial expansion of PMO coverage rules that did not originally include gastric bypass surgery or IVF treatments as part of the basic health plan.[32] The accumulation of cases triggered in the next step of this first phase, *T2*, could occur either through increasing numbers of individual claims or through the filing of collective claims to signal a more extensive reach of the demand for coverage. In our cases, the

Figure 3.5. Process of cluster formation: Implementation- and regulatory-gap cases

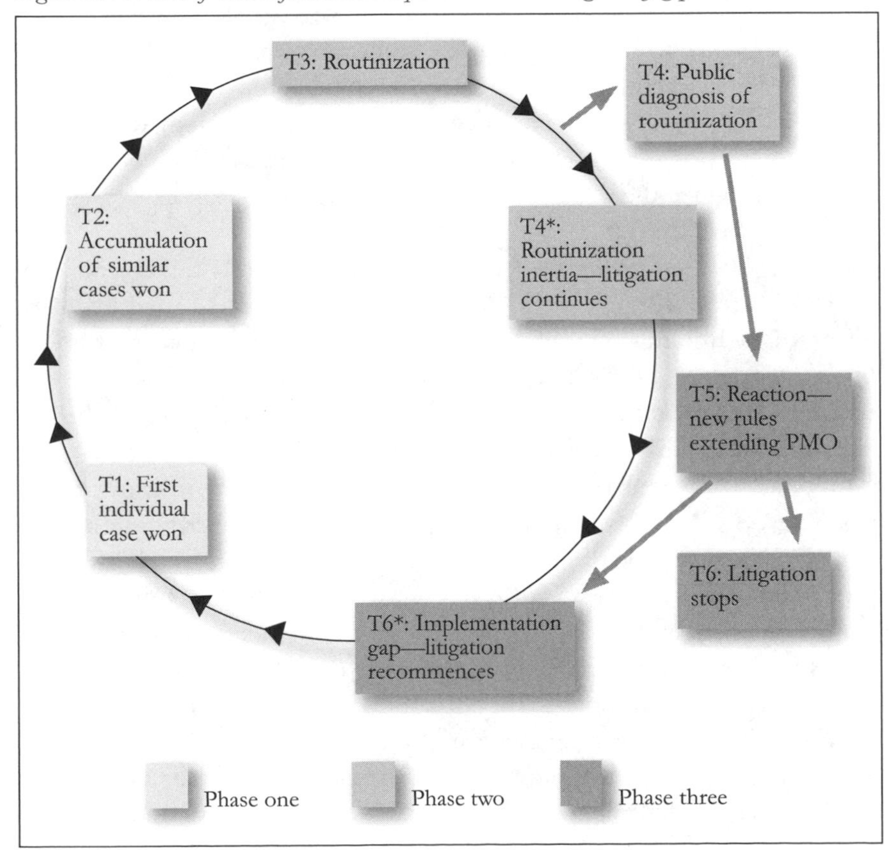

filing of collective claims first occurred around issues related to HIV/AIDS treatments, multiple sclerosis treatments, and people with disabilities. There was at this point not yet any evidence of increasing collective litigation for coverage regarding gastric bypass or IVF treatments (although in some of the first gastric bypass and IVF cases, it is possible to identify the role of legal advocacy NGOs filing test cases).[33]

While it is not possible to precisely mark the shift between *T2* and *T3*—and thus the move to the second phase—at a certain point in *T2*, the cluster of cases begins to be part of a routine whereby judicial intervention acts as a precondition for accessing a particular health service or for obtaining supplies from an identified insurer or provider.[34] This occurred during the years of sustained litigation to attempt to bridge PMO implementation gaps against PAMI and IOMA. Over the past decade, routinization has been observed in claims filed for medical services by people with disabilities and, as mentioned above, more recently, for gastric bypass surgery and IVF.

Once at step *T3*, the process of routinization may either continue through *T4**—where the inertia of the accumulation of individual cases recurs without being noticed or effectively addressed—or it may move into *T4*. *T4* is the point at which the legislature, policy makers, or courts could publicly recognize the routinization of PMO regulatory-gap cases and propose a way to address it.

The third and final phase begins at *T5*, with a legislative, executive, or judicial call for PMO reform or PMO compliance around a particular cluster of cases. In right-to-health cases in Argentina, only legislative or executive reactions have been observed. However, courts could also diagnose and react to the accumulation of individual litigation. In a sense, this is what the Supreme Court did in the *Badaro* case when it demanded that Congress take a more systemic approach toward pervasive implementation gaps in pension rules. An even more ambitious reaction from the judiciary can be seen in Colombia, when the diagnosis of accumulated litigation and the systemic problems of the health system that were to blame led the Constitutional Court to gather various claims under a single structural case, T-760/08.[35]

In Argentina, *T5* can be observed with regard to gastric bypass surgery claims, where reactions to routinization adopted different forms. At the provincial level, for instance, Catamarca was the first province to pass a law extending PMO rules to its provincial OSSs, followed by Tucumán and Mendoza. Within the federal government, executive reactions were identified in the draft of the administrative rule—ultimately not approved—that had been prepared by the SSSalud to extend coverage of bariatric surgery in certain extreme cases (see *La Nación* [Argentina] 2006b). Moreover, in 2008, Congress passed new legislation on the subject when it approved Law 26396. The new law established the National Nutrition Program and extended mandatory PMO coverage to include gastric bypass and other obesity treatments.[36]

By contrast, in other cases, diagnosis of or reactions to the accumulation and subsequent routinization may simply not take place or may be only partially undertaken. As a result, inertia may sustain litigation that seeks to increase access to certain drugs and treatments, as *T4** suggests. Inertia may be the consequence of a lack of diagnosis or of a lack of will to publicly acknowledge that court decisions are revealing a regulatory gap. The overhang may extend only for short periods, as was the case with the gastric bypass coverage rules. Or inertia may persist much longer, as is the case with the lack of federal regulation of IVF coverage. In IVF-coverage claims, even though Congress and the executive branch have diagnosed the accumulation of litigation and the regulatory gap,[37] no federal reaction has ensued to extend IVF coverage or to set up procedures for assessing the duty to cover IVF in certain cases. This is what several draft bills before Congress are proposing,[38] yet they remain to be considered and litigation continues.[39] These bills represent the type of regulation that was approved in the province of Río Negro in 2010 (see *Clarín* 2010).

Inertia has also been a prominent feature in the accumulation of regulatory-gap cases against certain insurers, such as IOMA or the public OSSs not voluntarily affiliated with the general regime of Laws 23660 and 23661 that makes PMO rules automatically applicable. Again, lack of reaction to routinization does not necessarily imply a lack of awareness. In fact, there may be multiple reasons why institutional actors with the capacity to offer more structural or systemic solutions to the routinization of cases—or to sanction lack of compliance to reverse it, as is the case of the SSSalud—may be unwilling to move forward.

Lastly, in some experiences with regulatory-gap litigation, after *T5* has been achieved and PMO reform has extended coverage for a certain medical benefit, the process of cluster formation could recommence in an effort to seek implementation of the newly reformed PMO rules. In the case of gastric bypass surgery, for instance, a new cycle of implementation-gap litigation may be recommencing. This is signaled by recent cases—such as those decided by the Supreme Court of Salta in February 2010 and a federal court in Mar del Plata in October 2010—ordering provincial OSSs to comply with the PMO under Law 26386.[40]

A last point on compliance should be made here. At different stages of the routinization cycle, positive court judgments do not necessarily imply compliance with the court's order. In fact, in fifteen of the sixty cases included in Database F01/08, courts had to impose a fine on defendants for their failure to comply with court orders. Only after imposition of the fines did these plaintiffs report compliance with the court orders. Even in such cases, however, the material effects of the cases were positive for litigants.

A Note on the Judicialization of Health and Its Impact

A comprehensive observation of the direct and indirect impacts of the judicialization of health would require further research. As a first step in such a project, I present in this section a brief exploration of the potential effects of the accumulation of individual cases from both an individual and a policy perspective. When available information allows, these effects are illustrated below with references to the gastric bypass cases that completed the cycle of routinization described in the previous section. I also clarify differences in litigation impact throughout the routinization cycle. It should be emphasized that this enquiry is still exploratory and is not intended to make causality claims. Most of the observations are restricted to conceptual descriptions of potential effects based on available secondary sources, interviews, and data collected concerning the context under which the cases developed. The focus here as it relates to policy effects is, in particular, on the absence of certain impacts in terms of more structural policy changes. This is important because the lack of policy changes addressing the causes and consequences of litigation suggests a cautionary assessment of the judicialization of health as we know it.

Effects on Individual Litigants

Individual litigants benefit, of course, when they achieve a victory in a right-to-health claim extending coverage of a certain need. This is so both when the litigation was caused by breach of a clear coverage rule and when the litigation was caused by the absence of a rule altogether. A court decision that actually acknowledges a right—bringing it out of the realm of mere aspiration—has a positive initial effect, especially for certain vulnerable groups that lack access to other resources and mechanisms for channeling their claims. This was arguably the case for people suffering from acute morbid obesity.

For potential litigants, too, successful cases can have positive effects when the accumulation of such cases leads to a policy change that extends coverage for all similarly situated patients. However, when litigation becomes a precondition for accessing a certain benefit, and no diagnosis of or reaction to the accumulation of cases takes place, the expenditures of insurers may increase as a result of court fees, thus diverting already scarce health resources away from the health system. Moreover, barriers that certain marginalized groups face in accessing the courts may in fact marginalize these groups even further.

In the previous section, I offered some preliminary data on the potential profile of those who have actually accessed the courts in right-to-health claims. In the surveyed dockets, it appears that people from poorer communities within the city of Buenos Aires did not, for the most part, participate in such litigation. Although one cannot draw firm conclusions from this limited exercise, the data point to the need for further research on the potential inequities of litigation from the perspective of litigants.

On another level, the potential inequalities exacerbated by routinized litigation also need to be evaluated regarding the patients of a particular health-care insurer being affected by the reallocation of resources generated by litigation and the extension of PMO coverage rules. In certain cases, litigation may have regressively distorted effects among people in need, especially with regard to the poorest patients or the more overloaded social health insurers. This may occur as a consequence of the queue-jumping effects that follow a court's intervention or the additional budgetary burdens imposed on OSSs already incapable of complying with the PMO's coverage demands. During the period of my research, at least, no public information was available regarding the potential demand different health insurers faced for gastric bypass surgery, the costs thereof, or potential budgetary impacts. What is known, however, is that not all insurers respect the existing PMO promises and that great inequalities in terms of PMO coverage pervade the social security system.[41]

Effects on Health Policy

PMO regulatory- and implementation-gap cases regarding claims on the right to health, particularly gastric bypass procedures, may have had aggregated impacts on health policy at the micro, meso, and macro levels. However, as the observations below on the meso and macro policy impacts of litigation suggest, little has been accomplished to close the broader health policy gaps that contributed to generating the cases.

Meso-Policy Effects

At the meso level of health policy making, right-to-health litigation could have strong effects on the design and monitoring of the PMO. Yet this has not been the case, in spite of the clear relationship between many of the cases and PMO flaws. Since its inception, the PMO has had serious governance problems related to the procedures for defining its standards of coverage and the monitoring of insurers' compliance with the plan.

One of the PMO's flaws arises from the fact that its standards of coverage are defined by Congress and the National Health Department but are applicable to provincial contributory insurers, about whom neither Congress nor the Department has basic information, particularly regarding their financing structure or health expenditures. Hence, the PMO operates within the context of state coordination incapacities characteristic of the weak governance of the Argentine health system.

The definition of the current procedures for establishing the PMO began in 2005 within the National Health Department. After consultations with various health-care actors, a commission of experts recommended a structural reform to the PMO, which was approved through Resolution 1991/2005 of the National Health Department.[42] The new resolution suggested submitting the new PMO model for the approval of a National Advisory Council on Health (*Consejo Nacional Consultivo de Salud*). Yet after several meetings, the Council (which was neither a paid nor permanent commission) made clear that further definitions and acceptance of new treatments and drugs required additional evidence, including technical and actuarial data that were apparently being produced by consultants at the Universidad de Buenos Aires. Two years later, the National Health Department issued Resolution 1714/2007, which unilaterally defined the valid PMO, declaring that, given the Council's demand for a "study of the costs by scholars at the Economics Department of the Universidad de Buenos Aires, who had been convened by the SSSalud and whose report is still pending,"[43] the valid PMO was the one established in 2005 by Resolution 1991. After several broad references to the need for cost-effectiveness calculations, Resolution 1714 also provided very general guidelines for the establishment by the National Health Department of a

> mechanism for PMO's update that should be based in a systematic analysis and detailed studies of charges imposed by diseases, and in evidence based medicine, in order to adopt decisions for the incorporation or removal of the services contemplated in the PMO.[44]

In practice, however, PMO determination resulted not only from small and scattered reforms at the ministerial level but also from several pieces of legislation, such as the one extending coverage of gastric bypass surgery and other legislation connected to the increase in PMO-related litigation. The criteria used for the original definition of the package were not outlined in any public document. Furthermore, in neither the elaboration of the original PMO nor its subsequent congressional[45] or executive reforms was there any cost analysis or technological assessment of the services for which coverage was mandatory; there was also no evaluation of the relationship between health benefits, health needs of the covered population, and the income and resources of each of the subsector insurers (Torres 2004, 200).[46] Moreover, many of the benefits secured by PMO coverage were not supported by either evidence or cost-effectiveness studies (Torres 2004).

Additionally, the persistence of PMO implementation-gap cases, along with the transformation of regulatory-gap cases into implementation-gap cases when a new rule extends the PMO, reflects the failure of monitoring mechanisms such as the SSSalud. Supervision of OSSs' compliance with the PMO is performed through essentially three tools: (i) a review of information contained in the contracts that OSSs distribute to beneficiaries; (ii) the collection of beneficiaries' claims by offices created especially for that purpose; and (iii) auditing reviews (Alonso 2007).[47] Even if the operation of such mechanisms is flawed, litigation seems to have had no impact in changing them.

In fact, the different clusters of right-to-health cases around the PMO could have been observed as, together, bringing the PMO's structural problems to the surface and demonstrating the need for a major reconfiguration of the PMO. The litigation, however, did not lead to an overthrow of the PMO's determination proceedings or the development of a more effective supervision mechanism for OSSs' and EMPs' compliance with existing PMO rules. In Colombia, on the other hand (as Yamin et al. discuss at length in their chapter), it was a diagnostic process of this type—the identification of a systematic pattern of right-to-health violations in the definition of coverage rules under the *Plan Obligatorio de Salud* and other generalized problems within the health system—that led to the T-760/08 decision of the Constitutional Court.

To date in Argentina, none of the right-to-health litigation surveyed seems to have affected PMO policies on a structural level, or the lack of political will to effect changes in the PMO's design or monitoring structures. Instead, litigation has often been connected to piecemeal PMO coverage reforms focused on certain diseases or on the needs of groups of patients, with the potential to cause unexpected distributive effects that have yet to be evaluated. Although litigation seems to have been the only alternative in the face of political blockages for the plaintiffs examined here, there is room to question the ultimate fairness of such litigation after years of absent structural change. This is all the more evident when one examines larger policy impacts.

Macro-Policy Effects

From a macro-policy perspective, it might be important to look at how PMO-centered litigation relates to some of the structural flaws of the Argentine health system, its institutional incapacities, and the political blockages that prevent a more systemic reform. These structural problems provide the context for litigation and may even be exacerbated by it, given the particularized and limited approach of the cases.

Firstly, the Argentine health system is characterized by high expenditures and poor performance. As James McGuire's (2010) recent comparative study shows, from 1960 to 2005, the country provided a good example of how high health expenditures were followed by a slow decline in infant mortality and one of the world's smallest rises in life expectancy. The poor comparative health performance of the system is illustrated in table 3.4, which compares Argentina's basic health indicators and total health expenditure with those of neighboring countries Chile and Uruguay.

Secondly, besides its comparative inefficiency, the Argentine health system is also defined by its inequalities, its huge curative bias, and over-fragmentation (McGuire 2010). Inequalities are present both within and between different health subsectors and insurers. Inequality between jurisdictions is shown by the gap in basic health indicators. For instance, although maternal deaths at the national level reached a ratio of approximately 40 deaths per 100,000 live births for 2004, significant disparities can be seen across provinces: in Corrientes, the ratio was 104 deaths per 100,000 live births; in La Rioja and Jujuy, 136 and 131, respectively; and in the city of Buenos Aires, just 20 (Pan American Health Organization 2007). When available, health data disaggregated by gender, ethnicity, age, and national origin also suggest disparities across these groups.

In addition, various studies show that almost every part of the health system suffers from a heavy bias toward expensive curative treatments at the expense of basic interventions and public health initiatives (Lloyd-Sherlock 2005). This is further exacerbated not only by the systemic fragmentation of the health system but also by the system's centralized regulation regarding priority-setting rules, in which decisions are made without basic information on local epidemiological situations, public health needs, state and private institutional capacities, or budgetary resources.

Thirdly, structural problems are also evident in the weak or nonexistent federal regulation and governance institutions plagued by corruption (Lloyd-Sherlock 2005). Research on state incapacities in the health sector, such as the SSSalud's study conducted by Guillermo Alonso (2007), provides examples of these problems, which also illustrate the description, above, on PMO rules design and implementation.

In spite of what many consider a health system desperately in need of structural reforms to correct its inequities, inefficiencies, and institutional incapacities (McGuire 2010), there have been few proposals for or discussions of systemic political reforms for the realization of a right to health since the 1986 failure of Raúl Alfonsín's program for unification. Most of the neoliberal reforms prompted during the 1990s introduced solutions that offered little more than a Band-Aid effect (Lloyd-Sherlock 2005). None of Argentina's political forces—including the Peronist party that ruled for sev-

Table 3.4. Basic health indicators and total health expenditure

Country	Under-5 mortality (2007)	Maternal mortality rate (maternal deaths per 100,000 live births) (2005)	Life expectancy at birth (2007)	Total expenditure on health as % of GDP (2006)
Argentina	16	77	74.8	10.1
Chile	9	16	78.3	5.3
Uruguay	14	20	75.9	8.2

Source: World Health Organization (2009b).

enteen years of the last two decades, unions, and organized civil society—have put forward a broad discussion on the adequacy of the health system when it comes to the realization of the constitutional right to health according to the principles of fairness and equality.

Also absent in the face of these systemic problems has been structural reform litigation in right-to-health claims (Abramovich 2009).[48] As this chapter has exposed, except for the important *Mendoza* case seeking to clean the Riachuelo River, right-to-health cases have predominantly sought individualized remedies for PMO implementation or regulatory gaps, and they have not affected PMO policies. Not one of the cases examined in the five databases seems to have addressed broader systemic flaws or policy constraints of the system. Moreover, in suggesting individualized solutions or legitimizing piecemeal reforms of PMO coverage rules, these cases raise doubts about the ability of the judicialization of health to approach—in a more structural manner—the unfairness, systemic flaws, and political blockages of the broader context in which the most vulnerable may claim their right to health.

Conclusion

The assessment of courts' role in the enforcement of the right to health depends on multiple variables and should be further studied and explained from perspectives that consider the evolution of litigation over time as well as litigation's multiple underlying variables and causes. The symbolic effects of litigation, together with the effects on the democratic inclusion of marginalized groups, should also be further studied through different areas of right-to-health litigation. The routinization of individual right-to-health claims extending PMO rules, however, should call our attention to a style of litigation that may—in the name of constitutional and human rights—result in further intensifying inequalities, systemic flaws, state incapacities, and political blockages.

Courts' failure to identify the aggregated effects of their interventions; Band-Aid or piecemeal political reforms; the failure of politicians, unions, and the health community to confront and debate larger systemic flaws; and the absence of a strong social movement concerned with the right to health are variables that await empirical observation, measurement, and evaluation in order to reach a better conclusion about the rights and wrongs of courts' role in the judicialization of health in Argentina.

Once such an assessment is undertaken, it will be important to avoid the oversimplified approach that contrasts strong judicial enforcement of social rights with alternatives precluding their judicial enforceability. Instead, courts could continue to play a role in the enforcement of the right to health. To avoid potentially regressive effects, however, such a role may be best realized if it is not limited to the traditional bilateral style of private-law litigation, in which individuals get to satisfy their needs regardless of the aggregated consequences of their cases. As Roberto Gargarella proposes in his chapter, a redefinition of courts' role in social rights litigation may in fact require weaker remedial interventions, such as those advocated by supporters of the dialogic approach, for example, and which are also presented in the Argentine Supreme Court's recent decisions in *Badaro* and *Mendoza* urging the other branches of government to seek a structural solution to the causes of litigation.

NOTES

1. These ideas led to the adoption, in 1949, of a new constitution containing a long catalog of workers' rights. Among such rights, the text made several references to health. The 1949 Constitution was short-lived, however. In 1955, military rulers abolished it and reinstated the original 1853 text.
2. Article 75.2 requires that the distribution of nationally levied taxes be "based on principles of equity and solidarity giving priority to the achievement of a similar degree of development, of living standards and of equal opportunities throughout the national territory." Article 75.8 mandates the annual allocation of the budget following the principles set forth in article 75.2. Article 75.9, known as the "progress clause," authorizes Congress to take actions conducive to "economic progress with social justice." Article 75.23 lists among Congress's powers the mandate "to legislate and promote positive measures guaranteeing true equal opportunities and treatment, the full benefit and exercise of the rights recognized by this Constitution and by the international treaties on human rights in force, particularly referring to children, women, the aged, and people with disabilities."
3. The last paragraph of article 75.23 includes a reference to the country's commitment to maternal and infant health. It mandates Congress to create a special and integral social security system to serve this goal.
4. The treaty provisions specifically delineating a right to health include, among others, article 25 of the Universal Declaration of Human Rights, G.A. Res. 217A (III), U.N. Doc A/810 at 71 (1948); article 12 of the International Covenant on Economic, Social and Cultural Rights, G.A. Res. 2200A (XXI), 21 U.N. GAOR Supp. (No. 16) at 49, U.N. Doc. A/6316 (1966), 993 U.N.T.S. 3, entered into force January 3, 1976; article 5 of the International Convention on the Elimination of All Forms of Racial Discrimination, G.A.

Res. 2106 (XX), Annex, 20 U.N. GAOR Supp. (No. 14) at 47, U.N. Doc. A/6014 (1966), 660 U.N.T.S. 195, entered into force January 4, 1969; articles 11(1)(f) and 12 of the Convention on the Elimination of All Forms of Discrimination against Women, G.A. Res. 34/180, 34 U.N. GAOR Supp. (No. 46) at 193, U.N. Doc. A/34/46 (1979), entered into force September 3, 1981; and articles 22 and 23 of the Convention on the Rights of the Child, G.A. Res. 44/25, Annex, 44 U.N. GAOR Supp. (No. 49) at 167, U.N. Doc. A/44/49 (1989), entered into force September 2, 1990.

5. Some of the most important federal regulations include Law 18610 on social health insurers; Laws 23660 and 23661 reorganizing the national health system; Law 24754 establishing the PMO; Law 24901 regulating benefits for people with disabilities; Law 25649 for the use of generic medicines; and a set of laws creating special health programs, such as Law 23798 creating the national program to fight HIV/AIDS.
6. See, for instance, the Constitution of the City of Buenos Aires, adopted in 1996, whose section 20 provides for the city's guarantee of an integral right to health, broadly conceived as "directly related to the satisfaction of needs in terms of food, housing, employment, education, clothing, culture and environment." In addition, articles 21 and 22 provide guidelines for the approval of a Basic Law on Health and for budgetary allocations. Along the same lines, article 19 of the Constitution of the Province of Santa Fe protects health "as a fundamental right of individuals and interest of the community."
7. One of the Court's frequently cited decisions in this regard is *Campodónico de Beviacqua, A.C. v. Ministerio de Salud y Acción Social*, October 24, 2000. For a later articulation of the same idea, see *Sánchez, N. R. v. Estado Nacional y Otro*, December 20, 2005.
8. *Campodónico de Beviacqua, supra* note 7.
9. *Asociación Benghalensis y Otros v. Ministerio de Salud y Acción Social – Estado Nacional*, June 1, 2000.
10. See, e.g., *N., L.M. y Otra v. Swiss Medical Group S.A.*, August 21, 2003; *Martín, S. G. y Otros v. Fuerza Aérea Argentina*, June 8, 2004.
11. *Etcheverry, R. E. v. Omint S.A.*, March 13, 2001; *V., W. J. v. OSECAC*, December 2, 2004; *F., S. C. v. Obra Soc. de la Act. de Seguros Reaseguros Capit. Ahorro*, December 20, 2005.
12. See *Campodónico de Beviacqua, supra* note 7.
13. *Monteserín, M. v. Estado Nacional*, October 16, 2001.
14. *Asociación de Esclerosos Múltiple de Salta v. Ministerio de Salud*, December 18, 2004; *Cambiaso Péres de Nealón, C. M. A. et al. v. CEMIC*, August 28, 2007.
15. *Defensor del Pueblo v. Estado Nacional y Otra (Provincia del Chaco)*, September 18, 2007.
16. From March 2005 to March 2010, public trust in the judicial system, according to Di Tella's confidence index, fluctuated between 47% and 50.5%.
17. In 2004, there were 285 OSSs run by unions (Torres 2004). An additional number of OSSs are run by provincial governments or created by law in order to protect particular groups of people, such as retirees who belong to the national social health system, PAMI.
18. In 1974, Congress established the National Integrated Health System (SNIS), stipulating the creation of a single, unified health insurance system. Another 1974 law created the National Health Career, requiring the competitive selection of public-sector doctors and nurses and prohibiting participants in the SNIS from working a second job. Pressure

from union leaders and physicians' associations watered down the original bills, and by 1977, the military government had ended the program. Moreover, in 1984, then Minister of Health Aldo Neri filed a bill for the creation of a unified health system, which failed after strong opposition by unions and doctors and forced his resignation in 1986 (McGuire 2010).

19. In her work on the right to health in Latin America, Alicia Ely Yamin has described the omission of a human rights framework by health-care supply reforms promoted by international financial institutions: "the current World Bank-sponsored health sector reforms have introduced into the region a new paradigm of health care that views health largely in terms of productivity" (2000, 130).
20. This mechanism reformed and extended the prior lists of mandatory health services established by law in late 1989 for the coverage of the social health system.
21. Originally, the PMO was applicable only to the social health subsector; Law 24754 extended it to private insurers.
22. Since there is no official publication for judicial decisions, except for Supreme Court cases, the database is also representative of the most relevant information available to lawyers and even judicial officers on right-to-health litigation. It may be fair to say that the court decisions included in the database represent most of the knowledge about judicial decisions on the right to health that is accessible to lawyers and claimants.
23. This is the jurisdiction to which the Supreme Court decided, in 2004, to channel most right-to-health claims filed against social health insurers. As a result, the Federal Civil and Commercial Courts became known as the *fuero de la salud*, or the health jurisdiction.
24. During seven of the ten surveyed years, health cases represented over 70% of the general *amparo* caseload, showing a decrease during the 2001–2 crisis.
25. This information was retrieved after filing formal petitions for information before courts in six provinces.
26. EMPs objected to Law 24754's extension of PMO rules to EMPs. They argued their case on the basis of the right to health. *Hospital Británico et al. v. Estado Nacional-Ministerio de Salud y Acción Social*, March 13, 2001.
27. *Mendoza, B.S. y Otros v. Estado Nacional*, June 20, 2006.
28. *Cambiaso, C.M. A. y Otro v. Centro de Educación Médica e Investigaciones Médicas*, September 5, 2007.
29. This phase may be preceded by a step in which similar types of cases are filed and then either rejected or lost.
30. *H., H. v. Dirección de Obra Social Personal Municipal*, Administrative Court of Appeals, La Plata, June 4, 2006; *M., R. S. v. Obra Social del Personal de Telecomunicaciones*, Federal Civil and Commercial Court of Appeals, October 5, 2006; *S., M. A. v. Obra Social Union Personal*, Federal Civil and Commercial Court of Appeals, November 9, 2006. The first gastric bypass surgery reported in the newspapers appeared in *Clarín* in June 2006 (in an article commenting on a case taken to court under the auspices of a major civil rights organization and successfully decided that month) (*Clarín* 2006).
31. *A., M. R. y L., M. v. OBSBA*, Tax and Administrative Court of First Instance of the City of Buenos Aires, No. 6, November 20, 2007. The case was also discussed in *La Nación* (Argentina) (2007).

32. In fact, in the above-cited article in *La Nación*, the head of the SSSalud recognized that the agency received approximately seventy petitions for IVF treatment each year, filed against OSSs denying coverage.
33. See *supra* note 30 and *La Nación* (Argentina) (2006a) (commenting on the first test case taken to court with the support of the Asociación por los Derechos Civiles).
34. Interviewees offered several anecdotes showing how to recognize the move to routinization. In one of the departmental offices of PAMI, patients entering the office would have the option of going through the "regular" counter or the *amparos* counter, a special counter processing service demands in which judges have already ordered PAMI to provide a certain supply. Others have mentioned that in the worst moments of the 2001–2 crisis, HIV/AIDS patients requesting the supply of antiretrovirals would be referred by officers at the National Health Department to nongovernmental organizations that could represent them in the filing of an *amparo.*
35. Sentencia T-760 de 2008. See further discussion by Yamin et al. (this volume).
36. For an explanation of the extension of PMO coverage to obesity treatments, see, for example, Ybarra (2008) and Azarkevich (2007).
37. In the case of IVF, Congress had draft coverage bills even before the first judicial cases were won. See, for example, Project 0949-D-2004, filed by a representative of Formosa in 2004.
38. Between 2004 and 2009, thirteen draft bills were filed with Congress in order to expand PMO coverage of IVF.
39. See, for example, a comment on the persistence of contradictory court decisions in Camps (2010).
40. *G. de F., G. v. Instituto Provincial de Salud de Salta*, Expte. No. CJS 30.742/07, February 9, 2010; *B., S.P. v. OSEPJANA*, Federal Court of Dolores, October 13, 2010. For the news distributed by the Supreme Court on the cases, see also *Centro de Información Judicial* (2010).
41. See, for example, the Ministry of Health's *Bases del Plan Federal de Salud 2004–2007*, which expressly declares that PMO rules are too difficult to fulfill. Along the same lines, ministries of health have repeatedly acknowledged difficulties in compliance with PMO rules by different insurers.
42. The resolution's introduction acknowledged that the design of the PMO was much more extended than that of its Latin American counterparts or its equivalent in the European Union, and that "it missed taking into account the resources that the health system provides for its own survival" (National Health Department Resolution 1991/2005, pt. 3).
43. National Health Department Resolution 1714/2007, considerando 10.
44. Ibid., art. 4.
45. It is telling that in the passage of laws demanding medical services for pregnancy, obesity, bulimia, and anorexia, the bills were not even analyzed by the Congressional Budgetary Committee.
46. There are no accessible public records on the different commissions and consultations organized by the National Health Department or SSSalud.
47. The SSSalud handles most of the supervision of OSSs' performance through the recording of activities. However, the agency limits its surveillance activities to the collection of reports filed by the OSSs—thus abdicating substantive control of the OSSs'

performance. Though, since 1999, the SSSalud created several short-lived initiatives for processing the claims of patients encountering problems with the OSSs and for audits of OSSs' compliance, Alonso (2007) reports that no sanctions came out of these investigations, which were driven mostly by political and opportunistic motives. In addition, in spite of the provisions requiring the compulsory dissolution or merger of OSSs that failed to comply with the PMO, as well as the perceived incapacity of many OSSs to fulfill the PMO's demands, no single OSS was dissolved.

48. Some have pointed to the *Mendoza* case, regarding the cleaning of the Riachuelo River, as a structural case. For a discussion of the lack of truly structural litigation in the country, see Abramovich (2009).

Chapter 4

Brazil

Health Inequalities, Rights, and Courts: The Social Impact of the Judicialization of Health

Octavio L. Motta Ferraz

The so-called judicialization of health—the large and growing volume of claims involving the right to health that reach the courts on a daily basis across Brazil—has achieved significant (and for many, worrying) proportions. Across the country, municipal, state, and federal health departments must respond to thousands of lawsuits every year in which individuals—and on a lesser scale, groups—claim some kind of health good (medication, surgery, medical equipment, and even food and diapers) based on the right to health, which is included in articles 6 and 198 of Brazil's 1988 Constitution. Moreover, since the late 1990s, most of these lawsuits have been successful for the claimant, in great part due to an expansive interpretation of the right to health that has been adopted at all levels of the Brazilian judiciary, from the lowest first instance courts to the Supreme Federal Tribunal. According to this interpretation, the right to health is an individual entitlement to *any* health procedure, equipment, or product that a person can prove she needs, irrespective of its costs. Such an expansive interpretation has led inevitably to a high success rate for this type of lawsuit and is partly responsible for the exponential growth of litigation into what health administrators often refer to as an "epidemic of judicialization." The scale of this phenomenon led the Supreme Federal Tribunal to call a public hearing (*audiência pública*) in March

With the support of the Norwegian Research Council and the Chr. Michelsen Institute (Bergen, Norway), I traveled to Brazil twice in 2009 and once in 2010 to collect data for this chapter. I have benefited from the invaluable research assistance of Daniel Wang, Fernanda Terrazas, and Luiza Teixeira.

and April 2009, when, for six days, it heard from fifty people representing government, academia, civil society, and the legal professions on how to solve what is now seen as the problem of the judicialization of health. Such public hearings, a new procedure resulting from the judiciary's reform in 2006, are intended to provide judges with additional information for deciding complex and controversial issues in a more enlightened and knowledgeable manner (Collucci and Pinho 2008).[1]

Given the novelty of the phenomenon (the first claims reached the courts in the mid-1990s and the numbers grew exponentially only around 2005) and the size of the country's territory and population (about 190 million people across 8.5 million square kilometers), there has yet to be a comprehensive study on the judicialization of health that encompasses the whole country—that is, on litigation against all governmental spheres (Brazil is a federal union, with 27 federative units, or "states," and more than 5,500 municipalities). However, there is a growing volume of data emerging from governmental reports and academic studies that confirms that the judicialization of health has become an important issue in several regions of the country and in all spheres of government (Ferraz 2009b). The leading regions, in terms of numbers of lawsuits and costs incurred by the government to fund them, are the richest and most populous regions of the south and southeast, such as São Paulo, Rio de Janeiro, Minas Gerais, Rio Grande do Sul, and Santa Catarina states. But the problem is also significant or growing rapidly in other states and municipalities across the country (see Brazilian National School of Public Health 2008).

In this chapter, I try to build the most comprehensive picture possible of the phenomenon, using data from academic studies, press reports, official documents, case-law analysis, and fieldwork carried out especially for this project. I start by presenting the legal framework within which the phenomenon must be analyzed, explaining how the right to health was included in the 1988 Constitution and the subsequent implications with regard to judicialization. I then move on to the phenomenon of judicialization itself, starting with the numbers currently available in terms of volume of cases and costs incurred by all levels of government, followed by an analysis of the phenomenon's social impact. This analysis is structured around four main questions: Who brings claims? What type of claims are brought? How are they received by the judiciary? And how are they enforced by government? Finally, the last section presents the main conclusions that I believe one can draw from the available data.

The Right to Health in the 1988 Constitution and the Creation of the Unified Health System

Health is recognized as a fundamental right in the Brazilian Constitution in a complex and sophisticated way. At the most abstract level, health is included in the list of fundamental rights found in title II of the Constitution. This title immediately follows the fundamental principles of the Brazilian Republic in title I, which are contained in articles 1 to 4. The fundamental rights are contained in articles 5 to 11—that is, in a prominent place in the beginning of the constitutional document, which contains a total of 250 articles. Article 5 is dedicated to civil and political rights and has no fewer than seventy-seven subsections. It includes traditional rights, such as the right to be free from torture (iii), freedom of expression (iv), freedom of association (xvii), and due process of law (liv). Articles 7 to 11 contain so-called labor rights. Article 7, with thirty-four subsections, regulates conditions of work, including unemployment insurance (iii), the minimum wage (iv), and maximum working hours (xiii). Then follows freedom of association to form trade unions (art. 8), the right to strike (art. 9), and the right to representation in governmental institutions (art. 10) and large private companies (art. 11). The remaining social rights are found together in article 6, in a single, short paragraph: "Education, health, work, housing, leisure, security, social security, protection of motherhood and childhood, and assistance to the destitute, are social rights under this Constitution."

This highly abstract clause is explained in great detail in later chapters of the Constitution that deal specifically with each of the areas of the "social order" (tit. VIII). There is a separate chapter for social security (ch. II), which includes health (sec. II), pensions (sec. III), and social assistance (sec. IV). There are also separate chapters for education, culture, and sports (ch. III); science and technology (ch. IV); social communication (i.e., the media) (ch. V); the environment (ch. VI); family, children, adolescents, and the elderly (ch. VII); and indigenous peoples (ch. VIII). The "social order" spans articles 193 to 232 of the Constitution, with several subsections and subparagraphs, regulating each of these areas to a level of detail that many commentators find inappropriate for a constitutional document. Whether or not this criticism is correct, the fact is that the social rights recognized in article 6 cannot be interpreted in isolation from their specification in the later chapters of the Constitution. In the case of health, it is important to look at articles 196 to 200, whose main passages are quoted below:

> Article 196 – Health is the right of all persons and the duty of the State and shall be guaranteed by means of social and economic policies aimed at reducing the risk of illness and other hazards and at the universal and equal access to actions and services for its promotion, protection and recovery. . . . Article 198 – Health actions and public services integrate a regionalized and hierarchical network and constitute a single system, organized according to the following directives: I. decentralization, with a single management in each sphere of government; II. integrated service, priority being given to preventive activities, without prejudice to assistance services; III. participation of the community; (1) The unified health system shall be financed, as set forth in article 195, with funds from the social welfare budget of the Union, the states, the Federal District, and the municipalities, as well as from other sources. . . . Article 200 – It is incumbent upon the unified health system, in addition to other duties, as set forth by the law; I. to supervise and control proceedings, products and substances of interest to health and to participate in the production of drugs, equipment, immunobiological products, blood products, and other inputs; II. to carry out sanitary and epidemiological vigilance as well as those relating to the health of workers; III. to organize the training of personnel in the area of health; IV. to participate in the definition of the policy and implementation of basic sanitation actions; V. to foster, within its scope of action, scientific and technological development; VI. to supervise and control foodstuffs, including their nutritional contents, as well as drinks and water for human consumption; VII. to participate in the supervision and control of production, transportation, storage, and use of psychoactive, toxic, and radioactive substances and products; VIII. to cooperate in the preservation of the environment, including that of the workplace.[2]

Thus, the Brazilian Constitution is rather complex and detailed in the way it envisages how the right to health, recognized in abstract terms in article 6, is to be implemented. Most important for our purposes, it should be noted that the Constitution adopts a broad conception of health and the measures for its promotion, going far beyond the narrow idea of health care to include actions and policies involving many other important social determinants of health. This is made clear throughout the health section of the Constitution, which mentions "social and economic policies" (art. 196) in general as a means of implementing the right to health, "preventative activities" (art. 198), "sanitary and epidemiological actions," "health of workers," "preservation of the environment" (art. 200), and so forth. Yet health litigation, as we shall see, is concentrated heavily on health care, particularly medicines.

It is also important to note that a wealth of ordinary infra-constitutional legislation and regulations from before and after the 1988 Constitution exists in relation to health. These infra-constitutional rules further specify the workings of the health system but cannot, of course, contradict the Constitution, which is the highest norm in the Brazilian legal system. Of particular importance for the issue of judicialization is Law 8.080 of 1990, a federal law that specifies how the constitutional right to health should be implemented, including detailed rules on the principles, organization, and functioning of Brazil's newly created unified public health system (*Sistema Único de Saúde*, or SUS). Before the 1988 Constitution, the Brazilian government had no explicit constitutionally based duty to implement health actions or provide health services on a universal basis (i.e., covering the whole population). It did of course carry out some relevant public health actions and run some public hospitals, though not on any significant scale. For health services in particular, a large part of the population had to rely on private providers either through direct out-of-pocket payment or through insurance schemes available only to the employed. Many jobless and poor people thus had no access to health services before the creation of the SUS by the Constitution.

It should be observed, finally, that all governmental spheres (federal, state, and municipal) share a joint responsibility to carry out the constitutionally mandated obligations regarding health, including the funding and administration of the SUS. From a health-litigation perspective, this means that individuals or groups can sue any sphere they believe to have failed to fulfill these obligations. This creates some complication since litigants can choose which sphere of government to sue and can also sue more than one at the same time. To acquire an exact picture of the judicialization of health, therefore, one would need to assemble data on all litigation directed against all spheres of government, which, if not impossible, would demand an inordinate amount of time and resources. What follows in the next section, thus, is based only on the available data.

There is also no space here to go into further detail on the functioning of the public health system as a whole, and the SUS in particular, as specified in Law 8.080/90 and a myriad of other legislative and regulatory instruments.[3] This is not too important for our purposes, however, since most litigation to date has relied directly, and often exclusively, on the constitutional norms, which lay out the basic principles of the system.

The Judicialization of Health in Brazil: Data and Analysis

This section attempts to sketch the most comprehensive picture possible of the judicialization of health in Brazil by compiling the available data involving all spheres of government. It relies on academic studies, press reports, and official documents, as well as on case-law analysis, interviews, and an electronic survey that were all carried out especially for this project. I do not claim that the currently available data enable an utterly seamless picture of this important phenomenon. I do believe, however, that the data presented here and their corresponding analysis allow us to significantly advance our understanding of the phenomenon, shedding light on important aspects hitherto not captured by existing studies.

This section is divided into two parts. The first part presents raw quantitative data on judicialization within all spheres of government, focusing on the volume and costs of health litigation. The second part moves on to a more detailed and qualitative analysis of the data, structured around four main questions: Who brings claims? What type of claims are most often brought? How are they received by the judiciary? And how are they enforced by the government?

The Available Data on Volume and Costs of Health Litigation

The Ministry of Health reports that it responded to 5,323 lawsuits between 2003 and 2009 claiming some kind of health benefit based on the right to health—resulting in an expenditure of R$159.03 million (US$80 million). This large volume of litigation has a considerable potential impact on health equity and is noteworthy in terms of its rapid and continuous growth. Indeed, in 2009 alone, the expenditure reached R$83.16 million (US$42 million), more than expenditures for the previous six years combined. This cost represents around 0.4% of the ministry's total health budget (US$20 billion) and 4% of its budget for medicines (US$2 billion).[4]

A more detailed picture can be drawn from litigation processed by the Secretariat of Science and Technology of the Ministry of Health (SCTIE-MS). This department processes the majority (around 80%) of the lawsuits to which the federal government responded. This is easily explained by the fact that most right-to-health litigation in Brazil, as we shall see below, involves claims for drugs, and the SCTIE-MS is the department entrusted with the organization and administration of pharmaceutical assistance. In November 2009, I was granted access to the database of health litigation of the SCTIE-MS by its secretary, Mr. Reinaldo Guimarães.[5] According to the database, from 2005 to 2009, the number of lawsuits grew from 387 to 2,174, more than a fivefold increase, and the costs spiraled up from R$2.4 million (US$1.2 million) to R$53 million (US$26.5 million), a staggering twenty-two-fold increase (see figure 4.1). The exponential growth in costs can be explained by a high concentration of cases demanding expensive patented drugs, such as etanercept and adalimumab (for rheumatoid arthritis), indursulfase (for mucopolissacaridosis II, or Hunter syndrome), human insulin analogs (for diabetes), sildenafil (for pulmonary hypertension), and peginterferon alfa and ribavirin (for hepatitis C).[6]

The principle of "decentralization" included in the constitutional provisions cited above, although imperfectly implemented so far, requires that the execution of health services be gradually decentralized to states and municipalities, especially the larger ones. In the context of judicialization, this means that, as a general rule, more claimants will choose to sue their municipality or state rather than the federal government. This explains why the number of lawsuits

Figure 4.1. Growth in lawsuits against Ministry of Health

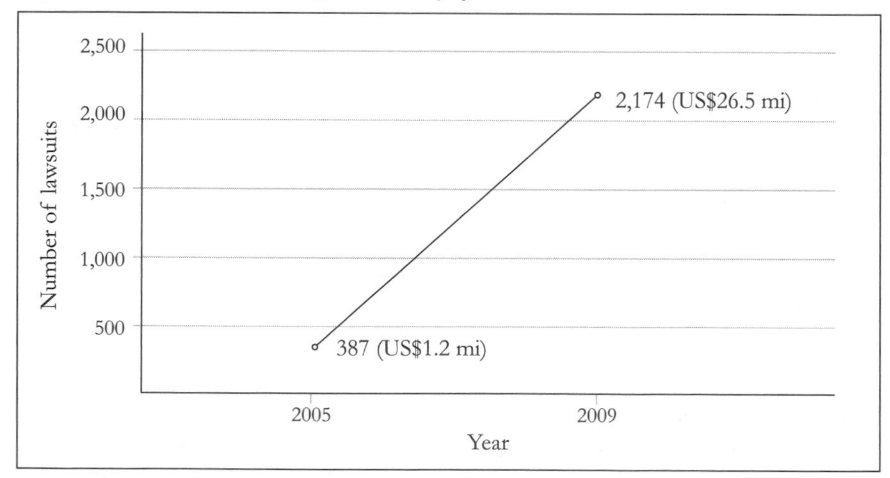

Source: SCTIE-MS.

against the federal government, although large and growing, is still only a fraction of the number against states and municipalities, to which we now turn.[7]

According to one of the most assiduous critics of the judicialization of health in Brazil, Senator Tião Viana of the incumbent Labour Party, R$2 billion (US$1 billion) were spent between January and October 2009 to fund treatment ordered by courts against all spheres of government (*Correio Braziliense* 2009). If these data are accurate, litigation at the state and municipal levels in 2009 would have exceeded federal litigation by nineteen times in terms of costs, consuming around 8% of state and municipal health budgets. While it is not clear how accurate this information is, it is certainly clear that judicialization is rampant at the state and municipal levels as well, significantly exceeding the phenomenon at the federal level for the reasons stated above. Indeed, even if we take into account only a few key states of the south and southeast, where data are more readily available, this scenario is confirmed.[8]

São Paulo State alone, for instance, the largest in population and richest in the country, claims to have spent R$400 million (US$200 million) on health-related litigation in 2008—around 30% of its budget for drugs and almost five times what the federal government spent in 2009 (see figure 4.2). Rio Grande do Sul, another major state, spent R$78 million (US$39 million), and Minas Gerais another R$40 million (US$20 million) in 2008. So, even leaving out, for lack of data, twenty-four of the twenty-seven Brazilian states, expenditure at the state level in 2008 is still six-and-a-half times larger than

Figure 4.2. Expenditure on litigation

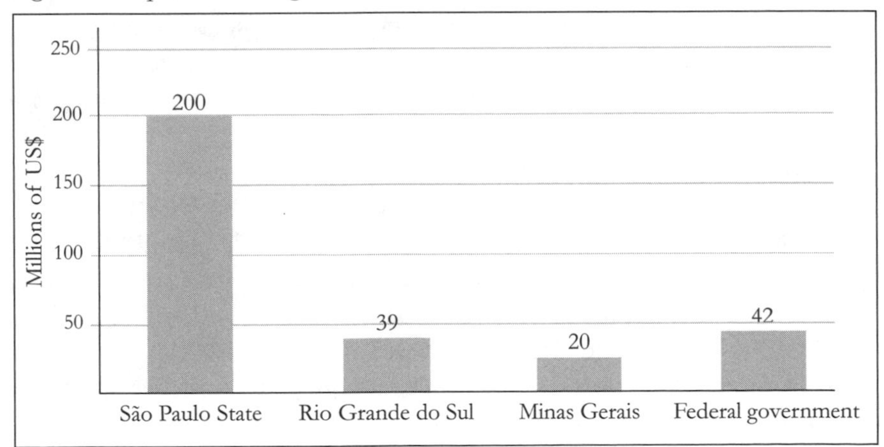

Source: Ministry of Health and state secretariats of health.

the federal expenditure in 2009, confirming that if judicialization is rampant at the federal level, it is significantly more so at the state level (Collucci 2009).

Several academic studies and reports from health departments confirm that judicialization is happening on a significant scale and is growing in terms of numbers of lawsuits in individual states and municipalities of the south and southeast. In the state of Rio de Janeiro, for instance, a recent study found 2,245 cases in 2006, up from 1,144 in 2002. In Rio Grande do Sul, there were 1,846 cases in 2002 and 7,970 in 2007, according to the legal advisor to the state's Secretariat of Health. In Santa Catarina, the growth was even more pronounced according to that state's legal advisor, growing from 24 in 2002 to 2,511 in 2007. In the Federal District (Brasilia), lawsuits grew from 281 in 2003 to 682 in 2007. Finally, a recent study from the state of São Paulo found 4,123 lawsuits in 2006 alone. The total accumulated number of individuals currently receiving treatment under judicial decisions stood at 25,000 in São Paulo in 2009, and 20,527 in Rio Grande do Sul in 2008.[9]

Not many studies focus on municipalities, but there is some evidence from press reports that judicialization has been growing at that administrative level as well. An electronic survey with municipal secretariats of health carried out for this project between November 2009 and March 2010 confirmed this scenario. Questionnaires were sent to all 5,566 Brazilian municipalities asking whether the judicialization of health was an important issue in that municipality and, if so, requesting data on the volume and costs of health litigation. We received responses from 1,337 municipalities (24% of the total). Of these, 34% said that the judicialization of health was growing and was an important issue; 23% responded that it was growing but was not yet an important issue; and 43% stated that they did not have that problem. Six hundred twenty-four municipalities reported on the number of individuals currently receiving treatment through judicial orders. The aggregate total was 44,708 (an average of 71.64 per respondent municipality), and the total volume of lawsuits stood at 12,766 in 2007, 15,735 in 2008, and 14,560 in the first six months of 2009. Costs also grew from R$47 million (US$24 million) in 2007 to R$73 million (US$37 million) in 2008, and had already reached R$57 million in the first six months of 2009. In addition, most of the claims were for medication, confirming the same trend as at the federal and state levels.[10]

The estimate presented in figure 4.3—highly conservative, since it is based on the very incomplete available data on states and municipalities—nonetheless shows that the judicialization of health in Brazil has indeed become a relevant issue (and, for many, a problem) in terms of volume and costs. Even with this conservative estimate, we reach the inordinate number of approximately 40,000 lawsuits per year. We must turn now to the social impact of this vast phenomenon.[11]

Analysis of the Data in Terms of Social Impact

What is the social impact of this colossal volume of litigation? Does it enhance the effectiveness of the constitutional right to health, as often claimed by its supporters? Or does it actually produce mostly negative consequences, such as disorder in health policies or distortion of health priorities and health equity, as often claimed by its detractors? A third possibility, frequently absent from the heavily polarized debate, is that the effects of judicialization are largely neutral.

It is impossible to arrive at a precise answer to these questions. The problem is not only the lack of sufficient quantitative data but also the contested nature of the concepts involved and the lack of an established methodology

Figure 4.3. Estimated volume of litigation in selected states and municipalities and at the federal level

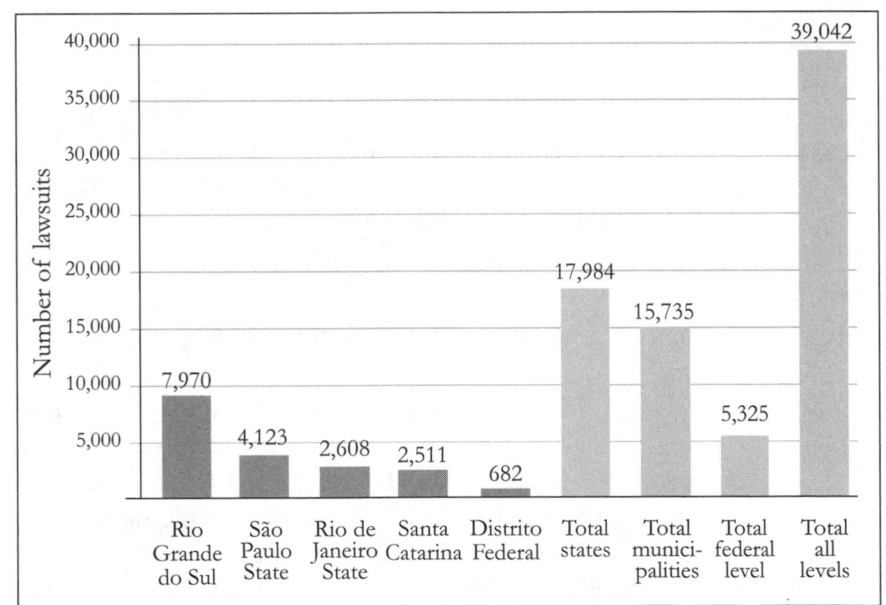

Source: Naundorf (2008); Chieffi and Barata (2009); Borges (2007); Pereira et al. (2010); Romero (2008); survey conducted with municipalities, 2010; Ministry of Health, personal communication, 2009.

to reach these answers. One major hurdle is the lack of consensus on what the constitutional right to health entails in terms of concrete benefits to citizens. If we do not know whether a certain treatment or surgery, for instance, should be part of the right to health, it is impossible to determine whether a court order enhances or harms the right to health. Similarly, if we don't have a precise and consensual idea of which health benefits should receive priority in necessarily limited health budgets, it is impossible to gauge whether a judicial decision furthers or detracts from health equity. The extremely contested nature of these interrelated concepts (right to health and health equity) makes it difficult to establish a clear methodology to judge the social impact of the judicialization of health. Any attempt to do so, therefore, must be necessarily tentative and based on some contested presumptions and stipulations.

In light of these hurdles, I propose to analyze the social impact of health litigation in Brazil by basing my consideration and discussion on the following premises, which I believe are plausible. Given the expressly transformative character of the Brazilian Constitution—that is, its pledges to reduce social inequalities in general and health inequalities in particular—and its strong focus on social determinants of health, I assume an interpretation of the right to health that incorporates these same aims. This means that the state, when implementing socioeconomic and health policies in order to advance the right to health, should aim to reduce health inequalities among its citizens. In a country as unequal as Brazil, this necessarily implies a strong preference for policies that have a positive impact on the health of the most disadvantaged. The social impact of court orders should be evaluated within the same framework. Our main question, therefore, should be, does litigation enhance the health conditions of the most disadvantaged?[12]

In order for such enhancements to occur for this population, at least the following conditions would need to be met. Firstly, most litigation would need to focus on health problems that are a priority for the most disadvantaged. Secondly, this type of litigation should be well received by courts. Thirdly, court orders would need to be strictly complied with by the state—that is, effectively enforced. Finally, court orders would need to be funded with extra resources (e.g., increased health budgets), or, if funded with existing resources, the money would need to be reallocated from programs that are not a priority from the perspective of the most disadvantaged.

The following discussion is structured around the following questions as they elicit important information on these conditions: Who brings claims?

What types of claims are most often brought? And how are claims received by courts and complied with by the state?[13]

Who Brings Claims?

If the majority of litigation focused on health problems that are a priority for the most disadvantaged, one would expect to find a great number of disadvantaged individuals as individual claimants and/or represented in collective suits (e.g., class action suits) filed by nongovernmental organizations (NGOs) or public attorneys. Let us see what the available data can tell us about the profile of claimants.

All studies carried out in Brazil to date converge on the finding that the vast majority of cases for which data are available are individual cases (cases brought by a single claimant) as opposed to collective lawsuits (lawsuits brought by public attorneys or NGOs in favor of large groups). The data I collected at the SCTIE-MS confirmed this finding. Of the 4,343 accumulated lawsuits during the years studied (2005–9), only 124 (less than 3%) were collective ones. The vast majority of lawsuits (97%) were individual ones in which the claimant was a single person demanding an individualized health benefit.

In and of itself, of course, this finding is not determinant in terms of social impact. If the majority, or at least a significant proportion, of individual claimants were disadvantaged individuals, litigation could potentially have a positive social impact—at the very least, a restricted one for the individuals involved, but potentially also a larger one, depending on how the state decided to implement the judicial decision. Given that judicial decisions in Brazil are binding only to the parties to a case, a successful outcome of an individual lawsuit benefits in principle only the individual claimant. But the state is free to decide to extend that benefit to the whole of the population affected by a similar health problem.

It seems a more plausible scenario, however, that the most disadvantaged do not figure as claimants in a significant proportion of individual cases. Given the prevalence of important socioeconomic barriers to accessing the courts, it is unlikely that the poorest citizens, who arguably need more health benefits from the state, are able to access the courts on the scale occurring in the judicialization of health. This scenario, moreover, is beginning to be confirmed by research, including my own, on the socioeconomic profile of litigants. To know the socioeconomic profile of individual claimants involved in right-to-health litigation, one can use a set of indirect indicators, such as *place of residence*, *type of legal representation used*, and *nature of health services used*. Let us look at each of these in turn.

Place of residence

Brazil, as is well known, is a highly unequal country in terms of income distribution and other related indicators, including health. These inequalities have a strong geographical component. The states of the south and southeast are richer and have better average health and other socioeconomic indicators than those of the poorer northeast and north. The states of the center-west fall somewhere in between these two poles, with the exception of the Federal District (Brasilia), which is highly developed. There are also significant inequalities within each state and even within municipalities. Given the stark segregation between poor and rich areas, it is possible to fairly accurately gauge socioeconomic profile by place of residence.

Applying this strategy to the data collected at the Ministry of Health, presented above, I have found an extremely high concentration of lawsuits (85%) in the most developed states of the south and southeast, even though their population represents just 56.8% of the country's total population. The north and the northeast together, with 36% of the Brazilian population, accounted for only 7.5% of the total.

The volume of lawsuits therefore bears a close relationship with levels of economic and social development. That is, the higher a region's level of socioeconomic development, the more likely it is to have a high volume of health litigation. When we use the United Nations' Human Development Index (HDI), this correlation becomes even more striking (see figure 4.4). Out of the ten states with the highest number of lawsuits, only one, Ceara, is not also one of the top ten in terms of HDI. The ten states with the highest HDI (above 0.8) together have generated 93.3% of lawsuits at the federal level (4,013), whereas the other seventeen states with the lowest HDI (below 0.8) together have originated a meager 6.7% of lawsuits (330). The same pattern, as we shall see below, was found at the state and municipal levels in several studies.[14]

It is important to note that this strong correlation remains when we adjust for population size. The country's average, based on the lawsuits in the database of the SCTIE-MS, is one lawsuit against the federal government for every 42,364 inhabitants. But there is huge variation when one disaggregates that number by region. The northeast, the poorest region of Brazil, has a very low ratio of lawsuits to inhabitants (1/177,704)—over four times lower than the country's average—whereas the south, the region with the highest HDI, is the champion of litigation, with a ratio of 1/11,902—almost four times higher than the country's average. Figure 4.5 shows the ratios for all regions of the country.

The available data on lawsuits against states and municipalities seem to confirm the same pattern. In the states and cities of the south and south-

Figure 4.4. Correlation between HDI and volume of litigation

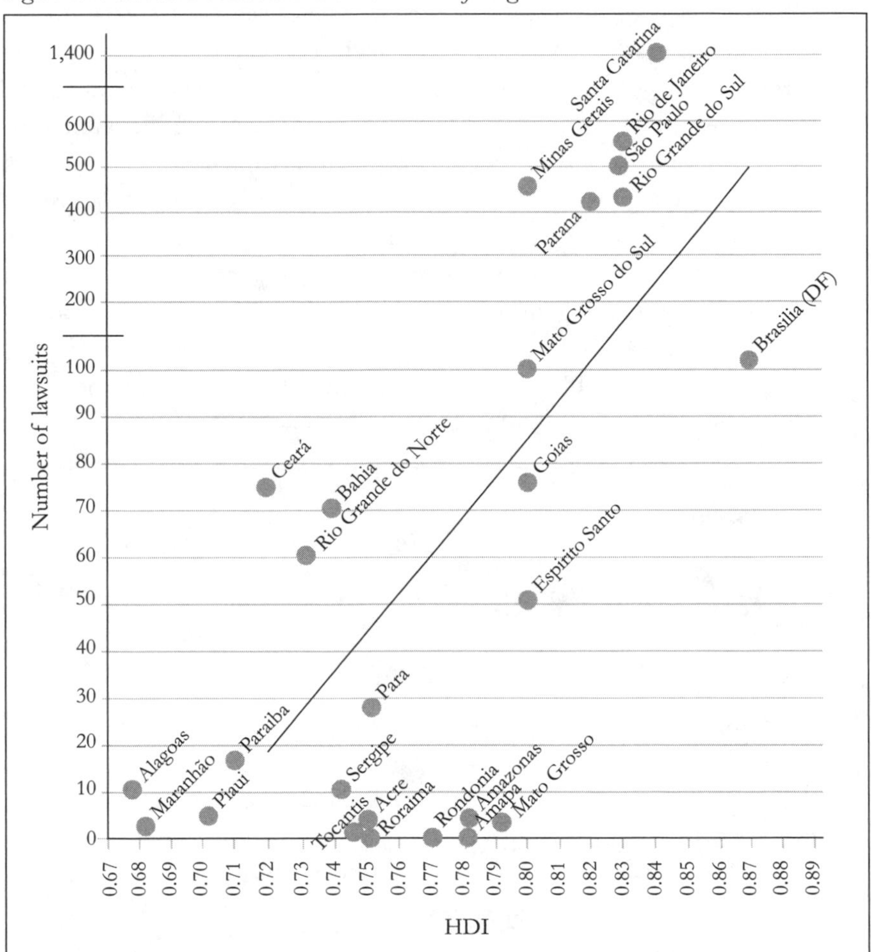

Source: Author's formulation using data from the SCTIE-MS and United Nations Development Programme (2009).
Note: Diagonal line indicates perfect correlation between HDI and litigation, whereas dots show actual correlation.

east, there is a significant and growing number of cases, whereas in the states of the north and northeast, the number is growing, but from a much lower base.[15] In the relatively poor northeastern state of Bahia, for instance, litigation, although growing fast, has not yet reached the scale of the southern states. The comparison between Rio Grande do Sul (a southern state) and Bahia is illustrative (see figure 4.6). The former, one of the most developed in the country, has much higher levels of litigation than the latter (1 lawsuit per 1,393 inhabitants and 1/125,973, respectively).

Within states, the same pattern repeats where data are available. Richer municipalities in a state tend to have higher levels of litigation than poorer ones. Take the state of São Paulo, for example. One finds, again, a striking correlation between the level of socioeconomic development and the number of lawsuits. According to the state's Secretariat of Health, the highest municipality in that state's ranking (with 3.13 lawsuits per 1,000 inhabitants) is São Jose do Rio Preto, one of its richest regions, whereas the lowest (0.04 lawsuits per 1,000 inhabitants) is Registro, one of the poorest areas of that state.[16]

It is of course true that the origin of a claim in a rich state or rich municipality is not definite proof of a claimant's high socioeconomic status. In principle, litigation could well be concentrated in the poorest areas of these rich

Figure 4.5. Lawsuits per capita

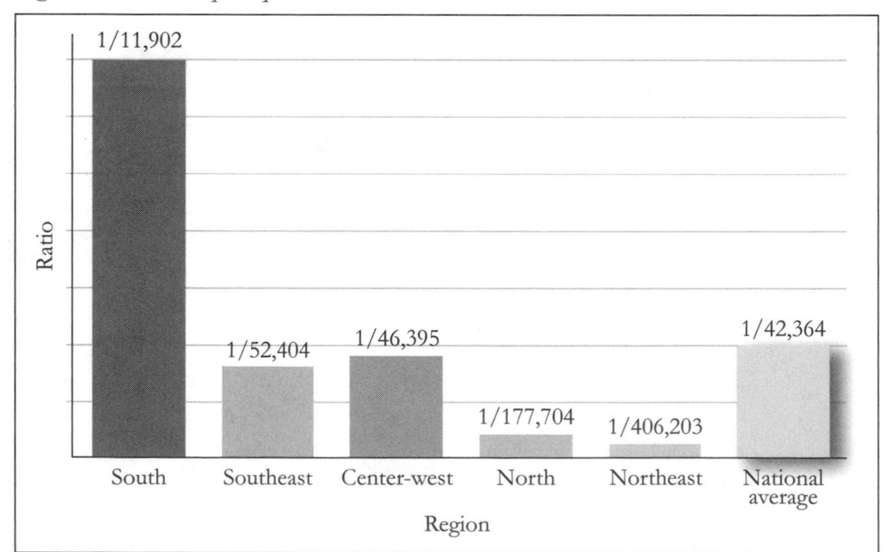

Source: Author's formulation using data from the SCTIE-MS and Instituto Brasileiro de Geografia e Estatística.

states and municipalities. We would need to look at litigants' exact addresses, therefore, to have a more precise idea of their socioeconomic status. It seems a rather plausible assumption to make, however, that most of the litigation originating in the most developed states and municipalities is brought by claimants with relatively advantaged socioeconomic status. This is because, as already noted, access to courts and legal services are much easier for these individuals. Often, the most disadvantaged are unaware of a constitutional right to health, have restricted access to legal assistance and, importantly, are not comfortable with the formalities of the legal system.

Two studies of the municipality of São Paulo confirm this assumption, having looked at the precise address of claimants to gauge their socioeconomic status. Fabiola Vieira and Paola Zucchi (2007) analyzed all litigation for medicines against the municipality of São Paulo in 2005. They found that 63% of the claimants in their sample resided in districts with the lowest degrees of social exclusion. In a more recent and comprehensive study, Ana Chieffi and Rita Barata (2009) used the São Paulo Social Vulnerability Index (which divides the city into six homogenous areas) and found that 74% of the claimants lived in the three areas with the lowest social vulnerability rates.

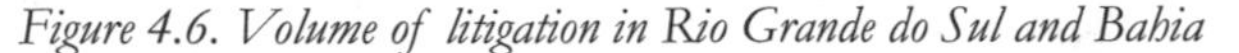

Figure 4.6. Volume of litigation in Rio Grande do Sul and Bahia

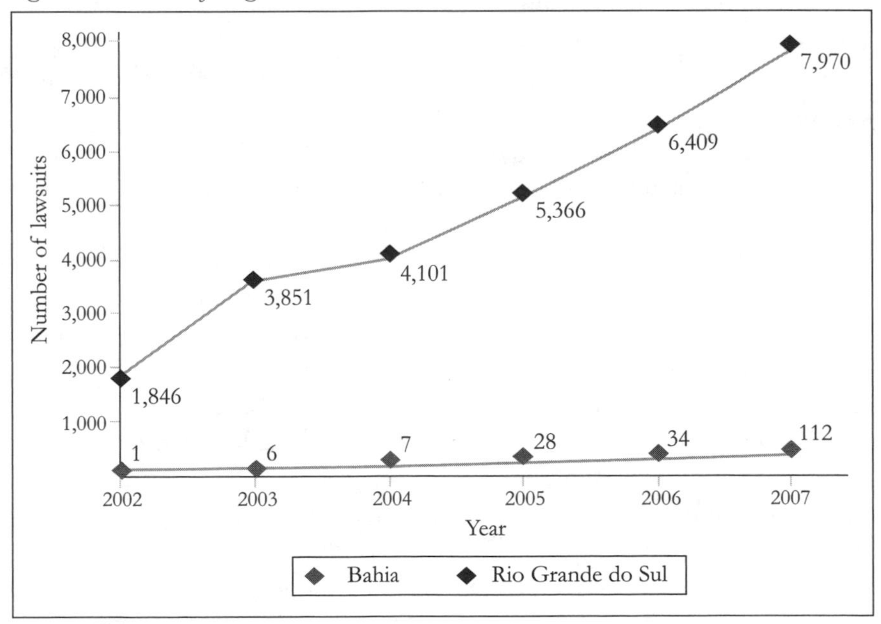

Source: Naundorf (2008); Costa (2009).

The available data on the geographical origin of claims and the place of residence of claimants suggest, therefore, a strong positive correlation between high socioeconomic status and volume of claims. This apparent higher capacity of individuals of a relatively advantaged socioeconomic status to litigate is confirmed by other indicators discussed below.

Legal representation and medical services

Two other indicators that can be used in Brazil to try to gauge the socioeconomic profile of claimants are the type of legal representation and the nature of medical services (public or private) they normally use. Legal representation can by and large reflect socioeconomic position because private lawyers' services are, as a rule, unaffordable for the most disadvantaged. The same goes for the use of private doctors as opposed to public ones. Given that only around 24% of the population has access to private health insurance that covers consultations with private doctors, and that the level of access to these doctors is expectedly much higher in the highest quintiles of income, one can confidently assume that a litigant who habitually uses the private health system is likely not to be in the lowest echelons of income in Brazilian society. One cannot confidently assume, however, that all or even most individuals represented by public lawyers and seen by public doctors are the most disadvantaged, since comparatively better-off people (i.e., those in the three intermediate quintiles of income) can and do use the services of public doctors and public lawyers, although not very often.[17]

Using both indicators together can give us a fairly accurate idea of the proportion of litigants who might come from the lower socioeconomic groups of society. A high prevalence of claims filed by private lawyers and supported by private doctors' prescriptions is a strong indication that this proportion is not very large. Most studies examining these indicators have found a high percentage of litigants who use private legal and medical services (see figure 4.7). Only Rio de Janeiro stands out with a high proportion of claims filed by attorneys from the Public Defender's Office (*Defensoria Pública*). Yet, when one looks at the type of medical services used in these cases, the proportion of private prescriptions is significantly higher, indicating that many clients of the public defender are not likely to be economically disadvantaged.

The data so far analyzed, although admittedly limited, nonetheless seem to confirm rather than challenge the intuitive and plausible assumption that litigation is not a tool often used by the most disadvantaged. The absence or paucity of claims in the poorest states, municipalities, and districts, and the significant proportion of claims filed by private lawyers and supported by private doctors' prescriptions seem to confirm that the "haves" are more likely to benefit from litigation. I am not claiming, it is important to emphasize, that right-to-health litigation is the exclusive preserve of socioeconomic elites. This is not warranted by the data just analyzed. The very rich are in fact unlikely to litigate or, when they do, they are more likely to litigate against their private health insurance companies, not against the state.[18] My interpretation of the data is more in line with Varun Gauri and Daniel Brinks's conclusion that the benefits of litigation accrue mostly to individuals "in the middle of the social spectrum"—in other words, "neither the most disadvantaged nor the wealthiest citizens" (2008, 336–37). This is in great part due to the *opportunity structure* for litigation in Brazil. "Rights awareness; organizational strength and ability to mobilize; and access to legal assistance, technical expertise, and financial resources" are not easily available to the least advantaged socioeconomic groups. So, even where legal assistance is available through public attorneys and defenders and court fees are waived (something easily done in

Figure 4.7. Percentage of lawsuits according to type of legal representation and medical services

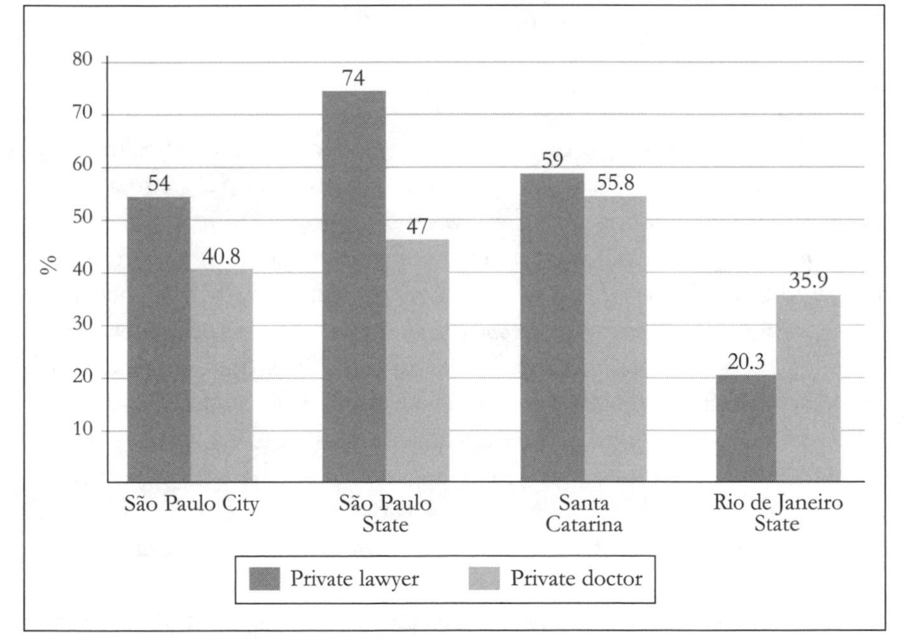

Source: Vieira and Zucchi (2007); Chieffi and Barata (2009); Pereira et al. (2010); Messeder et al. (2005).

the Brazilian system), the lowest socioeconomic groups struggle to make use of this structure (Galanter 1974).[19]

It is also important to emphasize that the picture presented so far is based on individual claims alone, which represent the vast majority of claims. Collective lawsuits sponsored by public attorneys, in particular the Public Prosecutor's Office (*Ministério Público*), are in principle more capable of benefiting the worst-off, provided that they focus on health issues that are a priority for that group. Moreover, the fact that collective suits are a tiny minority of current right-to-health litigation does not mean that their impact should be negligible. One single collective lawsuit has the potential to have a greater impact than thousands of individual suits combined, since it can conceivably affect the whole Brazilian population. Unfortunately, data on collective lawsuits are even scarcer than on individual ones. The available data, however, show a pattern similar to that found in individual suits: collective lawsuits are also highly concentrated on the ten states with the highest HDI (75%). The two least developed states of Brazil, Maranhão and Alagoas, have no collective suits against the federal government at all.[20]

We will now move from the profile of claimants to the profile of claims, which can also elicit interesting information about the social impact of litigation on health policies and health equity.

What Type of Claims?

According to the available data, the vast majority of right-to-health claims reaching the courts in Brazil are for *access to medication.* There is also a smaller proportion of claims for *surgical and diagnostic procedures*, mostly abroad or in the private system, which the public system is not equipped to carry out or prepared to fund; *medical equipment* (e.g., wheelchairs, prosthetics, and insulin infusion pumps); *special dietary products* (e.g., special milk for people with allergies); and *hygiene products* (e.g., geriatric diapers). Given that, as seen above, the vast majority of claims are individualized and not collective, the remedies demanded also tend to be individualized—that is, they seek the *provision of a health benefit* for an individual litigant rather than a change in policy to benefit a whole group or the population as a whole. Cases dealing with the social determinants of health as outlined in General Comment 14 of the United Nations Committee on Economic, Social and Cultural Rights[21]—such as basic sanitation, nutritious food, and safe water—are much rarer and not yet studied in any depth.

This strong focus on health care, in particular access to medication, has an important social and economic impact, since many claims are for expensive new medicines available in the market (in Brazil or abroad) yet not made available by the public health system. In Vieira and Zucchi's study (2007), cancer drugs, although representing only 7.5% of the cases, were responsible for a staggering 75% of the costs incurred by the municipality of São Paulo to comply with judicial orders in 2005. At the federal level, judicial orders forcing the government to provide thirty-five drugs not available in the Brazilian market represented as much as 78.4% of the costs of all right-to-health litigation in 2009 (*Folha de S. Paulo* 2010). Another study carried out by the Secretariat of Health of São Paulo State reemphasizes this point. Whereas the per capita expenditure for high-cost drugs incorporated by the public system is R$2,500 (US$1,250), it shoots up to R$10,600 (US$5,300) when only the judicially mandated drugs are taken into account.[22]

Given that the health budget is limited and is determined by law and other formal regulations at least a year in advance, these judicial orders, which must be complied with immediately, force an inevitable reallocation of resources that is potentially harmful to the rational use of funds and to health equity. Indeed, resources are being diverted from health policies—planned by health experts to serve the population as a whole—to the judicially ordered individual treatment of a few thousand patients who managed to access the courts. It is hard to determine with any degree of precision who the inevitable losers are in this reallocation of resources. Government health officials are unsurprisingly wary of publicizing which health policies lost funding due to the need to cover treatment ordered through litigation.[23]

One point of contention between supporters and detractors of judicialization relates to whether or not litigated drugs are included in the "official lists" (i.e., the government's pharmaceutical assistance programs). Those trying to justify the legitimacy of litigation argue that most lawsuits involve drugs that have already been incorporated into the official lists but that, because of some administrative failure, are not available in the public system. When this is the case, they claim, the judiciary is not distorting health programs and priorities but rather simply making sure the government complies with its own policies. There is little hard evidence, however, to support this argument. Some studies have indeed found that many of the drugs claimed through litigation are present in official lists (e.g., Borges 2007, 52%; Vieira and Zucchi 2007, 62%). But others have found the opposite (e.g., Chieffi and Barata 2009, 23%; Pepe et al. 2010, 48.1%). Moreover, while litigation for a drug included in an official list may indicate an administrative failure, it may also indicate several other possibilities:

- A doctor did not follow the therapeutic guidelines for the prescription of drugs, either deliberately (because she believed her patient required special treatment) or inadvertently (because she was not aware of the guidelines). In these cases, health authorities might deny the request and the request could proceed to litigation.[24]
- The lawsuit involved a single prescription calling for various drugs, some of which were included in an official list and some of which were not. When this happens, the patient's entire request might proceed through litigation.
- A patient was not a habitual user of the public system. Many of the drugs that feature regularly in litigation, such as cancer medications, are provided by the public system only when assigned as part of an entire treatment. In such cases, individuals who use the private system might often simply want the state to provide the drug while they continue to obtain their broader treatment through the private system (Chieffi and Barata 2009; Sant'ana 2009).

It is difficult, with the information available, to disentangle these possible explanations to know what percentage of claims fall under each of these categories. But it is important to realize that they exist—otherwise one runs the risk of oversimplifying the causal explanations of the phenomenon. What is clear is that the vast majority of right-to-health litigation in Brazil is concerned with access to medicines, many of which have not been incorporated in the official lists. Many of these drugs, moreover, are extremely expensive, and some without a clear significant additional benefit to the patient. Others have a proven benefit, yet at an inordinate cost compared to the alternative therapies available. This type of litigation represents the bulk of the costs of judicialization and has a significant, and potentially perverse, social impact.

How Are Claims Received by Courts and Enforced by Government?

Perhaps the most unanimous conclusion among studies on right-to-health litigation in Brazil is that Brazilian courts are receptive to such litigation and have an expansive interpretation of the constitutional right to health (Ferraz

2009a; Hoffman and Bentes 2008; Chieffi and Barata 2009; Pepe et al. 2010). This produces an extremely high success rate for litigants.

Cases begin in first instance courts, where one judge makes a decision. When appealed, the cases move up to the court of appeal, where three (and potentially five) judges hear the case. Finally, if the cases are appealed on a point of federal law, they move up to the Superior Tribunal of Justice, or if they are appealed on a point of constitutional law, they move up to the Supreme Federal Tribunal. Some right-to-health cases have gone all the way up to the superior courts. Most cases, however, go up only to the court of appeal of the state in which the claim originated; some do not even reach that stage, ending with the decision of the first instance judge. In an overwhelming majority of cases, the final judgment has been in favor of the claimant. This is an important element in the opportunity structure for litigation, as observed by Siri Gloppen (2008a), and it has been confirmed in a recent comparative study of Brazil, India, Indonesia, Nigeria, and South Africa (Gauri and Brinks 2008). Gauri and Brinks highlight how, in Brazil, the judiciary's receptiveness to health claims—not to be found in Indonesia and Nigeria for instance, and not as strong in South Africa—can be seen as one of the main factors leading individuals to choose the courts as a channel for health demands. Such receptiveness spurred an explosion in health claims, which they call the Brazilian "rights revolution" (309–12). India is the only studied country where receptiveness is equally strong; yet problems with compliance there have pushed claimants away from the courts and instead toward political channels (ibid.).

Once court orders are issued, how effective is compliance? The authorities who must comply with court orders are the health departments of the administrative unit sued by the claimant (federal, state, or municipal). Compliance is by and large high, but it varies across the country. According to the report *Remédio via Justiça* (Brazilian Ministry of Health 2005), the city of Florianopolis is among the most efficient in terms of compliance, whereas the state of Rio de Janeiro exhibits severe delays. In the state of São Paulo, a special separate pharmacy was set up simply to dispense court-ordered medicines, and a second one is about to be opened.[25] The same is the case in Rio Grande do Sul. According to the civil servant of the health department who led the initiative in São Paulo, this pharmacy was necessary primarily to avoid the risk of the health secretary falling into contempt of court, which can result in a prison order issued by the judge. This recurrent use of contempt-of-court orders and threat of prison is arguably one of the reasons why compliance seems so high in Brazil as compared to other countries. But it has its problems, not only creating a bad relationship between judges and health officials but also resulting in higher costs for the state. This is because the amount of time that judges often give for a court order to be implemented, such as forty-eight or seventy-two hours, is not long enough for the health authority to carry out the necessary procurement procedures required by law in order for the state to get the best price.

A potential problem with compliance reported by Hoffman and Bentes (2008) is related to claimants' available resources for following up on court decisions. Well-resourced HIV/AIDS NGOs, for instance, or private lawyers representing individuals, apply constant pressure on the authorities to ensure compliance with a decision, whereas poorer claimants represented by resourced-strapped public attorneys cannot do the same and might not even follow up on a favorable decision. The social gradient of judicialization, therefore, is present even at the compliance stage.

By and large, however, it seems fair to conclude that judicial resistance to right-to-health claims is virtually nonexistent in Brazil and compliance by state authorities is not a major hurdle, at least in individual lawsuits, which so far have been studied in more depth than collective lawsuits.[26]

Conclusion

If litigation were to focus on the health issues that are a priority for the most disadvantaged, its social impact would be at least potentially positive according to the criteria proposed in the previous section. The reason why such litigation would still be only *potentially* positive has been explained above: a real and overall positive impact would occur only if resources to fund the enforcement of court orders were not diverted from other health programs that are also a priority for the most disadvantaged. That would produce, at best, a neutral impact. A positive impact would require either an (unlikely) expansion of the health budget or a reallocation of existing resources from health programs that are not a priority for the most disadvantaged.

An expansion of the health budget is unlikely for legal and political reasons. Legally, only Parliament can decide to increase the health budget; this decision is made at least one year in advance, whereas court orders are issued daily and, through interim injunctions, compliance must take place within a matter of hours or days. As a result, it would be virtually impossible for Parliament to increase the health budget to account for the costs of judicialization, even if the political will existed. But the political will to do so, as is well known, is not there. The financing of public health in Brazil seems to have reached a political ceiling of around 3.5% of gross domestic product, as confirmed by Parliament's recent rejection—largely supported by the public—of a new "health tax," or *Contribuição Social da Saúde* (*Folha On Line* 2009).

The more plausible scenario is that Brazil is indeed experiencing a reallocation of funds from existing health programs in order to cover the costs of judicialization. As already noted, it is not easy to determine with precision where the funds used to comply with court orders are coming from. Health officials are quick to disclose and publicize the spiraling costs of judicialization, yet much less ready to divulge where the resources are being reallocated from. This is to some degree understandable, for if they publicize that some programs are losing resources in order to cover the costs of judicialization, the "losers" would become easily identifiable and might be able to complain. It would create an additional problem for the health administration to deal with.

At any rate, even if the "losers" of the judicialization of health are not precisely known, we are nonetheless beginning to shape a representative image of the majority of the "winners." We can say with some confidence, for instance, that they are neither those most deprived of health services nor the most disadvantaged in terms of other social determinants of health. Indeed, the total absence or paucity of judicialization in the regions, states, and municipalities of Brazil where human development is lowest shows that those at the bottom of the socioeconomic ladder are not going to court, whether individually or through public attorneys and NGOs, to claim their right to health. The high concentration (more than 90%) of claims in the rich states and municipalities of the south and southeast indicates exactly the opposite. Moreover, detailed micro-studies of the socioeconomic profile of litigants (often based on their place of residence) show a very low prevalence of claims originating in the poorest districts within municipalities. This is true for individual lawsuits and also for the comparatively fewer collective suits, which have the potential to benefit more individuals.

As to the object of claims, there is also consistent evidence that most of the cases (including collective lawsuits) demand medication. Sometimes the drugs are new and have not been incorporated into the public system; sometimes they are already part of the state's health policy, appearing on its "official list." It is not clear what percentage of claims fall into either category. What is clear is that the bulk of the costs of judicialization are generated by the former type of claim, especially claims for drugs that are not available in Brazil, and sometimes for drugs that have been rejected as cost ineffective in public health systems of more developed countries.

When we combine these two key elements of the current Brazilian model of right-to-health litigation, it seems plausible to conclude that the model's overall social impact is negative. Rather than enhancing the provision of health benefits that are badly needed by the most disadvantaged—such as basic sanitation, reasonable access to primary health care, and vaccination programs—this model diverts essential resources of the health budget to the funding of mostly high-cost drugs claimed by individuals who are already privileged in terms of health conditions and services.

For health litigation to produce a positive social impact in Brazil, this model would need to change in several ways. Judges would need to be more restrictive in their interpretation of the right to health. They would need to recognize that resources are limited and priorities need to be set, and that ability to access the judiciary is not a fair criterion for the allocation of health resources. Courts would also need to demand that health authorities provide clear and rational justification for the priorities they set, and should interfere only when they fail to do so. Judges would have to pay particular attention to whether the government's health programs aim to reduce the dismal health inequalities prevalent throughout the country, as the Constitution pledges. The legal profession could also help. It would be naive to ask private lawyers to stop representing better-off clients in their pursuit of expensive and complex therapies. But it is not outlandish to demand that public attorneys at least focus on representing the health interests of the most disadvantaged.

NOTES

1. Although there are various perspectives on the judicialization of health, there is now consensus that it does represent a problem that needs to be solved. It is too early to tell whether the public hearing on the judicialization of health will produce any change in the jurisprudence of Brazilian courts. The Supreme Federal Tribunal has decided only a handful of cases after the public hearing. Despite some indication that at least one of the judges, Gilmar Mendes, sees a need to restrict the expansive interpretation mentioned in the text, the practical outcome in all these cases has nonetheless remained unchanged; that is, the plaintiff was successful in all of them. It remains to be seen whether other judges will follow a more restrictive interpretation and, if so, whether that will produce any effective change in the outcome of cases.

2. Constitution of Brazil, 1988. Article 195 states simply that health services and actions are of public relevance, and the state will thus "regulate, supervise and control" their execution, which can be done directly or through third parties. Article 199 states that private companies can operate in the health sector on a complementary basis but can neither be owned by foreign capital nor receive public subsidies.
3. For a wealth of information on this topic, see the Ministry of Health's website at http://portal.saude.gov.br.
4. For the sake of simplicity, all currency conversions in this chapter from Brazilian reais to American dollars use the conversion rate of two reais for one dollar, which is an approximate average of the years 2008–9. Most of the data on costs are from these years (*Folha de S. Paulo* 2010). For data on the health budget, see Siga Brasil, www9.senado.gov.br/portal/page/portal/orcamento_senado/SigaBrasil.
5. The Ministry of Health has two subdepartments in addition to the SCTIE that also deal with lawsuits: the *Secretaria de Vigilância em Saúde* (Health Vigilance Secretariat) and the *Secretaria de Atenção à Saúde* (Health Attention Secretariat). The numbers presented here do not include lawsuits handled by these departments, which represent about 20% of the lawsuits against the Ministry of Health. These suits involve mainly vaccines, operations, oncology drugs, and ophthalmology services and products. Precise data on these lawsuits were not available when I visited the Ministry of Health in July 2009.
6. Ferraz and Vieira (2009) estimate that it would cost more than 100% of the health budget to provide 1% of the Brazilian population with only four of these drugs.
7. For a discussion of decentralization and its difficulties, see Spedo et al. (2009).
8. I tried to establish how these data were collected and where they came from by emailing Senator Tião Viana, with no success.
9. Borges (2007); Naundorf (2008); Romero (2008); Chieffi and Barata (2009); Maria Cecilia Correa (director of litigation department, Secretariat of Health of São Paulo State), interview, São Paulo, July 2009.
10. The survey was conceptualized by myself and Daniel Wang, and carried out through email and postal correspondence in partnership with CONASEMS, the National Council of Municipal Health Secretariats. I am particularly grateful to Blenda Pereira, who managed the survey logistics. The data were processed through Makesurvey software (www.makesurvey.net).
11. This is a conservative estimate not only because of the incomplete data on states and municipalities but also because some of the available data are already outdated (from as far back as 2006). For my calculations, I have used the most recent year for which data were available.
12. Due to the limited scope of this chapter, I cannot defend my interpretation of the right to health. See Ferraz (2009a) for a more detailed development of my argument.
13. The analysis builds to some extent on Gloppen's proposed framework (2008) dividing the phenomenon of right-to-health litigation into four stages: claim formation, adjudication, implementation, and social outcomes.
14. What might explain Ceara's high position in the ranking of litigation is its large population of 8,547,809 (the eighth most populated state of Brazil). In terms of the ratio of lawsuits to inhabitant (1/113,970), Ceara ranks well below the Brazilian average (1/42,364) and the average of the states of the south, southeast, and center-west.
15. Ceara and Rio Grande do Norte are possible exceptions, but there are no precise data on these states yet.

16. São Paulo's Secretariat of Health uses a different method for measuring the ratio of litigation to inhabitants (i.e., number of lawsuits per thousand inhabitants).
17. Public attorneys, especially public defenders, are representing an increasing number of middle-class people (Hoffman and Bentes 2008, 142; Vania Agnelli Sabin Casal, Luciana Jordão da Motta Armiliato de Carvalho, and Vitore André Zilio Maximiano [public defenders], Adriana Daidone [private lawyer specializing in health litigation], and Luiz Duarte de Oliveira [state's council specializing in right-to-health lawsuits], interview, São Paulo, July 2009).
18. There is a large volume of litigation against private health insurers demanding drugs and treatment. I decided not to analyze it in this chapter because it is not based on the constitutional right to health and thus not considered part of the phenomenon of the judicialization of health in Brazil. Rather, it is seen as an issue of private contract law.
19. Legal aid is liberally granted by the courts through a mere "self-declaration of poverty" by the claimant.
20. I am currently performing a case study of collective lawsuits claiming basic sanitation measures for entire municipalities in the south of Brazil. My initial impression is that collective lawsuits are more difficult to implement than individual ones.
21. United Nations Committee on Economic, Social and Cultural Rights, General Comment 14, U.N. Doc. E/C.12/2000/4 (2000).
22. Correa interview, *supra* note 9.
23. When interviewing health officials from the Secretariat of Health of São Paulo State, I pressed them to inform me which health policies suffered cuts due to the need to spend US$200 million on litigation in 2008. They were unwilling to disclose that information.
24. The Secretariat of Health of São Paulo State currently has an administrative procedure in place to try to avoid this situation. If a doctor wants to prescribe a type or dose of medication different from that established in the official guidelines, the patient can file an administrative request that will be reviewed by the health department (Correa interview, *supra* note 9).
25. Ana Luiza Chieffi (pharmacist of the Secretariat of Health of São Paulo State), interviews, São Paulo, July and November 2009.
26. Collective lawsuits, for which no in-depth studies yet exist, would seem intuitively more complex to enforce, since they might require more extensive and costly measures from the state.

Chapter 5

Colombia

Judicial Protection of the Right to Health: An Elusive Promise?

Alicia Ely Yamin, Oscar Parra-Vera, and Camila Gianella

Colombia is a country of many contrasts and even paradoxes. A long tradition of creating democratic institutions coexists with authoritarianism and alarming levels of political and social violence, including notably a brutal, fifty-year-long civil conflict. Entrenched poverty persists despite years of strong economic growth, and the country's extreme social inequality is reflected in its health statistics, where national averages mask deep disparities that run along urban versus rural divides, as well as racial, ethnic, and class lines (Instituto de Estudios Políticos y Relaciones Internacionales 2006, 11–32; Sánchez and Vargas 2009).[1] A weak civil society and fragmented social movements stand in sharp contrast to a vibrant and civically engaged academic community, especially in urban centers. In this context, the Colombian Constitutional Court has developed some of the most progressive jurisprudence in the world with respect to economic, social, and cultural rights, including health rights.

It would be impossible, in a chapter of this length, to detail the full extent of the Court's interventions with respect to the right to health. Not only has the Court since its creation in 1991 decided more than a thousand

---

Space does not permit including everyone's names, but we gratefully acknowledge the invaluable insights of the dozens of key informants we interviewed from government, civil society, and the private sector. This study would not have been possible without their collaboration. We especially appreciate the access and information provided by current and former magistrates of the Constitutional Court. We also wish to thank Helena Alviar in particular for her tremendously helpful insights and suggestions on an earlier version of this chapter. Much of this chapter is based on Yamin and Parra-Vera (2010).

cases explicitly addressing access to health care but it has also issued extraordinarily important judgments relating to other aspects of state obligations to respect, protect, and fulfill the right to health as set out in article 12 of the International Covenant on Economic, Social and Cultural Rights[2] and explicated in General Comment 14 of the United Nations Committee on Economic, Social and Cultural Rights.[3] For example, in a staunchly conservative Catholic country, the Court has issued controversial judgments regarding reproductive and sexual rights, including abortion and the rights of sexual minorities to health care. Amid an ongoing civil conflict and humanitarian crisis, it has ordered attention to underlying preconditions for health for internally displaced persons (IDPs). It has also issued decisions regarding water and sanitation, and state obligations to protect health and other rights from actions by private actors, such as extractive industries. Furthermore, the Court has issued rulings relating to important social determinants of health, such as housing and nondiscrimination.[4]

This chapter focuses on the evolution of the Court's interventions with respect to the definition of an autonomous right to health under the Colombian Constitution, and the extraordinary judicialization of demands for access to care. According to a report by the Human Rights Ombuds Office of Colombia, between 1999 and 2008, a stunning 674,612 actions for protection of constitutional rights were filed before the courts in relation to access to health care and treatment (Defensoría del Pueblo 2009, 30). By 2008, it was clear that courts had become an essential "escape valve" for Colombians who were denied access to medicines, surgeries, and treatments by a health system incapable of regulating itself (Procuraduría General de la Nación and Dejusticia 2008). In July of that year, the Court issued a sweeping decision that sought to improve the equity and functioning of the health system and stem the tide of litigation.

In that T-760/08 judgment, the Court examined systemic problems regarding the health system, definitively asserted the fundamental and actionable nature of the right to health, and called for significant restructuring of the health system based on rights principles, including nondiscrimination, participation, and accountability. The full implementation and impact of this sweeping structural judgment is yet to be seen as of this writing. Nevertheless, in this chapter we examine the responses to T-760/08 thus far and assess some of the potential as well as limitations regarding the judiciary's ability to create greater equity in the Colombian health-care system.

However, the Court's impact on the right to health cannot be discerned by examining cases regarding health care alone. Therefore, in addition to tracing the story of the Court's intervention in the health-care system, we will also mention a number of other cases that illustrate the diversity of the Court's concerns in relation to health rights. We argue that a consistent theme across the interventions of the Court is that through its innovative use of structural remedies and other mechanisms, it has sought to open executive decision making to greater public scrutiny and to permit greater democratic deliberation around fundamental issues regarding health, as well as other rights. The cases relating to health exemplify in many ways how the Court has not limited itself to what might be considered "politically acceptable," as scholars arguing for the constrained nature of judicially promoted social change have asserted with respect to other contexts (see Rosenberg 1991). On the contrary, it has challenged both powerful institutions and prevailing discourses in Colombian society.

Moreover, with respect to the health system in particular, the Court's actions have evolved as a response to the shortcomings of policy-making processes in Colombia and to the government's evident lack of institutional capacity for designing, implementing, and monitoring policies. We argue here that despite the enormous symbolic impact of the Court's decisions, the very factors that have led to the Court's strong interventions may also limit the impact of its decisions in material terms.[5] That is, as *The Federalist Papers* stated over two hundred years ago, like all courts, the Colombian Court must "ultimately depend upon the aid of the executive arm even for the efficacy of its judgments" (Hamilton et al. 1788, 464). Much of the impact of the Court's judgments concerning health will ultimately depend on the will of political elites and the strength of political processes.

Origins: The 1991 Constitution and the Creation of the Court

The adoption of a new and plainly aspirational constitution in 1991 occurred in the context of enormous political violence related to the internal armed conflict and drug trafficking.[6] The Constituent Assembly that led to the adoption of the 1991 Constitution and, in turn, the creation of the Constitutional Court, was a historic moment in Colombian history. There was broad participation in the process, including that from former insurgent groups such as M-19. Many of the delegates hoped that the new constitutional charter would usher in a new chapter in Colombian history, marked by greater democracy and social justice (Cepeda 2004, 549).

However, the coming together of Colombian society in the Constituent Assembly did not last long. Soon, the Court remained the only institution left to preserve the democratic vision set out in the Constitution (Uprimny and García Villegas 2006). As in other countries that have experienced significant judicial activism, the Court has often stood as the only bulwark of protection for vulnerable populations and unpopular causes (see, e.g., Gauri and Brinks 2008; Langford 2008, 19).

Health-related cases—as well as cases involving issues traditionally excluded from public debate by powerful actors in Colombian society, such as abortion—exemplify the kinds of protection the Court has afforded to marginalized minorities.[7] The Court has addressed treatment for HIV/AIDS patients and the right to insurance coverage for same-sex couples, among other issues.

However, it is too simplistic to assert that the Court has stood merely as the defender of the individual against the majority. Rather, it is more accurate to argue that it has also upheld a starkly different notion of Colombian society than that being pursued by the executive branch with respect to both economic and social policies, as well as democratic policy making (Uprimny and García Villegas 2006).

The Court in Context

Colombia has historically been a country of "haves" and "have-nots," with very disparate levels of development and an extremely unequal distribution of income. In the 1980s and 1990s, along with many countries in Latin America, Colombia adopted neoliberal economic policies that followed the so-called Washington Consensus, which, among other things, liberalized labor policies and undermined universal claims to health care and other economic and social rights (see, e.g., de Currea-Lugo 2006).

Further, Colombia is notable for the number of reforms that were rushed through the legislative process with virtually no opportunity for democratic debate. Indeed, the enactment of sweeping health-sector reform through Law 100 in 1993 has been cited as the paradigm of reform instituted by "change teams"—reforms defined and implemented by teams of technocrats, insulated from public debate and accountability (Plaza et al. 2001, 44–51).[8] Reform was necessary; however, the enactment of Law 100, which enshrined a managed-care model, was highly controversial. Nevertheless, it was pushed through the legislature shortly before the Christmas holiday and then implemented as quickly as possible through decrees, before a change of presidential administration took place just months later. Similarly, despite a presentation of alternative proposals for the health system in 2007 when Law 100 was being reformed through Law 1122, the legislative debate regarding that law lasted literally only a few minutes before approving then president Uribe's proposal.[9]

If normal legislative and political channels for complaints regarding health care were blocked, so too were avenues for social mobilization (Instituto de Estudios Políticos y Relaciones Internacionales 2006, 1–32). The armed conflict that has wracked the country for half a century, coupled with authoritarian repression of dissent, has had particularly devastating effects on the possibilities of social mobilization around health policy.

Colombia exemplifies Asa Laurell's insight that a country's pursuit of neoliberal policies aimed at diminishing the intervention of the state is often achieved through a vigorous state intervention colored by authoritarian trends (2000, 43). In Colombia, labor leaders and workers in the health sector have been killed and brutally repressed in the context of a politics of aggressive privatization.[10] Some complaints allege that the government has repeatedly deployed military units as well as death squads (e.g., *águilas negras*) to harass dissident health workers and leaders, and to occupy public hospitals slated to be privatized or shut down.[11] At the same time, especially in rural areas, attacks on medical facilities and personnel by illegal armed actors have been common, which has affected access to care and vaccination in some cases (*Cambio* 2009). In some regions, paramilitary groups have controlled and essentially managed health-care budgets, converting health care into another domain of so-called armed patronage (Ossa 2004; Briceño 2009; *El Tiempo* 2006; Rueda 2006).

Legal Opportunity Structure and the New Constitution

At the same time that other avenues of recourse were virtually closed, the legal opportunity structure created by the 1991 Constitution made seeking redress for health and other social claims through the Colombian courts extremely appealing. In addition to incorporating economic and social rights, the new Constitution enshrined various structural innovations. Among the most important innovations that explain the extent of health-related interventions by the courts generally and the Constitutional Court in particular are (i) the establishment of the Court as a specialized tribunal overseeing a new "constitutional jurisdiction" that includes all Colombian judges; (ii) the application of constitutional judicial review to specific cases through a protection writ (*tutela*); (iii) the extension of abstract reviews of legislation through *ex oficio* and *actio popularis*, including the virtual abolition of standing requirements; and (iv) reliance on expert opinions and outside evidence sources, including medical and scientific experts (see Cepeda 2004).

This chapter focuses on the use of the *tutela*, which, in the health arena, has been used to a far greater extent than other suits, such as popular actions (*acciones populares*) and class actions (*acciones de grupo*).[12] The *tutela* is analogous to the *amparo* of many other Latin American countries, but has taken on particularities in Colombia that have made it pivotal in securing health and other social rights. First, it involves very few formal requirements, which principally relate to stating sufficient facts to amount to a cause of action. Individuals may file petitions, orally or in writing, without the assistance of an attorney. Second, whichever judge receives the petition is bound to give it priority over all other matters and to reach a decision within ten days, including issuing an order when necessary. Third, any *tutela* judgment can be reviewed by the Constitutional Court in order to correct a decision or advance its own jurisprudence. When the Court chooses to do so, it may issue unification judgments (*sentencias de unificación*) clarifying jurisprudence regarding a specific subject, such as access to certain medicines (Cepeda 2004).

Finally, *tutelas* can be both simple and complex. That is, they may order an individual or government agency to carry out or to abstain from a particular action, and in these cases their effects are *inter partes*. As we shall see when we discuss cases relating to the health-care system and IDPs, judges may also adopt orders that are directed at a number of different authorities, which require a coordinated set of actions.

The Colombian Health-Care System: From Conception to Crisis

Notwithstanding the social and political context and the appealing legal opportunity structure, the extraordinary number of health claims seen by the Colombian courts and the scope of the Constitutional Court's interventions can be only partially explained by sociopolitical factors. The health system's inability to regulate itself has also played a decisive role.

The reforms implemented through Law 100 in 1993 were premised on the superiority of market-based allocation of health care. However, Law 100 envisioned something far from an unregulated market. Rather than setting up a normal private insurance scheme, Law 100 established a hybrid scheme whereby private insurance companies did not set the capitation rates, did not define deductibles or premiums, did not set the content of benefits packages, and did not control whom to insure.[13]

Under Law 100, a managed-care system was coupled with a defined benefits package to be provided under a national insurance scheme (*Plan Obligatorio de Salud*, or POS) through an individual capitation. Law 100 also introduced a two-tier system of benefits: (i) the contributory regime (POS-C), for those formally employed or earning more than twice the minimum wage, and (ii) the subsidized regime (POS-S), which had a capitation set at one-half of that for the contributory regime and included approximately half the benefits (Plaza et al. 2001; Savedoff 2000; Glassman 2007).

Although it has fallen short of the universal coverage called for under Law 100, insurance enrollment progress has quite steadily increased, as has health spending.[14] As of 2008, Colombia was spending 5.9% of its gross domestic product on the health sector, which is substantially more than it spent in 1993 (see Colombian Ministry of Finance and Public Credit 2008). In addition to public expenditure, the system is financed through payroll taxes, and there is a cross-subsidy from the contributory regime to the subsidized regime.[15] This reliance on payroll taxes has proven to be a fatal flaw in a country where neoliberal policies produced increasing informalization of labor.

Since 1993, Colombia's health reform has at times been cited as a success story in international circles.[16] Within Colombia, however, the system established under Law 100 has been criticized by actors from all sides of the political spectrum, even before the system's economic collapse. A basic source of inequity lay in the design of the system itself—that is, while those who were able to participate in the contributory regime received more benefits, those who were unable to pay were assigned to the subsidized regime, which provided far fewer benefits (Colombian Ministry of Social Protection 2005). Law 100 called for the two schemes to be unified by 2001 but the government failed to take steps to make this happen.

A second fundamental problem lay in the definition of the benefits packages themselves. They lacked clarity, an evidence base, and prioritization mechanisms. Although Law 100 was ostensibly intended to make social choices about health care explicit by establishing a defined benefits program, it left an inordinate number of what have come to be called "gray zones" that failed to specify whether a given procedure, medication, or service is covered. For example, for a colostomy, it was unclear whether the colostomy bag was included in the coverage.

The complexity of the system demanded significant state capacity to oversee an array of private and public actors. However, despite the existence of multiple oversight bodies, including the Superintendency and the National Commission on Social Security and Health (which was later replaced by the Commission on Health Regulation, hereinafter "Commission"), the system was plagued with regulatory failure. Policies to improve efficiency and consistency were not implemented and complaints were not addressed in any systematic manner. Furthermore, reimbursement processes have been dysfunctional (see, e.g., Procuraduría General de la Nación and Dejusticia 2008; López Medina 2008; Defensoría del Pueblo 2009); that is, when goods and services are not included in the POS but are nevertheless ordered by a court, the government reimburses the insurance companies (EPSs, for their Spanish acronym) through a solidarity fund (FOSYGA, for its Spanish acronym).[17] However, such reimbursement has been inordinately slow and inefficient, especially with respect to pharmaceuticals.[18]

In addition to an evident lack of institutional capacity within the health system, the neoliberal precepts enshrined by Law 100 led to an affirmative effort to reduce state regulation, including the active deregulation of the pharmaceutical industry beginning in 2004 and accelerated in 2006.[19] Studies show that these reforms made drug prices in Colombia, especially for brand-name drugs, higher than in other countries of the region (*Portafolio* 2010; Cortés 2010).

The financial crisis in the health sector that President Santos's administration faced upon assuming power was partially attributable to a failure to regulate pharmaceutical prices and insurers' conduct (*El Tiempo* 2010a). The Observatory on Medications of the Colombian Medical Federation documented that the average reimbursements from FOSYGA to the EPSs for medications rose from Col$1 billion (1997–2000) to Col$1 trillion in 2007; by 2008, they had exceeded Col$1.15 trillion (Andia 2009). Such reimbursements represented the only area where court-ordered provision related far more to non-POS items than to items already included in the POS. For their part, pharmaceutical companies claimed that the EPSs added markups that resulted in brand-name drugs costing as much as two hundred times what they did in other countries in the region (Cortés 2010). In 2009, the Ministry of Social Protection estimated that mark-ups on drugs reimbursed by the FOSYGA cost the government approximately Col$400 billion a year.[20]

The lack of a coherent policy, together with the evident manipulation of the reimbursement system by EPSs, was perhaps most blatant with respect to pharmaceuticals. However, far from being unique, this chaotic state of affairs prevailed across the health system.

Judicial Protection of the Right to Health

Evolving Legal Basis for Enforcement

Early on, the Court determined that the right to health was enforceable under three circumstances: (i) when the case involves a person or group of people in especially vulnerable circumstances, such as children, the disabled, or the elderly;[21] (ii) when the case involves the right to receive care in the POS;[22] and (iii) "when not providing care [or some other good or facility] to the ill person would threaten his/her [fundamental] right to life."[23] This last category was developed through the *doctrina de conexidad*, which enabled the right to health to be considered a "fundamental" right by virtue of its connection to the right to life, interpreted as a life of dignity (*vida digna*).

By finding the right to health enforceable when it was inextricably related to enabling a life of dignity—and not merely preventing imminent death—a wide range of goods and services not included in the POS have been conceded to petitioners. For example, the Court has ordered the provision of antiretroviral and costly cancer medications, and even the financing of patients' treatment abroad when appropriate treatment was unavailable in Colombia.[24] The Court has also approved medical attention for severe psychiatric disorders, post-mastectomy breast implants, the administration of growth hormones, and care for severe vision problems, among others.[25]

However, the Court progressively abandoned the doctrine of fundamental rights by connection, considering it "artificial" and erroneous to conceive of certain categories of rights as purely positive and programmatic, given that all rights have positive, programmatic facets to them.[26] In T-760/08, the Court affirmed that it was setting aside the doctrine of fundamental rights by virtue of connection and that, in turn, the doctrine of "special protection for vulnerable groups" was no longer relevant in determining that the right to health was indeed fundamental.[27]

Thus, after T-760/08, rather than determine whether the right to health is susceptible to protection through the *tutela* in a given case, the relevant inquiry became the extent to which aspects of the fundamental rights to health were enforceable—whether immediately or subject to progressive realization. The benefits contained within the POS, as well as "other required services" established through jurisprudence, were immediately enforceable. With respect to progressive realization, jurisprudence from the Court has established that although the state can allege a lack of resources to implement a specific obligation, it needs to outline its plan to obtain the necessary resources, and the respective policies that such a plan will entail developing, which should in all cases include opportunities for public participation and deliberation.[28]

Context for T-760/08: Magnitude and Impact of Tutela Claims

Between 1999 and 2008, the number of tutelas filed regarding health claims increased continuously. As figure 5.1 illustrates, the Human Rights Ombuds

Figure 5.1. Proportion of health tutelas among all tutelas

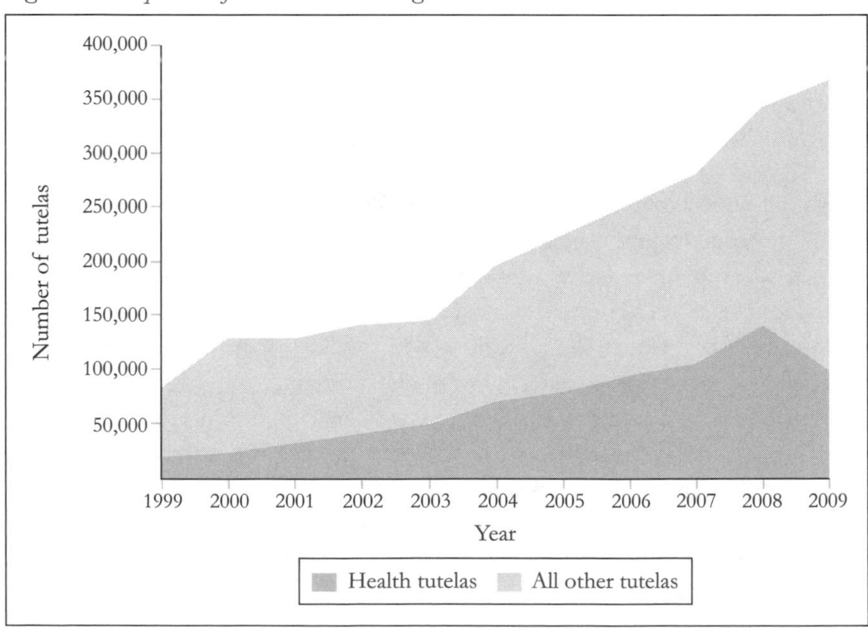

Source: Ombudsman.

Office calculated that 674,612 tutelas relating to health rights were presented between 1999 and 2008 (Defensoría del Pueblo 2009, 30). After T-760/08, however, the trend of increasing health tutelas was reversed, and there was a sharp decline in the number of tutelas filed (Defensoría del Pueblo 2010, 28). Nevertheless, this did not lead to fewer reimbursements, as there was a simultaneous increase in the number of claims filed for reimbursement from FOSYGA after being resolved in the Scientific Technical Committees of the EPSs.

Between 2006 and 2008, in approximately 86% of the cases involving health claims, the *tutela* was granted (Defensoría del Pueblo 2009, 35). Most of these *tutelas* were to enforce the provision of treatments and services that the insurance companies should have been covering. Indeed, between 2003 and 2008, 54% of the *tutelas* were for treatments and services that were contained within the POS (Defensoría del Pueblo 2007, 50, 78; 2009, 55). Similarly, between 2006 and 2008, 75% of the surgeries, 63% of the exams, 67% of the treatments, and 78% of the procedures sought through *tutelas* were services that people were entitled to under the POS (Defensoría del Pueblo 2009, 65, 74, 77). In 2009, the first full year post-T 760/08 for which data were collected, over two-thirds (69%) of the *tutelas* were for treatments and services contained within the POS.

Thus, with respect to the majority of the nearly 800,000 cases filed between 1999 and 2009, judges were enforcing either clear, pre-existing legal obligations—laid out in policies designed and enacted by the political branches of government—or obligations that had been read into the POS over years of jurisprudence (Procuraduría General de la Nación and Dejusticia 2008, 155–56). That is, a substantial proportion of the reimbursements from the government solidarity fund, FOSYGA, was attributable to the "gray zones" in the POS and to the systematic failure on the part of insurance companies to take into account constitutional jurisprudence attempting to make those gray zones less gray. For example, in its exhaustive review of the use of *tutelas*, the Human Rights Ombuds Office documented that in relation to surgeries, between 2006 and 2008,

> the principal source of denials are surgeries that require some additional input or added material in order to be realized, such as lenses for cataract surgery, stent implants for cardiac catheterizations, and orthopedic surgeries requiring joint replacements. (Defensoría del Pueblo 2009, 59)

There is an important distinction to be drawn between these cases and those in which the courts—especially the Constitutional Court—established entitlements to additional services that were never contemplated in the POS. Based first on the interpretation of what was necessary for a "life of dignity" and, more recently, the elements of an autonomous right to health, many of the Court's judgments have called directly for medications, care, and services outside of the POS, which have required funding from the government FOSYGA. Figure 5.2 presents data from the Colombian Association of Integral Medicine Companies (an association of private insurance companies), which is based on information from FOSYGA, regarding the amounts of reimbursement claims from FOSYGA for medications not included in the POS—the only area in which *tutelas* for non-POS care have exceeded those *tutelas* for care included within the POS.

As *tutelas* are awarded on a first-come, first-served basis and not all treatments are or could be universalized, the Court can be justifiably criticized for awarding health benefits based on the morally irrelevant criterion of who possesses greater access to justice. This inequity has been exacerbated greatly by the fact that those who have historically benefited from the *tutelas* are the

Figure 5.2. FOSYGA reimbursements

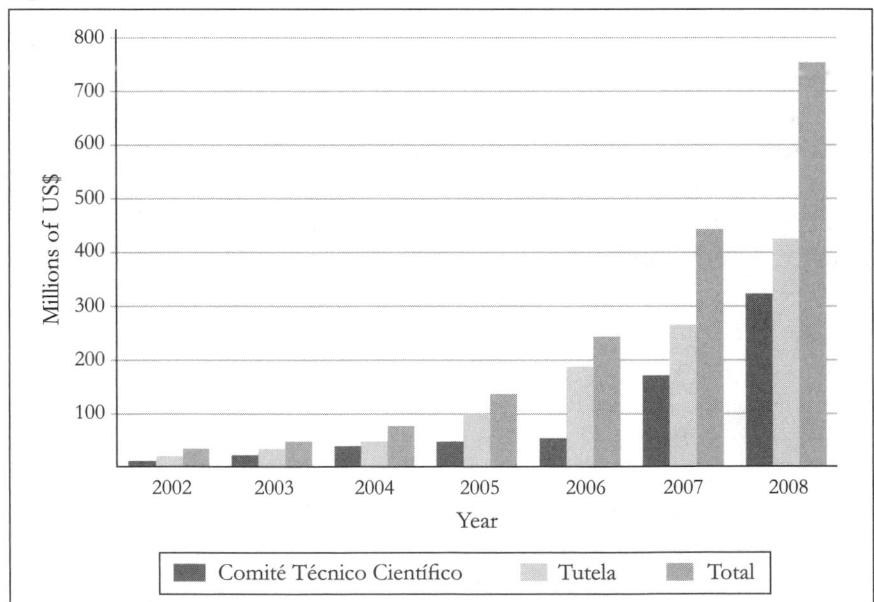

Source: Asociación Colombiana de Empresas de Medicina Integral, based on reports from the Fondo de Solidaridad y Garantía.

better-off, who have a more comprehensive defined benefit package. The studies carried out by the Human Rights Ombuds Office and the Attorney General's Office with the nongovernmental organization Dejusticia indicated that over half of the claims between 1999 and 2008 were brought by individuals in the contributory regime. In contrast, fewer than 20% were brought by individuals in the subsidized regime. Based on the numbers of affiliated persons in the regimes, the Attorney General's Office and Dejusticia calculated that in 2003, rates of the use of *tutelas* for enforcing health claims were almost six times higher for the contributory regime than for the subsidized regime (184/100,000 versus 33/100,000) (Procuraduría General de la Nación and Dejusticia 2008, 13).

Moreover, based on a review of data from 2006 to 2008, *tutelas* were brought at higher rates in wealthier departments than in poorer departments (see figure 5.3) (Defensoría del Pueblo 2009, 28). Given the effects

Figure 5.3. Department poverty levels (2008) and concentration of tutelas per 10,000 inhabitants (2006–8)

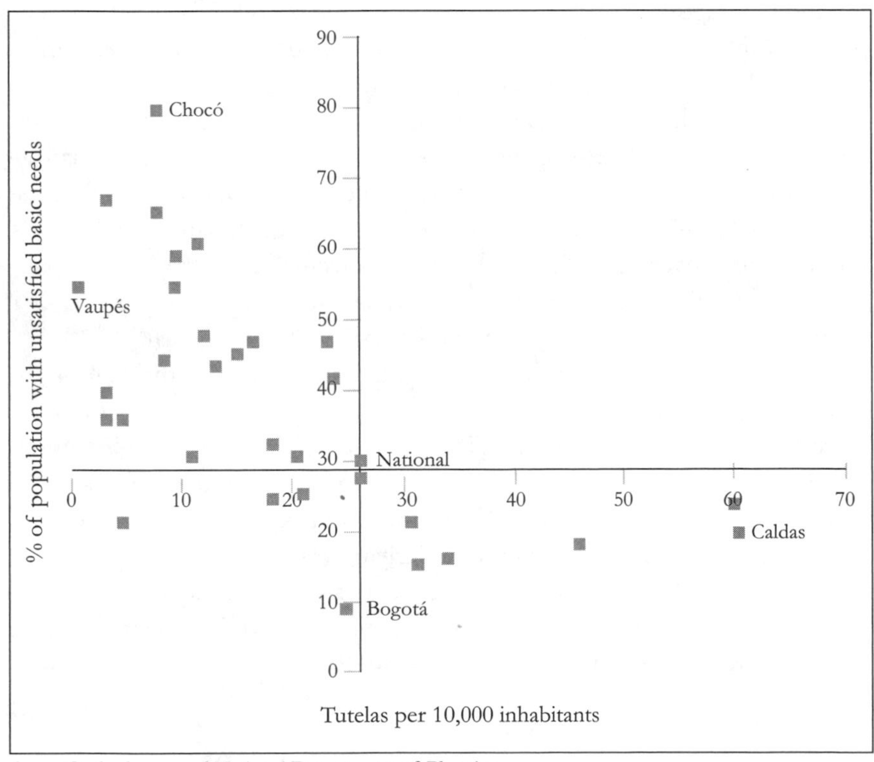

Source: Ombudsman and National Department of Planning.

of marginalization and armed conflict on many regions of the country—departments where access to justice is most difficult—people whose access to health is limited are likely to face double burdens in seeking redress.

The indirect, population-level equity impacts of the judicialization of health claims are more difficult to assess. It is clear that although *tutelas* have only *inter partes* effects, the wave of individual litigation led to new health policies, some of which have greatly benefited poor and marginalized sectors of society. For example, the Court's jurisprudence led to the inclusion of viral load tests within the POS, given that treatment for HIV/AIDS is dependent upon such a test.[29] The Court has exercised judicial control over the procedures used to determine beneficiaries of subsidized care, which by definition benefited many poor people in the country.[30] Similarly, the Court found that attempts by the government to reduce the budget for the subsidized regime constituted impermissible retrogression.[31]

On the other hand, some studies indicate that the funds disbursed by the FOSYGA for non-POS benefits could have been better applied to expand coverage directly in the subsidized regime or to fund crucially needed public health measures (Pinto and Castellanos 2004, 56).[32] As noted earlier, Colombia's extreme inequality is reflected in its health statistics; some parts of the country have undergone the epidemiological transition while others continue to face problems relating to basic sanitation and health infrastructure. For example, by 2008, while 94% of the urban population had access to improved drinking-water sources and 96% to adequate sanitation facilities, these numbers were only 73% and 60%, respectively, for the rural population (Joint Monitoring Programme for Water Supply and Sanitation 2010a, 2010b). Such disparities exist for a number of key health indicators.

In short, by 2008, not only the health system but also the role of the courts in the health system had become highly controversial in Colombia. Were the courts draining the public purse of needed resources for public health or were they defending individuals against the abuses of insurance companies? There was no question that structural reforms were needed, but there was little consensus as to the underlying problems or the appropriate solution. In T-760/08, the Court responded to its own diagnosis of the problems, which primarily concerned structural inequities in the system, systemic failures of regulation, and the overuse of *tutelas*.

Setting in Motion Health-System Reform? Judgment T-760/08 and Its Aftermath

The Judgment

T-760/08 collected twenty-two *tutelas* (twenty brought by individuals and two brought by EPSs), which the Second Review Chamber of the Court selected in order to illustrate systemic problems in the health system. The Court asserted that a structural approach to the health system's failings was necessary because "the organs of government responsible for . . . the regulation of the health system have not adopted decisions that guarantee the right to health without having to seek recourse through the *tutela*."[33]

Beyond resolving the twenty-two individual cases, the Court called for reforms to (i) ensure transparency in determinations of POS benefits as well as implement institutional performance audits to inform users about the performance of different providers and insurance entities, in particular regarding the numbers of *tutelas* their affiliated patients must bring in order to secure care; (ii) facilitate the execution of *tutelas* and the adoption of a contingency plan to ensure appropriate and timely reimbursements in the event of costs associated with care not covered under the POS-C or POS-S; and (iii) conduct a comprehensive revision of the capitation rates, which had not been fundamentally reviewed and revised in years.[34]

The Court did not declare the health-care system to be in an "unconstitutional state of affairs," as many activists and analysts had recommended.[35] However, it did call for restructuring the health system in significant ways. The Court directed the Commission to immediately and on an annual basis comprehensively update the benefits included in the POS-C/POS-S through a process that includes "direct and effective participation of the medical community and the users of the health system,"[36] in particular those who would be most affected by policy changes.

Law 100 had established the aim of unifying the two benefits regimes by 2001. Prior to 2008, the Court issued judgments that allowed the differentiation in schemes based on ability to pay but that urged the government to, in keeping with its own stated objectives, formulate a plan for the unification to occur within a specified time frame.[37] In T-760/08, citing the government's failure to take steps toward a unification of plans since the adoption of Law 100, the Court ordered the Commission to unify the POS-C and POS-S, initially for children and later for adults; in the latter case, this was to be done progressively and was to take into account financial sustainability as well as the epidemiological profile of the population. The Court itself did not propose contents of a unified POS or automatically equate unification with equalization; rather, it left that to the relevant agencies but stipulated that the process of devising a unification plan was to be participatory, transparent, and evidence based.[38]

Furthermore, the Court noted that achieving universal insurance coverage was an established public policy goal of the government, and, setting a 2010 deadline, called on the government to adopt deliberate measures to progressively realize universal coverage.[39]

Situating the Court's Approach to the Right to Health

The Court reiterated its previous jurisprudence, which established that health care falling outside the POS can be immediately enforced through *tutelas* when the following conditions are met: (i) the lack of the medical service threatens the patient's right to minimum level of subsistence (*mínimo vital*); (ii) the service cannot be substituted by one contained within the POS; (iii) the patient cannot afford to pay the price of the required treatment or medication and cannot obtain such treatment or medication through any other health-care regime, such as insurance plans provided by employers or prepaid complementary plans; and (iv) the service has been ordered by a physician familiar with the patient's case.[40]

In this regard, both T-760/08 and the Court's overall jurisprudence on the right to health are very much in keeping with General Comment 14 and can be sharply distinguished from the South African Constitutional Court, which has rejected a minimum core that can be enforced regardless of resources, in favor of a reasonableness review. In T-760/08 in particular, the Court attempted to establish a minimum essential level as distinct from any particular set of interventions that might be currently legislated through the POS. However, the Court's definition of a minimum essential level, which is immediately enforceable, was broad: "a vital minimum, without which organic deterioration would impede a normal life."[41] Other than what had already been excluded, such as cosmetic procedures, there were no firm lines drawn as to the extent of an immediately enforceable right to health care.

Furthermore, in assessing medical necessity, T-760/08 did not depart from the constitutional jurisprudence that has placed extraordinary importance on the opinion of the attending, and sometimes other, physicians. When determining the patient's need for a given medication or service, the Court has repeatedly characterized the issue as a conflict between the physician—who is presumed to be able to make decisions "based on scientific criteria" as well as his or her knowledge of the patient—and the EPS, which tends to make decisions based on financial, bureaucratic, or other criteria.

The Court's unwillingness to set out principles that might meaningfully limit the right to health, together with its continued deference to physicians in determining medically necessary care, has been criticized by actors from different political positions.[42]

On the other hand, the Court's approach to a remedy can be seen as consistent with theories of "experimentalist regulation" and the kinds of dialogic justice described by Roberto Gargarella in this volume. In T-760/08, far from dictating the content of an enforceable right to health, the Court sought to foster meaningful social negotiation over the parameters of that right as it relates to care. Gargarella argues that the Court's decision can be read as an attempt to ensure that political decisions regarding health priority setting respond to an exchange of arguments in public forums rather than to the pressure of interest groups and that structural problems unaddressed by the Colombian legislature—which in turn had resulted in the systematic violation of fundamental rights—be actively considered. As we will see below, this is not the first time the Court has used such a structural remedy to unblock political channels and open more democratic debate.

More specifically, the Court's approach to redefining a unified POS appears compatible with Norman Daniels's (2008) proposals for just processes in priority setting in health, discussed elsewhere in this volume. Daniels argues that we lack fine-tuned principles that tell us how to meet health needs fairly—such as what priority to place on the worst-off—when we cannot meet them all. Therefore, he argues that we need to fall back on a process that affords at least "accountability for reasonableness." According to Daniels, such a process must be (i) transparent, in that the grounds for decisions are made public; (ii) based on "relevant" reasons (e.g., appropriate patient care versus racial or gender stereotypes); (iii) revisable through some kind of appeals procedure because there will always be new factors to consider as well as atypical cases; and (iv) subject to regulation and enforcement (2008, 118–19).

Implementation of T-760/08 and the Context of Broader Health Reform

Although to date there has been nominal compliance with many of the orders in the judgment, from the outset the Uribe administration demonstrated reluctance to implement T-760/08. At times the administration made arguments based upon lack of resources; at others it stated that the time line for implementation was unrealistic (see *Cambio* 2008). Finally, both the Uribe and Santos administrations have until now shown profound reluctance to foster the kind of participatory process that was called for by the Court (Gianella-Malca et al. 2009).

Given the context and what was at stake, it was arguably foreseeable that the Court's emphasis on reasoned public debate as a means of constructing citizenship was almost completely ignored by the government (see, e.g., Yamin 2009; Gargarella et al. 2006). As Nancy Fraser (1992, 66) has argued about the preconditions for effective participation, "it does require the sort of rough equality that is inconsistent with systemically-generated relations of dominance and subordination." Not only does the Colombian context present extreme social inequalities but also certain interest groups—such as the EPSs—are well organized and exercise great economic clout in contrast with patients who have little or no economic means and are unorganized. Thus, the "rules of the game" for a democratic deliberation about the parameters of the right to health might be expected only to entrench profound imbalances in power. Indeed, during the first twenty months after the decision, this is exactly what seemed to occur, as the Commission appeared incapable of real implementation and overseeing the powerful interest groups.

For example, on July 30, 2009, one day before the deadline for doing so and after having met only twice, the Commission issued an accord "clarifying and comprehensively updating" the POS (Cortés 2009).[43] Just months later, through Decree 008, the Commission again "clarified and comprehensively updated" the POS, derogating the previous decree, but again neither provided a thorough revision nor the criteria on which its decisions were based (Andia 2010). Similarly, on September 30, 2009—again one day before the deadline set by the Court for unification—the Commission issued an accord whereby "temporarily" the POS-S for children up to twelve years of age defaulted to the POS-C, given that the Commission had not come up with an alternative "unified" POS for children.[44] Shortly thereafter, the Court issued a specific order affirming that "children" were defined as zero to eighteen years old and demanding that the Commission expand the equalized coverage.[45] Toward the end of 2009, the Commission seemed institutionally incapable of implementing the judgment.

However, the most telling governmental response to T-760/08 was then president Uribe's "Declaration of a Social Emergency" in December 2009.[46] Among other reasons, the government alleged that the reimbursement costs for non-POS care were bankrupting the system. Pursuant to this declaration, the government moved swiftly to issue a series of decrees that circumvented any popular discussion whatsoever. Some of these decrees were aimed at injecting much-needed resources into the health system through centralizing reimbursements, eliminating fraud and corruption, and imposing new taxes on beer, cigarettes, and gambling (although taxes on imported cigarettes were reduced).[47] However, efforts to control costs notably did not attempt to re-regulate the pharmaceutical industry.[48] Nor were emergency powers used to attempt to restrict the irregularities and arbitrary behavior of the EPSs (see, e.g., *Portafolio* 2009; *La Libertad* 2009).

In total, the government issued thirteen decrees that implied a substantial reform to the health system, while circumventing public debate as called for under T-760/08. The decrees created a furor among both patient and medical associations, as well as the general public (see, e.g., Federación Médica Colombiana 2010). By February 2010, mass protests were taking place across Colombia using the slogan "health is not a favor; it's a right" (see, e.g., *El Espectador* 2010; Agence France Press 2010). Importantly, these protests included people who were not typical social dissidents, such as physicians and members of the Catholic hierarchy (see, e.g., *El Tiempo* 2010a).

If the initial implementation of the judgment seemed to entrench rather than destabilize the steep asymmetries of power in the Colombian health-care context, the government's declaration of a state of social emergency changed the dynamic for a variety of interest groups—and even for the legislature and the Court itself. Indeed, one effect of T-760/08 may well have been to create what Charles Sabel and William Simon (2004, 1020) refer to as "destabilization rights":

> claims to unsettle and open up public institutions that have chronically failed to meet their obligations and that are substantially insulated from the normal processes of political accountability.

For the first time, the right to health became a matter of broad public debate in Colombia, and the design and feasibility of the entire health system were being actively discussed (see, e.g., *El Espectador* 2010; *El Tiempo* 2010b). In Cesar Rodríguez Garavito and Diana Rodríguez Franco's typology, these might be considered symbolic impacts of the judgment, changing the health discourse from a technocratic issue to one of democracy (2010a).

In April 2010, the Court declared the emergency decrees unconstitutional while allowing a provision relating to sin taxes to remain in effect temporarily.[49] The Santos administration, which assumed power in August 2010, faced health system reform as one of the first major issues it had to tackle, given the financial crisis within the system. One of the first proposals of the new administration and Congress was to divide the Ministry of Social Protection into a Ministry of Health and a Ministry of Labor (see, e.g., Radio Santa Fé 2010).

Implementation of T-760/08 must now be seen in a larger context of the broader health reforms in Colombia. That is, issues that were addressed in T-760/08 (such as the definition of benefit schemes and regulatory failures), as well as issues that were alluded to but not addressed (such as the unsustainability of reliance on payroll taxes for financing) will call for attention from the Santos administration and Congress. In addition, in its legislative proposals, the Santos government has recognized that issues that were omitted by the judgment but that are critical to the efficiency and equity of a health system—such as pharmaceutical policy, priority setting, the significance of primary care, and health promotion and prevention—will also need to be addressed in short order (Colombian Ministry of Social Protection 2010).

The extent to which T-760/08 precipitated broader health reforms, as well as whether such reforms would have occurred in the absence of this sweeping decision, is debatable. However, the level of scrutiny exercised by the Constitutional Court will unquestionably play a role in the shape that health reform takes and in the number of the judgment's orders that are ultimately implemented. It will also play a critical role in determining whether the symbolic discursive effects evidenced in protests during early 2010 will be transient or lasting, and whether they will translate into material effects in the course of institutionalization of reforms to the health system.

In March 2009, the Court's composition had changed substantially, including the departure of Justice Manuel José Cepeda, who drafted the T-760/08 opinion. The new Court tasked one of its Review Chambers with overseeing the implementation of the judgment's complex structural orders. As of this writing, the Court has issued over twenty orders (*autos*) requesting information regarding the implementation of the judgment. The Review Chamber has also invited a series of civil society groups— including representatives of Afro-Colombian and indigenous organizations—and members of Congress to provide information and observations concerning implementation of the decision.[50]

However, in contrast with the earlier structural decision regarding internally displaced persons—T-025/04, mentioned below—T-760/08 has not been linked with a strong social movement struggling for implementation of the decision. In fact, key members of the national movement for health have argued that the decision is not worth supporting because it distracts attention from the structural failings of a health system based on private insurance.[51] It is also unclear how sustained the Review Chamber's commitment will be in monitoring an extraordinarily complex judgment, especially if there are significant political reforms to the health system in 2010–11 that obviate some of the orders in T-760/08.

Other Judicial Protections of the Right to Health: Diversity of Cases, Mixed Results

T-760/08 has been criticized for overemphasizing access to care rather than focusing on preventive public health measures (Uprimny and Rodríguez 2008). Indeed, it is possible that the overall impact of the judicialization of health, coupled with the restructuring of the system in the aftermath of T-760/08, may be a substantial reinforcement of the investment in individual care reflected in Law 100, to the detriment of preventive public health measures.

The Court has, however, also protected the right to water and sanitation—though without resulting in the same magnitude of claims or financial impact. The right to water and sanitation is established as a component of the right to health under article 12 of the International Covenant on Economic, Social and Cultural Rights and more fully elaborated in General Comment 15.[52] In fact, the *doctrina de conexidad* (fundamental rights by virtue of connection) was first elaborated on in the context of a case involving access to these essential preconditions of health.[53]

The Court has also issued judgments related to informed consent, discrimination against unmarried couples (as it relates to health benefits), and other underlying preconditions of health, such as food.[54] In one controversial case involving sexual health rights, the Court issued a decision regarding hermaphrodism, in which it held that surgery to assign a particular sexual identity required a higher-than-ordinary level of informed consent and must be postponed until the person was of age to make that decision.[55] As a general rule, the effects of these judgments have been restricted to the specific litigants. Nonetheless, these judgments have also had important effects on policies, such as changes in insurance coverage for unmarried and same-sex couples.

The Court has also issued *erga omnes* judgments and structural orders related to reproductive health. For example, in a May 2006 holding having *erga omnes* effects, the Court struck down Colombia's absolute ban on abortion, legalizing the procedure under three circumstances: (i) when the continuation of pregnancy presents a risk to the life or health (physical or mental) of the woman; (ii) when pregnancy is the result of a criminal act of rape, incest, unwanted artificial insemination, or unwanted implantation of a fertilized ovule; and (iii) when grave fetal malformation makes life outside the womb unviable.[56] The Court found that Colombia's prior abortion law—one of the most restrictive in the world—unduly hampered women's exercise of their human rights, including their rights to health, life, bodily integrity, and reproductive autonomy (Undurraga and Cook 2009).

Even though in subsequent judgments the Court attempted to reduce barriers to accessing this critical reproductive health right, evidence suggests that women continue to face significant hurdles in accessing safe abortion under the circumstances permitted by law (*Semana* 2010). These include geographic and economic barriers relating to the organization of the health system, as well as resistance from providers to comply (so-called conscientious objection) (La Mesa por la Vida y la Salud de las Mujeres 2009, 43–55). Moreover, a new attorney general has also instituted obstacles to the judgment's implementation (Procuraduría General de la Nación 2010).

Through this series of decisions, the Court has forced the contested issue of abortion rights—blocked entirely from the political arena in this conservative Catholic country—to be placed into public discussion, which itself is a challenge to dominant powerful interests in Colombia. However, the Court's necessary reliance on the cooperation of political actors and institutions in questions of implementation has limited the effects of such decisions on women's health rights in practice. Five years after the decision, questions remain as to the extent to which the Court can translate its ability to unblock political debates into the adoption of effective policies and programs.

Another example of the Court's boldness in bringing marginalized issues into the political process relates to the conditions of internally displaced persons (IDPs). The principal precedent for the structural orders in T-760/08 was a 2004 case (T-025) in which the Court declared the existence of an "unconstitutional state of affairs" in relation to the situation of the millions of IDPs in the country, including their lack of access to care and deplorable living conditions that affected their health.[57]

As in the case of the health system in T-760/08, prior to this judgment the Court had already issued numerous judgments concerning IDP rights and aspects of the IDP situation. Just as the Court did not attempt to define the contents of a new POS in T-760/08, the Court did not impose a specific policy on the government with respect to IDPs. Rather, it required the government to develop a policy that met certain standards. After substantial input from both the government and civil society, the Court adopted indicators that measured the "effective enjoyment" of various rights of IDPs—including indicators relating to their right to health—and IDPs' effective participation in the development and decision-making process regarding internal displacement in Colombia.[58]

The implementation of T-025/04 has been monitored by a number of civil society groups organized into the Follow-up Committee on Public Policy on Forced Displacement, which has been formally recognized by the Court and submits periodic reports. Rodríguez Garavito and Rodríguez Franco (2010a) argue that this judgment had major instrumental (direct and indirect) as well as symbolic effects for the situation of IDPs in Colombia, including with regard to their health rights. Multiple programs have been created, budgets have been substantially increased, and public perception of the IDP crisis has been transformed from one of collateral damage of the internal armed conflict to a situation of massive human rights violations.

However, actual outcomes for IDPs have changed less than might be expected. The health situation of IDPs in Colombia is still abysmal and, despite progress, the government has failed to overcome the structural conditions that led to the declaration of the unconstitutional state of affairs.[59] Forced displacement is still a pronounced and ongoing phenomenon in Colombia despite changes in the public discourse (according to official data, in 2009 alone 111,414 people were forcibly displaced); leaders are frequently subjected to death threats and even killed; and IDPs continue to denounce barriers to receiving the social benefits to which they are entitled, including those in relation to healthy preconditions, such as food security, and health care (Comisión de Seguimiento a la Política Pública sobre el Desplazamiento Forzado 2010).

Moreover, despite the creation of programs since T-025/04, grossly inadequate registration systems often do not permit the identification of beneficiaries. Further, IDPs continue to face substantial barriers to participation in policy decisions affecting their welfare, including health care (Mesa de Seguimiento al Auto 006 de 2009 Desplazamiento y Discapacidad 2010).

Evaluations of impact are inevitably subjective in terms of "the glass being half full or half empty" and are challenged by being snapshots in time. Nevertheless, we believe that these cases collectively suggest that despite the Court's extraordinarily proactive role—including its development of indicators for monitoring the effective enjoyment of rights, its holding of public audiences, and its official recognition of an interested coalition of groups to monitor compliance in T-025/04—the implementation of decisions regarding the structural conditions that underlie the enjoyment of health rights is necessarily dependent on the execution of public policies by the political branches of government. On the one hand, respect for judicial review in Colombia means compliance with judgments that strike down discriminatory or retrogressive legal provisions regarding health and health care, and these impacts should not be underestimated. On the other hand, effective public policy making in this area requires sustained political commitment, as evidenced by allocation of resources as well as institutional capacity. Despite the Court's commitment to championing the health-related rights of the poor and excluded, it has limited power over these other factors in the Colombian context, constraining the material impact of its decisions.

Conclusion

The story of judicial intervention in health rights illustrates many of the paradoxes of the Court's role in Colombian society. The judicial protection of programmatic dimensions of the right to health has steadily increased in Colombia since 1991, and jurisprudence regarding the enforceability of the right to health is among the most progressive in the world. However, generous concessions of individual health-care benefits without regard to whether they could be universalized appear to have exacerbated rather than ameliorated inequities within the Colombian health-care system. This conclusion regarding judicialization might not be cause for concern, given that historically the middle class is often at the forefront of vindicating rights, as it has greater access to justice, and those rights are often later extended to the poor. Yet the complex and under-regulated system set up under Law 100, in combination with judicial interventions, has seemed to lend itself to manipulation by better-off patients, the EPSs, and pharmaceutical companies.

Through T-760/08, the Constitutional Court acknowledged many of the problems associated with resolving individual cases—both for the judiciary and the health system—and called for structural reforms. T-760/08 may be the most sweeping judgment regarding health rights issued by any court in the world to date, calling for significant restructuring of the health system in keeping with rights principles of equality, participation, and accountability, as well as for measures to reduce recourse to the courts. However, we have argued here that the Court did not seek to legislate health policy or displace the executive branch. Rather, it carefully followed what had been envisioned in prior legislation and called for the political branches of government to undertake the functions that corresponded to them. Also, critically, the Court attempted to foster a broad-based debate about the contours of a right to health care in Colombia's highly plural society.

Although T-760/08 has been criticized for potentially reinforcing a health-care system based on individualized curative care at the expense of preventative public health measures, it would be unfair to assess the Court's health rights interventions solely on the basis of that decision. The Court has protected other aspects of the right to health that go beyond access to care, including water and sanitation. The cases briefly mentioned in this chapter illustrate the breadth and depth of the Court's commitment to ensuring that health rights are respected, protected, and fulfilled. We have also noted the persistent gap between the expansive conceptualization of rights and the innovative remedies, on the one hand, and the material impact on outcomes, on the other.

Although we concur that the Court has played a significant role in unblocking political processes and debates in order to ensure that issues systematically excluded from political consideration are brought into the public sphere, we have argued that the very sociopolitical reasons that led to a heightened judicialization of health rights—and other social issues—also limit the possibilities for creating transformative social change through the courts in Colombia. That is, in the absence of a representative legislature, an administration capable and conscientious enough to execute public policies relating to health, and strong social movements to demand accountability for implementation, the Court's progressive jurisprudence does not effectively translate into the actual enjoyment of health-related rights by the worst-off in Colombia.

In short, the Colombian context presents profound challenges for "dialogic" judicial activism, in that steep social and power inequalities, violence and its attendant consequences for social mobilization, and the precariousness of the rule of law make true democratic dialogue extremely difficult. As of this writing, Colombia is undergoing yet another process of health reform. But there is no reason to believe that this will be a definitive reform. Indeed, system-wide reform is far more likely to entail an iterative process. Time will tell whether the destabilization achieved through the public's overwhelming rejection of the state of emergency regarding the health system will now or in the near future be channeled into a productive process of political debate about the scope of the right to health—or at least health care—as a fundamental asset of citizenship for all Colombians.

NOTES

1. Colombia has a Gini index of 58.5, reflecting a level of economic inequality that is among the highest in the world (United Nations Development Programme 2009).
2. International Covenant on Economic, Social and Cultural Rights, G.A. Res. 2200A (XXI), 21 U.N. GAOR Supp. (No. 16) at 49, U.N. Doc. A/6316 (1966), 993 U.N.T.S. 3, entered into force January 3, 1976.
3. United Nations Committee on Economic, Social and Cultural Rights, General Comment 14, U.N. Doc. E/C.12/2000/4 (2000).
4. See, e.g., Sentencia T-270 de 2007 (where the Court said that the right to water is a fundamental right in the case of a woman needing water in order to perform in-home dialysis); Sentencia T-585 de 2008 (where the Court protected the right to housing for a family not included in a relocation program for populations inhabiting high-risk zones); Sentencia T-769 de 2009 (where the Court ordered the suspension of the Muriel Mining Corporation's megaproject Mandé Norte, which took place in lands traditionally occupied by indigenous and Afro-Colombian communities, until the informed consent of the peoples and communities was obtained).
5. For some examples of the dichotomies related to symbolic and instrumental impacts of judicial decisions, see García Villegas (1993) and Rodríguez Garavito and Rodríguez Franco (2010a).
6. Constitution of Colombia, 1991.
7. See analysis of Sentencia C-355 de 2006 on abortion at the end of this chapter.
8. For a definition of change teams and a discussion of Law 100 reform, see Bossert (2000).
9. Analysts have pointed to heavy lobbying from the pharmaceutical industry and insurance companies (Felipe Galvis, interview, Bogotá, March 2009).

10. For example, the Asociación Nacional de Trabajadores Hospitalarios de Colombia has reported that 132 of its members were killed between 1996 and 2007. Moreover, the Asociación has reported threats, burglaries, and several instances of arbitrary detention of its members. See Martínez Guevara (2008).
11. Interview with workers and ex-workers from Instituto Materno Infantil, March 2009. See also Martínez Guevara (2008).
12. See Constitution of Colombia, 1991, art. 88.
13. Juan Manuel Díaz Granados (president of Asociación Colombiana de Empresas de Medicina Integral), interview, Bogotá, March 2009.
14. By 2009, close to 90% of the population had health insurance. Most uninsured people remain in rural areas and comes from the lowest quintiles.
15. The 12.5% payroll tax, 4% of which is paid by the employee, is among the highest in the region, and is additional to payroll taxes for social security. Further, 1% of payments made within the contributory regime is used as a cross-subsidy for the subsidized regime.
16. The World Health Organization (2000) ranked Colombia thirty-third out of all health systems in its 2000 *World Health Report*, while the United States was ranked thirty-seventh. See also Glassman et al. (2009).
17. When goods and services are not included in the POS-S but are nevertheless ordered by a court, the state reimburses the EPSs providing such goods or services if they are included in the POS-C. That is, the municipalities and regions cover the difference between the POS-C and the POS-S, if and when a service or medication is ordered through a *tutela*, and the FOSYGA covers anything beyond the POS-C.
18. *El Tiempo* (2009); Díaz Granados interview, *supra* note 13; Correa (2009).
19. Ministerio de la Protección Social, Circular 004 de 2006.
20. Ministerio de la Protección Social, Decreto 4975 de 2009.
21. See, e.g., Sentencia Su-225 de 1998 (where children's meningitis vaccine was declared part of their fundamental right to health); Sentencia T-1081 de 2001 (where the intraocular lens and medications related to eye surgery were conceded as protecting an elderly person's right to health); Sentencia T-025 de 2004 (where the Court determined that deplorable conditions and lack of services for displaced persons violated their right to health, among other rights).
22. See, e.g., Sentencia T-859 de 2003 (where the Court decided that when there is doubt about inclusion of a joint for joint-replacement surgery under the POS, coverage should be interpreted in line with providing a functional life of dignity); Sentencia T-261 de 2007 (where the denial of an intraocular lens in an intraocular-lens implant procedure included in the POS was interpreted as a violation of the fundamental right to health).
23. See, e.g., Sentencia T-571 de 1992 (where the Court said that denial of treatment for acute arachnoiditis—a debilitating condition characterized by severe stinging, burning, and neurological problems—affected life with dignity).
24. See, e.g., Sentencia T-499 de 1995 (where concession of antiretroviral therapy was deemed necessary for HIV treatment); Sentencia Su-111 de 1997 (where the Court issued a "unification judgment" announcing general rule that *tutelas* without recommendation by attending physician would generally be denied); Sentencia Su-819 de 1999 (where the Court ordered that a minor suffering from acute leukemia—for which the only treatment identified by the attending physician was to be found abroad—could receive such treatment abroad), reiterated in Sentencia T-414 de 2001 and Sentencia T-344 de 2002.

25. See, e.g., Sentencia T-409 de 2000 (where a *tutela* was conceded for treatment of severe depression that included suicide attempts); Sentencia T-119 de 2000 (where a *tutela* for breast reduction was denied on the grounds that it was considered an aesthetic treatment); Sentencia T-572 de 1999 (where a *tutela* for breast implants was granted when it was necessary to avoid severe depression and problems of self-esteem post-mastectomy).
26. Sentencia T-760 de 2008, sec. 3.2.5, citing Sentencia T-016 de 2007 (granting a *tutela* that ordered surgery on a nodular lesion on the patient's ear, a surgery that had previously been denied on the grounds that it was purely cosmetic).
27. Sentencia T-760 de 2008.
28. Sentencia T-595 de 2002 (where the Court addressed a plan for the needs of disabled persons in the public transport system, including ramps), reiterated in Sentencia T-760 de 2008.
29. This was later extended to other diagnostic tests, such as biopsies. See, e.g., Sentencia T-500 de 2007 (where the Court declared a violation of the fundamental right to diagnosis in a case where the EPS had classified a patient's skin problem as cosmetic before diagnostic tests were performed).
30. Sentencia T-1083 de 2000 (where the Court ordered that situations of vulnerability—such as pregnancy—and manifest conditions of infirmity be taken into account when allocating the benefits under the subsidized regime).
31. Sentencia C-1165 de 2000 and Sentencia C-040 de 2004.
32. The authors argue that approximately 199,000 additional individuals in 2002 and 327,000 additional individuals in 2003 could be insured using the revenues from the contributory regime and their associated administrative costs for those same years.
33. Sentencia T-760 de 2008, sec. 2.2.
34. Sentencia T-760 de 2008. See *El Tiempo* (2009).
35. According to Manuel José Cepeda, author of the judgment, a declaration of an "unconstitutional state of affairs" would have allowed the government a long period to analyze the flaws in the system and come up with proposals to address them, which in this case would have merely led to greater delays (interview, Bogotá, March 2009).
36. Sentencia T-760 de 2008, sec. 6.1.
37. Sentencia C-1032 de 2006. The judgment found constitutional the two-scheme health system set up under Law 100.
38. Sentencia T-760 de 2008, sec. 6.1.
39. Sentencia T-760 de 2008.
40. See, e.g., Sentencia T-760 de 2008; Sentencia Su-480 de 1997.
41. Sentencia T-760 de 2008, sec. 3.2.4.
42. Uprimny and Rodriguez (2008) argue that the Court can be faulted for having said almost nothing about principles through which to limit the right to health in a constitutionally permissible and financially sustainable manner. Santa María and Perry (2008) point out that universalization will increase payroll taxes on the formal sector for those in the contributory regime, which will lead people to transfer to the informal sector and the POS-S, which will again increase payroll taxes on the formal sector, in a vicious cycle.
43. Comisión de Regulación en Salud, Acuerdo 003 de 2009.
44. See Comisión de Regulación en Salud, Acuerdo 004 de 2009.

45. See Auto 342A de 2009.
46. Ministerio de la Protección Social, Decreto 4975 de 2009.
47. See, e.g., Ministerio de la Protección Social, Decreto 4975 de 2009; Decreto 073 de 2010; Decreto 074 de 2010; Decreto 075 de 2010; Decreto 127 de 2010; Jaramillo (2010).
48. See, e.g., Comisión Nacional de Precios y Medicamentos, Circular No. 1 de 2004 and Circular No. 4 de 2006; Cortés (2010).
49. Judgment C-252/10 said that legislative statutory regulations should be issued to overcome the structural problems of the health sector.
50. Auto S-34 de 2009.
51. Organizers of Tercer Congreso Nacional por la Salud, interview, Bogotá, March 2009. See also Pacheco (2009).
52. International Covenant on Economic, Social and Cultural Rights, *supra* note 2; United Nations Committee on Economic, Social and Cultural Rights, General Comment 15, U.N. Doc. E/C.12/2002/11 (2003).
53. Sentencia T-406 de 1992.
54. Sentencia T-216 de 2008; Sentencia T-856 de 2007; Sentencia T-224 de 2005.
55. Sentencia Su-337 de 1999.
56. Sentencia C-355 de 2006.
57. Sentencia T-025 de 2004.
58. See, e.g., Auto 109 de 2007; Rodríguez Garavito and Rodríguez Franco (2010a, 466–67).
59. Auto 008 de 2009.

Chapter 6

Costa Rica

Health Rights Litigation: Causes and Consequences

Bruce M. Wilson

Costa Rica, a small Central American country with a population of 4.4 million, is generally regarded as one of the oldest, most democratic countries in the Americas (Freedom House 2009; Wilson 1998). Compared to its neighbors on the Central American isthmus, Costa Rica enjoys a high gross domestic product (GDP) per capita;[1] but its GDP is somewhat lower than that of many South American countries (World Bank 2009). Although Costa Rica's poverty levels are the lowest in Central America, they remain moderately high, with approximately 24% of the population living below the state-determined poverty level. The impact of income inequality, however, has been ameliorated by an extensive state-funded welfare system that includes universal health-care coverage, pensions, education, and many other services. While the country's economic indicators are those of a middle-income developing country, its social indicators resemble those of economically developed countries. For example, life expectancy at birth in Costa Rica is 78.7 years, which is close to the level of the wealthiest countries in the world and a full six years higher than that of the next closest American country.[2] Using the United Nations' Human Development Index—a more sophisticated measure of development—as a metric, Costa Rica ranks fifty-fourth in the world, outperforming its GDP–per capita world rank by twenty places (United Nations Development Programme 2009).[3]

The author would like to thank the following people for their comments on and/or research help with this chapter: Daniel Brinks, Ross Cotton, Siri Gloppen, Kerstin Hamann, Sigrid Morales, Ole Frithjof Norheim, Olman Rodríguez, Kurt Weyland, Kieran Wilson, Alicia Ely Yamin, and the two anonymous referees.

Of Costa Rica's state-provided social services, its health-care system is particularly remarkable. A 2008 World Bank study concluded that Costa Rica is "an outstanding example of a middle-income country that provides its people, including the poor, with broad and deep health care coverage, considerable financial protection, and an extensive package of services" (Cercone and Pacheco 2008, 183). An earlier World Bank study concluded that "the health sector in Costa Rica has exhibited a record of exemplary standards" (Lisulo 2003, 2) and a United Nations report noted that Costa Rica and Cuba are the only two countries in the Americas with "optimum access" to essential medications and virtually universal coverage of health care (United Nations Development Programme 2003).[4]

With no constitutional guarantee to health rights, and nearly universal access to health care and health-care statistics among the best in the Americas, Costa Rica was an unlikely location for a rapid rise of health rights litigation. This chapter examines the transformation in Costa Rica, where health changed from a "blessing to be wished for" to a "human right to be fought for."[5] Despite the success of the country's health-care system, the last fifteen years have witnessed a rapid increase in the use of litigation by individuals to obtain treatments and medications denied by the state-funded health system. Why did patients begin filing health rights claims in the Supreme Court in the early 1990s, and why, since then, did the Court's jurisprudence gradually change from favoring the health system's administrators to favoring health rights claims? Has the Court's health rights jurisprudence derailed the state's ability to pursue its health priorities and effectively treat the most essential health conditions and illnesses?

These questions structure this chapter. First, I describe the historical development of Costa Rica's health system since the end of the 1948 civil war and the creation of a new constitutional chamber of the Supreme Court, which immediately and aggressively acted to protect individuals' constitutional rights. The next sections discuss the Court's initial refusal to protect health rights and its gradual construction and enforcement of a fundamental justiciable right to health.[6] Subsequently, the chapter analyzes key health rights cases and the Court's arguments in favor of health rights. The final section examines a frequently voiced argument that the Court's health rights jurisprudence is harming the health system by forcing the reallocation of funds away from general health priorities to high-cost treatments for uncommon illnesses.

Costa Rica's Health-Care System

Costa Ricans enjoy virtually universal access to a well-functioning state-funded health-care system. The percentage of the population covered by the health-care system expanded from 5% in the early 1940s to 17% by the 1960s, followed by a rapid growth to 46% by 1970 and 80% by 1980. At the end of the 1990s, 88% of the population had access to state-funded health care (Clark 2002, 3), and by 2006, approximately 93% of the population "had adequate access to primary care service" (Cercone and Pacheco 2008, 183). The national health system (*Sistema Nacional de Salud*) is composed of several autonomous institutions, while the Ministry of Health bears responsibility for developing the national health plan. The *Caja Costarricense de Seguro Social* (Costa Rican Social Security Agency, or CCSS, also commonly referred to as the "Caja"), a state institution established in 1941, has become the single most important actor in the health-care sector.[7] It currently runs all state-owned hospitals and health-care facilities; only a very small number of health facilities in Costa Rica are in private hands.[8] The Caja employs over 90% of all registered doctors in the country, although a significant number of them also maintain private clinics (Clark 2002, 3). The Caja contributes over 90% of the health-sector revenue via mandatory contributions from all of Costa Rica's employees and employers as well as the state.[9] The Constitution mandates operational autonomy for the Caja (over its targets, objectives, and strategies), which, coupled with its ability to raise its own revenues, grants it a great deal of policy-making freedom. The Caja's financial independence makes it less vulnerable to government influence than other autonomous institutions that rely on the state for their budgets. Indeed, article 177 of the Constitution requires that the executive branch cover any Caja budget shortfall in the subsequent year's national budget, which effectively further enhances the Caja's financial independence.[10]

A number of other state institutions play a smaller role in the health-care system. The National Insurance Institute (*Instituto Nacional de Seguros*)[11] covers work- and transportation-related accidents and their health-related consequences; the Costa Rican Institute of Water and Sewerage Systems (*Instituto Costarricense de Acueductos y Alcantarillados*) is responsible for the quality and provision of water supply and wastewater management; and the University of Costa Rica is responsible for health research (Pan American Health Organization 2010).

The health system underwent a major reform in the 1980s in response to systemic problems of an aging population, rising medical costs and increasing waiting times for treatments, reduced lists of available medications, and shortages of usable hospital beds and equipment (Lisulo 2003, 2). The severe economic crisis of the 1980s compounded the Caja's economic problems, with the state and employers reneging on their required contributions to the fund (Clark 2002, 5). A major goal of the reforms was to strengthen the Caja's financial base and modernize the administration of the health-care system. In the 1990s, these reforms were further enhanced through the creation of comprehensive health-care teams (*Equipos Básicos de Atención Integral de Salud*) "to bring essential services closer to the population and to increase the capacity of district-level clinics" across the country, especially in the poorer regions.[12] This particular reform has been credited with reducing the infant mortality rate from 14.0 per 1,000 in 1995 to 10.1 per 1,000 in 2002 (Rodríguez Herrera 2005, 46).

In spite of the many successes of Costa Rica's health-care system, the state's need to target its limited medical resources also sets the stage for contemporary health rights litigation. Historically, teams of medical professionals and health-system bureaucrats made decisions, based on medical criteria, about which medications and treatments the state health-care system would provide and fund. While the universalization of health-care coverage was gradually achieved, Costa Rica—like many middle-income countries operating on limited budgets—necessarily rationed its health-care services and drug formulary so that major diseases were treated before less common ones (Tinoco-Mora 2005).

People with illnesses not covered by the Caja's programs could, with difficulty and little chance of success, contest the Caja's initial decision.[13] Through the creation of a constitutional chamber of the Supreme Court in 1989, though, these patients were increasingly able to file cases forcing the Caja to provide free access to treatments and medicines that it had previously refused to provide. Thus, until the second half of the 1990s, costly medications, treatments, or surgeries required by specific groups of patients were routinely denied coverage by the Caja if they were not included in the government's official medicines list (*Lista Oficial de Medicamentos*, or LOM) or were not part of the Caja's broader health-care plan. Indeed, the LOM's guiding principle is to cover essential medicines necessary for "the health treatments of the majority of the population" (Chaves 2008).[14] Caja directors routinely argued that these specific treatments were too expensive, benefited only small numbers of people, and threatened to drain scarce resources away from the Caja's broader health-care priorities (Ávalos 1997).[15]

Pre-1989 Supreme Court Behavior and the Creation of the Constitutional Chamber

A 1989 constitutional amendment added a new seven-member constitutional chamber to the existing three chambers of the Supreme Court. Unlike the previously structured Supreme Court, the new chamber (*Sala Constitucional*, also known as the "Sala IV") quickly became a major actor in Costa Rican political life and one of the most assertive courts in the Americas. Today, the newly energized Supreme Court exercises both a forceful horizontal accountability function, limiting the actions of the other branches of government (Gloppen et al. 2010), and a willingness to support (and an ability to enforce) an expansive range of individual rights (Wilson 2005, 2007, 2009). The Sala IV's aggressive enforcement of a broad range of individual rights stands in stark contrast to the pre-reformed Supreme Court's behavior, which afforded little protection of individual rights and recognized few constitutional limitations on the actions of other governmental branches (Rodríguez Cordero 2002).

Costa Rica's contemporary Constitution,[16] promulgated in 1949, is a rights-rich document that grants the Supreme Court equal status with the executive and legislative branches of the state,[17] as well as a very high level of political and financial autonomy.[18] Despite the Court's independence, until its reform in 1989, it behaved in a similarly passive manner as other Latin American superior courts operating in a civil-law legal system. The Court exhibited extreme deference to popularly elected officials and assumed that decrees and laws emanating from the legislative or executive branches were constitutional unless there was powerful evidence to demonstrate otherwise (Gutiérrez 1999, 49–50; Wilson 2010).[19] Indeed, an institutional rule required a two-thirds super-majority vote of the full Court (*Corte Plena*) to declare any law or decree unconstitutional, which, according to Sala IV Magistrate Fernando Cruz Castro, resulted in a "presumption of constitutionality for all laws" (2007, 557). In addition, the Court largely ignored individuals' constitutional rights,[20] as evidenced by the dearth of individual rights (*amparo*) cases.[21] The Court generally operated very slowly and adhered to strict formal requirements, tending to reject cases that did not meet those requirements. Together, these factors appeared to produce a high level of judicial immobilism that rendered the Supreme Court politically irrelevant and left constitutional rights largely unprotected. It is thus not surprising that the Court was widely disregarded as an avenue for protecting individuals' health rights.

The 1989 Constitutional Reform

A 1989 constitutional amendment[22] revised articles 10, 48, 105, and 128 of the 1949 Constitution, creating a new chamber of the Supreme Court: the Sala IV, with centralized judicial review powers. The expansive rule granted to the Sala IV has transformed the Court into one of the most influential judicial bodies in the Americas.[23] The Sala IV's willingness to exercise its legal mandate has resulted in a profound impact on the balance of political power in the country (see Wilson 2005, 2010) and has brought the Constitution to life, placing it at the center of all political and rights questions.

The Sala IV can "declare, by the absolute majority vote of its members, the unconstitutionality of provisions of any nature and acts subject to Public Law" (art. 10, para. 1). That is, a simple majority—and not the super majority previously required—can declare a law or decree unconstitutional, and the Court's decisions are binding on all parties and cannot be appealed. This has been particularly important in contentious constitutional cases,[24] but less so in health cases. For example, in the three-year period from 2006 to the end of 2008, approximately 1,500 health rights cases were filed before the Sala IV, over 90% of which were resolved with unanimous decisions.[25]

The enabling law that accompanied the creation of the Sala IV, *Ley de la Jurisdicción Constitucional*,[26] mandated the Court to

> guarantee the supremacy of the norms and constitutional principles, international law, and community law in force in the republic, their uniform interpretation and application of fundamental rights and freedoms consecrated in the constitution or in international instruments in force in Costa Rica.[27]

The newly appointed magistrates of the Sala IV abandoned the Supreme Court's historical commitment to judicial formality and fully accepted the new, broad definition of standing. The *Ley de la Jurisdicción Constitucional* removed virtually all barriers to accessing the Court: today, anyone in Costa

Rica—regardless of age, gender, or nationality—may file a case directly with the Sala IV at any time of day, 365 days a year, without legal representation or the need to pay court fees. Indeed, the claimant does not even need to know the point of law upon which his or her claim is based[28] and can handwrite or type the claim on anything and in any language, including Braille.[29] According to Magistrate Eduardo Sancho, the Sala IV should be understood "not as an institution created to be at the service of the executive branch, but quite the reverse: to protect the rights of people" (Corte Suprema de Justicia, Sala Constitucional 1999).

Amparo cases filed with the Sala IV are resolved quickly. In the Court's early years, the average time needed to resolve a case was twelve weeks; recently, this has been reduced to less than nine weeks (Corte Suprema de Justicia, Sala Constitucional 2010a). Such speedy resolution and low-cost access to the Sala IV clearly makes the Court an attractive forum for individuals, social and business groups, and political parties to seek redress (Wilson and Rodríguez 2006).[30] Yet, initially, the Court's aggressive protection of individual rights did not extend to health rights. The next section illustrates how the Court came to protect and enforce individual rights while severely restricting health rights claims (Wilson 2009).

Enforcing Individual Rights

Figure 6.1 illustrates the rapid growth in caseload immediately after the Sala IV's creation in 1989. In 1990, the Court received 1,600 cases. This number increased rapidly in each subsequent year, reaching almost 19,000 in 2009, with over 90% of the cases being writs of *amparo* (Corte Suprema de Justicia, Sala Constitucional 2010a). This huge caseload does not "automatically signal the strengthening of individual or group rights" (Sieder et al. 2005, 3); even if the Court routinely protects individual rights, a lack of compliance will not advance those rights. In this section, I suggest that the exponential growth in caseload might reflect an increased recognition of the availability of a new legal opportunity that can be harnessed to seek judicial resolutions to disputes, including rights infringements.

The ability of marginalized individuals and organizationally weak groups in Costa Rica to seek protection and/or enforcement of their constitutional rights has been well covered in the existing literature (Murillo 1994; Solano 2007; Wilson and Rodríguez 2006; Wilson 2007, 2009). For many of these individuals and groups, their political weakness and social marginalization meant that political parties were not predisposed to facilitate the pursuit of their agendas (Wilson and Rodríguez 2006). A brief illustrative case concerning homosexuals—a socially marginalized and politically powerless group—demonstrates the profundity of the individual rights protection afforded by the Sala IV as well as the impact of such decisions. After years of gays being harassed and abused by the police and having their plight ignored by politicians, a group of gay people filed and won a case in 1994.[31] The Court's ruling in favor of gays to be free of police harassment resulted in a national program to train police officers to respect the rights of gay people. The implementation of the training program, although not perfect, ended routine harassment of gays by police in Costa Rica (Eijkman 2006a, 2006b). Some of the weakest and most marginalized groups—including women, senior citizens, disabled people, and children—similarly have won significant victories before the Sala IV in protection of their rights.[32]

Despite issuing repeated judgments protecting individual rights, the Sala IV routinely denied health rights claims until the mid-1990s, when it gradually constructed a constitutional right to health and began to uphold that right without concern for the resource implications of its decisions (which, as we will see below, was one of the Court's concerns when it first began hearing health rights cases). Health rights cases are of particular interest due

Figure 6.1. Sala IV caseload

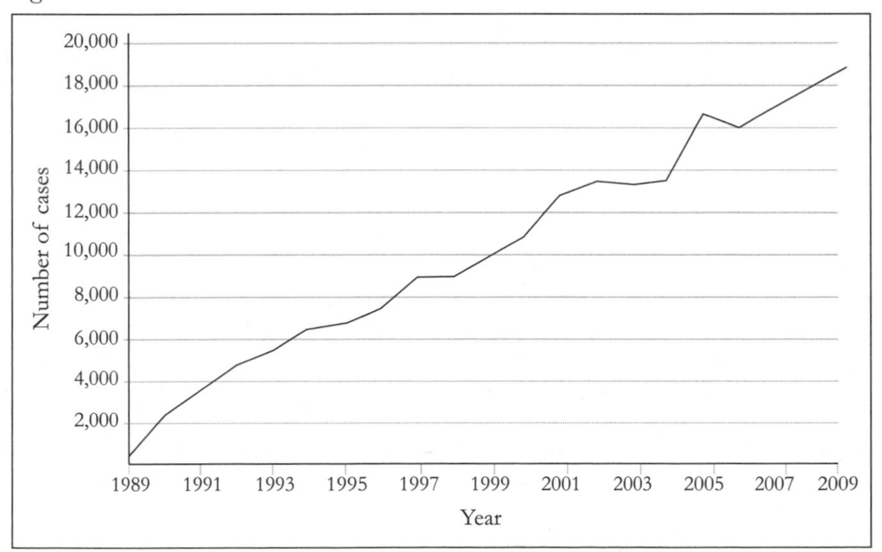

Source: Corte Suprema de Justicia, Sala Constitucional (2010a).

to the lack of a fundamental right to health in the 1949 Constitution and the high financial costs imposed on the state by the Court's decisions.

Explaining the Rise of Health Rights Litigation

In a recent internal report, Dr. Carlos Zamora of the Caja's actuarial services department presented data on the number of Sala IV cases filed against the Caja from 1989 through 2005. The higher of the two rising lines in figure 6.2 shows the number of cases claiming a right to any type of health care except for medications. While figure 6.1 shows a rapid growth in the Sala IV's overall caseload during its first years of operation, figure 6.2 shows that few *health* cases were filed before the Sala IV in its early years. After 1999, however, health-related cases rose at a much faster rate than the Court's total caseload. Clearly, the Court has moved from largely ignoring health rights to being a central actor in their protection.

While the Sala IV signalled from the outset that it would protect people's constitutional rights and would do so swiftly, the lack of a constitutional right to health, coupled with a few early failed health rights cases, made the Court an unlikely avenue for claiming a right to health. However, once the

Figure 6.2. Health and medicine cases filed with the Sala IV

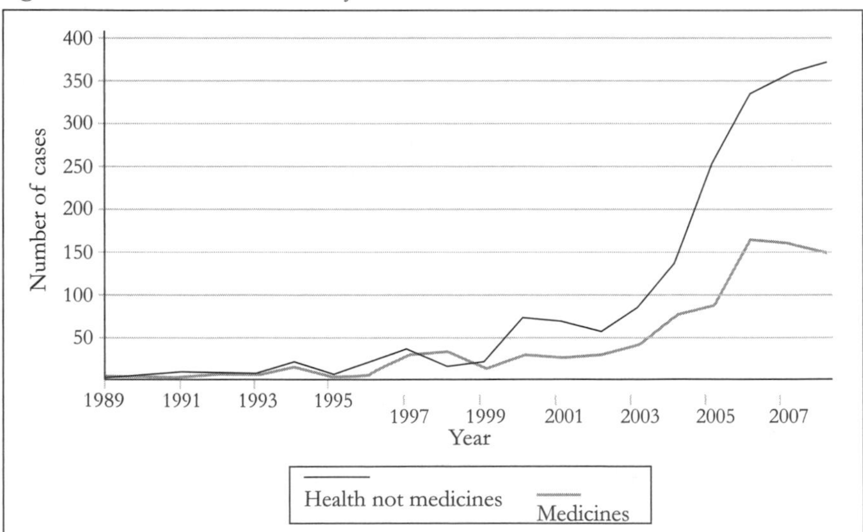

Source: Data for 1989–2005 from Zamora (2007); data for 2006–8 from Rodríguez and Morales (2010).

Court had constructed a fundamental right to health—and once it became clear that the Caja routinely complied with the Court's rulings—the legal opportunity structure became increasingly obvious.

Further promoting the filing of health rights cases at the Sala IV is the speed with which the Court rules on those cases. When a health case is filed, it is automatically given priority over all pending cases (with the exception of habeas corpus cases), and a *letrado* (clerk to the Court) is required to begin the legal process immediately.[33] The relatively high success rates of health rights claims, especially ones claiming access to a particular medication, are another signal of the Court's willingness to hear such cases: while the average success rate for *amparo* cases is approximately 25%, the success rate in recent years for health rights *amparo* claims against the Caja is over 60% (Doryan Garron 2008).[34] The rapid growth of health rights cases in the second ten years of the Court's existence perhaps reflects patients' growing awareness of a new, low-cost avenue for seeking medications and treatments denied by the Caja that promises high success rates, rapid resolution by the Court, and high levels of compliance by the Caja.

In the following sections, I examine the rise and success of health rights litigation through the newly available legal opportunity structure of the Sala IV. This, in turn, was a consequence of four fundamental changes in the judicial system: (i) the 1989 creation of a constitutional chamber of the Supreme Court, which greatly opened access to the Court and created an easy and economical venue for patients (and others) to have their claims heard; (ii) the amendment of constitutional article 48, permitting individuals to file writs of *amparo* with the Sala IV to seek protection of rights contained in the Costa Rican Constitution as well as in international human rights instruments; (iii) the Sala IV's gradual construction of a justiciable right to health, which is not contained in the Constitution; and (iv) the Caja's high compliance rate with the Court's health rulings, demonstrating that health rights victories are not hollow but enforced, and encouraging subsequent health rights claims.

Constructing a Right to Health

Although health rights in many Latin American countries are constitutional rights that are justiciable, this is not the case in Costa Rica.[35] Health rights were largely ignored in the Sala IV's early years of existence; but over the last ten to fifteen years, the Court gradually reversed its earlier jurisprudence, abandoned its deference to the Caja's technical experts, and generally ignored the financial implications of its rulings. Given the fact that the Costa Rican Constitution contains no explicit right to health, the volume of health rights cases filed with and decided by the Sala IV is somewhat surprising.

The development of Sala IV health rights jurisprudence and the construction of a right to health is detailed by sitting Magistrate Luis Fernando Solano Carrera (2007, 141–44). Magistrate Solano acknowledges the lack of an explicit right to health in the 1949 Costa Rican Constitution and notes that it is a derived right, constructed from two constitutional articles: the protection of human life (art. 21)[36] and the right to social security protection (art. 73).[37] These two provisions are strengthened by the 1989 constitutional amendment that created the Sala IV and amended article 48 to give international human rights treaties the same force as domestic law (Vargas 2007, 150). Solano (2007, 142–43) also notes that the right to health is either explicitly or implicitly contained in instruments of international law ratified by Costa Rica, including the Universal Declaration of Human Rights,[38] the American Declaration of Rights and Duties of Man,[39] the American Convention on Human Rights,[40] and the International Covenant on Civil and Political Rights.[41] These international instruments facilitated the creation of an expansive fundamental right to health. Magistrate Cruz Castro notes that Sala IV jurisprudence has treated international human rights treaties as having "an almost supra constitutional value" (2007, 560).[42]

While Magistrate Solano can point to cases from the early 1990s where the Court articulated and applied a nascent constructed fundamental right to health, the Sala IV's understanding of health rights was expanded and enhanced in subsequent decisions. In some of the earlier cases, the Court applied a more restricted definition of health rights. For example, a case filed in 1992 by the Asociación de Lucha contra el SIDA (Association of the Fight against AIDS) involved a person living with HIV/AIDS (PLWA) claiming a right to a state-funded antiretroviral medication, azidothymidine, that a Caja pharmacy had declined to fill. In defense of its refusal to fund and supply the prescribed medication, the Caja argued that the drug was not included in the LOM, was too expensive, and was not a cure for HIV/AIDS. In this instance, the Court accepted the Caja's arguments concerning the resource implications of supplying azidothymidine and agreed that "the cost of acquiring the medications implies a very large sacrifice for socialized medicine."[43] The Court also deferred to the Caja's medical expertise, stating, "the scientific data presented [by the Caja] indicates that [azidothymidine] is not a cure for the patient." Thus, the Court demonstrated its deference to the Caja's medical judgments, recognized clear financial limits on the extent of an individual's right to health, and stated its restrictive definition of the Caja's obligation to provide medications that do not cure illnesses. The Court ruled against the claimant, denying state-funded access to the medications.

In 1997, the Court returned to the question of state-funded antiretroviral medicines in a case similar to the one it rejected in 1992. This new case was filed by three seriously ill HIV/AIDS patients with prescriptions from Caja doctors for antiretroviral medications. Because the medications were not included in the LOM, the Caja pharmacies refused to provide them. In this case, the Caja made the same cost-based argument that it had successfully employed in 1992: it maintained that antiretroviral drugs were not on the official LOM, were too expensive, and still did not offer a cure for HIV/AIDS. The Sala IV, however, in a reversal of its unanimous 1992 decision, ruled (again unanimously) in favor of the plaintiffs and ordered the Caja to supply and pay for the necessary medications. The Court argued, "What good are the rest of the rights and guarantees . . . [or] the advantages and benefits of our system of liberties, if a person cannot count on the right to life and health assured?"[44] The justification for the Court's ruling in this case became the foundation for health rights jurisprudence and is frequently cited in subsequent health rights decisions. Interestingly, although the ruling was originally *inter partes* (applying only to the people involved in this particular case), a series of similar cases filed on behalf of other PLWA by the same lawyer were understood to be included in the 1997 decision and were successful in granting the patients their medications.[45] Since 1997, the Caja has provided antiretroviral medications not just to the patients who litigated for the right to such drugs but to any PLWA who was a Caja patient with a valid prescription from a Caja-affiliated doctor. By 1999, at a cost of over 11% of the Caja's total medicine budget, 680 PLWA were being treated with antiretroviral medications (*La Nación* [Costa Rica] 1999).[46]

Figure 6.3 shows the impact of the 1997 decision on access to antiretroviral medications in Costa Rica compared to its regional neighbors, where the legal opportunity to litigate for this particular health right was absent. Since the 1997 ruling, access to antiretroviral medications for PLWA in Costa Rica has increased to over 95%, representing the highest coverage in the Americas. Indeed, Costa Rica's coverage is significantly higher than the next highest country in the region, Chile, which has 82% coverage. In the Central American region specifically, Costa Rica's coverage is almost double the average

(Avert 2009). It could be argued that the Caja would have eventually accepted international evidence of the effectiveness of the newer antiretroviral medications and added them to the LOM, even without a Sala IV ruling, but this seems unlikely, given that the Caja argued vociferously against providing the medications at the time of the 1997 *amparo* case.

The impact of the Court's 1997 decision is seen not just in Costa Rica's almost-universal antiretroviral coverage but also in the mortality rates for HIV/AIDS patients, which dropped significantly after years of increases. A third impact has been the use of the Court's same legal arguments by patients with other uncommon, chronic illnesses who were routinely denied access to state-funded medications or treatments that the Caja deemed too costly. In the subsequent two years after its antiretroviral ruling, the Sala IV ruled in favor of patients requiring expensive medications, including multiple sclerosis medications for thirty-two patients that absorbed almost 1% of the Caja's medicine budget and medications for nineteen amyotrophic lateral sclerosis patients that cost 0.4% of the budget (*La Nación* [Costa Rica] 1999).

Figure 6.3. Antiretroviral coverage in Central America (2007)

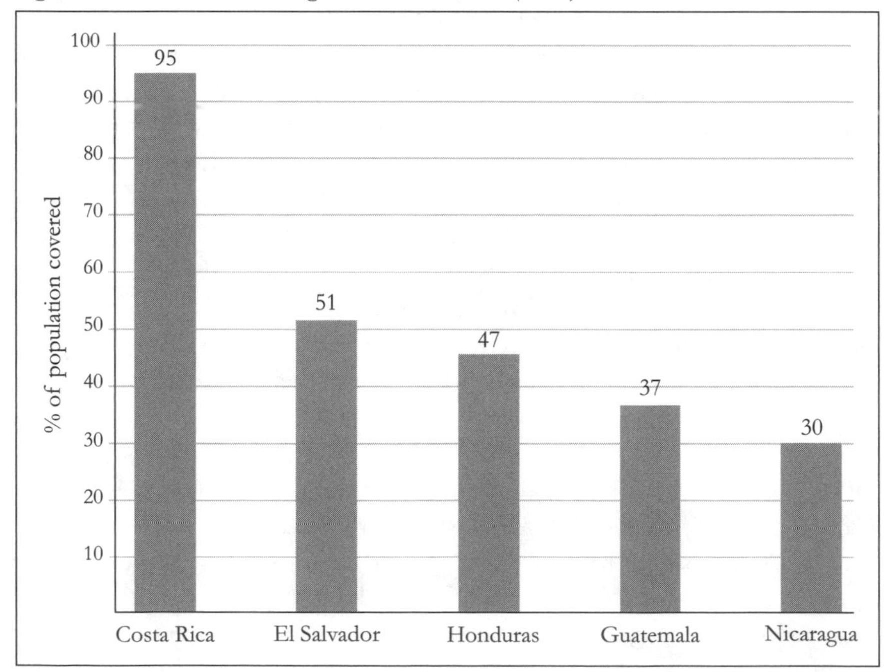

Source: Avert (2009).

Indeed, Albin Chaves Matamoros, the Caja director of Farmacoterapia, noted some years later that, of all the Court's medical decisions, the 1997 antiretroviral decision had had the largest impact on the Caja; in subsequent cases, patients claimed a "right to health and a good quality of life" while the Caja argued technical and economic points and maintained that the public health system must be prioritized in order to attack the principle causes of death. He noted that 21% of the Caja's medicine budget is required to treat just 6,789 patients (Ávalos 2005).

The Sala IV has also regularly ruled in favor of transplant patients and keeping clinics open that the Caja wanted to close, among other things. For example, in a 2004 case filed by the Ombuds Office on behalf of four very ill women in need of liver transplants, the Sala IV handed down a unanimous decision within four weeks of the filing—and after just one hour of deliberation—requiring the Caja to perform the operations immediately. In spite of the Caja's inability to perform liver transplant surgery because it lacked the facilities and protocols to do so, Caja director Alberto Sáenz Pacheco said that he would comply with the Sala IV's decision and order the surgeries "as he must" (Ávalos 2004). Open disagreement on the part of Caja directors with the Sala IV's health rights rulings is a common response, but it is coupled with general compliance at a much higher level than for other Sala IV decisions. A recent pilot study of compliance with Sala IV rulings revealed that 86% of health rights case decisions are complied with, compared to an overall case compliance rate of 40% (Corte Suprema de Justicia, Sala Constitucional 2010b).

Criticism of the Sala IV's Health Rights Decisions

Although the Caja complies with the vast majority of health rights decisions, it has sometimes done so under protest. Indeed, recent interviews with senior Caja personnel reveal some of them to be acting under an implicit threat of being sent to jail if they refuse to comply.[47] The main criticism of the health rulings is that the costs are so high that they are harming the national health system by redirecting limited resources to expensive treatments for uncommon diseases. This cost issue has played a role in many medication cases and in a public debate between the Caja and the Sala IV. For example, a 2003 case regarding a child with type 1 Gaucher disease[48] relied on the Sala IV's 1997 antiretroviral decision to argue that the child be treated with Cerezyme (imuglucerase) at a cost of approximately US$175,000 per year (Heuser 2009). The Sala IV, in this case, acknowledged the treatment as being financially "undoubtedly onerous," but argued that because the child needed the medicine to "maintain her life," the medicine had to be supplied and funded by the Caja.[49] In its ruling, the Court also addressed the Caja's protestations about the budgetary impact by admonishing the Caja to be more efficient in its use of its resources.

A recent study randomly selected thirty-seven Sala IV cases regarding access to medicines and categorized these cases according to the type of medication sought by each claim. Cases were placed into a series of groups ranging from one to four, with group I representing drugs deemed high priority for Costa Rican society and group IV representing drugs deemed very low priority. The study found that only 2.7% of the medications mandated by the Court's decisions fell into priority group I (highest priority), 24.3% in group II, 51.4% in group III, and 21.6% in group IV (experimental treatment). The study revealed that 73% of the successful cases resulted in court-mandated patient access to medications classified as low priority or experimental—that is, medications that produce "marginal" health benefits for very severe conditions at a high cost for the health-care system. Of all these cases, only three of them sought drugs already available on the World Health Organization's essential drugs list (Norheim and Wilson 2010).

The Sala IV's continued deafness to the Caja's budgetary concerns is reflected in a series of breast cancer cases that began in 2006, which forced the Caja to fund and provide Herceptin (trastuzumab), a very expensive drug, to twenty-two breast cancer patients. The Caja complained that the cost of complying with the Sala IV's Herceptin ruling and nine other recent high-cost medication cases would absorb 1% of the Caja's total medicine budget. Again, the Court dismissed the Caja's complaints about the budgetary impact of the decision, stating, "sick people should not have to pay for the results of bad planning on the part of the [Caja]" (*La Nación* [Costa Rica] 2006). This sentiment was recently echoed by another Sala IV magistrate who responded to the potential ethical problem of the Sala IV's decisions directing the Caja's budget away from combating common diseases to treating those that are uncommon and affect only a small number of patients. The magistrate noted that obviously the Caja's "resources are limited, but this is only an ethical dilemma to the extent that you have utilized all your resources properly. . . . If you are wasting your resources, the ethical argument does not apply."[50] He went on to note that

> nothing that has happened as a result of court decisions [in terms of health litigation] has affected [the Caja] from a budgetary point of view. . . . If you can prove that costs will affect others, show me, then we will consider it.[51]

This position is supported by the public health lawyer of the Ombuds Office, who argued, "We do not think that economic issues are reasons not to defend a human right for medical attention. We tell [the Caja] we do not accept that kind of explanation, they must simply find the budget for that. Sala IV holds the same position as we do."[52]

In addition to budgetary concerns, exploitation of the system is another key worry. Some members of the Caja's medical staff have expressed fear that specific doctors and drug companies are using the openness of the judicial system and the Court's jurisprudence to push their own companies' prescription drugs.[53] Since neither the Caja nor the Court keeps detailed data on the claimants, it is difficult to establish, at this point, if there is systematic abuse of the system. Some cases, such as the 2003 Gaucher case mentioned above, may have involved opportunism on the part of drug manufacturers. In that case, a Boston-based pharmaceutical company specializing in high-cost medications for uncommon diseases identified a patient in Costa Rica. Once the company established the drug's effectiveness for the patient, it sought to have the Caja pay for the medication through a lobbying effort before the Caja and the minister of health. Eventually, the case was taken to the Sala IV, which ordered the Caja to supply the medication.[54] In addition, recent evidence indicates that certain drug companies have approached HIV/AIDS patients asking them to file cases with the Sala IV to stop the Caja from switching their medications to generic alternatives (Stern 2010).

In a recent interview on *Radio Reloj*, Magistrate Cruz Castro admitted the possibility of doctors inappropriately and unethically prescribing medications not on the LOM in order to benefit a pharmaceutical company, which he recognized as a potential threat to the financial well-being of the health system. But Cruz Castro (2009) also argued that the Sala IV's decisions are correct and that it is not the Court's responsibility to investigate doctors. The real problem is not the costs but "a lack of self constraint and ethics on the part of the doctor, which is not an issue the Sala can resolve because the Sala assumes the doctor always makes his medical decisions with the greatest responsibility." Cruz Castro's fear may also be misplaced: a recently constructed database of all medical cases filed with the Sala IV from 2006 through 2008 (Rodríguez and Morales 2010) shows that very few doctors participated in more than one case before the Court. That is, very few doctors prescribing medications not on the LOM have helped more than one patient file a case before the Sala IV. The same is true for lawyers. Because it is not necessary to hire a lawyer to file a health rights case before the Sala IV, very few claimants use lawyers. Indeed, less than 2% of the approximately 1,500 cases filed between 2006 and 2008 had legal representation and the vast majority of the lawyer-filed cases were unsuccessful (Rodríguez and Morales 2010).[55]

In most cases, the Court has argued that the prescription from the patient's treating doctor outweighs the technical-medical criteria used by the Caja's *Comité Central de Farmacoterapia* (Pharmacotherapy Central Committee) to determine which medicines should be on the LOM (Vargas 2007, 177). This was emphatically stated in a 2007 medication decision[56] in which the Sala IV addressed the large number of *amparos* filed for medications denied by the Caja. The Court noted that in some cases the Caja rejected the best medical treatment for a patient—as recommended by the treating doctor—"for eminently economic reasons." The Court rejected this justification, arguing that

> the only reason the Caja could refuse its obligation to supply such medications would be that those medications were not necessary to treat the patient (based on medications' composition) as determined by the attending physician, of if the patient rejected the medications for being contraindicated. Otherwise, the Caja is under the undeniable obligation to supply them.[57]

More recently, though, the Court has issued health rights decisions in favor of entire classes of people[58] and in a more dialogic manner. For example, a 2009 decision[59] ruled that everyone over sixty-five years old should receive vaccinations for pneumococcus (Oviedo 2009). Prior to this decision, the Caja had routinely provided pneumococcus vaccinations to all children under two years old (a high-risk category), but refused to offer it to other potentially at-risk groups. In the case, a group of senior citizens argued that they, too, were a high-risk group for pneumococcus. They successfully filed a claim with the Sala IV forcing the Caja to include them in their vaccination program against pneumococcus and rotavirus at a total cost of US$8 million (Ávalos 2008). Another interesting difference in the pneumococcus case is that Magistrate Adrián Vargas Benavides invited the minister of health to present her ministry's views to the Court before the Court made its decision, which, according to one senior *letrado*, "probably tilted the case in favor of the seniors' petition to have access to the vaccine."[60] That is, the Court's decision in this case resulted from dialogue with various stakeholders from the Caja and the Ministry of Health, in contrast to the Court's previous decisions, which tended to ignore cost considerations and follow the advice of the patient's treating doctor.

Conclusion

In many ways, the absence of successful health rights litigation before the mid-1990s is perhaps less surprising than the rapid rise of health cases after that date. Since the 1940s, Costa Rica has boasted one of the top-performing health systems in the Americas, with long-standing committees staffed by medical professionals that evaluate and assess which medicines and treatments should be included in the country's state-funded, near-universal health system. In addition to the health-care system's impressive performance, other factors mitigate against health rights litigation. First, before its reform in 1989, the Supreme Court was firmly embedded in a Latin American civil-law tradition in which superior courts defer to popularly elected branches of government. It was not until the creation of the Sala IV that a viable legal opportunity structure allowed for successful health rights litigation. People suffering from illnesses that required medication or treatments not covered by the national health plan had no readily available, realistic avenue for appealing the denial of those treatments, medicines, and/or surgeries.

The creation of the Sala IV in 1989 opened up a low-cost, broadly accessible legal opportunity for individuals to demand the protection and promotion of fundamental rights contained in Costa Rica's Constitution. But even with a new and assertive pro-rights superior court, there was still no recognized fundamental right to health, which discouraged the filing of health cases. Through its jurisprudence, the Court gradually constructed a right to health (based on other constitutional rights and international conventions) and incrementally expanded the application of that right. But it was not until the late 1990s that the Court's health rights decisions were no longer constrained by cost considerations; after that date, health rights litigation expanded even more rapidly than the rate of increase of the Court's total docket. The Sala IV's expansive application of the right to health—combined with the Court's low-cost, open access—allowed individuals, for the first time, to file all types of health rights claims. The relatively quick case resolution by the Sala IV and the high level of compliance by the Caja encouraged more cases, resulting in anything but the hollow victories predicted by Rosenberg (1991). Even though the legal system remains a civil-law system, the Court's decisions are binding on everyone, except the Court itself, and are regularly treated by the Court and subsequent claimants as precedents.

Thus, while health rights in Costa Rica remain in flux, they appear to be expanding both in number and in the breadth of their impact. As the Court starts to issue decisions in favor of the health rights of entire classes of people (such as in the pneumococcus case), the costs imposed on the Caja will likely be increasingly onerous. But while the Caja routinely complies with the Sala IV's decisions, it also publicly and vocally complains that those decisions are harming the financial health and performance of the socialized health-care system. At this point, however, there is no concrete evidence produced by the Caja (or any other agency) showing any areas of health provision that have been harmed by the Sala IV's decisions. Similarly, there is no evidence to demonstrate a decline in any major health indicators resulting from the misallocation of resources.

NOTES

1. US$6,060, or US$10,950 purchasing power parity.
2. Rosero-Bixby (2008) notes that Costa Rica's population has one of the highest levels of nonagenarians in the world, perhaps reflecting the success of its welfare state and its health-care system.
3. Panama, in fifty-eighth position, is the only other Central American country with a "top 100" ranking. El Salvador ranks 101st, Honduras 117th, Nicaragua 120th, and Guatemala 121st (United Nations Development Programme 2009).
4. A 2001 World Health Organization report on health-system performance ranks Costa Rica 36th out of 191 countries (de Bertodano 2003).
5. United Nations Secretary-General Kofi Annan (quoted in Nygren-Krug 2002, 2).
6. The transformation of Costa Rica's Supreme Court is covered elsewhere. See, e.g., Wilson (2010).

7. In 1943, the Caja was reformed and became an autonomous state institution. It was given constitutional status in the 1949 Constitution (art. 73). For an excellent history of the Caja, see Vargas (2007).
8. A 1973 law (*Ley de la Universalización del Seguro de Enfermedad y Maternidad, Ley No. 5349*, September 24, 1973) transferred control of all state-owned hospitals to the Caja.
9. Much of the information in this paragraph is drawn from Clark (2002), Rosero-Bixby (2004), and Picado et al. (2003).
10. A 2001 law removed "the finance ministry's budget authority powers, including caps on hiring and salaries," over the Caja (Clark 2002, 3–4).
11. Until recently, this was the only agency legally allowed to sell private health insurance in Costa Rica; very few Costa Ricans carry private health insurance (Clark 2002).
12. The reformed health system included twenty-nine hospitals across ninety health zones, with ten health-care teams per zone. Each team covered approximately four thousand people and was staffed by a doctor, a nurse, and a technician (de Bertodano 2003). The motivation for the creation of the teams and their impact is detailed in Rodríguez Herrera (2005).
13. An appeals process allowed patients to request that medications not on the official medicines list be provided by the Caja (Tinoco-Mora 2005, 33–34).
14. This list is currently about 190 pages long and is compiled by the *Comité Central de Farmacoterapia*, an agency composed of thirteen medical specialists (from various national hospitals) and two pharmacists. An explanation of the criteria and scoring rubrics used by the committee to select medications for the LOM is detailed in Tinoco-Mora (2005).
15. Both in academic publications (see, e.g., Chaves 2008; Zamora 2007) and in the national press (see, e.g., Ávalos 1997; Ávalos and Méndez 1999), Caja directors have frequently and publicly stated their concern over the significant costs incurred by complying with the Sala IV's medical rulings.
16. Constitution of Costa Rica, 1949.
17. Article 9 of the Constitution reads, "The Government of the Republic is popular, representative, alternative and responsible. It is exercised by three distinct and independent branches: Legislative, Executive, and Judicial. None of these Branches may delegate the exercise of their own functions."
18. Since 1957, the judicial branch, which is controlled by the Supreme Court, has been constitutionally guaranteed no less than 6% of the government's annual budget (Constitution, art. 177).
19. Between 1938 (when the Court centralized its power of judicial review) and 1989 (when its constitutional chamber was created), the Supreme Court received approximately 150 unconstitutionality cases. In contrast, the Sala IV received 228 unconstitutionality cases in its first twenty months of existence (Gutiérrez 1999, 50).
20. One of the first actions of the Court under the 1949 Constitution was to ignore appeals for protection by political and labor union leaders who were punished by the Junta immediately after the civil war (see Wilson 2007). Indeed, the unwillingness of the pre-reformed Supreme Court to hear rights cases became a major argument against the creation of the Constitutional Chamber in 1989—that is, that there would be no caseload for such a Court.

21. In 1980, for example, the Supreme Court received just eleven *amparo* cases (Rodríguez Cordero 2002, 43).
22. *Reforma de los Artículos 10, 48, 105 y 128 de la Constitución Política, Ley No. 7128*, August 18, 1989.
23. The Court has the power to adjudicate conflicts of competency between government branches; engage in judicial review both a priori (constitutional consultations) and a posteriori (unconstitutionality); engage in concrete (based on a case) and abstract (general interest) judicial review; and make its rulings broadly effective (*inter partes* in cases of habeas corpus and *amparo*, and *erga omnes* for all judicial review and jurisprudence) (Navia and Ríos-Figueroa 2005, 202–4).
24. Good examples of contentious cases where a two-thirds majority was not possible are the presidential reelection cases from 2000 (Resolution 7818-00) and 2003 (Resolution 2771-03).
25. There were 131 decisions during this period in which one or more magistrates dissented from the majority decision (calculations by the author based on Rodríguez and Morales 2010).
26. *Ley de la Jurisdicción Constitucional, Ley No. 7135*, October 11, 1989.
27. Ibid., art. 1.
28. The vast majority of these petitions are *amparo* cases that permit anyone the right to demand that the Sala IV maintain or reestablish any and all constitutional rights not already protected by the habeas corpus provision. Article 48 (as amended in 1989) states, in part, that everyone has the right to use writs of protection (*amparo*) to "maintain or reestablish the enjoyment of other rights conferred by this Constitution as well as those of fundamental nature established in international instruments on human rights, enforceable in the Republic." Costa Rican *amparos* are similar in scope to the *tutela* actions available in Colombia.
29. *Amparo* claims have been written on bread wrapping paper, and in 2009 the Sala IV accepted a claim written in Braille. The Court has declared its intention to create Braille versions of all its decisions (Terra.com 2009).
30. The use of the Court to address all kinds of issues has become so common that "Salacuartazo" has entered the popular lexicon to mean an *amparo* filed before the Sala IV.
31. Resolution 4732-94.
32. This is not to suggest that all of the Court's decisions favor marginalized members of society. In a number of cases, the Court has ruled against marginalized groups' rights, including the right to same-sex marriage, which the Court has rejected twice. Many of these decisions are discussed in Wilson and Rodríguez (2006) and Wilson (2007).
33. This statement was repeated in interviews with three *letrados* in San José, November 2009.
34. If all cases involving a right to health care are considered, the success rate at the Sala IV is approximately 50%. There is, however, a lack of data concerning the actual rate of compliance with the decisions.
35. Even though Brazil, Chile, Colombia, El Salvador, Nicaragua, and Venezuela, for example, have an explicit constitutional right to health (Brewer-Carías 2009), it is not a guarantee that those rights are justiciable.
36. Article 21, which states that "human life is inviolable," was motivated by a desire to ban capital punishment.

37. Article 73: "Social security is established for the benefit of manual and intellectual workers, regulated by a system of compulsory contributions by the State, employers and workers, to protect them against the risks of illness, disability, maternity, old age, death and other contingencies as determined by law."
38. Universal Declaration of Human Rights, G.A. Res. 217A (III), U.N. Doc A/810 at 71 (1948).
39. American Declaration of the Rights and Duties of Man, O.A.S. Res. XXX, adopted by the Ninth International Conference of American States (1948), reprinted in Basic Documents Pertaining to Human Rights in the Inter-American System, OEA/Ser.L.V/II.82 doc.6 rev.1 at 17 (1992).
40. American Convention on Human Rights, O.A.S. Treaty Series No. 36, 1144 U.N.T.S. 123, entered into force July 18, 1978, reprinted in Basic Documents Pertaining to Human Rights in the Inter-American System, OEA/Ser.L.V/II.82 doc.6 rev.1 at 25 (1992).
41. International Covenant on Civil and Political Rights, G.A. Res. 2200A (XXI), 21 U.N. GAOR Supp. (No. 16) at 52, U.N. Doc. A/6316 (1966), 999 U.N.T.S. 171, entered into force March 23, 1976.
42. International conventions are frequently cited in support of health rights claims in Costa Rica. In a 1997 health rights case, for example, the claimant argued that the hospital Rafael Ángel Calderón Guardia—owned and controlled by the Caja—routinely discriminated against PLWAs by refusing them treatment in the hospital's clinics. A significant part of the legal argument was based on the violation of a number of international conventions, including article 11 of the American Declaration of Rights and Duties of Man, *supra* note 39; articles 3, 7, and 25 of the Universal Declaration of Human Rights, *supra* note 38; article 26 of the International Covenant on Civil and Political Rights, *supra* note 41; and article 12 of the International Covenant on Economic, Social and Cultural Rights, G.A. Res. 2200A (XXI), 21 U.N. GAOR Supp. (No. 16) at 49, U.N. Doc. A/6316 (1966), 993 U.N.T.S. 3, entered into force January 3, 1976. The role of international human rights instruments in the development of Sala IV jurisprudence is discussed by Magistrate Gilbert Armijo (2003).
43. Resolution 280-92.
44. Resolution 5934-97.
45. I thank Marco Castillo for taking the time to provide me with the details of how these cases were filed and decided (interview, San José, November 2009).
46. Gustavo Picado and Luis Sáenz conclude that the cost of antiretroviral medications for PLWA declined in subsequent years—to 9.7% by 2000 and 5.4% by 2002—due to a significant decline in drug prices (quoted in Rodríguez Herrera 2005, 25).
47. Interview with senior Caja personnel, San José, June 2008.
48. Exp. 2003-8377.
49. Ibid.
50. This has also been publicly addressed by other Sala IV magistrates. See, e.g., Solano (2007).
51. Interview with a *magistrado suplente* (alternative magistrate), San José, June 2008.
52. Interview with a health lawyer in the office of the *Defensoría de los Habitantes*, San José, June 2008.
53. This was a constant theme in interviews conducted with medical professionals in Costa Rica in June 2008 and November 2009.

54. But if the company had been aware of the litigation avenue, it arguably would have used the legal opportunity immediately rather than spending time and resources on fruitless lobbying strategies (Heuser 2009).
55. This data was collected by Rodríguez and Morales (2010); interpretation and analysis of the data was conducted by the author.
56. Resolution 00043-07.
57. Ibid.
58. In Resolution 2009-15666, the Court argued that old people are specially protected by the Constitution (art. 51).
59. Resolution 2009-8339.
60. Personal communication, April 2010.

Chapter 7

India

Citizens, Courts, and the Right to Health: Between Promise and Progress?

Sharanjeet Parmar and Namita Wahi

For the average Indian, maintaining good health is no easy task. Although key health indicators vary greatly from region to region, reflecting the country's demographic diversity, nationwide averages remain abysmally low, with basic health and social indicators close to the level of the world's least developed countries. For example, an estimated 117,000 maternal deaths occurred in 2005—reportedly almost one-quarter of the world's total (World Health Organization 2007; Center for Reproductive Rights 2008). This situation is startling in light of India's reputation as one of the world's strongest emerging economies, particularly as measured by growth in gross domestic product in recent years (J. Shankar 2009). Instead, India ranks 153 out of 193 countries regarding total expenditure on health per capita; in 2008, general government expenditure on health as a percentage of total health expenditure was only 28%, with the remaining 72% spent on private care (World Health Organization 2010b).

This chapter examines whether litigation provides an effective mechanism for supporting the realization of the right to health. Improvements in health outcomes are dependent on various factors, including health policy and expenditure, delivery and accountability mechanisms, medical education

---

The authors would like to thank Anita Parmar and Hannah Simpson for their invaluable research assistance. This chapter has benefited enormously from the editorial comments of Alicia Ely Yamin and Siri Gloppen, as well as inputs from Jackie Dugard, Pratap Bhanu Mehta, Partha Mukhopadhyay, and Varun Gauri.

and training of health workers, and levels of education and awareness of patients. Accurately ascertaining the overall impact of health rights litigation on each of these elements for a country the size of India requires a study beyond the scope of this chapter. Instead, we describe here the body of Supreme Court and High Court cases that have sought court-enforced remedies for violations of the right to health, and identify the outcomes that have followed. We also track particular outcomes from specific cases or groups of cases and consider how litigation can affect the welfare of petitioners and/or the population. In so doing, we demonstrate the importance of adopting a "fine-grain" analysis, which, together with past analyses based on the totality of health rights cases, presents a comprehensive and nuanced basis from which to assess impact.

In this chapter, we define "health rights litigation" as encompassing all cases seeking enforcement of the constitutional right to health by the Supreme Court and High Courts. We consider two primary sources of information: (i) Supreme Court and High Court cases that involve claims regarding the right to health, with a particular focus on the Supreme Court, and (ii) interviews with petitioners, lawyers, judges, public sector health officials, and health activists. Secondary sources presenting empirical data on health indicators and public health spending, as well as socio-legal commentary and analysis, are also highlighted.

Our analytical framework is based on a broader comparative country study on health rights litigation, which involves consideration of claims formation, adjudication, implementation, and corresponding social outcomes (Gloppen 2008a). In the first section, we present our methodology for reviewing health rights litigation in India. In the second section, we summarize important features of India's health system—including governmental policies over the last sixty years and health expenditure—with a view to presenting a snapshot of the country's deep and systemic health inequities. In the third section, we describe the socio-legal development of fundamental rights litigation in India, which enabled judicial recognition and enforcement of the right to health. In the fourth section, we present the health rights jurisprudence of the Supreme Court. Finally, in the fifth and sixth sections, we review a particular set of Supreme Court cases to map the key litigation outcomes that are relevant to measuring impact for litigants, the population, and/or public policy.

Through this analysis, we highlight both the strengths and limitations of health rights litigation in India. We find that the two primary strengths of litigation lie in (i) its ability to highlight problems of access, availability, and quality of health care and (ii) its role in devising procedures to prompt policy responses by public and private actors. The overall effectiveness of general relief orders, however, appears to be mitigated by a lack of responsiveness by government actors, for litigation outcomes lack the sanction of strong penalties to trigger prompt responses. This situation is compounded by weaknesses that characterize India's health-care system. Without a deeper empirical exercise tracking individual outcomes from the large body of applicable cases, it is difficult to conclude authoritatively how they, together, affect the delivery of health services. For now, we conduct a thorough mapping of the relevant elements and present preliminary findings from which this question may be considered in the future.

Methodology

In assessing the impact of litigation, this chapter considers how claims concerning the right to health have been argued, adjudicated, and implemented in India. Both private and publicly minded petitioners have brought a large number of cases seeking remedies for breaches of the right to health; and both kinds of petitioners have founded their claims on fundamental rights in the Constitution. But while private claimants seek remedies that serve the narrowly defined interests of individual petitioners, public interest litigation (PIL) is brought by petitioners who do not necessarily have a direct interest in the matter and/or who seek broader remedies that affect the well-being of the public at large or a particular marginalized group.

This chapter examines 218 cases before India's Supreme Court and High Courts that concern potential violations of the right to health. Collecting a comprehensive and/or representative set of health rights cases is difficult, since not all cases are published in case reporters and those that are reported are not necessarily available in legal databases and/or searchable through legal search engines. We collected our sample through keyword searches on Indian legal search engines.[1] We then cross-referenced the body of resulting cases with case references identified from existing legal commentary on health rights litigation (Desai and Mahabal 2007; Shankar and

Mehta 2008; Muralidhar 2008). From our sample of 218 cases, we identified ten categories of litigation claims (see figure 7.1).

We then undertook a detailed examination of a subset comprising all Supreme Court cases, which number sixty-six. As decisions of the apex court in the country, these cases constitute an important benchmark for evaluating the outcomes of health rights litigation. Moreover, the Supreme Court enjoys the confidence of citizens to uphold fundamental freedoms guaranteed under the Constitution (Sathe 2002). We examined several aspects of these Supreme Court cases, including questions as to who brought the cases; what and how claims were made; how the claims were adjudicated; and the litigation outcomes that followed.

We also conducted thirty-five interviews with petitioners, attorneys, judges, academics, and other civil society actors working on public health and human rights issues. Finally, we researched the resulting legislative and policy responses, followed up by interviews with government health officials.

An Overview of Health Indicators, Spending, and Policy

Based on India's performance on basic health indicators and public health spending, the state of the country's public health appears grim. Drawing on India's history of health policy initiatives, this section depicts the gaps between policy and implementation and highlights the political failure to prioritize the development of a robust public health-care system.

Distribution of Powers

Within India's federalist system, state governments possess primary responsibility for public health and sanitation, including both the funding and the programmatic and structural development of public health-care systems, hospitals, and dispensaries.[2] Moreover, they contribute 80–85% of the total public expenditure on health (Duggal 2006). The central government, however, exercises considerable influence over health. It prescribes health policy through its "Five-Year Plans," which outline its upcoming policy and budgetary commitments. In addition to making budgetary allocations for state-level public health programs, the central government sponsors various disease eradication and treatment schemes—including those for malaria, tuberculosis, and HIV/AIDS—that are undertaken at the state level (J. Das Gupta 2001).

Health Indicators

India performs poorly on all health indicators, which is reflected in its ranking of 134 out of 182 countries in the United Nations' Human Development Index for 2009. Life expectancy at birth in India is sixty-four years (United Nations Children's Fund 2008b). Childhood mortality is a key social indicator because its main causes include avoidable factors such as infectious diseases, diarrhea, and pneumonia; infant mortality statistics are strongly correlated to and indicative of access to and availability of health systems (Cutler and Lleras-Muney 2006). Though India's under-five mortality and infant mortality rates declined between 1990 and 2008,[3] the United Nations Children's Fund (UNICEF) found that 47% of children in India are underweight—more than the number for the entire continent of Africa (United Nations Children's Fund 2006). India's country rank for under-five mortality remains at 49 out of 196 countries (rank 1 reflects the worst), putting India well above neighboring South Asian countries (United Nations Children's Fund 2008a). Moreover, India's infant mortality rate is 52 per 1,000 live births. India's Millennium Development Goals include reducing the maternal mortality rate to 109 out of 100,000 live births by 2015; in 2009, the rate was well behind this goal, at 405. UNICEF attributes these failures to social inequalities and shortage of primary health-care facilities.

Health Expenditure

Average levels of public health spending in India have remained chronically low since the 1990s. The yearly total expenditure on health (public and private) in India as a percentage of gross domestic product from 1995 to 2008 ranged between 4.1% and 4.8%. Private expenditure accounts for the bulk of this spending: government health expenditure constitutes only about one-quarter of this total, ranging between 22% and 28% over the fourteen-year period (World Health Organization 2010b). The impact of this spending inequality has severe consequences for India, where 42% of the population lives below the international poverty line of US$1.25 per day,[4] and an even larger proportion of the population relies on public health facilities (United Nations Children's Fund 2008b; Ravallion et al. 2008; Economic Research Foundation 2006). Moreover, the bulk of public health spending is on recurrent items (e.g., salaries); little is spent on capital investment and the maintenance and upgrading of existing infrastructure (Bajpai and Goyal 2004).

Health Policy

Despite detailed policy frameworks and various governmental committees aimed at reforming the health care system,[5] India's health system fails to meet the basic health needs of its vast and largely impoverished population. Based on a review of India's health policy since independence, we attribute this failing to the following factors: (i) the absence of a political commitment toward realizing universal health care; (ii) a shift in budgetary priorities toward vertical disease-eradication programs and family planning; (iii) the failure to develop an integrated health infrastructure; and (iv) the implementation of ill-conceived and cost-ineffective health programs at the expense of universal care. Of note, the current Five-Year Plan also acknowledges most of these factors as responsible for India's poor health-care system. To supplement the discussion below, table 7.1 outlines notable features of health policy in India's Five-Year Plans.

Lack of Political Commitment Toward Development of a Universal Health-Care System

On the few occasions when India's policy makers have articulated a commitment to the provision of universal health care, they have been met with opposition from domestic and international actors, including the World Health Organization and the World Bank. Early recognition of the need for universality, equity, and comprehensiveness of health care was reflected in the initial development of primary health centers, community health centers, and district hospitals following the 1946 report of the Health Survey and Welfare Committee (Bhore Committee), which the government established in 1943 to suggest improvements to the public health system under the chairmanship of Sir Joseph Bhore. However, over the 1960s and 1970s, the focus of public policy shifted to vertical disease-eradication programs and family planning. It was not until 1983 that the National Health Policy reiterated a commitment to universal health care, which was inspired in part by the 1978 Alma-Ata Declaration.[6] Due to a strong domestic and international lobby questioning the financial viability of universal care, however, the 1983 policy recommendations were not followed. Recently, the 2002 National Health Policy (which remains in effect today) has carefully steered away from committing to universal access to health services on grounds of financial viability—despite openly acknowledging the deplorable state of the health-care system and India's poor performance on public health indicators.

Focus on Individual Disease Eradication Programs Administered Vertically and Family Planning

"Vertical" programs designed to control infectious diseases have been the focus of government health policy since the 1960s, with support from international agencies like the World Health Organization and the United Nations Children's Fund (Nundy n.d.). Simultaneously, family planning became a policy priority after India's ruling elite and development advisors from the International Monetary Fund and World Bank became increasingly preoccupied with an anticipated population explosion and potential food shortages.

Table 7.1. Highlights of health policy based on India's Five-Year Plans

Plan	Time period	Main features
First Second	1951–56 1956–61	Both plans: • Prioritized provision of water supply and sanitation • Introduced separate vertical programs for control of malaria, tuberculosis, filariasis, leprosy, and venereal diseases
Third	1961–66	• Shifted focus from preventive health services and prioritized family planning
Fourth	1969–74	• Strengthened primary health centers to improve rural care • Intensified vertical campaigns against communicable diseases
Fifth	1974–79	• Focused on population control by pulling basic health workers into the family planning program
Sixth	1980–84	• Reiterated the need to create a comprehensive health system that responded to environmental, nutritional, educational, socioeconomic, preventive, and curative needs
Seventh	1985–90	• Failed to follow 1983 National Health Policy recommendations for universal care; instead, prioritized the development of three-tier health services and oversight of personnel, equipment, and facilities
Eighth	1992–97	• Encouraged private initiatives (e.g., hospitals and clinics) through tax incentives • Prioritized vertical programs funded by multilateral agencies with conditionalities (e.g., HIV/AIDS, tuberculosis, malaria, and polio)
Ninth	1997–2002	• Highlighted the dismal condition of public health care • Proposed to invest in primary-level care and referral services
Tenth	2002–7	• Launched the National Rural Health Mission in 2005 • Highlighted the need for decentralization of health-care delivery systems to local government
Eleventh	2007–12	• Focused on the convergence of health care, hygiene, water, and sanitation under the National Rural Health Mission • Proposed launch of National Urban Health Mission in 2011 • Enhanced public–private partnerships at secondary and tertiary levels

The Ministry of Health was correspondingly partitioned into departments of health and family planning; moreover, a countrywide, incentives-based, target-oriented, and time-bound female sterilization program was introduced (M. Das Gupta 2005; Maharatna 2002). During the 1970s, particularly during the "Emergency" (1975–77), public funds were disproportionately allocated to family planning,[7] and health-care workers got sucked into the government's population-control drive (M. Das Gupta 2005). The corresponding neglect of public health services resulted in a decline in institutional public health capacity that has plagued the implementation of health programs ever since.

Lack of an Integrated Health Infrastructure

India's health programs are characterized by piecemeal health-care strategies. The introduction in the 1950s, and subsequent intensification in the 1960s, of vertical disease control programs prevented the development of an integrated health system (Nundy n.d.; Maharatna 2002). Later attempts at integration of health personnel were sidetracked during the population-control drive in the 1970s (Nundy n.d.). The central government's launch of the National Rural Health Mission in 2005, believed to be an important step in renewing government focus on health care in India (A. Sinha 2009), has been criticized for failing to integrate existing health systems (Ashtekar 2008; Duggal 2006). A 2008 performance audit of this program by the comptroller and auditor general found that many states, particularly the poorest, had failed to fully expend program funds due to lack of capacity (*Economic and Political Weekly* 2010). Similar capacity and execution problems have delayed the planned 2008 launch of the National Urban Health Mission, which was targeted at meeting the health needs of the urban poor across 429 cities. As of 2010, this program had still not been implemented (K. Sinha 2010). The situation presents considerable adverse consequences for future initiatives, including those potentially prescribed through litigation. For instance, yearly increases in budgetary allowances for health-care spending are dependent on the utilization of existing budgetary allowances.[8]

Prevalence of Ill-Conceived and/or Cost-Ineffective Programs

Where health programs have in fact been implemented, outcomes have been unsatisfactory given the high costs and limited success of such programs. For instance, the 2002 National Health Policy notes that the government has relied on a vertical implementation structure, which requires separate manpower for each of the major disease-control programs. While this system has eradicated certain diseases like smallpox, it has failed to eradicate diseases like malaria and tuberculosis. The policy finds that "'vertical' structures may only be affordable for those diseases which offer a reasonable possibility of elimination or eradication [with]in a foreseeable time-span,"[9] implying that much of India's vertical disease-eradication programs have been ill conceived and cost-ineffective. Moreover, vertical programs for eradication of diseases like malaria have not been accompanied by broader concerted action on public health and sanitation, thus limiting their impact.

Finally, following economic liberalization in 1991 and the concurrent structural adjustment program imposed by the International Monetary Fund, health-sector reforms were introduced at the state level by multilateral and bilateral funding agencies such as the World Bank, the European Commission, the United States Agency for International Development, and the UK Department for International Development. These "reform" projects favored commercialization of health care, including the adoption of user fees in public hospitals, privatization of a range of services within the health sector, and the promotion of public-private partnerships via franchising, social marketing, and the "contracting out" of services (Duggal 2006).

In sum, after decades of poor policy commitments and budgetary neglect, India's health infrastructure is weak and lacks institutional capacity. A 2007 study attributed the "weak voice" of citizens and the "low accountability between public sector employees and citizens in the healthcare sector" as the key binding constraints to effective delivery of public health services (Hammer et al. 2007). The remainder of this chapter considers how health rights litigation has responded to these shortcomings, and whether the remedies devised by courts in consultation with petitioners and the government have yielded positive individual and population outcomes.

The Development of Social Rights Litigation

The right to health emerged from the broader development of social rights litigation, which has been attributed largely to an activist Supreme Court's liberal interpretations of its powers of review, as well as to the substantive rights guaranteed under the Constitution of India.

The Indian Supreme Court was established in 1950 pursuant to the Constitution. As the apex court in a unified judicial system that includes twenty-one High Courts and the subordinate judiciary, the Supreme Court possesses original (art. 131), appellate (arts. 132–36) and advisory jurisdiction (art. 143). Under the Constitution, a law declared by the Supreme Court is binding on "all courts within the territory of India" (art. 141); moreover, the Supreme Court can issue any orders "to do complete justice" between the parties (art. 142). Both the Supreme Court and High Courts have the power to punish failures to abide by their decisions through contempt orders (art. 129 and the Contempt of Courts Act, 1971), which is underscored by the obligation of "all authorities, civil and judicial, in the territory of India" to "act in aid of the Supreme Court of India" (art. 144) (Muralidhar 2002).[10]

Part III of the Constitution guarantees certain fundamental rights, including the rights to life (art. 21), liberty (art. 19), and equality (art. 14). Articles 32 and 226 empower the Supreme Court and High Courts to grant appropriate remedies for violations of fundamental rights. Part IV lists the "Directive Principles of State Policy," which shall be applied by the state in making laws but are unenforceable as rights (art. 37). These principles correspond with rights guaranteed under the International Covenant on Economic, Social and Cultural Rights.[11]

Having asserted its power of judicial review as a "basic feature" of the Constitution,[12] the Supreme Court has used its review powers extensively. The origins of the Court's activism can be traced to the post-Emergency period. During the Emergency of 1975–77, the government led by Indira Gandhi imprisoned opposition politicians, centralized power by dismissing state governments, and ultimately suspended fundamental freedoms. Despite having previously invalidated constitutional amendments that contravened fundamental rights,[13] the Court's credibility was severely damaged when it ruled that fundamental rights could be suspended during a period of emergency[14]—thereby lending legitimacy to the regime's practice of political repression. In part out of atonement for the failings of the Emergency era,[15] the Supreme Court subsequently adopted an increasingly activist role to "extend legal protection to the interests of the weak and underprivileged sections of society" (Baxi 1988).

The Court liberalized rules of standing[16] to facilitate access to justice for disadvantaged groups, thereby expanding access to legal aid and entertaining petitions that were submitted as letters to the Court.[17] Considered a "judge-led and judge-dominated movement," these moves ushered in the use of "public interest litigation" (Baxi 1988). Over the same period, the Court expanded the nature and scope of fundamental rights through an expansive interpretation of the right to life[18] as the right to live a life with dignity,[19] which includes housing,[20] education,[21] health, and food (see below)—thus making social rights justiciable. In so doing, the Court has characterized fundamental rights and the Directive Principles of State Policy as complementary, with "neither part being superior to the other."[22] The impact of the Court's activist role on the realization of the economic, social, and cultural rights of the underprivileged, however, has been criticized as insufficient (Rajagopal 2007). Below, we explore to what extent this criticism holds true with regard to the right to health.

Nature and Scope of the Right to Health

India's public health policies and infrastructure are clearly inadequate to meet the needs of its population. As discussed in this section, the right to health emerged and developed out of litigation that responded to these inadequacies.

The Development of a Justiciable Right to Health

In a 1981 decision highlighting deplorable prison conditions, the Supreme Court interpreted the right to life to "include the right to live with human dignity and all that goes along with it, namely, the bare necessities of life such as adequate nutrition, clothing and shelter."[23] A 1992 minority opinion by the Court later recognized the right to health as falling within the right to life in a case concerning the provision for state workers' health and medical care.[24] Additional decisions between 1989 and 1995 included health-related issues within the right to life (such as access to medical treatment for prisoners),[25] as well as a "better standard of life, hygienic conditions in work place and leisure"[26] within the right to a livelihood. But it was only in 1996 that the right to health was made independently justiciable when the government was directed to pay compensation to a petitioner with a medical emergency after the petitioner had been denied treatment by seven hospitals.[27] Later, the Court affirmed that "it is now settled law that right to health is integral to right to life."[28] Health has since been routinely cited among the fundamental rights protected under the Constitution.[29] Table 7.2 highlights key jurisprudential developments in the justiciability of the right to health.

Deriving the Core Content of the Right to Health

International human rights instruments guarantee everyone the right "to the enjoyment of the highest attainable standard of physical and mental health," which is subject to progressive realization.[30] The Supreme Court has found the enforcement of this right to be "a most imperative constitutional goal whose realization requires interaction [of] many social and economic factors."[31] Over time, the scope of the right to health has evolved according to the remedies devised by the Supreme Court.

While Supreme Court and High Court decisions outline specific minimum obligations encompassed by the right to health, a comprehensive definition of the core content of the right has yet to be articulated. At a minimum, the right includes an individual's entitlement to adequate health care[32] (which has been held to include emergency health care) and to "adequate medical facilities."[33] The Court has repeatedly rejected government pleas of

Table 7.2. Key developments in Supreme Court right-to-health jurisprudence

1978–80s	Right to life interpreted expansively (*Maneka Gandhi*); "right to life includes the right to live with dignity" (*Bandhua Mukti Morcha*)
1987, 1989	Supreme Court's remedial powers under article 32 interpreted expansively (*M. C. Mehta*; *Union of India v. Raghubir*)
1989	Health recognized as integral to the right to life (*Francis Coralie Mullin*; *Parmanand Katara*)
1992	Minority opinion recognized justiciability (*CESC v. Chandra Bose*)
1995	Health deemed an integral component of workers' rights (occupational health and safety) (*CERC*)
1995, 1996	Medical negligence cases decided (*Indian Medical Association; Verma v. Patel*)
1996	Health recognized as a fundamental right; emergency medical care included as a core element of this right (*Samiti*)
1997	Health recognized as a fundamental right in awarding state employee reimbursement of health claim (*Mohinder Singh Chawla*)
1998	Health part of enforcement of right to life; state with limited resources is under obligation to provide health care to all citizens and not only public employees (*Bagga*)
2001	Right to a healthy environment recognized in case concerning pollution (*M. C. Mehta*) and a case involving smoking (*Murali Deora*)
2007	Right to health recognized "amongst the human rights protected under the constitution" (*Reddy v. Revamma*)

budgetary limitations, holding that "financial stringency may not be a ground for not issuing requisite directions when a question of violation of fundamental right arises."[34] Moreover, drugs must meet certain minimum regulatory standards,[35] and there should be specific standards and processes for medical negligence claims.[36]

It should be noted that the nature and scope of the right to health evolved largely out of cases involving egregious suffering or difficulties in accessing public health services. These cases concerned two groups of claimants. First, they concerned poor people who suffered loss or harm as a result of accessing public services of substandard quality. We considered these to be "public" negligence cases because they were brought against state providers and authorities and resulted in broader court orders affecting the quality of public health services. Second, they concerned government employees seeking reimbursement for private care because quality public health care, which would ordinarily have been covered under their insurance scheme, was not available. In upholding the right of government employees to access health care, however, the Court has noted that reimbursing employees' medical costs must be balanced against the state's duty to provide medical care for everyone.[37]

The Supreme Court has also enforced the right to health for mentally ill detainees and industrial workers. It has prescribed minimum standards of care for the mentally ill, such as the integration of mental health treatment into primary health-care services.[38] Moreover, the Court has held the health of workers to be an essential component of the right to life, thus imposing an obligation on "the State and the employer to provide facilities . . . for ensuring sustained good health and leisure to the workman"[39] and ensuring minimal workplace health and safety standards.[40]

The Supreme Court regularly cites India's health-related obligations under the Universal Declaration of Human Rights[41] and the International Covenant on Economic, Social and Cultural Rights.[42] Though noted as "part of a conscious strategy of social transformation wherein previously disadvantaged groups have been made aware of their basic rights," these references are not generally accompanied by a rigorous analysis of the relevant normative frameworks and underlying guiding principles (Balakrishnan 2008).

Core Obligations and Underlying Determinants

The United Nations Committee on Economic, Social and Cultural Rights considers the provision of food and nutrition; shelter, housing, and sanitation; safe and potable water; and underlying determinants such as education and healthy environmental conditions as core components of the right to health.[43] Derived from the right to life under article 21 of the Indian Constitution, social rights are similarly regarded as indivisible in India. The Supreme Court first recognized the right to food as part of the right to life in a case addressing starvation deaths in the state of Orissa,[44] and later in a case concerning the ineffective public distribution system throughout India in the face of mass starvation[45] (hereinafter "the right-to-food case"). The Supreme Court has also recognized the right to "pollution free water" within the right to life.[46] Lower courts have upheld claims for the provision of adequate water and sanitation facilities, as mandated by the right to life.[47] The Court has also upheld "the State's constitutional duty to provide adequate facilities for . . . shelter . . . to make the right to life meaningful."[48] However, its decisions on shelter have been criticized for siding with state interests against those of the poor in terms of the remedy granted.[49] The maintenance of a healthy environment has been indispensably linked to the right to life,[50] and environmental standards have been applied to municipalities and private entities.[51]

Categories of Health Rights Litigation

From the 218 cases sampled for this chapter, we identified nine categories of health rights cases; the remaining cases were categorized as "other," and included mostly cases on assisted suicide. Figure 7.1 depicts each category as a percentage of the total sample cases reviewed.

A majority of the cases involve claims regarding medical negligence, environmental (as related to public health) issues, and the provision of drugs and public health services. These finding resemble those of a 2007 study of Supreme Court and High Court cases, which found that 43% of the cases related to public health issues, 26% to medical malpractice and hospital management, 14% to medical reimbursement and insurance, 6% to HIV/AIDS, and 11% to an undefined "other" category (Shankar and Mehta 2008). In the sections below, we undertake a deeper qualitative examination of our subset of Supreme Court cases and consider the profile of petitioners, claims, and outcomes from these categories of cases.

Health rights litigation appears to have provided additional means of holding public actors accountable for health-related matters. In one case, for example, the Medical Council of India was directed by the Supreme Court to institute a formalized mechanism for hearing patient complaints concerning medical negligence.[52] Following this decision, the Council initiated the process of formulating guidelines for investigation into cases of medical negligence (Padmini 2003). However, given the recent dissolution of the Council in wake of a corruption scandal, the guidelines have not yet been adopted and the body's future status is unclear at this time (Deccan Herald 2010). In another case, the Court empowered village administration bodies (gram sabhas) to monitor the distribution of food supplies under the public distribution scheme and set up a grievance redress mechanism.[53] Outside our subset of Supreme Court cases, the High Court of Madras applied the right to health to uphold a procedure under the 2005 Patent Act enabling third parties to file oppositions to patent applications.[54] The decision preserved a mechanism allowing affected parties to review the Patent Controller's decisions regarding patent applications for drugs, thus maintaining an additional check on potential monopolistic drug pricing. The Supreme Court has directed petitioners—in this case, organizations working on behalf of people living with HIV/AIDS—to negotiate public policy and protocols with government actors over the provision of second-line antiretroviral HIV/AIDS treatment.[55]

Figure 7.1. Nature of health rights cases

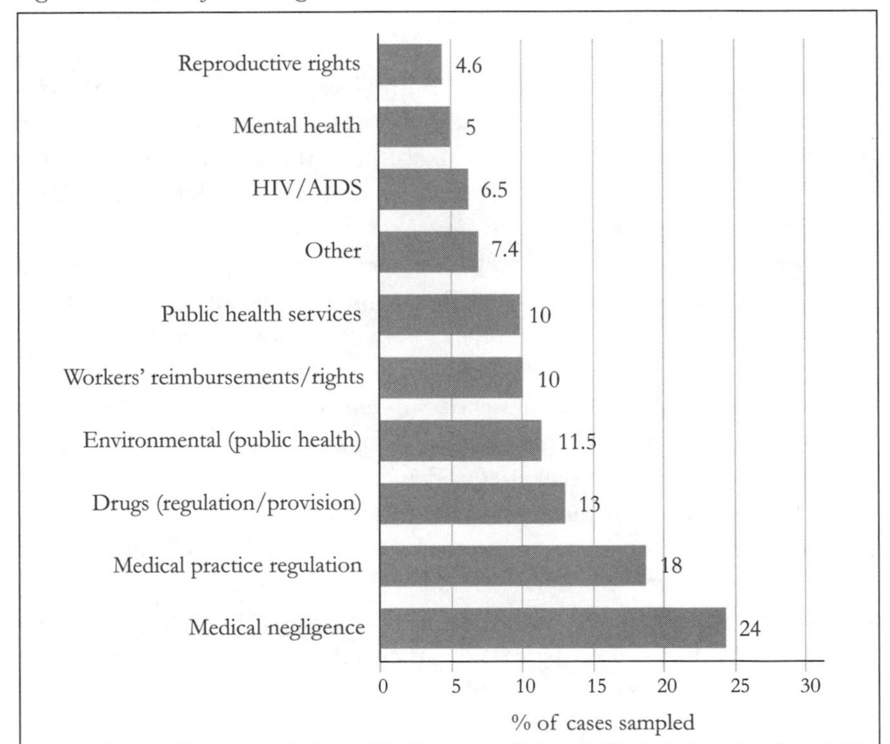

Claims Formation and Adjudication

We now take a closer look at our sample of sixty-six Supreme Court cases and examine how the claims were formed and adjudicated. Our analysis demonstrates the breadth of interests involved and the Court's varied approaches in devising judicial remedies.

Petitioners and Health Claims

Both private and public petitioners have sought to make state actors accountable for failures to comply with existing health obligations or to highlight gaps within the relevant legal or regulatory framework. In our sample of sixty-six Supreme Court cases, individual petitioners brought claims for medical negligence (eleven) and reimbursements for health expenses (four). However, they also raised public interest claims (eight) on issues such as disability rights, environmental health (air and water pollution), and drug regulation. Group petitioners, including unions and community associations, raised health claims that affected the welfare of their members (seventeen), including medical negligence and employee health reimbursement.

We thus found that just over two-fifths of the Supreme Court cases involved social justice, or public interest, claims (twenty-eight); of these, over half were brought by interested individuals (fifteen) and just under half were brought by nongovernmental organizations and unions (thirteen). A 2007 study of Supreme Court and High Court cases found that only one-fifth of the cases were PILs brought by nongovernmental organizations (Shankar and Mehta 2008). Shylashri Shankar and Pratap Mehta determined that this was a low rate and concluded that health rights litigation was a negligible public action strategy in India (due to resource and enforcement barriers). However, a qualitative examination of our subset of Supreme Court cases brought by individuals suggests a more complex picture. While a number of individual petitioners sought individual relief, a considerable proportion of individual petitioner-led cases sought broader public interest or social justice goals. Moreover, these latter claims concern sizable populations. Finally, certain public health claims that were intended to have an impact beyond the individual petitioner were not necessarily formally filed as a PIL. This cursory sketch of claims from our Supreme Court sample suggests the importance of qualitatively evaluating health rights cases in terms of individually tracking potential outcomes.

Health activist groups such as the People's Health Movement[56] and patients' rights groups such as those working on behalf of people affected by HIV/AIDS,[57] injecting drug users,[58] and cancer patients[59] have served as petitioners and/or provided litigation support for health rights cases. These groups rely on their networks to raise public awareness, collect data, and lobby public officials to ensure that public policy and government services best serve their constituencies.[60] International organizations such as the Center for Reproductive Rights and Doctors Without Borders have also provided litigation and/or advocacy support to domestic health rights cases.[61] Although none arose within our sampled Supreme Court cases, we found several *suo moto* cases before the High Courts, in which the government was required to respond to concerns over the delivery of public health-care services.[62]

The petitioners interviewed for this chapter highlighted the importance of working with public interest lawyers and/or organizations and lamented the insufficiency of public interest lawyers to support their claims in court.[63] Moreover, while some petitioners felt that their lawyers kept them duly informed and treated them as an equal partner throughout the litigation and advocacy processes,[64] other petitioners cited the need for greater collaboration with lawyers—especially in terms of communicating litigation developments and outcomes. Petitioners also bemoaned the need to secure a "senior" advocate[65] to ensure that claims are seriously and expeditiously heard by the judiciary, especially the Supreme Court; yet such advocates are costly and rarely provide pro bono services. The situation exposes a serious "access to justice" failure perpetuated within the Indian legal system, whose class bias and hierarchy valorizes certain lawyers—and therefore their clients—over others.

Claims Adjudication

In its decisions, the Supreme Court has granted both specific and general relief. Specific relief usually takes the form of monetary compensation for medical negligence, or directions for reimbursement of health expenses in medical reimbursement cases. General relief—the adjudication of which has resembled that undertaken in social rights cases generally—usually seeks directions for addressing systemic public health failures. Furthermore, the Court has employed a variety of remedial techniques in adjudicating health rights cases.

These approaches include (i) appointing amicus curiae to provide assistance on legal issues;[66] (ii) exercising supervisory jurisdiction through the use of "continuing mandamus" over the matter;[67] (iii) establishing commissions or expert bodies to ascertain facts or to independently verify facts presented by the parties, and asking these bodies to report to the court on the implementation of interim orders; (iv) passing mandatory orders, including preliminary and final injunctions; and (v) delivering detailed directions to public and private respondents to develop requisite policy and regulatory responses and practice. Some of these approaches are discussed in greater detail below.

Retaining Supervisory Jurisdiction through Continuing Mandamus

The Supreme Court has liberally interpreted its powers under article 32 of the Constitution to issue prerogative writs in order to retain supervisory jurisdiction over cases. This enables the Court to issue a series of interim orders through which it can address complex issues comprehensively and over time. For example, the Court employed continuing mandamus to issue several orders to the central government and corporate actors concerning occupational health and safety in the asbestos industry. In the right-to-food case, the Court passed a series of interim orders whose implementation has been overseen by a Court-established committee; parties must answer to the Court when compliance issues arise.[68] In a case concerning access to second-line HIV/AIDS treatment, the Court retained supervisory jurisdiction while the parties negotiated a treatment protocol and reported to the Court on progress.[69] Lawyers for the petitioners reported having worked with government lawyers to outline an agreed-upon basis for the delivery of such treatment, which was later adopted in an order by the Court.[70]

Mandatory Orders and Directions

The Supreme Court has issued mandatory orders regarding the provision of accessible, available, and quality primary health care. The Court has also prescribed minimum standards regarding the provision of emergency medical facilities, calling on state and central governments to take the following actions: ensure adequate facilities at primary health centers and upgrade hospitals at the district and subdistrict levels; increase availability of specialized treatment; create a centralized communication system to ensure availability of beds; and improve overall ambulatory availability and care.[71] Government actors have been ordered to fulfill their public health responsibilities in environmental health cases, including the collection and disposal of garbage,[72] the development of emissions standards,[73] and the implementation of compensation schemes for victims affected by industrial pollution.[74] It may also be noted that High Courts have followed with similar actions: ordering measures for improved sanitation in Rajasthan;[75] ordering the establishment of a primary health center for an impoverished village in Orissa;[76] and prescribing severe punishments for individuals convicted of the manufacture of spurious drugs.[77]

Interim rulings by the Supreme Court have also ordered reforms of health-related policies and regulation, though the details for such policies have been determined by other actors. The Supreme Court has directed the central government to devise a regulatory system to control the supply of spurious drugs, including establishing laboratories and undertaking research.[78] The Court also ordered the government to regulate and upgrade the functioning of blood banks and complete the licensing of all blood banks.[79] Both public and private actors were required to adopt asbestos regulations prescribed by the International Labour Organization and undertake a ten-year review of implementation thereof. In the same case, the Court also directed the government to appoint asbestos inspectors and ordered the National Institute of Occupational Health to undertake the routine medical re-examination of asbestos workers.[80] In a case reviewing female sterilization practices across India, the Court's numerous directions included the establishment of an approved panel of doctors to carry out sterilization procedures in accordance with criteria to be provided by the central government; the introduction of a checklist of patient data for doctors; the circulation of uniform patient consent forms; the creation of uniform standards for compensation for workers who have suffered health complications from exposure to asbestos over the course of their employment; and the introduction of an insurance scheme.[81]

The Supreme Court has also responded with measures to raise awareness or highlight areas of need in order to elicit prompt responses. For example, the Court has directed law journals, national newspapers, public television stations, and radio channels to publish or broadcast the Court's judgments informing private and publicly employed doctors of their obligation to treat medical emergencies. Moreover, state governments have been ordered not only to maintain but also make public overall statistics about sterilization procedures and resulting deaths. They are also required to disseminate information about the central government-sponsored insurance policy to cover necessary medical treatments resulting from failed sterilization procedures.[82]

Oversight Mechanisms

In addition to appointing amicus curiae to provide assistance on legal issues, the Supreme Court has delegated its authority to commissions or expert bodies to investigate situations or provide independent verification of facts presented by the petitioners or the government, as well as to oversee implementation of the Court's orders. Below are some examples.

- Court-established committees have been employed to fill vacancies and improve the recruitment of health personnel for primary health centers.[83]
- A special committee of Court-appointed experts was directed to examine which pharmaceutical drugs were to be banned from manufacture and sale in India, based on specific orders that were passed regarding the drug Analgin.[84]
- The Court ordered the establishment of state "quality assurance committees" to investigate breaches of sterilization procedures under the national sterilization guidelines.[85]
- In the right-to-food case, the Court appointed commissioners who are empowered to inquire about violations of the Court's interim orders and demand redress from the government, with the full authority of the Court.[86]
- The Court delegated its authority to other bodies to oversee implementation of orders in mental health cases. High Courts were ordered to monitor the conditions of "mentally ill and insane" women and children in prisons and pass appropriate orders from time to time; and judicial magistrates were ordered to oversee examinations of mentally ill patients performed by mental health professionals.[87]

Ultimately, successful outcomes resulting from the Court's decisions depend on the government's ability and willingness to act and comply with the Court's orders, putting a high premium on the effectiveness of supervisory bodies and contempt powers. Moreover, additional means of verification are required to ascertain whether these measures have successfully further democratized health policy discourse. The following section considers these aspects of health rights litigation.

The Varied Impacts of Health Rights Litigation

This section considers the potential impact of health rights litigation on petitioners and the interests they represent, on the substance and process of health policy making, and on universal outcomes for the population. In doing so, it recommends areas for future investigation.

Impact on Litigants and Population

A review of the sixty-six Supreme Court cases sampled for this chapter reveals variety in terms of the nature and number of litigants. The bulk of the cases reviewed (forty-nine) addressed remedies sought by petitioners in relation to a particular health claim or public health issue. A smaller number of cases (sixteen) involved broader socioeconomic claims that possessed a health element and/or affirmed normative elements of the right to health.

Of the forty-nine health-specific cases, forty-one petitioners—that is, 84% of petitioners—obtained successful relief orders from the Court. This group of "winning cases" demonstrates the breadth of litigants that have benefited from health rights litigation, as well as the range of specific and general remedies that followed (some cases involved more than one type of claim):

- *Individual claims.* In one-third (thirteen) of the cases, orders were issued granting specific relief for individual litigants. Most of the orders involved monetary damages for public medical negligence (nine), and the rest were for government employee reimbursements (four). Notably, many of the medical negligence petitioners belonged to economically disadvantaged sections of society and sought compensation for poorly performed public health services.[88]
- *Group claims.* In another third (sixteen) of the cases, specific and general relief orders were issued for a particular group of litigants. These groups represent diverse social groups and included, for example, mentally ill patients, indigent women and children, retired army members, and beneficiaries of workers' compensation schemes. Specific relief included monetary compensation, including contributions to group insurance schemes. General relief orders targeted the systemic conditions that could be attributed to health rights failures and included the adoption and/or implementation of procedures and protocols as recommended by Court-appointed experts.

- *Public health claims.* One-third (fifteen) of the cases involved orders that affected a public health matter or led to outcomes with a universal impact on the realization of the health rights of the population. General relief orders directed public actors to adopt specific policies, programs, regulations, or legislation to address systemic public health failures, often concerning environmental issues but also regarding emergency medical care.

Ascertaining the extent to which affected groups and communities benefited from the litigation would involve tracking each individual

Novartis v. Cancer Patients Aid Association

Pharmaceutical company Novartis was granted exclusive marketing rights (EMR) for the cancer drug Glivec. The EMR allowed only Novartis and three out of nine generic manufacturers to distribute the drug. Unfortunately, the three generic companies that were included on the EMR lacked the combined capacity to service the entire patient population.

Novartis sells Glivec for about US$2,500 per month, while generic manufacturers sell the drug for about US$180 per month. Glivec is thus sold at a nearly 1,400% mark-up of the generic price. Used to treat chronic myeloid leukemia, an extremely life-threatening form of cancer, the drug is known to produce remission in over 90% of patients and thus is required for lifelong use as part of disease treatment. Each year, there are an estimated 30,000 new chronic myeloid leukemia cases in India.

The petitioner, a patients' rights group, provides free cancer drugs to its members. It successfully challenged the EMR grant based on applicable patent law (including scientific argument) and the right to health.[89]

In light of the considerable mark-up of the brand-name drug, this case significantly affected public health. However, the magnitude of the impact is difficult to measure, even in broad terms. Ascertaining the number of patients seeking the drug—which would allow us to most easily demonstrate impact—is not a straightforward task. While data is available for the number of chronic myeloid leukemia patients and the number of Novartis users, it would not be accurate to assume that the remainder of the patient population is purchasing a generic version of the drug, since some patients may be pursuing alternative therapies (such as ayurvedic or homeopathic treatment) or no therapy at all. Further investigation would also involve monitoring implementation of the Glivec International Patient Assistance Program, implemented by Novartis in India in September 2002, and the practices of other drug assistance programs, such as that operated by the Cancer Patients Aid Association.

case—a difficult exercise, especially considering the myriad of applicable variables. The box below serves as an example of the difficulties inherent in measuring the potential benefits of litigation. Here, cancer patients successfully opposed a patent application by including arguments grounded in the right to health.

Impact on Policy Process

As described earlier, the Supreme Court has devised processes for the formulation of policy and regulations, including the establishment of investigative, monitoring, and reporting bodies to oversee the implementation of its interim orders. This approach corresponds with existing characterizations of the "discursive role" the Court has played throughout its adjudication of social rights litigation. Specifically, the dialogic remedies described above reflect an "incremental, dialogic and systemic remedial approach required to achieve fuller compliance" with social rights by calling on legislators to revise laws and policies without the Court itself directing details or processes for policy formulation (Roach 2008).

It is worth noting that our interviews suggested that in certain instances where the Supreme Court has diverged from this "discursive role" and independently prescribed policy, the ensuing directions have encountered difficulties in implementation. In a recent case concerning sterilization, for example, the Court's pronouncement that the procedure must be conducted by a doctor with a post-graduate degree has been criticized by both petitioners and doctors.[90] This order, which was not sought by petitioners, imposes an unnecessary requirement that is difficult to fulfill, and ultimately affects availability of the health service by reducing the total number of sterilization operations that may be conducted.

These process-oriented litigation outcomes are critical for addressing a common criticism that "in the last twenty years, the Indian Parliament has almost stopped legislating" (Sathe 2002). Unfortunately, Court-prompted processes involve slowly paced consideration of new policies and regulations, only a few of which are eventually adopted. The discussion below depicts the mixed record experienced by these policy processes.

Impact on Policy

Health rights litigation appears to have influenced the deliberation, and in some cases the adoption, of policy in the areas of regulation of blood banks;[91] regulation of drugs;[92] emergency care; mental health care;[93] medical negligence and malpractice by public entities;[94] tobacco control laws; and reproductive rights.[95] In each of these instances, Court guidelines have recommended the adoption of measures to fill existing policy gaps, which have in turn prompted initiatives by the government. There is no way to conclude whether these policy and legislative initiatives would have been adopted in the absence of health rights litigation. However, some evidence is available to identify a correlation between the Court's pronouncements and subsequent policy and legislative development. Table 7.3 outlines some major policy and regulatory outcomes from our case sample.

These examples support broader commentary that social rights litigation prompts "catalysing changes in law and policy" (Muralidhar 2008). However, Court directions to fill policy gaps are frequently met with delays; for example, drafts by Court-appointed expert committees often remain under

Table 7.3. Policy impacts of health rights litigation

Case	Litigation outcome	Policy outcome
Blood banks (1998)	Licensing system outlined for blood banks	Blood bank legislation extensively revised in 1999 to include good manufacturing practices, standard operating procedures, and validation of equipment (Blood Index 2007)[a]
Drugs and vaccines (1995, 1996)	Specific orders issued banning the drug Analgin	Directives issued by central government in 1996 banning the manufacture, sale, and distribution of fixed-dose combinations of Analgin and antispasmodics (Pharmainfo.net 2009) Mashelkar Committee appointed by Ministry of Health to comprehensively review the drug regulatory system to prevent the manufacture and sale of substandard and spurious drugs
Emergency care (1996)	Committee appointed to investigate the provision of emergency medical care State governments ordered to formulate time-bound plans for implementing measures recommended by the committee and the Supreme Court	Expert group appointed by National Human Rights Commission recommended national accident policy and the establishment of centralized accident and trauma services in all districts (2004) (Indian National Human Rights Commission 2006) Proposed legislation and regulations by Law Reform Commission (2006)

consideration by government actors for extended periods of time without enactment or follow-up. Such dynamics indicate the Court's weak enforcement powers over its own orders and threaten to undermine its legitimacy. The following examples depict mixed performances in terms of the implementation and/or enforcement of health rights decisions.

Table 7.3 (continued)

Medical negligence (2001)	Guidelines framed under which a doctor could be held criminally liable for professional negligence or deficiency of service Medical Council of India ordered to institute a formalized mechanism for hearing complaints	In 2002, regulations on professional conduct, etiquette, and ethics adopted by Medical Council of India; chapter 8 concerns punishment and disciplinary action (Medical Council of India Notification 2002)[b]
Mental health care (1991)	Government ordered to improve mental health institutions and integrate mental health into primary care	National Human Rights Commission delegated oversight of three mental institutions (Indian National Human Rights Commission 2006, 2), which later reported progress in practice[c]
Reproductive rights (2003)	Guidelines issued for regulating the performance of sterilizations; negligence standards and compensation scheme established	Family Planning Insurance Scheme adopted in 2005[d]
Tobacco control laws (2001)	In the absence of statutory provisions, smoking prohibited in public places (e.g., hospitals, health institutions, educational institutions) All levels of government directed to take necessary action to implement the ban	Tobacco-control legislation passed[e]

[a] Compare the results of a 1992 study that sampled blood banks and found nearly 50% of their samples contaminated with hepatitis B (Irshad et al. 1992) and a 1995–96 survey that found "testing transfusion-transmitted infections unsatisfactory and poorly regulated" (Kapoor et al. 2000) with a 2003 study finding that "safer transfusion practices are slowly evolving but they may be enhanced by prospective audits into the use of blood in surgical practice" (Naraj et al. 2003).

[b] The Medical Council of India is a national body funded by the Indian Ministry of Health and Family Welfare.

[c] Oversight of mentally disabled patient cases by the Indian National Human Rights Commission found that over 90% of admissions to mental health institutions are reported to have become voluntary, and shifts from custodial care to treatment and rehabilitation have also been reported between 1997 and 2005 (Indian National Human Rights Commission 2006, 2).

[d] See also Indian Ministry of Health and Family Welfare (2005).

[e] "Judicial activism has played a major role in providing impetus to the tobacco control legislation, both by directing government to take much needed steps for tobacco control and by creating a climate of public support for such legislation" (Reddy and Gupta 2004).

- *Emergency care.* Despite the Supreme Court's important role in highlighting policy and implementation shortcomings, detailed recommendations and proposed legislation remain under consideration by the respective government entities in draft form.
- *Medical negligence.* Procedures and guidelines governing the investigation of medical negligence cases by the Medical Council of India are yet to be designed. Moreover, the Council has recently been dissolved following corruption charges and will be replaced by another body. Finally, it remains to be determined whether the high proportion of public medical negligence cases has influenced the delivery of care by public providers.
- *Sterilization.* Neither the judgment nor subsequent policy has set standards in terms of noncompliance, which makes it difficult to collect information on noncompliance and hold the government accountable.[96]
- *HIV/AIDS treatment.* Under Supreme Court directions, a protocol on second-line treatment was under negotiation between affected groups and government representatives. After being deadlocked for over a year, the negotiations finally came to an end in December 2010, when the Court ordered the government to extend second-line treatment to HIV-positive patients.
- *Public-private partnerships.* In 2007, the Delhi High Court directed private hospitals to provide free health services to the poor in compliance with long-standing agreements made with the municipality in exchange for valuable land concessions (Krishnan 2010). Later, in September 2009, the High Court issued directions to one private hospital to provide free treatment to the poor and imposed an "exemplary fine" of 2 lakh rupees (approximately US$5,000).[97] The fine appears disproportionately small compared to the profits earned by the hospital after years of noncompliance with the original agreement. The Court later received notice that the hospital had yet to comply with the order and continues to charge poor patients for services (*The Tribune* 2009).
- *Draft bills on health rights, HIV/AIDS, and the right to food.* Each of these draft bills has been prompted by and involved participants in related health rights litigation. However, even after several years, the bills remain under consideration by the central government.

The mixed character of these policy outcomes confirms an absence of judicial follow-up and sustained implementation of Court orders by all parties involved. Calls for the provision of additional resources—including financial, capacity-building, and organizational resources—could assist health activists in cementing a foundation for sustained post-litigation advocacy and follow-up (Epp 1998). However, weak judicial penalties are a problem. Examples of such penalties can be seen in the low amounts of damages awarded in public medical negligence cases, which consequently do not generate the necessary reforms to public health care, and in the penalty recently levied against a private hospital, described above. Further study is needed to track the results from contempt orders delivered in noncompliance cases.

Impact on Population

Identifying the populations concretely affected by Supreme Court decisions is a difficult exercise. Nonetheless, it is possible to identify areas of impact on the population that merit deeper examination. Table 7.4 illustrates universal policy outcomes resulting from litigation that affect the general population or specific groups of people.

Conclusion

A frequent criticism of social rights litigation is that this method of ensuring delivery of socioeconomic entitlements is too ad hoc and too dependent on the ability and means of petitioners to bring a case to court, as well as the shifting composition of the judiciary (Ely 1980). As discussed, a major failing of India's health system has been the adoption of piecemeal policies

Table 7.4. Population impacts of health rights litigation

Policies affecting the general population
• Right-to-food schemes (42% of the population below the poverty line, or 456 million people, are affected) (World Bank 2008) • Licensing and quality of blood banks • Regulation of drugs and vaccines • Family Planning Insurance Scheme (regulation of sterilization procedures) • Tobacco control legislation (tobacco-attributable deaths range between 800,000 and 900,000 each year) (Reddy and Gupta 2004) • Medical ethics and medical negligence guidelines
Policies affecting particular groups
• Reimbursement of medical expenses for government employees • Workers' health insurance (both public and private) • Regulation of delivery of mental health services • Antiretroviral treatment for people living with HIV/AIDS

as opposed to the financing of an integrated and comprehensive health-care system. The potential of health rights litigation thus appears counterintuitive in terms of its ability to render the delivery of health services more equitable. Instead, our study paints a complex picture of health rights litigation with no clear answers in terms of its overall impact on equity.

The persistence of India's executive and legislative health failures renders the enforcement of a right to health an important tool for citizens to hold the state accountable for its constitutionally mandated obligations and to seek concrete relief. Petitioners appear to represent varied interests and groups, and the Supreme Court has used its review powers creatively. Health rights litigation has highlighted areas of dire need, including basic necessities like food, water, and essential medicines. Moreover, it has opened a discursive space that has forced the government to defend its record on certain health rights issues and negotiate with petitioners and civil society groups before adopting policies. This latter dynamic is particularly important for petitioners from marginalized and vulnerable groups, who typically lack the means to influence government policy (Liebenberg 2010; Galanter 1974). We have been unable to concretely establish causation between health rights litigation and reallocation of budgetary priorities, especially since budget priorities are influenced by multiple factors. Nonetheless, certain correlations are evident from specific cases, including the cases on blood banks, India's Family Planning Insurance Scheme, HIV/AIDS treatment, and medical negligence in public hospitals.

At the same time, our study has described the limitations of health rights litigation. Specifically, the record on implementation of Supreme Court orders has been mixed, making it difficult to assess the overall effectiveness of judicial accountability on the health system. We find that because the Court's remedies are not backed by serious penalties for noncompliance, enforcement challenges, particularly in cases of structural reform, will continue to abound—notwithstanding the use of oversight mechanisms. Moreover, litigation is neither necessary nor sufficient for achieving structural reform on a particular issue. Cases considered relatively successful, such as the right-to-food and access-to-treatment cases, have employed litigation within a broader public advocacy campaign. Civil society networks have also been actively involved in follow-up regarding implementation of the Court's remedies.

In conclusion, without a deeper empirical and qualitative review of the entirety of health rights litigation, we cannot answer definitively whether health rights litigation in India has led to a more equitable delivery of health services. However, health rights litigation does *not* appear to be deepening health inequities between competing health interests. At best, it has highlighted areas of serious need and thus supported access for certain sections of the population. At worst, it has failed to significantly improve the persistent systemic failures that plague the Indian health system.

Judging from existing literature, health rights litigation in India may represent a more promising subset of cases regarding the potential of litigation to bring about social change. Given the gravity of the health-care crisis in India, any improvements in health outcomes through litigation are noteworthy and deserving of fuller and detailed consideration by lawyers, academics, and health practitioners.

NOTES

1. These included keyword searches on legal search engines available through Manupatra, Indian Kanoon, and the Supreme Court of India ("right to health," "article 21," "blood banks," "directive principles and public health," "drug policy," "emergency care," "environmental health," "healthy environment," "HIV/AIDS," "medical negligence," "medical malpractice," "reproductive health," "right to food," "right to water," and "workers' health").
2. The Constitution of India, 1950, art. 246 read with schedule VII, list II.
3. India's under-five mortality rate per 1,000 live births dropped from 116 to 49 and its infant mortality rate per 1,000 live births dropped from 83 to 52 (United Nations Children's Fund 2008b).
4. India's population was 1.16 billion in 2007 (World Health Organization 2009c).
5. Ten governmental committees of note have been established to review public health care: Health Survey and Welfare Committee, 1946 (Bhore Committee); Health Survey and Planning Committee, 1962 (Mudaliar Committee); Chadha Committee, 1963; Mukherjee Committee, 1965 and 1966; Committee on Integration of Health Services, 1967 (Jungalwalla Committee); Basic Health Services Committee, 1968 (Mukerji Committee); Committee on Multipurpose Workers under Health Family Planning Programme, 1973 (Kartar Singh Committee); Shrivastav Committee, 1975; and Health Manpower Planning, Production and Management Committee, 1986 (Bajaj Committee).
6. Declaration of Alma-Ata, International Conference on Primary Health Care, Alma-Ata, USSR, September 6–12, 1978.
7. Notwithstanding spending on such programs, India's population increased from 351 million in 1951 to over a billion in 2001 (M. Das Gupta 2005).
8. Interview with a senior official at the Ministry of Health, New Delhi, January 2010.
9. National Health Policy 2002, sec. 2.3.2.1.

10. *Union of India v. Raghubir Singh*, (1989) 2 SCC 754 at 766 (finding that the Supreme Court has the final word on the interpretation of the Constitution; its orders, being law, are binding and enforceable by executive, legislative, and judicial authorities).
11. International Covenant on Economic, Social and Cultural Rights, G.A. Res. 2200A (XXI), 21 U.N. GAOR Supp. (No. 16) at 49, U.N. Doc. A/6316 (1966), 993 U.N.T.S. 3, entered into force January 3, 1976. Consider constitutional articles 42 (provision for just and humane working conditions and for maternity relief) and 47 (state's duty to raise people's level of nutrition and standard of living and to improve public health).
12. *L. Chandrakumar v. Union of India*, (1997) 3 SCC 261(striking down certain articles of the Constitution as violative of the "basic structure" of the Constitution because they exclude the jurisdiction of the High Courts and Supreme Court).
13. *I. C. Golaknath v. State of Punjab*, AIR 1967 SC 1643 (holding that fundamental rights were sacrosanct and could not be modified, restricted, or impaired by Parliament); *Kesavananda Bharati v. State of Kerala*, AIR 1973 SC 1461 (power of judicial review a "basic feature" of the Constitution).
14. *A. D. M. Jabalpore v. Shiv Kant Shukla*, AIR 1976 SC 1207 (upholding a presidential order prohibiting bringing a writ of habeas corpus during a state of internal emergency).
15. Commentators have noted that it was no coincidence that Justices P. N. Bhagwati and Y. V. Chandrachud, who initiated the PIL movement, were in the majority in *A. D. M. Jabalpore* (Sathe 2002). The PIL movement was led by activists and social scientists as opposed to lawyers (Baxi 1988).
16. *Bandhua Mukti Morcha v. Union of India*, AIR 1984 SC 803 (relaxing the rule of *locus standi* to address the rehabilitation of bonded laborers); *Hussainara Khatoon v. State of Bihar*, AIR 1979 SC 1360 (right to life includes the right to a speedy trial).
17. *Sunil Batra v. Delhi Administration*, AIR 1978 SC 1675 (considering a letter written by a prison inmate as a writ petition); *Hussainara Khatoon*, *supra* note 16; *PUDR v. Union of India*, AIR 1982 SC 1473 (permitting PIL by "public spirited citizens" on behalf of socially or economically disadvantaged groups who are unable to approach the Court, for which standing should be liberally considered).
18. See, e.g., *Maneka Gandhi v. Union of India*, AIR 1978 SC 597 (holding that articles 14, 19, and 21—on equality, liberty, and life, respectively—formed a composite code and declaring that a refusal to grant passport to a petitioner without pre-decisional hearing is subject to scrutiny on grounds of fairness, reasonableness, and nonarbitrariness); *Hussainara Khatoon*, *supra* note 16.
19. *Bandhua Mukti Morcha v. Union of India*, *supra* note 16.
20. *Olga Tellis and Others v. Bombay Municipal Council*, (1985) 2 Supp SCR 51 ("No one has the right to make use of a public property for a private purpose without requisite authorisation").
21. *Mohini Jain v. State of Karnataka*, AIR 1992 SC 1858 (the right to life includes the "facilities for reading, writing and expressing oneself"); *Unni Krishnan, J. P. and Others v. State of Andhra Pradesh and Others*, AIR 1993 SC 217 (right to education up to age of fourteen is an enforceable fundamental right).
22. *State of Kerala v. N. M. Thomas*, (1976) 2 SCC 310, para. 134 (considering the extended period for passing special tests for promotion of employees belonging to Scheduled Castes and Scheduled Tribes), considering *State of Madras v. Champakam Dorairajan*, 1951 SCR 525 ("The directive principles have to conform to and run subsidiary to the chapter

on fundamental rights"); *Kesavananda Bharati v. State of Kerala, supra* note 13 (defining the extent to which the government can restrict the right to property: "In building up a just social order it is sometimes imperative that the fundamental rights should be subordinated to directive principles").

23. *Francis Coralie Mullin v. Union Territory of Delhi*, (1981) 2 SCR 516 (rights of prisoners and conditions of detention).
24. *CESC Ltd. v. Subash Chandra Bose*, AIR 1992 SC 573, 585 ("Health is thus a state of complete physical, mental and social well being and not merely the absence of disease or infirmity").
25. *Parmanand Katara v. Union of India*, (1989) 4 SCC 286 (PIL seeking provision of emergency medical care for injury following newspaper report of doctors' refusal to treat injured motorist).
26. *Consumer Education and Research Centre v. Union of India*, (1995) 3 SCC 42 (issuing extensive occupational health and safety guidelines for asbestos workers).
27. *Paschim Banga Khet Mazdoor Samity v. State of West Bengal*, (1996) 4 SCC 37; AIR 1996 SC 2426 (extending the right to speedy medical assistance to workers).
28. *State of Punjab v. Mohinder Singh Chawla*, (1997) 2 SCC 83 (constitutional obligation to provide health facilities to government workers under article 21, when read with Directive Principles of State Policy articles 39[c], 41, and 43).
29. *P. T. Munichikkanna Reddy and Others v. Revamma and Others*, AIR 2007 SC 1753 (considering the right to property in a case of adverse possession).
30. United Nations Committee on Economic, Social and Cultural Rights, General Comment 14, U.N. Doc. E/C.12/2000/4 (2000).
31. *State of Punjab v. Mohinder Singh Chawla, supra* note 28.
32. *Mahendra Pratap Singh v. State of Orissa*, Orissa High Court, AIR 1997 Ori 37 (requiring government to provide a primary health center in village).
33. *Paschim Banga Khet Mazdoor Samity v. State of West Bengal, supra* note 27.
34. *Kapila Hingorani v. State of Bihar*, (2003) 6 SCC 1 (payment of salary arrears of public-sector employees ordered after reported starvation deaths due to such nonpayment on the basis of their right to life); *Paschim Banga Khet Mazdoor Samity v. State of West Bengal, supra* note 27, citing *Khatri (II) v. State of Bihar.*
35. *Vincent Pannikulangura v. Union of India*, (1987) 2 SCC 165 (ordering the regulation of the manufacture, sale, and distribution of thirty drugs alleged to be hazardous, some of which are already banned in other countries; state must also ensure that drug pricing is accessible); *Drug Action Forum v. Union of India*, (1997) 6 SCC 609 (directing a ban on the manufacture of fixed dose combinations of Analgin).
36. See, e.g., *Malay Ganguly v. Respondent: Medical Council of India and Others*, W. P. (C) No. 317 of 2000 (ordering the Medical Council of India to institute procedures for hearing medical complaints); *Jacob Mathew v. State of Punjab and Another*, (2005) 6 SCC 1 (guidelines for medical professionals regarding criminal negligence).
37. *State of Punjab v. Mohinder Singh Chawla, supra* note 28.
38. *Sheela Barse v. Union of India*, (1993) 4 SCC 204 (declaring placement of mentally/physically handicapped children in jails unconstitutional); *Rakesh Chandra Narayan v. Union of India*, 1991 Supp. (2) SCC 626, (1989) Supp. (1) SCC 644, 1994 Supp. (3) SCC 489 (remedying deplorable conditions in a mental hospital).

39. *CERC v. Union of India*, (1995) 3 SCC 42; *Kirloskar Brothers Ltd. v. Employees' State Insurance Corporation*, (1996) 2 SCC 682 (denial of employee benefits found to violate applicable statute); *State of Punjab v. Mohinder Singh Chawla*, *supra* note 28.
40. *State of Punjab v. Mohinder Singh Chawla*, *supra* note 28; *Kirloskar Brothers Ltd. v. Employees' State Insurance Corporation*, *supra* note 39 ("the right to health is a fundamental right of worker, and should be provided for both state and private employers").
41. Universal Declaration of Human Rights, G.A. Res. 217A (III), U.N. Doc A/810 at 71 (1948).
42. International Covenant on Economic, Social and Cultural Rights, *supra* note 11.
43. General Comment 14, *supra* note 30, paras. 11, 43.
44. *Kishen Pattnayak and Another v. State of Orissa*, AIR 1989 SC 677 (acknowledging the right to food as part of the right to life).
45. *People's Union for Civil Liberties (PUCL) v. Union of India and Others*, W. P. (C) No. 196 of 2001 (affirming the right to food under the right to life)
46. *Subhash Kumar v. State of Bihar*, AIR 1991 SC 420 (pollution of a river by the release of slurry/sludge by an industrial unit); *Rural Litigation and Entitlement Kendra, Dehradun and Others v. State of UP and others*, (1985) 2 SCC 431 (recognizing right to a clean environment when considering "issues relating to environment and ecological balance") (Muralidhar 2006).
47. E.g., *Dr. K. C. Malhotra v. State of MP and Others*, High Court of Madhya Pradesh, AIR 1994 MP 48 (nonperformance of municipal functions resulting in spread of water-borne diseases); *Prasanta Kumar Rout, Orissa Law Reviews v. Respondent: Government of Orissa, Represented by Secretary, Urban Development Department and Others*, Orissa High Court, 1994 II OLR 444 (municipality failing to drain excess water).
48. *Ahmedabad Municipal Corporation v. Nawab Khan Gulab Khan*, (1997) 11 SCC 123 (pavement dwellers avoiding removal by municipality; right to shelter includes all the infrastructure necessary to enable them to live and develop as human beings).
49. *Olga Tellis and Others v. Bombay Municipal Council*, *supra* note 20, dictum followed in *Municipal Corporation of Delhi v. Gurnam Kaur*, (1989) 1 SCC 101 and *Sodan Singh v. NDMC*, (1989) 4 SCC 155.
50. *Subhash Kumar v. State of Bihar*, AIR 1991 SC 420 (pollution-free water and air). See also *Virender Gaur v. State of Haryana*, (1995) 2 SCC 377 (municipal land earmarked for public use cannot be leased out to a private party); *Murli S. Deora v. Union of India*, (2001) 8 SCC 765 (ban on passive smoking in public places until statutory provisions implemented).
51. *Municipal Council, Ratnam v. Shri Vardichand*, 1980 Cri LJ 1075 (environmental health; public health a paramount principle of government).
52. *Malay Ganguly v. Respondent: Medical Council of India and Others*, *supra* note 36.
53. *People's Union for Civil Liberties (PUCL) v. Union of India and Others*, *supra* note 45.
54. *Novartis v. Union of India and Others*, Madras High Court, W. P. Nos. 24759 and 24760 of 2006 (upholding a provision of the Patent Act allowing pre-grant oppositions to patent applications in light of Parliament's objective to "provide easy access to the citizens of this country to life saving drugs and to discharge their Constitutional obligation of providing good health care to its citizens").
55. *Sahara House v. Union of India*, Delhi High Court, W. P. (C) No. 535 of 1998; *Sankalp Rehabilitation Trust v. Union of India*, Supreme Court, W. P. (C) No. 512 of 1999; *Voluntary Health Association of Punjab v. U. O. I.*, W.P. (C) No. 311/2003; *Common Cause v. Union of India*, W. P. (C) No. 61/2003 (seeking, inter alia, government provision of second-line antiretroviral drugs for HIV-positive persons).

56. This group was a petitioner in the case *Ramakant Rai and Health Watch UP and Bihar v. Union of India*, W. P. (C) No. 209 of 2003 (considering the need for improved sterilization services and negligence insurance).
57. For example, the India Network of Positive People (INP+) and Delhi Network of Positive People (DNP+) in *Sahara House v. Union of India, supra* note 55.
58. Sankalp Rehabilitation Trust in *Sankalp Rehabilitation Trust v. Union of India, supra* note 55.
59. *Novartis AG, Switzerland v. Cancer Patients Aid Association, India,* Order of Chennai Patent Controller, January 25, 2006 (challenging a patent application for the drug Glivec).
60. Eldred Tellis (director, Sankalp [organization providing front-line services for injecting drug users]), interview, Mumbai, August 2009; Y. K. Sapru (chair, Cancer Patients Aid Association), interview, Mumbai, August 2009; Pratibha Siva (legal officer, Lawyers Collective HIV/AIDS Unit), interview, New Delhi, July 2009.
61. The Center for Reproductive Rights provided research support to the petitioners in *Ramakant Rai and Health Watch UP and Bihar v. Union of India, supra* note 56; Médecins Sans Frontières provided advocacy support to petitioners in *Novartis AG, Switzerland v. Cancer Patients Aid Association, India.*
62. See *Suo Moto v. State of Rajasthan*, Rajasthan High Court, AIR 2005 Raj 82; *The Registrar, Aurangabad Bench of the Bombay High Court v. State of Maharashtra, Director of Health Service, Deputy Director of Health Service, Civil Surgeon, Government Hospital, et al.*, Bombay High Court, W. P. No. 403 of 2009 (taking *suo moto* cognizance of January 2009 news reports of a health survey by the Centre for Enquiry into Health and Allied Themes depicting the condition of district hospitals and rural health services in thirty-two districts of the state of Maharashtra).
63. Abhijit Das (director, Centre for Health and Social Justice), interview, New Delhi, January 2010.
64. Hari Shankar (peer educator, Delhi Network of Positive People), interview, New Delhi, January 2010.
65. Both the Supreme Court and the High Courts can designate certain advocates as senior advocates based on their seniority and competence.
66. This tool has been used extensively in environmental cases (Harish Salve [amicus curiae in Supreme Court case *T. N. Godavarman Thirumulpad v. Union of India*], interview, New Delhi, August 2009).
67. A writ of continuing mandamus is issued to a lower authority in the general public interest asking the officer or authority to perform its task expeditiously for an unstipulated period of time in order to prevent a miscarriage of justice. The writ of continuing mandamus was first introduced by the Court in *Vineet Narain v. Union of India*, AIR 1996 SC 3386.
68. *People's Union for Civil Liberties (PUCL) v. Union of India and Others, supra* note 45.
69. *Sahara House v. Union of India, supra* note 55; *Sankalp Rehabilitation Trust v. Union of India, supra* note 55.
70. *Sahara House v. Union of India, supra* note 55; *Sankalp Rehabilitation Trust v. Union of India,* order dated December 16, 2010. Shivangi Rai, an attorney for the petitioners, explained how the Supreme Court, during oral argument, rejected arguments made by the state-sponsored National Aids Control Organization that the potential costs of such a plan were prohibitive; the Court's rejection was based on the petitioner's arguments grounded in the right to health (personal communication, January 19, 2011).
71. *Paschim Banga Khet Mazdoor Samity v. State of West Bengal, supra* note 27.

72. *Municipal Council, Ratlam v. Vardhichand and Others*, 1980 Cri LJ 1075.
73. *Subhash Kumar v. State of Bihar*, AIR 1991 SC 420; *M. C. Mehta v. Union of India*, (1987) 4 SCC 463 (environmental pollution causes several health hazards and therefore violates the right to life).
74. *M. C. Mehta v. Union of India, supra* note 73.
75. *Suo Moto v. State of Rajasthan, supra* note 62 (ordering the relevant statutory body under the state government of Rajasthan to maintain sanitary conditions in the city of Jaipur).
76. *Mahendra Pratap Singh v. State of Orissa, supra* note 32.
77. *People's Union for Civil Liberties (PUCL) v. Union of India and Others, supra* note 45.
78. *Vincent Pannikulangura v. Union of India, supra* note 35. See Mashelkar Committee for Review of Drugs Regulatory System in India, Interim Report, 2003, http://cdsco.nic.in/html/Interim%20Report.htm (referring to Supreme Court decisions in this regard).
79. *Common Cause v. Union of India*, (1998) 2 SCC 367 (highlighting deficiencies in the system for collecting, storing, and supplying blood).
80. Following these actors' findings on the adverse health impacts of asbestos exposure, the Court ordered 100,000 rupees to be paid by the concerned factory or industry or establishment within a period of three months from the date of certification by the National Institute of Occupational Health (para. 32).
81. *Ramakant Rai and Health Watch UP and Bihar v. Union of India, supra* note 56; Das interview, *supra* note 63; Prasanna Hota (director, NIPI-UNOPS, and former health secretary, Ministry of Health and Family Welfare), interview, New Delhi, January 2010.
82. *Ramakant Rai and Health Watch UP and Bihar v. Union of India, supra* note 56.
83. *Salekh Chand Jain v. Union of India and Others*, Delhi High Court, 99 (2002) DLT 803; *Supreme Court Young Advocates Forum v. Union of India and Others*, Delhi High Court, 99 (2002) DLT 290.
84. *Drug Action Forum v. Union of India, supra* note 35. See Muralidhar (1997–98).
85. Interim Order, *Ramakant Rai v. Union of India*, W. P. (Civ.) No. 209 of 2003, March 1, 2005.
86. *People's Union for Civil Liberties (PUCL) v. Union of India and Others, supra* note 45 (PIL seeking implementation of government food distribution schemes).
87. *Rakesh Chandra Narayan v. State of Bihar*, 1989 SUPP 1 SCC 644 (extensive directions issued following consideration of the deplorable conditions in an institute for the mentally ill, including directive in 1997 to the National Human Rights Commission to monitor, supervise, and coordinate functioning).
88. Anand Grover (director, Lawyers Collective HIV/AIDS Unit), interview, New Delhi, August 2009; Justice S. Muralidhar (Delhi High Court), interview, New Delhi, August 2009 (affirming that medical negligence cases, particularly those brought under the consumer-protection regime, have benefited India's lower and middle classes).
89. *Novartis AG, Switzerland v. Cancer Patients Aid Association, India,* Order of Chennai Patent Controller, January 25, 2006.
90. *Ramakant Rai and Health Watch UP and Bihar v. Union of India, supra* note 56; interview with a senior health official of the Indian government, January 2010; Prasanna Hota, interview, New Delhi, January 2010. It is not clear, however, why parties did not seek removal of this direction from the Court.
91. *Common Cause v. Union of India, supra* note 79.
92. *Vincent Pannikulangura v. Union of India, supra* note 35; *Drug Action Forum v. Union of India, supra* note 35.

93. *Rakesh Chandra Narayan v. State of Bihar*, *supra* note 87.
94. *Malay Ganguly v. Respondent: Medical Council of India and Others*, *supra* note 36.
95. *Ramakant Rai and Health Watch UP and Bihar v. Union of India*, *supra* note 56.
96. Das interview, *supra* note 63.
97. *Supreme Court Young Advocates Forum v. Union of India and Others*, Delhi High Court, 99 (2002) DLT 290 (directing Apollo Hospital to reserve 33% of its beds and 40% of its outpatient services for free for the poor as enforcement of contract with public authorities). See also Thomas and Krishnan (2010).

Chapter 8

South Africa
Health Rights Litigation: Cautious Constitutionalism

Carole Cooper

This chapter finds that while litigation has played a significant role in promoting access to health services for poor and disadvantaged people in South Africa, the hopes and expectations regarding its ability to alleviate inequality and deprivation in the health arena have been unevenly met. The chapter begins by examining the various factors that enable litigation, and then moves on to provide an overview of some of the main health rights cases, highlighting the nature of claims and factors affecting litigation outcomes. Thereafter, it examines courts' approaches to these claims and the remedies provided. It concludes with a discussion of the extent to which judicial remedies have been implemented and the impact of litigation in terms of claimants' access to health.

Context of Health Rights Litigation

Health rights in South Africa may be contextualized within the country's political transition from a parliamentary sovereignty run by a white minority regime to a constitutional democracy based on majority representation. The new democratic government promised widespread social and economic reforms designed to address the deep systemic inequalities experienced by millions of people—a legacy of the iniquitous apartheid system (Terre-

---

I am greatly indebted to Siri Gloppen for her exceptional support during the writing of this chapter and for her helpful comments on and thorough edit of its contents. I am also indebted to Alicia Ely Yamin for her helpful comments and suggestions regarding the chapter's structure and to Brian Honnermann, formerly of the AIDS Law Project, for his generous assistance with information and statistics on HIV/AIDS.

blanche 2002; Seekings and Nattrass 2006). When it came to power, poverty-linked diseases were rife, and millions of people, especially in rural areas, lacked basic amenities necessary for health, such as running water, adequate nutrition, and access to clinics and hospitals. In addition, successive governments' failures to address the emerging HIV/AIDS epidemic have seriously undermined the country's health profile.

The level of inequality has placed enormous budgetary pressure on the government, forcing it to balance competing demands for improvements in health, education, social welfare, housing, and other areas. At the same time, efforts to be more competitive in the global economy have hampered social reform and exacerbated unemployment, thereby increasing levels of deprivation. Such deprivation has been further deepened by bureaucratic inefficiency and corruption, which have contributed to failures to transform budgetary allocations into tangible benefits for the poor. As a result, the poor have increasingly taken to the streets to protest against the nondelivery of services (Atkinson 2007; South African Institute of Race Relations 2010).[1]

The health system was—and is—marked by deep-seated inequalities between a well-resourced private health sector and an under-resourced and neglected public health sector (Coovadia et al. 2009). Private-sector health funding still significantly outstrips that of the public sector: in 2008, private health expenditure accounted for 5.2% of gross domestic product, while public health expenditure constituted just 3.7% (South African National Treasury 2009, 41). In line with its vision for a unified health system, the government has focused on developing an accessible and affordable primary public health-care system. Recent legislation aims to render health services more accessible and affordable, make medical insurance more equitable, and improve financial and administrative accountability.[2] Organizationally, health care has been rationalized (reducing health departments from fourteen to one national and nine provincial departments, among other changes) and divided between three levels of government,[3] and funding redistributed in favor of poorer provinces.[4]

While the government has made progress in addressing inequalities in the health sector—including the establishment of eighteen new public hospitals and over one thousand clinics—as of 2008, 10% of all clinics still lacked sanitation, electricity, and telecommunications; 20% lacked piped water; only 30% had weekly visits by a doctor; and only 40% had primary health-care nurses.[5] A significant fault line that has undermined the government's health reform is the HIV/AIDS epidemic, which was fueled by the Mbeki government's denial that HIV causes AIDS and its opposition to providing antiretroviral (ARV) medicines to treat it. With an estimated 5.6 million people living with HIV, the epidemic has placed enormous pressure on an already overburdened health-care system.[6]

Within this context, promises for a better future for South Africa's poor and marginalized are grounded in the transformative 1996 Constitution.[7] Its Bill of Rights accords not only civil and political rights but also socioeconomic rights, including health and water rights.[8] The Constitutional Court has emphasized both the justiciability of socioeconomic rights and their importance in a context where

> millions of people are living in deplorable conditions and in great poverty. There is a high level of unemployment, inadequate social security, and many do not have access to clean water or adequate health services. These conditions already existed when the Constitution was adopted and a commitment to address them and to transform our society into one in which there will be human dignity, freedom and equality, lie at the heart of our new constitutional order.[9]

Such statements by the Constitutional Court, the senior court in constitutional matters,[10] raised expectations of litigation as an avenue for social transformation generally and with regard to the right to health specifically.

Health Rights Claims

Health rights litigation in South Africa is facilitated by a range of constitutionally protected rights. Section 27(1) of the Constitution provides a general right to have access to health-care services, including reproductive health care, as well as access to sufficient food and water. These rights are qualified by subsection 2, which states that "the state must take reasonable legislative and other measures, within its available resources, to achieve the progressive realisation of each of these rights." Subsection 3 states that "no one may be refused emergency medical treatment." Other relevant rights (not dependent on the qualifier "access to" and not subject to the resource qualification) are the right to an environment not harmful to health or well-being (sec. 24[a]); prisoners' right to adequate medical treatment (sec. 35[2][e]);[11] and children's right to basic medical services (sec. 28[1][c]). Access to basic sanitation services, conducive to good health, has been interpreted as part of the right of access to adequate housing (secs. 26[1] and [2]).[12]

The health rights are supported, inter alia, by the rights to equality, dignity, life, bodily integrity, and access to information held by the state.[13] Section 7 of the Constitution obliges the state to respect, protect, promote, and fulfill the rights contained in the Bill of Rights. The duty to respect places an obligation on the state to refrain from actions that impair people's enjoyment of their fundamental rights, while the duty to protect enjoins the state to prevent the infringement of these rights by private actors. The duty to promote and fulfill the rights requires the state to take positive legislative and other measures to enable rights holders to access these rights (Liebenberg 1998, 41:25). The Constitution also requires that public administration be governed by democratic values and principles, including responsiveness to people's needs, accountability, and the fostering of transparency (sec. 195). Furthermore, all constitutional obligations must be performed diligently and without delay (sec. 237). The state must encourage the public to participate in policy making, giving effect to a deliberative form of democracy (sec. 195). In sum, this provides a broad basis for constitutional litigation on health. To pursue the rights in practice is, however, more problematic.

Of the nineteen health rights cases reviewed for this chapter (see table 8.1), most were brought by public interest bodies; only three were brought by individuals. The preponderance of public interest cases is a function of both positive and negative aspects of the judicial system. On the negative side, firstly, the high cost of litigation in general and the technical knowledge required to file a claim effectively hamper individuals' access to the courts.[14] In addition, while in criminal cases poor people are afforded the right to a legal practitioner at the state's expense, public legal assistance is virtually nonexistent in civil cases.[15] Furthermore, direct access to the Constitutional Court exists in theory but not in practice. The Constitution allows a person to bring a matter directly to the Court when the matter is in the interests of justice and with leave of the Court (sec. 167[6]), but the Court, reluctant to act as a court of both first and last resort, has required applicants first to exhaust all other remedies or procedures. With the expansive constitutional jurisdiction of the High Court, most constitutional cases reach the Constitutional Court only on appeal (Chaskalson et al. 2007) and only the "most persistent and well supported litigants are able to access the court" (Dugard and Roux 2006, 112–13).

On a more positive note, the Constitutional Court has adopted a rule shielding unsuccessful litigants in constitutional litigation from having to pay costs, since a costs award might have a chilling effect on litigants wishing to vindicate their constitutional rights (Chaskalson et al. 2007; Friedman 2007). This, however, presupposes that applicants are able to bring a claim in the first place.

A generous standing provision has facilitated public interest litigation on health and other rights. In the words of the first president of the Constitutional Court, Arthur Chaskalson,

> we should rather adopt a broad approach to standing. This would be consistent with the mandate given to this court to uphold the Constitution and would serve to ensure that constitutional rights enjoy the full measure of the protection to which they are entitled.[16]

In addition, a new amicus curiae provision allows a nonparty to request permission to intervene in litigation to advance its own argument, with entry depending, inter alia, on whether the argument will be of use to the Court.[17] Public interest litigators have actively used this provision, sometimes with great effect, as illustrated below.

Public interest litigation may thus provide an avenue for poor and disadvantaged groups to vindicate their rights—but it is a narrow avenue. Organizations conducting such litigation generally rely on limited donor funding and on the services of pro bono lawyers or lawyers operating on a contingency basis, which means that cases are relatively few in number. In practice, it also means that such organizations decide which cases deserve to be heard. The expense and difficulty in accessing the justice system is probably a main reason why South Africa, unlike the Latin American countries analyzed in this volume, has not seen a wave of cases by individuals claiming access to treatment.[18]

In line with the overall theme of this book, South Africa's health rights cases may be divided into three categories: (i) challenges to health policies and laws that are seen to block or undermine access to health rights (policy gaps); (ii) challenges to practices that are inimical to the health needs of poor and vulnerable groups (regulatory gaps); and (iii) challenges to the government's failure to enforce its own laws and policies, thus undermining health rights (implementation gaps). Table 8.1 gives an overview of the cases. The following

Table 8.1. Health rights litigation in South Africa, 1996–2010

Policy-gap cases					
Short case name	Full case reference	What the claim sought	Legal basis for claim	Ruling and remedies	Implementation status
Van Biljoen (1997)	*Van Biljoen v. Minister of Correctional Services*, 1997 (4) SA 441 (C)	Provision of ARVs to four prisoners (two of whom had already been prescribed treatment)	Constitutional right of detained persons to provision of adequate medical treatment at state's expense (sec. 35[2][e])	Ordered state to provide ARV treatment to the two for whom treatment had already been prescribed; as prisoners are more exposed to opportunistic infections, "adequate medical treatment" is not defined by availability in public health system; state unable to prove that treatment was unaffordable	Implemented
Soobramoney (1998)	*Soobramoney v. Minister of Health, KwaZulu-Natal*, 1998 (1) SA 765 (CC)	Provision of medical treatment (i.e., dialysis); refusal in terms of provincial policy contested as infringing health rights	Constitutional rights to emergency medical treatment (sec. 27[3]) and life (sec. 11)	Decided in terms of constitutional right to health-care services (sec. 27[1][a]); found policy rational and fair, given resource constraints; granting claim could undermine general provision of health services; public interest trumps individual need	Case dismissed
Grootboom (2001)	*Government of the Republic of South Africa and Others v. Grootboom and Others*, 2001 (1) SA 46 (CC)	Protection of children's right to basic medical services (in part)	Among other rights, constitutional right of children to basic medical services (sec. 28[1][c])	Held that provision of basic health services for children fell to parents in first instance, not the state	Aspect regarding children's right to health dismissed

Table 8.1 (continued)

Short case name	Full case reference	What the claim sought	Legal basis	Ruling and remedies	Implementation status
TAC–PMTCT (2002)	*Minister of Health and Others v. Treatment Action Campaign and Obers*, (No. 2) 2002 (5) SA 721 (CC)	State contested High Court decision on rollout of program (nevirapine treatment) to prevent mother-to-child-transmission of HIV	TAC relied on constitutional rights of access to health-care services (sec. 27[1]), life (sec. 11), dignity (sec. 10), and basic medical services for children (sec. 28[1][c])	Ordered state to remove restrictions on provision of nevirapine and permit and facilitate its use where appropriate, including training and counseling; held state responsible for children's health-care needs where parents are unable to provide care, as with poor HIV-positive women reliant on public health services	Accurate statistics unavailable but widespread rollout assumed
Westville (2006)	*N and Others v. Government of Republic of South Africa and Others*, (No. 1) 2006 (6) SA 543 (D); (No. 2) 2006 (6) SA 568 (D); (No. 3) 2006 (6) 575 (D)	Provision of ARVs to prisoners living with HIV/AIDS	Constitutional rights of access to health-care services (sec. 27[1][a]) and adequate medical services for prisoners (sec. 35[2][e]); relevant legislation	Ordered state to provide ARVs to relevant prisoners at facility in terms of supervisory order	Failure to comply led to further litigation and subsequent state compliance; remedy facilitated development of plan for nationwide ARV provision in prisons
Mazibuko (2009)	*Mazibuko and Others v. City of Johannesburg and Others*, 2009 ZACC 28	Declaration of city's free basic water policy as unconstitutional: amount supplied too low; prepayment water meters unlawful	Constitutional rights to water (sec. 27[1]), equality (sec. 9); National water standard regulations (sec. 3[b]); Water Services Act 108 of 1997 (secs. 4[3], 11); Johannesburg City bylaws (secs. 9C, 11); Promotion of Administrative Justice Act No 3 of 2000	Dismissed claim; overturned judgments by lower courts	Case dismissed, but the city partially amended its water policy during litigation

Table 8.1 (continued)

Regulatory-gap cases					
Short case name	Full case reference	What the claim sought	Legal basis	Ruling and remedies	Implementation status
PMA (2001)	*Pharmaceutical Manufacturers Assoc. of SA (PMA) v. President of the RSA* (TAC as amicus curiae), Case No. 4183/98 (TPD)	PMA's claim: order interdicting promulgation of Medicines and Related Substances Control Amendment Act 90 of 1997 designed to increase access to medicines Amicus's argument: in favor of legislation enabling access to cheaper HIV/AIDS drugs	PMA: constitutional right to property and economic rights (secs. 22 and 25) Amicus: constitutional rights to life (sec. 11), dignity (sec. 10), and access to health-care services (sec. 27[1][a])	Case withdrawn in April 2001	State able to promulgate amending legislation giving effect to 1996 National Drug Policy enabling access to cheaper medicines
Hazel Tau (2003)	*Hazel Tau and Others v. GlaxoSmithKline and Others*, Case No. 2002Sep226 (Competition Commission)	Lowering of ARV prices on the grounds that existing prices led to premature, predictable, and avoidable deaths	Competition Act 89 of 1998 (secs. 49B[2][b] and 8[a])	Complaint withdrawn when companies acceded to demand in December 2003	Market opened to generic ARV medicines, reducing prices in public and private sectors
Affordable Medicines (2005)	*Affordable Medicines Trust v. Minister of Health*, 2005 (6) BCLR 529 (CC)	Inter alia, declaration that regulations regarding licensing requirements for doctors and nurses to prescribe medicines were ultra vires Medicines and Related Substances Control Act 101 of 1965 as amended	Constitutional rights to choose profession (sec. 22), freedom of movement (sec. 21), and dignity (sec. 10); Medicines and Related Substances Control Act (sec. 22[C][1][a]); Regulation 18 in terms of Act	Dismissed most claims; struck down regulation hampering health-care providers' ability to dispense medicines	Greater access to medicines established by facilitating dispensation by doctors and nurses

Table 8.1 (continued)

Short case name	Full case reference	What the claim sought	Legal basis	Ruling and remedies	Implementation status
New Clicks (2005)	*Minister of Health and Another v. New Clicks South Africa (Pty) Ltd and Others (TAC and Another Amici Curiae)*, 2006 (2) SA 311 (CC)	New Clicks sought declaration of certain regulations as ultra vires main Act, including state-prescribed single exit price for medicines designed to cut costs for consumers	Regulations in terms of Medicines and Related Substances Control Act	Ruled that Medicines and Related Substances Control Act seeks to give effect to sec. 27(1) of Constitution; held that single exit price could adversely affect viability of pharmacies, thereby impairing access to medicines; ordered state to reconsider exit price	Protracted dispute over appropriate exit price
Goliath (2008)	*Minister of Health of the Province of the Western Cape v. Cedric Goliath and Others*, Case No. 13741/07 (CPD)	State's claim: permission for mandatory isolation in health facility of patients suffering from drug-resistant tuberculosis Counter claim: declaration of detention as inconsistent with right to freedom	State: National Health Act 61 of 2003 (secs. 7 and 25[2][w]); constitutional provision for action in the public interest (sec. 38) Counter claim: constitutional right to freedom and security of the person (sec. 12)	Permitted state to isolate respondents in terms of sec. 7 of Health Act; noted lack of regulatory guidelines; dismissed counter claim	Implemented
TAC–Merck (2008)	*TAC v. MSD (Pty) Ltd and Merck & Co. Inc. and Related Companies*, Case No. 2007Nov3328 (Competition Commission)	Finding that companies abused their dominant position (sec. 8[c] of Competition Act) in the market for the ARV efavirenz by refusing to license other firms to import and/or manufacture generic versions of the medicine on reasonable and nondiscriminatory terms	Competition Act (sec. 8[c]); constitutional right of access to health-care services (sec. 27[1]); binding international law via various human rights treaties	Complaint withdrawn when companies acceded to demands	Implemented

Table 8.1 *(continued)*

Implementation-gap cases					
Short case name	Full case reference	What the claim sought	Legal basis	Ruling and remedies	Implementation status
Woodcarb (1996)	*Minister of Health and Welfare v. Woodcarb (Pty) Ltd and Another*, 1996 (3) SA 155 (N)	Order prohibiting respondent from continuing with polluting activities without a certificate of registration	Atmospheric Pollution Prevention Act 45 of 1965; constitutional right to environment not harmful to health and well-being (sec. 24[a])	Granted interdict prohibiting respondents from continuing with activities	Implemented
Du Plooy (2004)	*Du Plooy v. Minister of Correctional Services and Another*, 2004 JDR 0521 (T)	Release on parole of prisoner with terminal illness	Constitutional rights to dignity (sec. 10), access to health-care services (sec. 27[1][a]), medical treatment for prisoners (sec. 35[2][e]), access to information (sec. 32[1][a]), and just administrative action (sec. 33); Promotion of Administrative Justice Act	Ordered release on parole of terminally ill prisoner	Implemented
Interim Procurement (2004)	Case not filed	Mandamus requiring state to implement legislation temporarily to bypass lengthy procurement procedures and thus expedite access to cheaper ARVs	Medicines and Related Substances Control Act	Case withdrawn when state implemented expedited process	Cheaper ARVs in some provinces one year prior to implementation of final tender

Table 8.1 (continued)

Short case name	Full case reference	What the claim sought	Legal basis	Ruling and remedies	Implementation status
Hichange (2004)	*Hichange Investments (Pty) Ltd v. Cape Produce Co (Pty) Ltd t/a Pelts Products and Others*, 2004 (2) SA 393 (E)	Mandamus requiring investigation, evaluation, and assessment of pollution impact; directive that state take steps in light of findings	National Environmental Management Act 107 of 1998 (NEMA); Atmospheric Pollution Prevention Act (APPA) giving effect to right to environment not harmful to health or well-being	Ordered state to direct respondent to undertake investigations regarding its polluting activities and ensure compliance with APPA and NEMA	Compliance presumed
TAC–Rath (2008)	*TAC and Another v. Rath and Others*, 2007 (4) SA 563 (C)	Order interdicting provision of vitamins and false advertising regarding treatment for HIV/AIDS; prohibiting unauthorized clinical trials; requiring state to adopt reasonable measures to investigate and prevent above actions, including supervisory order reporting on measures taken	Medicines and Related Substances Control Act	Interdicted respondents from undertaking unlawful clinical trials and publishing advertisements pending submission to Medicines Control Council; ordered state to investigate the above and take action in light of investigations	Rath left country after case

Table 8.1 (continued)

TAC–MM (2009)	*Treatment Action Campaign v. Minister of Correctional Services*, (2009) JDR 0043 (T)	Order requiring state to provide copy of the Judicial Inspectorate of Prisons' report on death of prisoner with HIV/AIDS	Promotion of Access to Information Act 2 of 2000 (secs. 78 and 82); constitutional right to access information held by state (sec. 32)	Deemed state's action "reprehensible" and showing "complete disregard" for Constitution and Act; ordered state to provide report to TAC	Implemented
Nokotyana (2009)	*Nokotyana and Others v. Ekurhurleni Metropolitan Municipality and Others*, [2009] ZACC 33	Inter alia, the provision of chemical toilets for every one or two households in the informal settlement while awaiting decision (long delayed) by province on future status of settlement	Among other rights, constitutional right to housing (secs. 26[1] and [2]); National Housing Code (chs. 12 and 13)	Declined to consider reasonableness of local government policy as applicants' claim had changed fundamentally on appeal; considered it inappropriate to order local government to accept assistance offered by provincial and national governments; not just and equitable to provide relief to applicants where thousands of others were in similarly unsatisfactory circumstances; ordered province to make final decision on application to upgrade status of the settlement within fourteen months of date of order	Claim for toilets to be provided immediately dismissed

sections examine key cases particularly illustrative of each category and analyze the reasons behind the litigation, the nature of litigants' demands, and the factors supporting or undermining litigants' claims.[19]

Policy-Gap Claims

Soobramoney

The first challenge to government policies on the right to access health services decided by the Constitutional Court was brought by Mr. Soobramoney, an unemployed man suffering from kidney disease. Relying on the rights to emergency medical treatment (sec. 27[3]) and life (sec. 11), he unsuccessfully challenged the refusal by the KwaZulu-Natal Department of Health to make dialysis available to him.[20] The department's refusal was based on its policy of prioritization in situations where demands for dialysis far exceeded resources. The Court considered Soobramoney's claim not in terms of the section 27(3) right to emergency medical treatment, on which he relied, but in terms of the right of access to health services (sec. 27[1]) instead, as the applicant's condition of chronic renal failure was an "ongoing state of affairs," and not an emergency arising from a "sudden catastrophe" requiring immediate medical attention to avert harm.[21] In dismissing the claim, the Court stated that in situations of limited resources, access to a right does not mean that it must be granted immediately, providing that policies and criteria for setting priorities are fair and rational.[22] The case raised a number of themes that would be developed by the Court in future health rights cases, including the issue of the immediacy of demands and the question of available resources, with the Court indicating that the needs of the poor majority would trump individual claims for expensive treatment. This signal may have had a chilling effect on the lodging of such claims, thus exacerbating the problems relating to individuals' access to the justice system mentioned above.

TAC–PMTCT

The Mbeki government's AIDS denialism has featured significantly in South African health rights litigation. The state's blocking of access to ARVs was first contested in a case regarding the prevention of mother-to-child transmission (PMTCT) of HIV. The situation demanded urgent attention, as statistics revealed that HIV prevalence among pregnant women attending public-sector antenatal clinics was growing rapidly. The incidence increased from 7.6% in 1994 to 30.2% in 2005,[23] and it was estimated that the nonavailability of ARVs for mothers and their newborn infants was causing approximately 35,000 babies a year to be infected with HIV. Absent medical intervention, about one-fifth to one-third of children born to mothers living with HIV would contract the virus (Kapczynski and Berger 2009, 47 [citing Coutsoudis et al. 2001]). International trials in 1998 had indicated the feasibility of applying short-course AZT therapy for PMTCT, with further Ugandan and South African trials proving the efficacy of nevirapine. It was estimated that one dose of nevirapine given to the mother during labor and one dose given to the child directly after birth could reduce transmission by up to 50% (Kapczynski and Berger 2009, 50, 55, 57).

In the face of government's refusal to make ARVs available for PMTCT,[24] the Treatment Action Campaign (TAC), a social movement, initiated a campaign to pressure the government to do so. TAC is comprised overwhelmingly of people living with HIV/AIDS and deploys a combination of strategies, including litigation, treatment literacy, mobilization, and advocacy, to enforce the right of access to treatment. Through educating vulnerable people about HIV, the benefits of treatment, and their rights, it has sought to create a basis for both self-help and social mobilization (Heywood 2009, 18). The philosophy that people in direct need of health care would "mobilise around tangible needs" informed the PMTCT campaign, which "caught the attention of young women with HIV and . . . began to galvanise a social movement that was made up of people who were poor, black and living with HIV" (Heywood 2009, 20). Continued government obduracy led TAC to believe that litigation was necessary to force the government's hand. However, it decided initially to postpone filing a claim until nevirapine had been registered for PMTCT, in order to provide a solid legal basis for the case.[25] In 2000, the government, no doubt influenced by the threatened litigation, introduced a pilot program for comprehensive nevirapine-based PMTCT at two research sites per province. It declared that if the program proved to be feasible after two years, nevirapine would be made more widely available. By April 2001, nevirapine had been registered, and given the government's inadequate response, TAC believed that morally and politically it had no alternative but to embark on litigation (Heywood 2003). Throughout the case, political mobilization and advocacy supported the litigation, with the litigation itself feeding back into strengthening those strategies.

The claim, filed against the national health department and the nine provinces in August 2001, asked the High Court to declare the government's policy unconstitutional, require that the government make nevirapine available in the public health sector to HIV-positive pregnant women and their babies, and order the government to plan and implement an effective PMTCT program. Further, it asked that the government be ordered to meet these demands within clear timeframes and subject to further scrutiny by the Court (Heywood 2003). The applicants argued that restrictions on the availability of ARVs for PMTCT in the public health sector and the failure to implement an effective countrywide PMTCT plan infringed the right to access medical services, children's right to basic health services, and the rights to life and dignity.[26] They also relied on section 195 of the Constitution, which requires the state to be governed by the principles of responsiveness to people's needs and participative policy making, to argue that the government's conduct was a breach of international obligations to which South Africa had committed itself.[27] In turn, the government argued that nevirapine would lead to widespread ARV resistance, that it was unsafe due to toxic side effects, that breastfeeding would undermine any beneficial effects, and that the health system lacked the capacity to supply the treatment.[28]

The case's dynamics were influenced by a split between some provinces, as well as between provinces and national government.[29] Evidence demonstrated a latent capacity to support a PMTCT program in eight out of nine of the provinces. Moreover, the support of experienced constitutional lawyers helped turn the case in TAC's favor (Heywood 2003). The High Court found for the applicants, declaring that a "countrywide [P]MTCT programme is an ineluctable obligation of the state."[30] The government took the case on appeal to the Constitutional Court, which found for TAC.[31] This was an important victory for TAC, demonstrating that litigation could contribute to developing policies in areas stifled by political blockages.

Westville

Prisoners are a vulnerable group with high HIV prevalence. Most are young, unemployed black men from marginalized communities, with limited access to health, education, and other sources of social welfare. Their frequent movement into and out of prison means that unless the illness is properly treated, it could severely affect prisoners and their communities (Goyer et al. 2004).[32] In April 2006, fifteen prisoners and TAC lodged a claim against the Department of Health and the Department of Correctional Services, seeking the provision of ARVs to prisoners at the Westville Correctional Centre, where over one hundred inmates had died of AIDS-related illnesses since the beginning of 2005.[33] Despite the government's 2003 operational plan for the universal provision of ARVs (implemented in May 2005), Westville prisoners were not receiving the medication. In December 2005, the Department of Correctional Services agreed to submit a progress report to the AIDS Law Project concerning the provision of ARVs at Westville. When it failed to do so, a decision was taken to litigate.

Relying on sections 27 and 35(2)(e) of the Constitution, the litigants asked the High Court to order the government to lift restrictions and provide ARVs to the fifteen prisoner claimants, as well as to all similarly situated Westville prisoners, in accordance with the government's operational plan and treatment guidelines.[34] Experts indicated that unless the applicants, whose CD4 counts were below 200 cells per milliliter, were treated immediately, they were likely to suffer irreparable harm and premature death.[35] The Court found for the applicants, noting that it was only after the launch of legal proceedings that the government had taken any action, and even then its action was inadequate.[36] It ordered the government to lift restrictions on the provision of ARVs and to draw up a feasible plan for providing ARVs to prisoners at the facility.[37]

Mazibuko

Water is a scarce resource in South Africa, especially for the poor. One-tenth of Johannesburg's 3.2 million people lack access to clean tap water within two hundred meters of their home, and one-fifth lack access to basic sanitary services.[38] In the *Mazibuko* case, poor residents in the Phiri township in Soweto challenged the city's policy on water rights. The applicants sought orders declaring that the policy, which granted 6 kiloliters of free water each month to every account holder, violated the right to sufficient water under the Constitution (sec. 27[1][b]) and the Water Services Act, and that the installation of prepayment water meters in the township was unlawful.[39] The city had introduced such meters in 2004 to reduce unaccounted-for water usage, rehabilitate the water network, reduce water consumption, and improve the rate of payment.[40] The claimants demanded that the city provide them with 50 liters of free water per person per day, with the choice of a credit meter. Phiri residents were required to choose between a yard tap with a restricted flow and a prepayment water meter; they were not given the option of a credit meter, the main form of water metering for residents in the rest of the city of Johannesburg.[41]

The Anti-Privatisation Forum, a social movement comprising community-based organizations and activists seeking to halt the commodification of basic needs, supported citizens' resistance to the introduction of prepayment water meters. Unlike TAC, which has always used litigation as a strategy, the Forum was wary of litigation, seeing law and rights "as legitimising privilege" (Dugard 2010, 1). Instead, its preferred strategies included mass action, community meetings, alliance building, and submission of memoranda to government (Dugard 2010). Resistance to the meters was expressed through mass marches to offices of the city and the service provider, Johannesburg Water. Physical attempts to prevent the digging of trenches resulted in an interdict banning such activities in August 2003. The Forum regrouped and formed the Coalition against Water Privatisation, but the interdict and arrests of protesting residents and activists undermined the campaign, and the first prepayment water meters were installed in February 2004.[42]

Thereafter, the Forum/Coalition decided to incorporate litigation into the campaign, with the concurrence of Phiri residents. This was a tactical decision made with the caveat that litigation should not replace or hamper other activities. Legal and logistical assistance from nongovernmental organizations[43] and counsel operating on a contingency basis provided the necessary support for the case. Litigation-related decisions were made in consultation with the community, giving people a sense of ownership of the case and enhancing political mobilization. The litigation re-energized the campaign, providing a focal point for political discussions and strategizing.[44]

The High Court[45] found the forced installation of prepayment water meters—which provided no choice of other kinds of water meters for residents—unconstitutional. It ordered the city to give Phiri residents the option of a credit meter and to provide them with a free basic water supply of 50 liters per person per day.[46] On appeal, the Supreme Court of Appeal,[47] inter alia, set the amount of constitutionally guaranteed "sufficient water" (sec. 27[1]) at 42 liters per person per day, which it ordered the city to provide to those unable to pay (when reasonable and with regard to available resources). It declared that the prepayment water meters installed in the township were unlawful and gave the city two years to legalize their use.[48] The Constitutional Court overturned the judgment on appeal, finding the city's free basic water policy (as developed during the course of litigation) reasonable and the installation of prepayment water meters lawful.[49]

These policy-gap cases—*Soobramoney*, *TAC–PMTCT*, *Westville*, and *Mazibuko*—highlight the shifts in government policy that may occur during the litigation process itself (e.g., the introduction of pilot sites for PMTCT and additional water supplies for the indigent). In addition, they demonstrate how findings on policy matters in successful cases may positively influence policy findings in future cases (*TAC–PMTCT* influencing *Westville*). They further highlight how skillful legal and mobilization strategies may together exploit latent policy differences within the state, favorably influencing a case's outcome (*TAC–PMTCT*). Lastly, they point to differing degrees of judicial intervention in determining policy development, depending on the particular circumstances of a case (*Soobramoney* and *Mazibuko* on the one hand and *TAC–PMTCT* and *Westville* on the other).

Regulatory-Gap Claims

Given that private actors (e.g., multinational pharmaceutical manufacturers) control essential health goods and services, governmental regulation of their activities is central to realizing the right to health.

PMA

Regulations on the cost and availability of medicines are important for achieving justice in health care. Under apartheid, the lack of appropriate regulations led to very high drug prices in the private sector (Heywood 2001). In 1997, the new government attempted to remedy this when it amended the Medicines Act[50] to allow, among other things, for parallel importation (sec. 15E) and the generic substitution of medicines (sec. 22F). Seeing this as a threat to their monopolies, in 2001, the Pharmaceutical Manufacturers Association (PMA) and about forty pharmaceutical companies sought an interdict to stop the amendments, basing their challenge on the constitutional rights to property (sec. 25); the freedom to choose and practice one's trade, occupation, or profession (sec. 22); and equality before the law (sec. 9[1]). TAC applied to intervene as amicus curiae under the legal provisions allowing nonparties to present their own arguments.[51] Viewing the case as a threat to the accessibility of ARVs in the public and private health sectors, TAC argued that the right of access to health trumps rights to private property and that the contested clauses were necessitated by the government's duty to realize the health right and to protect the rights to life, dignity, and equality, as well as the best interests of the child (Heywood 2001). To complement its legal efforts, the organization adopted a multifaceted campaign that included local and international mobilization and advocacy. When the case began, demonstrations were held in thirty countries, and, by then, over two hundred fifty organizations worldwide had signed a petition opposing the pharmaceutical companies' claim. Resolutions by the European Union and the Dutch government called for the case to be dropped (Heywood 2001). As a result of the pressure and TAC's legal arguments, including extensive supporting affidavits, the PMA withdrew its claim, apparently in exchange for an agreement that government would adhere to its duties under international trade law.[52]

This case was important in several respects. It gave public exposure to the argument that medicines should be treated differently from other commodities in terms of patent law; it led to a reduction in the price of ARV medicines in the private sector; it demonstrated that a social movement could successfully take on powerful multinational pharmaceutical companies and win, thus laying the ground for future legal attacks on the monopolistic practices of such companies (Heywood 2001); and it highlighted the role that an amicus curiae can play in vindicating health rights.[53]

Hazel Tau

After the PMA case, TAC engaged in a number of legal initiatives that sought to force multinational drug companies to permit the generic manufacture of their drugs and/or drop the price of ARVs (Berger 2008). Of these cases, the principal one is *Hazel Tau.* People living with HIV/AIDS, health workers, and several organizations (including TAC, the Aids Consortium, a trade union federation, and a trade union) brought a challenge against pharmaceutical companies GlaxoSmithKline and Boehringer Ingelheim to force them to lower the cost and address the lack of availability of ARVs.

The case was argued under the excessive pricing provision (sec. 8) of the Competition Act rather than under the Constitution, as the latter would have required legal arguments for the horizontal application of the relevant rights.[54] The claimants relied implicitly on the right to life, arguing that the high cost of ARVs was directly responsible for the premature, predictable, and avoidable deaths of people living with HIV/AIDS.[55] Medical experts testified to the need for access to a combination of drug choices within and between drug classes to treat HIV/AIDS effectively. Economic evidence demonstrated the high cost of drugs in South Africa compared to generic alternatives elsewhere.[56] In December 2003, the companies settled, agreeing to license certain companies to manufacture and import generic AZT, lamivudine, and nevirapine, subject to a maximum 5% royalty (Heywood 2009; Treatment Action Campaign and AIDS Law Project 2003).

This was an important victory. Apart from its implications for access to ARVs in the public health sector, *Hazel Tau* was the first case to bring affordable generic ARVs to the private-sector market (AIDS Law Project 2006). It acted as a catalyst for TAC to take further legal action under the Competition Act against a number of other drug companies, resulting in out-of-court settlements that effectively reduced drug prices and increased the availability of generic ARVs.[57]

PMA and *Hazel Tau*, two cases concerning the activities of corporations and the regulation of private actors, demonstrate how "the shadow of litigation" may enhance litigants' bargaining power and how a successful outcome may hinge more on a skillful use of this leverage than on actual judicial decisions.

Implementation-Gap Claims

The third and last category of health rights cases in South Africa discussed here addresses governmental failures to implement laws and policies already in place. Such failures can stem from insufficient resources, inertia, or political expediency. Political factors relating to AIDS denialism were prominent in both *TAC–Rath* and *TAC–MM*. In the first case, the state allowed an AIDS denialist to conduct unauthorized clinical trials and make false statements that his product could cure AIDS. The High Court, inter alia, interdicted and ordered the government to prevent the clinical trials and the publication of the misleading advertisements. In *TAC–MM,* the state refused access to a report on the death of an HIV-positive prisoner, in contravention of the Promotion of Access to Information Act (No. 2 of 2000) and the constitutionally protected right to information. The Court ordered the government to make the report available.

In the *Interim Procurement* case, a combination of inertia and political motives was responsible for the government's failure to apply an interim process in awarding the tender for ARVs, which would have allowed it to procure cheaper medicines while finalizing its operational plan. It was only when TAC threatened legal action that the state complied. This led to drastic price reductions in generic medicines prior to the implementation of the plan, which meant that more patients could be treated and many lives saved. In another case based on state inertia, *Woodcarb*, the High Court ordered the government to fulfill its obligation to prevent pollution by a tanning factory that was damaging the health and well-being of nearby residents.

The *Interim Procurement* case shows again that, if skillfully used, leverage provided by the litigation process may be sufficient for resolving the case even before it is adjudicated. Once in court, implementation-gap cases pose fewer challenges for the court than policy-gap cases and have been regularly decided against the state.

Overall, the analysis of South Africa's health rights cases shows that despite extensive constitutional rights, as well as liberal standing and amicus curiae provisions, few individuals are able to get their cases heard because the threshold for effective constitutional health rights litigation is high. Although these provisions enable public interest litigators to assist claimants who otherwise would not have been able to vindicate their health rights—and test cases won in court have potentially far-reaching consequences—litigation requires extensive resources. In this context, the effective use of a sound legal strategy (including incontrovertible scientific, medical, economic, and other relevant evidence), social mobilization by potential beneficiaries, and the garnering of local and international support were critical in leading to positive outcomes not only in judgments but also prior to the litigation process. These outcomes, in turn, provided leverage for further legal pressure, with positive results.[58]

Adjudication of Health Rights

The quotation from the Constitutional Court cited earlier in this chapter establishes a vision of South Africa as a transformative constitutional democracy, with a forward-looking Constitution aiming to ensure that all South Africans have access to a just and equitable society consonant with a dignified human existence. The Court envisages a system in which "continuous respect is given to the rights of all to be heard and have their views considered," which is "calculated to produce better outcomes through subjecting laws and governmental action to the test of critical debate," and in which, through litigation, the government is held accountable for its policies and legislation.[59] In this vision, the adjudication of socioeconomic rights, rather than being counter-majoritarian or antagonistic to democracy, may deepen democracy. To achieve this end, however, courts need "actively to interpret socio-economic rights" rather than merely to passively accept that such rights can serve that end (Roux 2006, 10:59). In the realm of health rights, the question is whether South African courts have played the requisite dynamic transformative role while maintaining a balance vis-à-vis the democratic branches of government. This section analyzes the way that courts have interpreted the boundaries of their role, the content of health rights, and the standard of review, as well as the remedies that courts have imposed.

The Constitutional Court's adjudicative role is governed by a principled stand on the appropriate role of courts in a democracy, where the determination of policy is properly the terrain of the legislature and executive. This does not mean that the Court has adopted a static approach in this regard, but the flexibility displayed seems more a question of context than of the Court developing a normative approach to its interface with policy issues. Thus, in *TAC–PMTCT*, where the lives of mothers and infants were at stake, the Court adopted a less deferential stance toward the executive branch. While acknowledging the separation of powers, the Court emphasized that this did not imply abstention from orders affecting policy:

> Where state policy is challenged as inconsistent with the Constitution, Courts have to consider whether in formulating and implementing such policy the State has given effect to its constitutional obligations. If it should hold . . . that the State has failed to do so, it is obliged by the Constitution to say so. Insofar as that constitutes an intrusion into the domain of the Executive, that is an intrusion mandated by the Constitution itself.[60]

This stance is reflected in the Court's orders in the case, which required significant policy shifts. By contrast, in *Mazibuko*, where the threat to life was less immediate, the Court adopted a more deferential stance, retreating to a process-oriented reasonableness approach in which the government was held to account primarily for the manner in which it pursued the achievement of social and economic rights.[61]

Integral to the Constitutional Court's approach to health rights litigation is the notion that courts are institutionally ill-equipped to adjudicate on issues that involve multiple social and economic consequences or determine budgets—hence its deference to the notion of available resources qualifying progressive realization. In *Soobramoney*, the Court acknowledged the province's budgetary constraints[62] but did not interrogate whether the allocation of resources by the central government was justifiable. Its deferential stance to the question of budgets was reiterated in *TAC–PMTCT* and *Mazibuko*.

Even though the Court acknowledged in *TAC–PMTCT* that a reasonableness review might have budgetary consequences, it underscored that its order was not directed at rearranging budgets.[63] In *Mazibuko*, it stated that the legislative and executive arms of government were best placed to investigate social conditions in the light of available budgets.[64] This coyness with regard to budgetary issues and resource allocation sits uneasily with the Court's decisions in civil and political rights cases, which have had significant budgetary implications (McLean 2010).

Interpretation of the Rights to Health and Water in Section 27

In line with its stance that courts should not develop substantive policy, the Constitutional Court has refused to give content to the rights to health and sufficient water in section 27(1). In the *TAC–PMTCT* case, the Court addressed the argument that it should define the minimum core content of the right to health in accordance with the notion of a dignified human existence. Following its finding in *Grootboom* against defining a minimum core,[65] it held that to do so would impose two self-standing positive obligations on the state: one in section 27(1) to give effect to a minimum core and another in section 27(2) progressively to realize the right. The Court found that the right in subsection 2 to which the state must progressively give effect is that in subsection 1.[66]

The Court's view of the contingent nature of this relationship was reiterated in *Mazibuko*. The litigants contended that as Johannesburg's free basic water policy was based on a minimum (25 liters of water per person per day set in the national regulations), the Court could—taking the context into account—determine a higher amount (50 liters per person per day) as constituting "sufficient" water necessary for dignified life. The Court rejected this contention on three grounds.

It held, firstly, that the section required the government to take reasonable legislative and other measures progressively to achieve the right of access to sufficient water, within available resources. It did not confer a right to claim sufficient water from the state immediately.[67] Determining a fixed content of the right would, held the Court, lead to immediate demands that the state would be unable to fulfill. The Court thus limited itself to a process-oriented role in which it held the government accountable for how it sought to pursue the right.[68] It is, however, unnecessary for the Court to vitiate section 27(1) out of fear that demands will swamp the state. Determining the content or normative purpose of section 27(1) does not mean that the state must give it immediate effect. Section 27(2) qualifies subsection 1 precisely because the Constitution recognizes that the state might not be in a position immediately to meet all demands placed on it.

The Court's second argument concerned the institutional inappropriateness of courts determining the content of any socioeconomic right, as the legislative and executive branches are better placed to investigate socioeconomic conditions in light of available budgets and determine achievable targets.[69] This constitutes "an almost complete abdication" of the Court's duty to interpret the "normative standards underpinning constitutional rights in the light of the considerations of section 39(1) of the Constitution" (Liebenberg 2010, 466–80).

Thirdly, the Court argued that giving content to the right to sufficient water in section 27(1) would lead to rigidity, since the right's requirements would vary over time and between contexts: "Fixing a quantified content might, in a rigid and counter productive manner, prevent an analysis of context."[70] This is overstating the case. The choice is not between determining an exact amount and avoiding any interpretation of the right whatsoever. The choice—or rather obligation—facing the Court is to determine the normative standard underlying the right as required by the Constitution in section 39(1). This would provide guidance to other courts in their assessment of the state's progress in giving effect to the right.

The Court made clear that the content of the section 27(1) right is contingent on the obligation of progressive realization within available resources, and that legislative and other measures are the primary instruments for achieving the right. Through such measures, "the rights set out in the Constitution acquire content and that content is subject to the standard of reasonableness."[71] This seems to mean that the content of the right is whatever the state decides its policy to be at the time, implying that the rights and obligations in 27(1) and (2), respectively, are coterminous. With no scope for determining the norms underlying the right, the only role left for the courts is to scrutinize the policy for reasonableness on an almost ad hoc basis.[72]

Standard of Review

The Constitutional Court's adoption of reasonableness review as the standard against which to assess the progressive realization of rights has been both condoned as an effective way for courts to scrutinize public policies while preserving respect for democracy and the separation of powers (Sunstein 2001b) and criticized as a weak form of review, especially in the context of limited available resources (see, e.g., Pieterse 2006b; Davis 2006; Bilchitz 2003; Roux 2002). Still others have interpreted it as a stringent test that "requires the court to substitute its view of what the Constitution requires" but that "stops short, however, of a full proportionality test" (McLean 2010, 174).

Over time, the Court has developed criteria informing the reasonableness standard that, if applied, could allow the Court to operate in a more robust fashion.[73] In *TAC–PMTCT*, the Court (following *Grootboom*) held that measures, in order to be reasonable, could not leave out of account those whose needs were most urgent and whose rights were most in peril. The development of comprehensive PMTCT programs, though important, did not justify withholding treatment until the best program was formulated, funds and infrastructure provided, and medical research completed. A program for the realization of socioeconomic rights, the Court stated, must be "balanced and flexible and make appropriate provision for attention to . . . crises and to short, medium and long-term needs. A programme that excluded a significant segment of society could not be said to be reasonable."[74] As the women concerned could not afford medical services, limiting nevirapine's availability to the research sites meant that the poor outside those sites suffered. The Court thus argued that state policy should take into account differences between those who could afford to pay and those who could not.[75] While this finding was context specific, it was also reflective of a more normative approach to the right of access to health in that it highlighted the necessity of attending urgently to the needs of the most vulnerable, who because of their poverty and marginalized status risked being excluded from goods and services necessary for their health and life.

In *Mazibuko*, however, the judiciary's context-specific approach seems devoid of normative underpinnings. A consideration of context, the Constitutional Court held, was central to a determination of reasonableness, and the basis for determining this was to require the state to explain its decisions and policy-making process.[76] This suggests that as long as the state can justify its choices, its policy will probably not be unreasonable. While a consideration of context is indeed important, if it is not linked to any normative purpose, it risks becoming self-serving. The Court's process-oriented approach meant that the Court was relieved of the obligation to scrutinize thoroughly whether the government's policy amendments did indeed serve to alleviate the hardships experienced by the applicants—who in some instances ran out of water halfway through the month.

Section 27 as a Negative Right

The applicants in *Mazibuko*, in addition to alleging an infringement of their positive right, argued that the installation of prepayment water meters was a retrogressive measure violating their negative right to water under section 27. Previously, the applicants had enjoyed a continuous water supply; under the new system, however, the supply was interrupted once the free allocation was used up (unless they bought more). They were rarely able to purchase enough water to last the whole month, causing hardship. The claimants rejected the city's argument that savings resulting from the installation of prepayment meters could be used to improve conditions of those with more urgent water needs, asking why the constitutional objective of improving the position of those without access to water had to be met by worsening the position of the—also impoverished—Phiri residents. Appearing to misunderstand the argument, the Constitutional Court focused on the cost, instead of the amount, of water. As residents were now given a certain amount of water free of charge—whereas previously they had to pay—the Court found no violation of the right (Liebenberg 2010). It seems that the Court failed to subject the city's reasoning to the level of scrutiny that elsewhere in the judgment was held to be an essential aspect of constitutional litigation on socioeconomic rights.[77]

Adjudicating "Unqualified" Health Rights

In litigation regarding prisoners' right to adequate medical treatment (sec. 24), children's right to basic medical services (sec. 28), and the right of everyone to an environment not harmful to health and well-being (sec. 36), courts are not constrained in the same way as they are with section 27 rights. These rights are neither qualified by the words "access to" nor subject to "progressive realisation within available resources," meaning that such rights should be protected fully and immediately.[78]

In *Westville*, the High Court reminded the government that the Constitution (sec. 237) requires all constitutional obligations to be performed diligently and without delay, and, reflecting the Constitutional Court's approach in *TAC–PMTCT*, noted that the state bears a duty not only to formulate programs but to ensure their reasonable implementation.[79] The government's plan for treating HIV-positive prisoners at the Westville facility was neither adequate nor reasonable, given its inflexibility, its irrationality (too few sites for administering ARVs), and the unjustified and unexplained delays in its implementation.[80]

The interpretation of children's right to "basic medical services" has been the subject of some contestation, particularly regarding whether it is the state or the children's parents who bear the obligation imposed by the right (Sloth-Nielsen 2005). In *Grootboom,* the Constitutional Court, overturning the decision of the High Court, held that the provision of basic health services for children fell to the parents in the first instance and not the state. In *TAC–PMTCT*, it amended this stance to take into account parent's ability to provide such care. Since HIV-positive mothers who depended on the public sector were mostly indigent and unable to access private medical treatment, it fell to the state to fulfill their children's health-care needs.[81]

Nature of Remedies

The Constitution accords courts broad powers to grant appropriate relief and make any order that is just and equitable (secs. 38 and 172). According to the Constitutional Court, constitutional relief might be a declaration of rights, an interdict, a mandamus, supervisory jurisdiction, or a new remedy.[82] The nature of the right infringed and the infringement provide guidance as to what constitutes appropriate and effective relief, giving expression to constitutional values. This is particularly important in socioeconomic rights cases, which are few in number and where litigation is often directed at systemic problems affecting a group of people. In health rights cases, remedies have included striking down, reviewing and setting aside, declarations, mandatory interdicts, punitive costs orders, supervisory orders, or a combination of these.

In *TAC–PMTCT*, the Court reaffirmed its authority to make a wide variety of orders, including mandatory orders.[83] Giving effect to the negative form of the right, it ordered the government to remove restrictions preventing public health facilities from prescribing nevirapine. It also imposed positive obligations on the government to permit and facilitate the use of nevirapine for PMTCT in state clinics and hospitals where medically indicated, including testing and counseling if necessary.[84] The Court held that there was no in-principle reason why it should not impose a structural interdict (which the High Court had done) in cases where this was "necessary"—for example, if the government "failed to heed a declaratory order or other remedy granted by a court in a particular case."[85] However, in this case, the Court refrained from imposing such an order, noting that the government had always cooperated and implemented its orders.[86] Considerations of comity seemingly predisposed the Court to place undue faith in the state. The reality was that the respondents were hostile to the provision of ARVs, and positive policy developments during the litigation process were driven by the legal proceedings. The Mpumalanga provincial government made no effort to implement the order until TAC instituted contempt-of-court proceedings.[87] Kent Roach and Geoff Budlender have argued that a structural interdict is warranted when the consequences of even a good-faith failure to comply with a court order are so serious that remedial action after the failure would not be adequate, such as in the *TAC–PMTCT* case, stating that

> it is not over-dramatic to suggest that as a result of the failure by the [Mpumalanga] province to comply effectively with the order of the Constitutional Court, a significant number of babies may have been infected with HIV where this was avoidable, with probably fatal consequences. (2005, 333–34)

In *Westville*, the High Court did impose a supervisory order, considering the context as well as the government's conduct. It considered the fact that most of the prisoners, according to expert evidence, faced death or irreparable harm to their health unless immediately provided with ARV treatment, and that, despite the government's operational plan, no rational or workable plan had been forthcoming regarding either the applicants or similarly situated Westville prisoners.[88] Delays, obstruction, and restrictions seriously compromised the health of the applicants and infringed their constitutional rights. The Court ordered the state to remove restrictions preventing prisoners from accessing ARV treatment at an accredited health facility and immediately to provide ARV treatment to the applicants and all similarly situated prisoners. The government was given two weeks to lodge an affidavit setting out its plan to comply with the order.[89] The necessity of the order was later borne out by the government's recalcitrance in adhering to it. TAC had to return to court twice to seek the order's implementation. After the Department of Correctional Services had drawn up (with ALP/TAC input) a framework agreement for ARV treatment in prison facilities, TAC decided not to proceed with further complaints under the order but rather to concentrate on solving problems directly with the department's officials (Berger 2008).

A deliberative and transformative notion of constitutional democracy requires courts actively to interpret socioeconomic rights in order to empower the poor and marginalized. The analysis in this chapter highlights the Constitutional Court's mixed track record in this respect. In the life-and-death context of *TAC–PMTCT*, the Court adopted a robust approach, ordering the countrywide extension of a PMTCT policy. This was made easier by policy developments during the litigation process that enabled the Court to treat this largely as an implementation gap. While not explicitly providing normative content to section 27, the Court's emphasis on the urgency of attending to the health needs of the poor and vulnerable, along with ensuring that all were included in the policy, imparted a normative purpose to the right. This robust stance, however, was not applied to the remedy (unlike in *Westville*). In *Mazibuko,* the Court's approach bordered on being passive. Although the city's amendment of its free basic water policy during the case achieved some redistribution of health goods and services, and although the Court aimed to secure public participation in policy making, the Court's failure to scrutinize the substantive aspects of the water right meant that what constituted fulfillment of the right (sufficient water) and whether the city could have afforded to provide a greater amount of water (available resources) remained unexamined.

Implementation and Impact

Whether litigation has a positive impact on the health system and on people's access to health services depends, in part, on the nature of the order (kind and extent of benefits); whether and how it is implemented; and whether it influences policy. To determine the extent to which a case has influenced subsequent policy developments or delivery of benefits is difficult, but the brief analysis below seeks to tease out some of these issues.

Policy and Budgetary Impacts

While it is often difficult to conclude that policy changes would not have occurred but for litigation, some cases do allow credible links to be established. The policy developments around the *TAC–PMTCT* case provide an example. The government's introduction of pilot sites for PMTCT and its extension of the number of these sites was almost certainly a response to the threat of and engagement in litigation; so too was the cabinet committee's decision to introduce a comprehensive PMTCT program announced in April 2002 (South African National Treasury 2002, 354; 2003, 87).[90] Furthermore, the Court's order accelerated the process of making nevirapine more widely available. The case also seemed to be a catalyst for further developments, such as the establishment of the Joint Health and Treasury Task Team in July 2002 to examine treatment options for supplementing comprehensive HIV/AIDS care in the public sector and the eventual adoption of the operational plan for the universal rollout of ARVs in November 2003 (Berger 2008).

It is difficult to attribute increased budgetary allocations directly to successful (or unsuccessful) litigation. The *TAC–PMTCT* case probably influenced the government's launch of its Enhanced Response to HIV/AIDS and Sexually Transmitted Infections Budget Strategy, which was developed during the case (South African National Treasury 2002) and led to dramatic increases in the government's conditional grant for HIV/AIDS to the provinces from R46 million in 2001–2 to R246 million in 2002–3 (434%) (South African National Treasury 2004b, 65).[91] While this budget was to be used more generally to give effect to the government's HIV/AIDS strategic plan, it also included expanding and strengthening the PMTCT program. The universal rollout of ARVs, intended to commence in April 2004 (in effect from May 2005), led to further steep increases in the conditional grant to R773 million in 2004–5 and R1,127 million in 2005–6 (South African National Treasury 2006, 39). As in the case of later policy developments, this could be seen as part of a snowball effect on the provision of ARVs that *TAC–PMTCT*, together with continued political mobilization, helped set in motion.[92]

Westville also shows a close link between litigation and policy developments. This was a function of the space created through the supervisory order, which compelled the parties to negotiate the terms of an acceptable settlement. TAC and the ALP took advantage of this opportunity by engaging the Department of Correctional Services and the Department of Health in a participatory process for drawing up a framework document for the treatment of HIV/AIDS in prison facilities nationally. Although the Department of Correctional Services in the end drew up its own framework document, finalized in October 2007, the ALP and TAC were able to comment on and make inputs into this document over a six-month period, thus contributing to the development of policy in relation to the management and treatment of HIV/AIDS in prisons (AIDS Law Project 2008).

Litigants need not be successful for litigation to have an impact on policy. In *Mazibuko*, for example, the city revised its free basic water policy to include an additional 4 kiloliters of free water each month for indigent households. It also provided for residents to apply for an additional 4 kiloliters each year for emergencies and led to a proposal to install fire hydrants in Phiri to ensure sufficient water in the case of fire-related emergencies (a result of applicants' evidence that two children died when a fire in a shack was not contained because of insufficient water). These policy amendments played a significant role in the Constitutional Court's finding that the policy was not unreasonable.[93] Whether they will benefit the poor, however, depends on implementation, and monitoring has revealed that the registration system for indigent people is not yet functioning properly.[94] The finding of reasonableness in this important test case is thus based on a policy that has yet to be properly implemented.

In *Goliath*, litigation played a role in pointing to and creating publicity around government inefficiency and lack of commitment, specifically the state's failure to give effect to its 2007 policy guidelines on drug-resistant tuberculosis. This heightened awareness seemed to be a significant factor in the process that culminated in the publication for comment of new regulations in April 2010.[95]

Finally, litigation has made available information that otherwise would not have been forthcoming. In *PMA*, for instance, the amicus's intervention led pharmaceutical companies to reveal offers they had made to the government for discounted medicines, a fact that the government had not made public, and provided the basis for TAC to pressure for discounted medicines in the private sector.

Implementation and Social Outcomes

Monitoring compliance with court orders is often critical for the realization of benefits. Successful monitoring, however, presupposes financial and logistical resources, and is especially problematic when a broad constituency is the beneficiary. In such circumstances, a supervisory order could relieve civil society of the burden of monitoring. In the *TAC–PMTCT* case, the main impediment to implementation was the government's hostility to ARVs. The Constitutional Court refused to impose a supervisory order, perhaps viewing TAC as capable of monitoring implementation. However, this did not occur, as the organization's "focus was largely on the bigger picture, seeing *TAC–PMTCT* as an entry point to develop the right to health in general and access ARV treatment in particular" (Berger 2008, 80).[96] Difficulties with monitoring implementation in the absence of a supervisory order are highlighted by the fact that estimates of implementation of PMTCT efforts range from 30% to over 90% (see, e.g., Chopra et al. 2009). Even the Department of Health in its 2008–9 annual report stated that it could not say how many HIV-positive women and babies were taking ARVs as its data collection system was not in place—six years after the *TAC–PMTCT* judgment (South African Department of Health 2009, 36).

Despite vagueness concerning the precise extent of PMTCT programs, such programs have undoubtedly had a positive effect on the health of HIV-positive women and their babies. A 2006 government study found that of 19,758 babies born to mothers living with HIV, a total of 16,288 tested negative (Heywood 2009, 25), and a study of infants with HIV-positive mothers in rural northern KwaZulu-Natal found that between 2001 (the time of the *TAC–PMTCT* case) and 2006, infant mortality declined by 57% after the application of both ARV therapy and PMTCT programs (Ndirangu et al. 2009).

Litigation also directly benefited prisoners at the Westville facility. TAC's monitoring indicated that after *Westville*, most prisoners needing ARVs received them. Further developments, indirectly linked to the litigation, included the prison hospital's accreditation by the Department of Health to provide on-site ARV treatment, as well as improved coordination between the Department of Health and the Department of Correctional Services regarding the delivery of HIV-related health-care services to prisoners (Berger 2008). The case was also a catalyst for the extension of treatment to other prisons in the country; the 2008–9 annual report of the Department of Correctional Services stated that the program had been implemented in 50% of the department's management areas (South African Department of Correctional Services 2009, 57).[97]

South Africa's HIV litigation has had financial consequences for the health system, leading to savings by preventing ill-health and thus freeing resources for further treatment (but also adding costs).[98] Again, cases need not be actually adjudicated in order for such effects to occur. The threat of legal action against pharmaceutical companies had a major impact on the price and accessibility of ARVs in both the public and private sectors, which facilitated more widespread access to treatment. (In some cases, though, it has taken concerted pressure to break companies' monopolistic practices—for instance, it took six years of pressure and the lodging of a complaint with the Competition Commission in November 2007 before U.S.-based Merck & Co. and its local subsidiary, MSD [Pty] Ltd, acceded to the ALP's demands for the generic licensing of its ARV product efavirenz required by two-thirds of people starting ARV treatment in the public sector.[99]) It has been argued that once these companies realized that the legal and political tide had turned against them, they (unlike the government) generally saw the benefit in reaching a settlement rather than attracting more negative publicity through a court case (Berger 2008). Table 8.2 illustrates the cost saving arising from legal action against these companies by comparing 2008 tender prices on ARVs with prices that would otherwise have applied.[100]

The drop in the price of nevirapine meant that the government saved R37 million in the 2008 tender, while the *TAC–Merck* settlement allowed the government to procure 600 mg efavirenz tablets for less than half the 2004 price (AIDS Law Project 2008). The lower cost and subsequent greater availability of both first- and second-line ARVs also provided alternative treatment regimes to patients who were resistant to or intolerant of specific drugs. Cheaper generic ARVs also helped secure the supply of ARVs—preventing shortages of medicines that had plagued some hospitals—which is essential for effective treatment.

Conclusion

In its early pronouncements, the Constitutional Court raised expectations that it would operate as a means for principled social transformation. These expectations were engendered amid the devastation of the HIV/AIDS epidemic, and in this context, the right to health became central to the vision of a more just society. This chapter has sought to investigate the role of health rights litigation in facilitating and/or undermining the social transformation to such a society.

We have seen that both litigation itself and settlements in the "shadow of litigation" have led to important policy changes and transfers of health

Table 8.2. Cost saving arising from legal action against pharmaceutical companies (annual prices per adult[a])

Drug	Private-sector price	Best international branded price	Best international generic price	2008 South Africa tender price
AZT (300 mg)	7,082	4,599	1,470	953
Lamivudine (150 mg)	7,787	2,457	693	400
AZT/lamivudine (300/150 mg)	9,733	6,515	2,142	1,231
Nevirapine (200 mg)	4,380	4,599	1,176	430
Efavirenz	. . .	. . .	US$237	US$169

[a] Prices for all drugs except efavirenz are listed in South African rand and are rounded to the nearest whole.

goods and services to poor and vulnerable groups in South African society. Moreover, although the Constitutional Court has eschewed a policy-making role,[101] the development of policies during the litigation process has accorded it the leverage to extend policy where warranted by the context (*TAC–PMTCT*).[102] Litigation has also created opportunities for parties to engage the Court over the interpretation of health rights in test cases, which, given the precedent-based nature of the judicial system, has potentially far-reaching consequences. Furthermore, litigation has broadened debates and created awareness in society about the distribution of health resources and—together with social mobilization, advocacy, and education—has empowered people in need of health care or the basic preconditions of health (*TAC–PMTCT*, *Mazibuko*). Finally, litigation has enhanced a culture of justification by requiring the government to justify its policies and decisions.

On the other hand, the Constitutional Court's reluctance[103] to give normative content to socioeconomic rights generally and health rights specifically suggests the retreat by the Court to a more procedural approach, in which it assesses whether criteria for priority setting are rational and fair (*Soobramoney*) or requires deliberative processes and consultation with all affected parties (*Mazibuko*). While this is constructive and reduces the risk of the judicial process being used to bypass legitimate priority setting,[104] a "culture of justification" can also play a negative role, making the process itself the core of the right and nullifying its substantive content. Furthermore, when the Court is overly restrained in its orders and remedies, the potential for litigation to lead to real benefits for poor and vulnerable people is reduced.

From the perspective of a deliberative model of democracy, adjudication of socioeconomic rights may deepen democracy, provided that the courts "actively . . . interpret socio-economic rights so as to serve this end" (Roux 2006, 10:59). They need to play a dynamic, transformative, yet balanced, role vis-à-vis the other branches of government. In the realm of health rights, it is questionable whether the courts have consistently played an adjudicative role consonant with this goal. At times, their overly deferential stance to the executive and legislative branches has arguably undermined the rights' transformative potential. The outcome of such deference is to deny poor people access to basic health goods and services essential for a healthful and dignified existence.

Litigation has not always met expectations in terms of providing a channel for the poor to advance their rights. South Africa still faces huge health system challenges with respect to the inequitable distribution of health resources, the quality of care, physical infrastructure, and the management of health services, among other things. It could be, however, that those expectations were too high. It is perhaps too much to expect litigation to achieve what can be gained more appropriately through political will and efficient government administration.[105]

NOTES

1. The South African Institute of Race Relations estimates that between January and October 2009, over one hundred community protests took place throughout South Africa. Such protests were fueled mainly by dissatisfaction with councillors and other officials, but also by the failure of service delivery (2010, 3).
2. The National Health Act (61 of 2003), the Medicines and Related Substances Control Amendment Act (90 of 1997), and the Medical Schemes Act (131 of 1998).
3. The national government is responsible for formulating health policy, building capacity, and allocating resources to provinces and local governments; provincial authorities are responsible for the development of district-wide primary health systems, including provincial health policies, norms, and legislation; and local governments' competencies include water and food control, waste management, and surveillance and prevention of communicable diseases (South African Department of Health 1997).
4. Most of the provinces' budgets come from the national government in accordance with the equitable share grant provided for in the Constitution. In 2009–10, district health services, including primary health care and district hospitals, accounted for 41% of provincial health expenditure (South African National Treasury 2009, 54). An additional conditional grant to the provinces is earmarked for particular purposes in line with national priorities (Hassim et al. 2007, 79).
5. Half of public health-care facilities did not have functional clinics or community health committees (South African Department of Health 2009, 7).
6. Cumulative AIDS deaths as of July 1, 2008, were estimated to be 2.5 million (South African Institute of Race Relations 2008, 438). As pressure mounted to deal more effectively with the HIV/AIDS epidemic, money for this purpose was increasingly made available through the conditional grant.
7. Constitution of the Republic of South Africa, 1996.
8. Health and water rights are dealt with separately in the Constitution. In this chapter, water rights are regarded as part of broader health rights. The chapter thus follows General Comment 14 of the United Nations Committee on Economic, Social and Cultural Rights, which has recognized that the right to health includes nutrition, water, and clean sanitation (U.N. Doc. E/C.12/2000/4 [2000], para. 4).
9. *Soobramoney*, para. 8. The justiciability of socioeconomic rights was also underscored by the Constitutional Court in *Ex parte Chairperson of the Constitutional Assembly: In re Certification of the Constitution of the Republic of South Africa, 1996*, 1996 (4) SA 744 (CC).
10. Any order of constitutional invalidity of legislation made by the Supreme Court of Appeal or High Court must be ratified by the Constitutional Court. In nonconstitutional

cases, the Supreme Court of Appeal is the highest court of appeal. In cases of dispute, the Constitutional Court decides whether or not a matter is constitutional (secs. 167 and 169 of the Constitution).

11. "Everyone who is detained, including every sentenced prisoner, has the right . . . to conditions of detention that are consistent with human dignity, including . . . the provision, at state expense, of adequate . . . medical treatment."
12. See *Nokotyana.*
13. Sections 9, 10, 11, 12, and 32, respectively, of the Constitution. All have been relied on by litigants in health cases.
14. See *Airey v. Ireland,* 3 ECHR (1979), para. 24; the *Canadian Bar Association v. British Columbia,* 2008 BCCA 92 (Canlii) (2008) 290 DLR (4th 617); *The Richtersveld Community v. The Government of the Republic of South Africa & Others,* LCC 63/05 (unreported) 341.
15. Civil cases comprised only 13% of 340,000 cases in 2005–6. Legal Aid Board, telephone interview, March 2007.
16. *Ferreira v. Levin NO*; *Vryenhoek v. Powell NO* 1996 (1) SA 984 (CC), para. 165.
17. Rule 10 of the Rules of the Constitutional Court. See Budlender (2006, 8.1–5).
18. For further analyses of *Soobramoney*, see McLean (2010), Bilchitz (2005), Van Bueren (2005), Scott and Alston (2000), and Moellendorf (1998).
19. Full case name is given in the table. In the chapter, cases are identified by their short names only, unless they do not appear in the table.
20. *Soobramoney*, paras. 5, 7.
21. Ibid., paras. 19–21, 31.
22. Ibid., paras. 28–31.
23. South African Institute of Race Relations (2008, 442) (citing South African Department of Health's *National HIV and Syphilis Prevalence Survey—South Africa 2006*). The survey may not be fully representative, as only an estimated 80% of pregnant women attended public clinics, 85% of them African.
24. The *Prevention of Mother-to-Child HIV Transmission and Management of HIV Positive Pregnant Women* policy document of October 2000 made no provision for this.
25. TAC chose not to propose AZT (already registered for PMTCT), since its greater cost and more complicated regime was believed to make success less likely (Heywood 2003).
26. *TAC–PMTCT*, paras. 4–5.
27. Ibid., para. 19.
28. Ibid., paras. 51–56.
29. The national government had apparently threatened the Western Cape with legal action when it began rolling out ARVs in January 2001. There were also divisions within KwaZulu-Natal between the premier and provincial health authorities. While most provinces complied with government's instruction not to reply to TAC's letter of demand, the Western Cape sent TAC a copy of its report to the Minister of Health, indicating that it planned to provide 90% of pregnant HIV-positive women with nevirapine by mid-2002 and 100% by 2003 (Heywood 2003, 292–94).
30. *TAC v. Minister of Health,* 2002 (4) BCLR 356 (T), para. 67.
31. For further analyses of *TAC–PMTCT*, see McLean (2010), Liebenberg (2010), Pieterse (2006b), and Bilchitz (2005).
32. In 2002–3, there were about 188,000 prisoners in jail, and over 30,000 were released each month (Goyer et al. 2004, 9 [citing South African Office of the Judicial Inspectorate 2002]).
33. *Westville*, para. 7.

34. Ibid., paras. 17–18.
35. Ibid., para. 19.
36. Ibid., para. 32.
37. Ibid., para. 35. For a further analysis of *Westville*, see Cameron (2006).
38. *Mazibuko*, para. 7.
39. The claimants held that regulation 3(b) published in terms of section 9 of the Water Services Act 108 of 1997 set a minimum and that the Court was free to determine a higher amount as sufficient water (Regulations Relating to Compulsory National Standards and Measures to Conserve Water, *Government Gazette*, No. 22355, Notice R509 of 8 June 2001). They also held, inter alia, that prepayment meters were unlawful as they resulted in unauthorized cut-offs in terms of section 4(3) of the Water Services Act or sections 9C and 11 of the bylaws (City of Johannesburg Metropolitan Municipality Water Services By-laws, *Provincial Extraordinary Gazette [Gauteng]*, Gazette No. 179, Notice 835 of 21 May 2004, published in terms of the Local Government: Municipal Systems Act 32 of 2000); the manner in which they were introduced infringed the Promotion of Administrative Justice Act 3 of 2000; and they violated the constitutional right to equality, among other rights.
40. This replaced a flat-rate system in which residents were charged for 20 kiloliters of water consumption per household per month, while actual usage per household was 67 kiloliters. As a result of poor infrastructure and nonpayment, Johannesburg Water estimated that 75% of the water to Soweto was unaccounted for (*Mazibuko*, paras. 11–13).
41. Ibid., para. 14.
42. Dale McKinley (co-founder of the Anti-Privatisation Forum), telephone interview, September 2010.
43. The Centre for Applied Legal Studies and Centre on Housing Rights and Evictions.
44. McKinley interview, *supra* note 42.
45. *Mazibuko and others v. City of Johannesburg and others (Centre for Applied legal Studies as amicus curiae)*, [2008] 4 All SA 471 (W).
46. Ibid., para. 183.5.1.
47. *City of Johannesburg and others v. Mazibuko and others (Centre on Housing Rights and Evictions as amicus curiae)*, 2009 (3) SA 592 (SCA).
48. Ibid., paras. 24, 58–60.
49. *Mazibuko*, paras. 27, 29, 82. For further analyses of *Mazibuko* and water rights in South Africa, see Ellmann (2010), Danchin (2010), and and Kapindu (2009).
50. Medicines and Related Substances Control Amendment Act 90 of 1997.
51. The PMA opposed its application, forcing TAC to go to court to seek admission, which was granted.
52. "It is not the [government's] intention to render nugatory the patent and other intellectual rights of the Applicants, but rather to activate the principle of exhaustion by importing more affordable genuine medicines placed by the applicants or their subsidiaries, or licencees on other markets" (Heywood 2001, 156 [quoting Government's Heads of Argument, April 17, 2001, para. 76.1]).
53. For further analyses of *PMA* and mobilization around generic drugs, see Mbali (2005), Fordhan (2008), Park (2002), and Fisher and Rigamonti (2005).
54. This was regarded as an unnecessary legal hurdle. Jonathan Berger (head of policy and research, AIDS Law Project), telephone interview, December 2009.

55. *Hazel Tau*, Statement of Complaint in terms of section 49B of the Competition Act 89 of 1998 to the Competition Commission, para. 107.
56. Ibid., paras. 38–45.
57. The ALP sent letters of demand to Abbott Laboratories SA (a local subsidiary of the U.S. company), which refused to license any company in respect of its combination drug lopinavir/ritonavir, and to Bristol Myers-Squibb concerning the excessively priced amphotericin B, an anti-fungal drug, no longer patent protected, over which it had an effective monopoly in South Africa. As a result, Bristol Myers-Squibb agreed to reduce the drug's price by 80% in the public sector and 85% in the private health sector (AIDS Law Project 2006, 29; 2007, 31). The matter against Abbot Laboratories was dropped when the company went some way toward addressing the ALP's concerns. Eventually, acceding to pressure, the U.S.-based Merck & Co. and its local subsidiary, MSD (Pty) Ltd., agreed to license four generic companies to market and sell efavirenz products to both the public and private health sectors in South Africa and southern Africa, and to waive any right to a royalty (AIDS Law Project 2008).
58. The *TAC–PMTCT* decision was relied on by the High Court in its finding in *Westville*, while *PMA* and *Hazel Tau* led to further pre-litigation victories against pharmaceutical companies.
59. *Democratic Alliance and Another v. Masondo NO and Another* 2003 (2) SA 413 (CC), paras. 42–43; *Mazibuko*, para. 160.
60. *TAC–PMTCT*, para. 99.
61. *Mazibuko*, para. 59.
62. It took into consideration that the province had overspent its budget by R152 million in 1996–7, and that overspending was likely to reach R700 million in 1998 (para. 24).
63. *TAC–PMTCT*, para. 38.
64. *Mazibuko*, para. 61.
65. The Court chose not to follow General Comment 3 of the United Nations Committee on Economic, Social and Cultural Rights regarding the provision of a minimum core (U.N. Doc. E/1991/23 [1991], para. 10) as amplified by General Comment 14.
66. *TAC–PMTCT*, paras. 29, 34–35. The Court's view that a purposive reading of the right does not allow for the defining of a minimum core has been contested. It has been argued that to give effect to the values of equality, human dignity, and freedom, a purposive reading could in fact require an interpretation of the minimum core (McLean 2010). It is also criticized for not making explicit the steps required for the progressive realization of the rights (Bilchitz 2005).
67. *Mazibuko*, para. 57.
68. Ibid., para. 59.
69. Ibid., para. 61.
70. Ibid., para. 60.
71. Ibid., para. 60, emphasis added.
72. In *Nokotyana*, the Constitutional Court declined to determine what constitutes "basic sanitation" in terms of the right of access to housing (sec. 26[1] and [2]), which has a similar formulation to sections 27(1) and (2) (see table 8.1). As stated by Bishop and Brickhill (2009), the Court's refusal to order the municipality to accept the national and provincial governments' offer to enable the provision of one chemical toilet for every four households should not be seen to mean that socioeconomic rights litigants are not

entitled to have a settlement made an order of the court because of the difficulties in providing the same services everywhere else. Rather, the principle should apply only to cases, as in *Nokotyana*, where the Court has rejected the substantive claim (on the basis that it was fundamentally changed on appeal); otherwise, the whole purpose of according socioeconomic rights would be defeated.

73. To meet the standard, the Court has held that measures must ensure that appropriate financial and human resources are available; must be capable of facilitating the realization of the right; must be reasonable in conception and implementation; must be balanced and flexible; and must attend to crises and the urgent needs of those in desperate situations. A wide range of measures may be reasonable. Unfairly discriminatory policies would not be reasonable. When other rights are also implicated, the criterion for reasonableness would be ensuring compliance with those rights (Bilchitz 2005).
74. *TAC–PMTCT*, para. 68.
75. Ibid., para. 70.
76. *Mazibuko*, para. 71.
77. Liebenberg (2010) notes that while retrogressive measures are not prohibited, they place a particular burden of justification on the state.
78. They are circumscribed only by internal modifiers, such as "basic" and "adequate." Any limitation of these rights, therefore, should occur in accordance with section 36 (the limitations section) of the Constitution.
79. *Westville*, para. 31.
80. Ibid., para. 30.
81. *TAC–PMTCT*, para. 79.
82. *Fose v. Minister of Safety and Security*, 1997 (3) SA 786 (CC) (per Justice Ackermann), paras. 19, 69, referring to *Pretoria City Council v. Walker*, 1998 (2) SA 263 (CC), para. 96; *Hoffman v. SAA*, 2001 (1) (SA (CC), para. 45.
83. *TAC–PMTCT*, para. 99.
84. Ibid., para. 135.
85. Ibid., para. 129.
86. Developments in state policy during the case seemingly influenced the Court, although it did not specifically give this as a reason for not imposing a structural interdict. Gauteng had added new pilot sites, and nevirapine was expected to be made available that year throughout the province. Likewise, KwaZulu-Natal had changed its policy; the government had made substantial additional funds available for the treatment of HIV, including PMTCT, removing budgetary impediments (*TAC–PMTCT*, paras. 118–20, 129). The Court's reluctance to impose a structural interdict seemed to stem from such a move being viewed as solely punitive. Such interdicts may, however, be useful in countering government inertia or administrative incapacity.
87. *TAC v. MEC for Health, Mpumalanga & Minister of Health* (TPD), Case No. 35272/02.
88. *Westville*, para. 32.
89. Ibid., paras. 32, 35.
90. The extension of pilot sites during the litigation included a major Johannesburg public hospital, which was declared a pilot site after the hospital's chief executive officer wrote a letter confirming the institution's capacity to run such a program (Heywood 2003, 293).
91. The National Treasury's 2004 *Estimates of National Expenditure* (2004a) give different figures of R54 million in 2001–2 and R210 million in 2002–3 for the conditional grant for HIV/AIDS. According to the National Treasury's 2003 *Intergovernmental Fiscal Review*

(2003, 87), the overall amount earmarked for HIV/AIDS under the Enhanced Response to HIV/AIDS Budgetary Strategy rose from R345 million in 2001–2 to over R1 billion in 2002–3, and to R1.8 billion in 2004–5 (estimate).

92. The HIV & AIDs and STI Strategic Plan for South Africa 2007–2011 estimated that about R45 billion was required for 2007–9, compared to the actual budgeted amount of R14 billion for that period (Heywood 2009, 27).
93. *Mazibuko*, paras. 90–97.
94. McKinley interview, *supra* note 42.
95. Regulations Relating to Communicable Diseases, *Government Gazette*, No. 33107, Notice R287 of April 13, 2010, secs. 21(1)–(3).
96. To facilitate more concerted monitoring of ARV rollout, a civil society monitoring forum was established to report on progress, including political obstacles (Heywood 2009).
97. The 2007–8 annual report of the Department of Correctional Services (2008) stated that 4,294 prisoners were receiving ARVs at twelve sites; but as the report did not state how many prisoners were living with HIV, the figure is hard to evaluate. In light of the fact that the government's obstructionist tactics delayed the extension of the program, and that the final agreement between the parties on a more universal framework was reached only in August 2008, the 50% rollout constitutes fairly positive progress.
98. Although the Court in *TAC–PMTCT* glossed over the cost of treatment, providing nevirapine required the training and appointment of counselors and the provision of medical staff and infrastructure, which did have cost implications.
99. The ALP was acting on behalf of TAC.
100. Brian Honnerman (researcher, AIDS Law Project), personal communication, January 21, 2010. The Medicines Control Council registered the first co-packaged product containing efavirenz, AZT, and lamivudine in December 2008.
101. In line with the doctrine of separation of powers.
102. By contrast, in *Mazibuko*, the Court was satisfied that the state's policy, including the fairly minimal developments during the litigation, was reasonable.
103. The lower courts have been prepared to go further than the Constitutional Court in imparting normative content to health rights, as evidenced by their judgments in *Grootboom* and *Mazibuko*. The Constitutional Court in *Mazibuko* (para. 68) found that the lower courts had erred in quantifying a specific amount of water, thereby giving content to sections 27(1)(b) and (2). In an implied admonition, the Constitutional Court noted that they had failed to consider the content of the obligation imposed by those provisions and to follow the jurisprudence of the Constitutional Court in *Grootboom* and *TAC–PMTCT*.
104. For example, as a route for the better-off to access expensive treatments at the state's expense, as has been the case in some of the other countries analyzed in this volume.
105. What may be achieved by a committed government is illustrated by the mass testing drive for HIV undertaken by the new minister of health, betokening, according to Justice Edwin Cameron of the Constitutional Court, a "freshly invigorated sense of purpose and commitment," which is "exhilaratingly different from 1993" (when he started the AIDS Law Project) (AIDS Law Project 2010, 65).

CROSS-CUTTING ISSUES

Chapter 9

Dialogic Justice in the Enforcement of Social Rights: Some Initial Arguments

Roberto Gargarella

In the last few years, we have seen an extraordinary, and perhaps surprising, increase in litigation in the area of health rights. However, the idea that courts should work for the enforcement of health rights—and, more generally, social rights—is still subject to numerous criticisms.

Some critics maintain that courts should not deal with positive rights in the same way they deal with negative rights because while the latter require the state simply to not interfere with people's initiatives, the former would require its activism. Others say that judges should not interfere with budgetary issues, which are better reserved for representatives in Congress. Still others consider that judges are not well equipped—technically speaking—to confront these questions, or that they are forced to address conflicts on a case-by-case basis, preventing them from having a "global" understanding of the issues at stake.[1] These criticisms, which I will not explore further, have been repeatedly examined (and discarded as implausible) by legal authors and the specialized literature on the subject (see Sunstein 2004; Tushnet 2008b).[2] However, there are still some objections that deserve additional careful study because they continue to carry a certain persuasive force. The first of these criticisms is the *separation-of-powers objection*, while the second related criticism is the *democratic objection*. Let me describe these two views and say something more about each of them.

The separation-of-powers objection. According to this view, the judiciary should not get involved in the enforcement of social rights because it would be interfering with a task reserved for the representatives of the people, thus breaking the equilibrium and distribution of functions between the different

The author would like to thank Lucas Arrimada and Ignacio César for their invaluable support, without which this chapter would not have been possible.

branches. In so doing, judges would become legislators in an area that is particularly sensitive because it directly involves the allocation of the budget; discussion in this area must instead be reserved for the different parliamentary actors, who come from different sections and regions of society. Moreover, judges would distract their attention from problems to which they need to give priority and—even worse—open the door to abuses of power that the entire system of separation of powers has tried to avoid.

The democratic objection. This new objection is intimately linked to the former one and refers to judges' *lack of legitimacy* to interfere with questions of public policy. The idea is that only the people, acting directly as the sovereign, or their representatives, are and should be authorized to define national public policies. While courts are part of the democratic schema, their members lack the legitimacy enjoyed by other democratic authorities: the majority of their members are not selected and cannot be removed by the people directly. This situation of diminished legitimacy gives us reason to prevent judges from interfering with our decisions concerning how to organize the basic structure of our society or how to distribute our resources.

Both objections are relevant. However, both are vulnerable to the same and obvious criticism—namely, to the question, What conception do you have in mind when you refer to the ideas of separation of powers and of democracy? When we examine this question in more detail, we discover that the objections lose most of their initial attraction.

Let us reflect, first, on the notion of separation of powers. What do critics *really* mean when they say that social rights' judicial activism violates the idea of separation of powers? In what sense is that true? Why would such activism offend the notion of separation of powers? The idea of separation of powers presumed in such criticism refers to the most rustic and unattractive definition of the term, which was discussed and discarded not only during the founding period in the United States but also in many other jurisdictions. This notion of a "strict" separation rejects any kind of interference between one branch of power and the other: each branch is in charge of its own affairs, and the others need to remain within their own limits, strictly respecting the jurisdiction of all others.

This view (which was maintained, for example, by some Anti-Federalists during the framing period)[3] was rejected by the new authorities of the newly independent countries (at least in most American societies), who abandoned the proposal of a *strict separation* for a different one: that of *checks and balances.* As we know, the notion of checks and balances would ultimately become the dominant, most popular, and most respected approach to the notion of separation of powers and was thus incorporated into the new constitutions of the new nations. The idea was not to strictly separate the different branches but rather to force each of them to interact with one another, partially interfering with the others' affairs (Hamilton et al. 1788, no. 47).

For those who adhere to this latter interpretation of the notion of separation of powers, judges' partial interference with the missions of the other branches (e.g., in the area of social rights) is not a problem in and of itself: it is the judicial branch's duty to subject the actions of the other branches to its controls. The discussion that requires attention is a different one, related to the modalities, scope, and limits of that intervention—but not to its mere existence.

My reply to the democratic objection would follow a similar route and have a similar structure. In this case the question is, What conception of democracy would be offended by such activism? It is not clear that all possible and reasonable versions of democracy would be so affected.

Two Notions of Democracy

Democracy is a fundamentally contested concept (Waldron 2002), which is why it is particularly important to clarify which notion of democracy is the one that—supposedly—would require us to reject judicial activism in the area of social rights. For the sake of simplifying a long and complex discussion, I would say that judges who invoke the concept of democracy when denying the invitation to enforce social rights use one of the following two notions of democracy.

Rousseauan Democracy

Perhaps surprisingly, some judges invoke a Rousseauan notion of democracy when refusing to intervene in the area of social rights. They say that democracy requires judges to step outside political questions and that any judicial interference with budgetary issues implies an offense to democracy: democracy requires a government by the people and for the people, rather than the ruling of a judicial elite. This view has profound roots in both the United States and France, based on these countries' revolutionary periods and the time when many of the founding fathers opposed (what can be considered) an early version of judicial activism (Kramer 2005). That critique against judicial review regained part of its force in recent decades (Bork 1990), after an unexpected wave of progressive judicial activism—particularly in the United States, after the years of the Warren Court. In a paradoxical twist of fate, the attack that was then launched against judicial activism, grounded in a Rousseauan version of the democratic argument, came to defend a status quo of inequality and injustice.[4]

The problems with this view are many. First, it is unclear why certain, localized, limited forms of judicial review would offend such a view of democracy. A Rousseauan democracy would certainly be offended by judges taking the place of legislators, but not by judges seeking to strengthen the democratic components of the system. Second, even during the most Jacobin period of the French Revolution there existed some limited versions of judicial review, in the form of the so-called referee legislative (which implied a kind of judicial remand to the legislature). Similarly, in the United States, those who opposed judicial review for democratic reasons did not criticize judicial review per se but rather the fact that judges had the *last say* regarding fundamental constitutional questions (Kramer 2005). Finally, legal scholars who propose majoritarian understandings of democracy (e.g., Waldron 2009), or populist approaches to it (e.g., Tushnet 2008b), do not reject judicial review *tout court* but instead the somewhat unlimited way in which it is presently exercised. In sum, defending a bold conception of democracy need not imply opposing all types of judicial activism.

Hamiltonian, or Pluralist, Democracy

An alternative reading of democracy, one commonly adopted by academics and judges in the United States, is one that I would call Hamiltonian, or pluralist, democracy. Those who advance this understanding argue that judges' only mission is to safeguard the constitution, without replacing the will of the people with their own will. U.S. legal authorities have used this reading to resist any kind of judicial intervention regarding social rights. The reasoning in such a case is simple: if "we the people" decided not to include social rights in the constitution—but decided instead to write a "negative" constitution—judges should not decide the contrary. Paradoxically, this more conservative view of democracy ends up with a conclusion similar to the one maintained by Rousseauan democrats: namely, that judges should leave the task of enforcing social rights to the legislature (Edelman 1988, 23–4; see also Easterbrook 1992, 349; Bork 1979, 69).

Although there are many things to say about and against this argument, I will mention only three of them. First, it is clear that this understanding of democracy is not applicable in contexts such as that of Latin America, where constitutions are explicitly committed to long lists of social rights. Second, the argument seems to depend on a specific interpretative theory—namely, one or another version of originalism—which seems very difficult to defend. Different interpretative theories could lead us along diverse routes and to different, more ambitious outcomes in terms of social rights.[5] Third, the very idea that the "will of the people" is frozen in the constitution seems theoretically untenable (see, e.g., Ackerman 1991).

What has been the consequence of readings of democracy such as the ones examined above in the area of social rights? More specifically, what do those readings imply in terms of judicial behavior regarding social rights? The main consequence has been, in my opinion, *judicial abstinence* (and judicial passivism): namely, a recurrent attitude among judges in which they decide not to intervene in the area of social rights by claiming that they have no competence, authority, or—most significantly—legitimacy to do so.

Curiously, this attitude contrasts with another typical judicial disposition, which I will call *judicial imposition* (and judicial activism): judges' tendency to enforce their own understanding of the constitution by challenging the legislature's approach to that text, and their assumption that they have the final say regarding the meaning of the constitution.

Both of these tendencies are problematic and respond to unattractive assumptions about democracy (the idea that democracy either forbids judicial activism or is not in tension with the—relatively limited—legitimacy of the judicial power). The problem with these views resides in their rigid understanding of democracy, resulting in a rigid understanding of the role of the judiciary. It is both possible and desirable to renew our thinking about these issues.

Deliberative Democracy

Other equally or more attractive theories of democracy require judges to deal with social rights in a completely different mode. Here, I will explore one of those theories: deliberative democracy (Elster 1998; Bohman 1996; Cohen 1989). Although there are several variants of this view, my proposed version is characterized by the following two features. First, public decisions must be adopted after an ample process of *collective discussion*. Second, the deliberative process requires, in principle, the intervention of *all those potentially affected* by the decision at hand (Elster 1998). These requisites help us distinguish this deliberative view from the alternatives so far explored.[6]

The deliberative view is and has been considered a crucial approach for the sake of making justifiable public decisions. This seems so particularly regarding areas as important and sensitive as those connected to social rights. In those areas, deliberative democrats maintain, it is especially important to ensure that decisions are fairly discussed and agreed to by those potentially affected (Gruskin and Daniels 2008; Daniels and Sabin 2002, 34; Daniels 2008; Dixon 2007).

In relation to judges' role in this process, deliberative democrats would support neither judicial activism nor judicial passivity in all cases. Instead, they would advocate an active intervention of the judiciary on certain occasions and in specific, justified manners. Among our reasons for supporting this (provisional) conclusion are the following: (i) the connection between certain basic rights (e.g., each person's right to question the government) and the preservation of the democratic procedure; (ii) the intimate connection between social rights and political participation; and (iii) the need to follow the constitution, particularly when it explicitly encompasses social rights, as is the case with most Latin American constitutions.

Such a mission would require judges to safeguard the inclusive nature of the decision-making process (Ely 1980), maintain the deliberative character of the decision-making process (Sunstein 1985), and ensure the equal status of those who take part in the democratic process (Sunstein 1994a, 1994b).

The Court, Deliberation, and Fundamental Rights

So far we have established that courts have important institutional duties to fulfill, which, on occasion, may call for courts' active intervention and even require them to challenge some legal decisions already in force (what some people may call *judicial activism*). A court's institutional mission is not only compatible with basic democratic ideals but also required by them. We need to ensure that our norms are the product of a *collective and inclusive discussion* rather than the imposition of a few voices, and courts are in an excellent position for helping us achieve that objective.

For those who share this view, judges can help us in the decision-making process by revising the way in which legal norms are *created* and *applied*; that is, they can ensure that the process through which those norms have been enacted has fulfilled its basic deliberative requirements and that the norms are applied in a manner compatible with our equal moral status.

What exactly could judges do in this respect? Below I will provide some suggestions and illustrate them with different examples related to the enforcement of social rights in general and health rights in particular. These ideas may provide a good, empirically grounded starting point for the development of a more general theory of *dialogic justice.*

Bringing Voices into the Public Forum

Frequently, the legislative process is organized in a way that excludes relevant viewpoints from the discussion of a norm (e.g., directly affected groups might not have representation in Congress, or they might not be consulted even though they are targeted by the norm at stake). In these situations, judges may properly decide to intervene simply in order to ensure respect for the deliberative process. This is what happened in South Africa in the *Doctors for Life* case.[7]

In this case, the doctors' organization Doctors for Life brought a complaint to the Constitutional Court claiming that the National Council of Provinces, "in passing certain health bills, failed to invite written submissions and conduct public hearings . . . required by its duty to facilitate public involvement in its legislative processes."[8] The Court properly recognized the strength of that claim. As Judge Albie Sachs stated,

> A vibrant democracy has a qualitative and not just a quantitative dimension. . . . Dialogue and deliberation go hand in hand. . . . It is constitutive of [the people's] dignity as citizens today that they not only have a chance to speak, but also enjoy the assurance they will be listened to. This would be of special relevance for those who may feel politically disadvantaged at present because they lack higher education, access to resources and strong political connections. Public involvement accordingly strengthens rather than undermines formal democracy, by responding to and negating some of its functional deficits.[9]

This decision is interesting particularly because of the centrality that judges attributed to the elements of voice and discussion in the decision-making process. The Court maintained that the intervention of the public in legislative debates is a necessary part of a process committed to achieving impartiality.

Taking Arguments Seriously

Other cases that justify judicial intervention are those falling under the label of *strict-scrutiny analysis.* We are referring, in this case, to norms that are grounded on clearly *impermissible legal arguments* or that are merely the product of interest groups' pressure. Here, I will define impermissible legal arguments as those that are based on suspect classifications, such as race, ethnicity, racial origin, or nationality. Legal violations of this type should be serious and clear.[10]

Of course, political authorities should have a broad space for maneuvering—an ample capacity to choose between different courses of action according to their ideologies and convictions. However, to respect representatives' freedom to choose is not to say that their actions should be legally unconstrained. Judges, for instance, should ensure that representatives "deliberate rather than respond mechanically to constituent pressures" (Sunstein 1985, 49). As a consequence, courts could be authorized to challenge norms that are not supported by a "reasoned analysis,"[11] as typically happens in "cases involving discrimination against blacks, women, aliens and illegitimates, [where] the Court has invalidated statues even when they were not raw exercises of power in the ordinary sense" (ibid., 56).

To take just one example, in the *Reyes Aguilera* case in Argentina, part of the Supreme Court used these types of arguments in order to challenge political authorities' actions.[12] The case examined Decree 432/97, which in practice required a totally handicapped girl, of Bolivian origin, to complete twenty years of residence in the country before she could have access to the pensions to which handicapped people are entitled under article 9 of Law 13478. In their vote, Judges Eduardo Petracchi and Carmen Argibay argued that the distinction promoted by the state was suspect and involved an invidious discrimination. In their opinion, the state failed to demonstrate that its distinction was based on a compelling interest and that the means it had chosen were the least restrictive for achieving that interest.

Defining the Boundaries of a Political Decision

Time Limits and Remand to the Legislator

Another way that courts can help the political discussion is to set the boundaries of a political decision, or provide politicians with criteria about basic constitutional demands—criteria to be taken into account by the legislators in their decisions. One way to do so, which is particularly interesting for the deliberative perspective proposed here, would be to *remand* the defied norm to the legislators, with specific indications regarding how to avoid future constitutional challenges. This is, for example, what happened in the *Badaro* case before Argentina's Supreme Court.[13]

In *Badaro*, a pensioner challenged the state's system for calculating and adjusting the amount paid to pensioners. Unsurprisingly, the Court recognized the legislature's capacity to decide the amount to be paid to pensioners. However, the Court also said that Argentina's Constitution required those amounts to be "mobile" (according to inflation/variables of prices) and reasonable, so as to ensure a decent subsistence for the sector. The Court then maintained that the norm under its examination systematically affected a large group of pensioners and thus offended the constitutional requirements. For this reason, it exhorted political authorities to correct their policy according to the demands of the Constitution. The Court decided to defer its final pronouncement on the topic while it waited for the legislators' response. One year after *Badaro*, the Court issued its second pronouncement on the same topic, known as *Badaro II*, where it challenged, again, the legislative omission. In this new decision, the Court declared that Congress had not respected the reasonable time limits established by the tribunal and urged Congress to dictate a new law that resolved the general problem that it had created.

Declaring What Political Authorities Are Not Authorized to Do

Another instance of the same principle would appear in cases where courts examine a specific political decision and declare whether legislators met their legal obligations in the decision-making process. This can be done without telling political authorities what the actual content of their policy should be.

The well-known *Grootboom* case, decided by South Africa's Constitutional Court in 2001, is a good example.[14] The case involved residents of a squatter settlement who occupied privately owned land and were coercively evicted by public authorities. In its historical—but at the same time quite simple and modest—decision, the Court condemned the state by maintaining that since the state's housing program made no provision for the relief of the appellants, the policy could not be considered reasonable. The state's obligation was to provide "legal and administrative infrastructure" to ensure access to housing on a "programmatic and coordinated basis, subject to available resources."[15] South Africa's Constitution, the Court concluded, "obliges the state to act positively to ameliorate" the housing conditions of the disadvantaged appellants.[16]

In its decision, the Court did not require the government to ensure shelter for all but rather insisted that the state design an emergency plan for those in need—whatever reasonable plan the government decided to adopt, according to its democratic authority. Nor did the Court ask political authorities to pass certain specific measures; rather, it requested a "coherent, coordinated program designed to meet" constitutional obligations.[17]

Promoting and Overseeing the Exchange of Arguments

Courts can also play a significant role in ensuring that legal norms are the product of an exchange of reasons, rather than the mere imposition of one interest group or sector of society on the rest (Sunstein 1985).[18] Courts' engagement in this crucial action to oversee the democratic procedure can take place in many different ways. For example, courts can require legislators to open the decision-making process to the public in order to avoid or reduce the influence of interest groups, or they can require political authorities to call on public audiences to supervise crucial aspects of the application of the law. More radically, courts can scrutinize the legislative process to ensure that legislative debate is genuine and not a mere facade.

One interesting illustration in this respect comes from the Colombian Constitutional Court.[19] Its awareness and commitment to democratic deliberative ideals can be recognized in its important T-760/08 judgment (discussed by Yamin et al. in this volume), through which the Court cooperated in the restructuring of Colombia's entire health system. The decision came after an intense judicialization of the area (more than 320,000 relevant cases came before the judiciary between 1999 and 2005). The Court's polemical decision tried to organize and clarify the profuse and sometimes contradictory regulations existing in the area, which were the result of so many legal reforms and judicial decisions. In its ruling, the Court took measures to reduce the use of *tutelas* (writs for the protection of constitutional rights), required the reorganization of existing health-care plans through transparent and participatory mechanisms, and demanded the reconstructive process to be supervised by public audiences (Yamin and Parra-Vera 2009). In this case, as in many others, the Court demonstrated its courage and commitment to deliberative democracy.[20] The Court showed its willingness to criticize, challenge, or strike down laws that had been approved without public debate or had not been the product of a reasonable process of public deliberation.[21]

Forcing the Consideration of Structural Problems

The "Estado de Cosas Inconstitucional"

On some occasions, courts can force legislators to address structural problems that politicians systematically refuse to consider. Undoubtedly, politicians, rather than judges, are in charge of defining which public policies to advance as well as which problems—among the many that a democracy may face—to address. However, political branches' failure to confront certain structural problems may become a source of permanent, massive, and manifest violations of rights. Environmental problems, prisoners' rights, and the needs of displaced people represent such structural situations.

The fact that the judiciary has no legitimacy for defining an exact remedy for such violations of rights says nothing against its participation in the process of finding a solution to that problem. In fact, it is the judiciary's duty to take part in the solution because—given its powers, capacities, resources, and institutional place—it shares responsibility for any systematic violations of rights that occur in the community.

Fortunately, there are many interesting examples that suggest what judges could do in those difficult situations of massive, structural violations of rights. For instance, the Colombian Constitutional Court (and more recently, the Argentinean Supreme Court, as we will see below) has been trying to find a way out of these complex situations, through its doctrine of *estado de cosas inconstitucional* (an unconstitutional state of affairs) (Ariza 2005; see also Cepeda 2004). This doctrine was first advanced by the Court in its T-153/98 judgment, in which the tribunal examined the living conditions of prison inmates.[22] The Court used this opportunity to set in motion a collective process in which representatives from all affected parties were required to participate. The Court also established a period of four years for these actors to define and implement a solution to the problem.[23]

Calling for Open Discussions

Another instance of the same principle would appear when the court itself calls a public meeting in order to promote an open discussion about the proper solution to a rights violation. This action is particularly relevant for problems that political authorities are not willing to address, and it may be justified in cases where the required knowledge is fragmented and dispersed, the voices and viewpoints to be considered are numerous, and the risks of making a biased decision are high.

Given that judges are not authorized to determine or carry out public policies, they should reserve such interventions for extreme situations—not to define and enforce a particular policy but rather to help put into motion the legislative machinery and, if necessary, oversee the dialogic process.

The series of public audiences called by Argentina's Supreme Court in the *Matanza-Riachuelo River Basin* case (*Mendoza*) are exemplar in this respect.[24] Furthermore, two very recent decisions, from the Brazilian and Mexican Supreme Courts, show that the inclination to call for public audiences is no longer an extravagant exception in the region. The Brazilian Court resorted to the mechanism of public audiences, for the first time, in a September 2009 decision.[25] In this case, concerning the state's obligation to provide medicines, the Court informed its decision through criteria collected in a public audience. Meanwhile, the Mexican Court resorted to a similar process in a controversial case about abortion.[26] On this occasion, the Mexican Court launched a process of public audiences in order to ground its decision (Ansolabehere 2009). In addition, the Court instituted a new decision-making process that included judicial discussions open to the public and the transmission of its sessions on television through a new "judicial channel."

Conclusion

In the previous pages, I have tried to demonstrate that judicial intervention in cases involving health rights in particular and social rights generally can be perfectly justifiable, if done under certain specific circumstances and developed in certain specific modes. I have maintained that even though there are numerous things that judges are not authorized to do, given their limited democratic legitimacy, there are also many others that they are *required* to do, in order to honor their constitutional obligations. This conclusion, I believe, challenges traditional views about judicial review, democracy, and the separation of powers, and also defies the ambiguous and unattractive notions of *judicial restraint* and *judicial activism*.[27]

NOTES

1. See, for example, Judge Richard Posner, famously stating that the constitution "is a charter of negative liberties; it tells the state to let people alone; it does not require the federal government or the state to provide services, even so elementary a service as maintaining law and order" (*Bowers v. De Vito*, 686 F.2d 616 [7th Cir. 1982]); or Judge Antonin Scalia's statement, "it is impossible to say that our constitutional traditions mandate the legal imposition of even so basic a precept of distributive justice as providing food to the destitute" (Edelman 1988, 24). Similarly, see Epstein (1997).
2. The best empirical analysis of the topic is Gauri and Brinks (2008).
3. For a discussion on the topic, see, for example, Vile (1967, 1991).
4. Remarkably, this Rousseauan democratic argument has been used not only regarding constitutions such as the U.S. Constitution, which is silent on social rights, but also regarding socially advanced constitutions, such as most Latin American ones. This was, for example, what Argentina's Supreme Court maintained in the case *Ramos, Marta y otros v. Provincia de Buenos Aires*, JA 2002-IV-466, March 12, 2002.
5. See, for example, articles by Forbath, West, Michelman, Balkin, or Siegel in Balkin and Siegel (2009).
6. On the one hand, while the deliberative model would have coincidences with Rousseauan versions of democracy concerning the value that both views give to political participation, it would differ from the participatory view, or at least important versions of it, as a consequence of its defense of public debate. On the other hand, deliberative democracy would also differ from Hamiltonian democracy, particularly as a consequence of its second distinctive feature.
7. *Doctors for Life International v. The Speaker of the National Assembly and Others*, 2006 (6) SA 416 (CC).
8. Ibid., para. 2.
9. Ibid., para. 234.
10. As Thayer put it, judges could defy statutes only "when those who have the right to make laws have not merely made a mistake, but have made a very clear one,—so clear that it is not open to rational question" (1908, 21).
11. See, for example, *Mississippi Univ. for Women v. Hogan*, 458 U.S. 718, 726 (1982).
12. *Recurso de hecho deducido por Luisa Aguilera Mariaca y Antonio Reyes Barja en representación de Daniela Reyes Aguilera en la causa Reyes Aguilera, Daniela v. Estado Nacional*, September 4, 2007.
13. *Badaro, Alfonso Valentín, v. ANSES s/ reajustes varios*, August 8, 2006.
14. *Government of the Republic of South Africa and Others v. Grootboom and Others*, 2001 (1) SA 46 (CC). In addition, in South Africa's famous *Treatment Action Campaign* case, the Constitutional Court went some steps further, ordering the state to prescribe the required HIV medicine in question (nevirapine) "without delay" and to take "reasonable measures" to facilitate its use. *Minister of Health and Others v. Treatment Action Campaign and Others*, (No. 2) 2002 (5) SA 721 (CC), paras. 95, 135.
15. *Government of the Republic of South Africa and Others v. Grootboom and Others*, *supra* note 14, para. 78.
16. Ibid., para. 93. See also the interesting decision *State of Punjab v. Mohinder Singh Chawla*, AIR (1997) SC (1225), where the Indian Supreme Court interpreted the right to health as integral to the right to life, and thus worthy of the most imperative constitutional protection.

17. *Republic of South Africa v. Grootboom, supra* note 14, para. 99. See also the crucial and more polemical case *Holiness Kesavananda Bharati v. The State of Kerala and Others*, AIR (1973) SC (1461), where the Indian Supreme Court decided that Parliament could not amend certain basic features of the Constitution.
18. Cases demanding a "public value" justification for statutory classification include *City of New Orleans v. Dukes*, 427 U.S. 297 (1976); *Daniel v. Family Security Life Ins. Co.*, 336 U.S. 220 (1949); *Tigner v. Texas*, 310 U.S. 141 (1940); *Rosenthal v. New York*, 226 U.S. 260 (1912); and *Engel v. O' Malley*, 219 U.S. 128 (1911). See Sunstein (1985, 50).
19. Criticisms of the Court's position may be found in Kugler and Rosenthal (2000, 14), Kalmanovitz (2000), and Pérez Salazar (2003, 89).
20. Other decisions where it showed its commitment to democratic debate as a precondition for the legitimacy of the laws include Sentencia C-013 de 1993; Sentencia C-386 de 1996; SC-222 de 1997; Sentencia C-760 de 2001; Sentencia C-915 de 2001; Sentencia C-1250 de 2001; Sentencia C-688 de 2002; Sentencia C-801 de 2003; Sentencia C-551 de 2003; Sentencia C-1056 de 2003; Sentencia C-839 de 2003; Sentencia C-1152 de 2003; Sentencia C-313 de 2004; Sentencia C-370 de 2004; and Sentencia C-372 de 2004. See García Jaramillo (2008).
21. A remarkable illustration in this respect is its 2004 decision striking down the so-called Anti-terrorist statute, which represented a crucial part of the executive branch's political agenda. The Court struck the statute down when it realized that more than a dozen of the representatives who voted for the polemical statute had changed their views on the topic from one day to the next, without giving any public explanation.
22. For the relationship between prisoners' rights and the right to live with human dignity, see the Indian Supreme Court's decision in *Francis Coralie Mullin v. Union Territory of Delhi*, (1981) 2 SCR 516.
23. See also Sentencia T-025 de 2004 (regarding the rights of "displaced people"); Sentencia T-590 de 1998 (regarding the protection of human rights defenders). Similarly, the Argentinean Supreme Court has been deciding "structural litigation" cases in recent years. See, for example, *Verbitsky, Horacio s/habeas corpus*, May 3, 2005 (regarding prisoners' rights) and *Causa Mendoza, Beatriz Silvia y Otros v. Estado Nacional y otros s/ daños y perjuicios (daños derivados de la contaminación ambiental del Río Matanza – Riachuelo)*, July 8, 2008.
24. *Mendoza, supra* note 23.
25. Supreme Federal Court of Brazil, 2009.
26. *Acuerdo General 2/2008*, March 10, 2008. The case appeared at a difficult moment for the Court, given its traditional lack of popularity and a particularly negative conjuncture after a decision on pederasty. The case therefore presented a good opportunity for the Court to reconstruct its legitimacy.
27. According to some, judicial activism means judges' imposition of their own, biased views about the law; and according to others, it means exactly the opposite of judicial restraint (judicial restraint would then be defined as the judicial tendency not to strike down laws unless they are obviously and openly unconstitutional).

Chapter 10

Litigating the Right to Health: Are Transnational Actors Backseat Driving?

Mindy Jane Roseman and Siri Gloppen

This chapter focuses on one of the puzzles motivating the research project that resulted in this book: the appearance of global, contemporaneous right-to-health litigation. As the country chapters show, similar types of health rights cases have emerged in different parts of the world at about the same time—in different legal systems and under different social conditions and health systems. Most notably, we see an early concentration of cases on HIV/AIDS medication in the late 1990s and early 2000s, and more recently, in the Latin American countries, around certain new drugs (e.g., for cancer, rheumatoid arthritis, Alzheimer's, and diabetes). Why are health rights cases—and similar ones at that—simultaneously arising in different countries? It is a coincidence?

The country chapters shed light on context-specific dynamics that have stimulated health rights litigation. In this chapter, we summarize those trends and use them to explore factors beyond the national context that may have contributed to such litigation—and that help us understand the global nature of this phenomenon. In doing so, we distinguish three types of (analytically distinct, but interwoven in practice) transnational influences: firstly, similar cases may arise independently in different countries in response to similar structural changes or global developments; secondly, domestic initiatives to litigate may be triggered or facilitated by diffusion and domestically driven learning from experiences elsewhere; and thirdly, transnational actors may actively initiate or facilitate litigation processes. We are particularly interested in exploring the third type of influence. If transnational actors are involved,

This chapter was researched with the assistance of Alison Davidian, then an LLM student at Harvard Law School. The authors also wish to thank Alicia Ely Yamin and the anonymous reviewer for their contributions.

who are they? What are their aims and interests? What is their relationship with national actors? What is the nature of their contribution?

This chapter only begins to explore this complex terrain. Based on patterns from the country cases, we outline an analytical framework with a set of hypotheses concerning how transnational processes and actors are likely to influence different types of litigation. In the last part of the chapter, we start exploring some of the linkages. The analysis, though tentative, aims to provide a basis for and inspire further investigation. Its focus is on understanding how transnational influences have contributed to cases that have arisen—not to explain why certain health rights cases arise in some contexts and not others. That would require a systematic investigation of "negative" cases, which is beyond the scope of the current study.

Patterns Emerging from the Country Studies

While our focus is on transnational influences, these must be seen in the context of the domestic factors that influence the individuals and organizations bringing right-to-health cases to court (their opportunity structure).[1] The country studies show great variation in how health rights cases are brought, by whom, and for what purpose.

Individuals litigating for medications or services that the health system has denied them[2] dominate right-to-health cases in the Latin American countries. The cases are usually decided on an individual basis in rulings that in principle do not have a general effect (although they may in practice set precedent and/or spur changes in policy or practice).[3] The claims vary in nature. Some claims seek treatment that the system offers in principle but fails to provide (in a timely manner or at all), while other claims seek drugs and treatment that are not (or no longer) part of the individual's health plan.[4] The aggregate effect of such cases, which often concern relatively costly drugs or treatment, may be substantial in terms of both cost and potential health gains; but the direct impact of each case on the health system is normally negligible (although individual claims for extremely costly treatments for rare diseases may represent a significant burden for the unit that bears the cost).

While individual right-to-health cases for private gain typify those in Latin American countries, other cases more directly and explicitly aim for structural change.[5] These are often collective and public interest cases undertaken or supported by nongovernmental organizations (NGOs).[6] Landmark cases of this nature are found in Argentina,[7] Brazil,[8] and Colombia.[9] In addition, courts have issued judgments that directly affect policy by signaling that all similar cases will be treated equally, as in the 1998 ruling from the Costa Rican Constitutional Court regarding access to HIV/AIDS drugs (see Wilson in this volume); by keeping cases open in order for new claims to enter, as is commonly done in Argentina (see Bergallo in this volume); or by constructing policy-directing judgments from individual cases, as the Colombian Constitutional Court did in its landmark structural judgment on the health system (T-760/08), in which it combined a number of individual cases and used them to review its own health rights jurisprudence and demand wide-ranging reform of the health system (see Yamin et al. in this volume). Still, the dominant pattern in the Latin American cases is individuals (or groups of individuals) litigating for private gain.

In South Africa and India, health rights claims from individuals seeking treatment are less common. The first such case before the South African Constitutional Court failed.[10] The Constitutional Court cited the need for reasonable priority setting by the health system in a context of resource scarcity, indicating that the Court's role as guardian of the constitutional right to health is not to grant individual relief counter to health policy priorities but rather to ensure that health policies are rational, reasonable, and respectful of the right to health. This sent a strong signal to potential litigants, and in a context where the threshold for accessing the courts is relatively high, few claims for individual treatment have subsequently gone to the courts. South Africa has, however, witnessed some important right-to-health decisions in cases brought by public interest NGOs (in this volume, Cooper; Norheim and Gloppen). Also, in India, the bulk of right-to-health cases has been brought by organizations or individual lawyers in the public interest—which gives the advantage of the cases being fast-tracked through an otherwise glacially slow justice system (Parmar and Wahi in this volume).

Transnational Influences Contributing to Contemporaneous Health Rights Litigation

Three different processes—or a combination thereof—may explain why health rights litigation (and similar types of lawsuits) increases around the same time across continents: (i) litigation may arise spontaneously and independently in response to similar changes in actors' opportunity structures due to what we may call *transnational structural changes*; (ii) it could be a result of *diffusion* processes by which local litigators are inspired by and learn from litigation processes elsewhere; or (iii) it could be the result of *active intervention by transnational actors* of various kinds.

Transnational Structural Changes

Four broad transnational processes relevant to the rise in right-to-health litigation have accelerated in the past two decades, changing the structural and normative conditions affecting the supply of and demand for health services, as well as legal opportunity structures.

First, there has been a rapid *development of pharmaceutical and other medical technologies*, resulting in increased possibilities for treating previously untreatable conditions and better treatment for a wide range of illnesses and conditions.

Second, health systems' and insurers' *economic ability and willingness to pay* for medical services have not kept up with the increased supply of and demand for potentially useful treatments. The growing gap between technologically possible disease-treating/life-extending regimens and their economic (and ethical) feasibility has led to attempts to restrict health spending, even in wealthy countries.[11] This has coincided with a global neoliberal economic trend and increased focus on reducing public expenditure through the privatization and commercialization of health services (co-payment, outsourcing, etc.)

Third, in the wake of the Cold War, there has been an international *rights revolution*, exhibited by a strengthening of human rights norms in the international system—including the development of the right to health—and a spread of rights awareness and rights discourses.[12] Many countries domesticated these norms in new, liberal, rights-rich constitutions that strengthened legal institutions and made them more suitable for legal mobilization around social issues, including the right to health.[13] This changed countries' legal opportunity structures, allowing actors to take advantage of judicial forums.[14]

Finally, there has been a *revolution in information technology*, most importantly the Internet, which has increased access to information on medical developments and on health as a human right.

Together, these four underlying transnational trends create conditions in much of the world where broad sections of the population are aware of an expanding array of cures and treatments that fall outside of the health system or health plan. This, in combination with a greater rights awareness and a sense of being entitled to health services that might keep us fit and alive creates fertile grounds for health litigation—provided the legal system is reasonably accessible and responsive to such claims, and the health system has a reasonable capacity to provide for what is litigated.[15] This changes the context within which health provision takes place and is undoubtedly important for understanding why we see litigation for similar drugs occurring in different countries at the same time, as awareness of technological advances spread—and why we see thousands of cases claiming individual access to treatment in Latin America, once patients become aware and litigation enters their perceived opportunity structure. This brings us to a second process—diffusion, or learning—that may spur a simultaneous rise in litigation.

Diffusion

For our purposes, diffusion refers to processes by which domestic litigators and/or their support structures (e.g., activists, lawyers, judges, doctors, and commercial interests) are inspired by and learn from litigation processes elsewhere, but without active, intentional efforts by transnational actors to influence or facilitate the litigation. Theories of legal diffusion and social networks are useful for understanding these processes, as is the notion of the "vernacularization" of human rights (see Risse et al. 1999; Merry 2006; Meyer et al. 1997). Such learning processes also take place at the national level, often with patient organizations as a catalyst, and this may help explain the exponential rise in individual cases once courts prove responsive to (particular types of) claims for individual benefit—and, conversely, why cases tend not to be filed where there is a principled/regular dismissal of such litigation.

Transnational diffusion is intertwined with the transnational structural changes discussed above. Litigation strategies and right-to-health jurisprudence from other jurisdictions are more readily available to lawyers and activists today than in the past.[16] The development of international human rights norms around the right to health has created the space and generated impetus for activists, scholars, and patient organizations, among others, to interact and form transnational networks. The 1990s witnessed an exponential growth in transnational civil society participation that had health and rights at its core; the United Nations conferences on human rights, reproductive health, women's empowerment, and social development[17] brought together governments, civil society, and donors to discuss and strategize about long-term global agendas to alleviate inequalities, ill-health, abuses, and unsustainable development. The International AIDS Conferences, which had begun in the mid-1980s as international scientific meetings, also became sites for political organizing as HIV infections reached pandemic proportions in the 1990s.[18] Such arenas for diffusion seem particularly relevant for understanding health litigation brought by activists in the public interest (although patients' organizations may play a role in stimulating individual litigation for access to treatment).

The development of international human rights norms on the right to health and the global availability of judgments also creates an enabling context for judges. It has been suggested that international human rights law itself is responsible for the judicialization of the right to health, convincing judges to loosen their restraint and deem such cases justiciable (Forman 2005).

Transnational structural changes and diffusion processes are important for understanding the simultaneous emergence of health litigation in different countries. But we are also interested in exploring intentional efforts by transnational actors to initiate, stimulate, or facilitate court cases on the right to health.

Intentional Interventions by Transnational Actors

Transnational actors are a diverse category of individuals, organizations, and firms whose common characteristic in this context is that they (seek to) influence health litigation processes in national contexts other than where they are primarily based.[19] In contrast to demand-led diffusion, where local litigators actively embrace experiences from elsewhere, the impetus here comes from transnational actors. In practice, there will often be elements of both, and they may be difficult to distinguish—for example, when transnational lawyers' networks or organizations like the ESCR-Net sow seeds of litigation in new settings, and local activists instigate litigation where the legal opportunity structures make the setting ripe (see Cummings and Trubek 2008; Santos 2007).[20]

Transnational actors differ greatly with regard to their motivations for seeking to influence litigation and with regard to the nature of their influence. "Transnational actors" as such is not an analytically useful category and needs to be broken down. We distinguish three, albeit still broad, categories of transnational actors likely to influence litigation in very different ways: civil society, commercial interests, and donors.

Transnational Civil Society

Transnational civil society comprises transnational *human rights NGOs* for whom the right to health is a specific focus or part of a broader social rights agenda. It also includes institutions, networks, and individuals engaged transnationally in health litigation as litigators, amici, or back-stop institutions providing assistance.[21]

Besides direct engagement in domestic litigation (alone or with domestic partner institutions), transnational organizations may stimulate or facilitate cases brought by national counterparts. Transnational civil society actors typically have a public health and human rights agenda. When trying to understand their potential influence, it is thus particularly relevant to investigate health rights cases brought in the public interest or otherwise aimed at bringing about changes in health policy advancing social justice.[22] Two transnational organizations noted for having undertaken pioneering, precedent-setting litigation around social rights generally and right to health in particular include the Center for Reproductive Rights (CRR) and the Centre on Housing Rights and Evictions (COHRE), whose cases focus on claiming low (or no-) cost health interventions for large or excluded sectors of the population.

It is important to acknowledge, however, that NGOs (whether domestic or transnational) are not necessarily purveyors of a general cause. Patients' organizations exist primarily to promote condition- or disease-specific interests that in some cases may run counter to a public health agenda.[23] And where the aim of civil society actors includes getting a patented medication on the registry of publicly provided drugs, they may share common interests with the pharmaceutical company holding the drug's patent.

Commercial Interests

Multinational (and national) pharmaceutical companies often have economic interests at stake in right-to-health litigation, particularly in access-to-medicines cases. Sometimes, multinational pharmaceutical companies are direct parties to cases of major importance for access to medications and the right to health, such as those regarding patent rights. What is less clear is whether these companies also influence cases brought by others—for instance, by stimulating or supporting (directly or indirectly, through funding or other means) litigation brought by individuals or organizations suing for access to a patented regimen of treatment.

Linkages with transnational pharmaceutical companies are of particular interest when exploring dynamics that drive litigation for access to patented medication—litigation that, as other chapters in this volume show, represents substantial costs in some of the countries studied here, most notably Brazil, Colombia, and Costa Rica. These linkages, however, are difficult to uncover and credibly establish, since all sides may be reluctant to disclose relations that could appear improper. But by combining a variety of methods and materials, it might be possible to shed light on this potentially very important phenomenon.

Donors

Litigation often depends on funding.[24] Besides pharmaceutical companies (which could be motivated to fund litigation due to material interests), potential sources of transnational funding for health rights litigation include international agencies,[25] bilateral donors,[26] and private foundations and organizations.[27] These funders may contribute to health rights litigation by financing cases that advance particular objectives (e.g., in the interest of public health or in support of vulnerable groups). Alternatively, they may provide general operational support for organizations whose activities include litigation.

That transnational donors provide funding for litigation does not mean that they provide the impetus to litigate. The recipient institution may still generate the initiative, with the transnational donor serving as facilitator. Still, it is interesting to explore whether in some cases donors (directly or indirectly) encourage partner organizations to litigate, thus contributing to the spread of health rights litigation as a transnational trend.

Exploring Transnational Actors' Influence on Health Litigation: An Analytical Typology

Based on the patterns emerging from the country cases and on the theoretical exploration of different transnational influences presented above, we have identified a range of dynamics that may explain the simultaneous rise of health rights litigation in various countries. In the following sections, we will explore one aspect of this picture more closely—namely, whether transnational actors contribute to the global trend by intentionally stimulating litigation and, if so, how this influence plays out in various cases and contexts. To this end, we outline a framework to guide empirical investigations, in which we formulate hypotheses based on characteristics of different types of cases.

We assume that the likelihood of transnational engagement in health rights litigation, as well as its nature (type of actors involved and form of influence), depends on the scope and aim of the litigation, the costs and profits involved, and the legal and political opportunity structures. This is illustrated in table 10.1.

Table 10.1. Types of health rights litigation and potential transnational influences

Cost/profit	Scope		
	Private gain ⟵⟶ Public interest / structural change Few beneficiaries ⟵⟶ Many beneficiaries		
High	High-cost interventions outside of health plan for rare conditions (orphan drugs, specific cancer drugs, dialysis, expensive operations) • Pharmaceutical companies • Patients' organizations/activists	High/medium-cost interventions outside of health plan for common conditions (cancer, Alzheimer's, rheumatoid arthritis, diabetes, HIV/AIDS) • Pharmaceutical companies • Patients' organizations/activists • Donors	High/medium-cost interventions outside of health plan relevant to large section of society/vulnerable groups (patent rights, HIV/AIDS, tuberculosis, vaccines, screening) • Pharmaceutical companies • Rights activists • Donors
Medium	Medium/low-cost interventions inside or outside of health plan relevant to few patients, (noncompliance, waiting time, off-patent drugs) • Influence from transnational actors unlikely	Medium/low-cost interventions inside or outside of health plan for common conditions (noncompliance, waiting time, off-patent/inexpensive drugs, standard treatment) • Influence from transnational actors unlikely	Low-per-patient-cost interventions outside of health plan relevant to large section of society/vulnerable groups (vaccines, screening, antenatal care, PMTCT, malaria prophylaxis, food safety, clean water/air) • Rights activists • Donors • Commercial interests
Low/no profit	Regulations to improve access to health for specific (vulnerable) individuals (discrimination on ethnic/cultural grounds, prisoners) • Rights activists • Donors	Regulations to improve access to health for specific (vulnerable) groups (discrimination on ethnic/cultural grounds, prisoners) • Rights activists • Donors	Regulations to improve access to health-related services/interventions for general population (abortion, contraception) • Rights activists • Donors

Scope is a matter of both whether the case concerns one individual, a group, or potentially "all" (if the case is for structural change) and the magnitude and nature of potential benefits. In table 10.1, the scope is represented by the horizontal axis. Generally, transnational engagement is assumed to be more likely in cases concerning many beneficiaries and where the potential benefit is large (the right side of the table). The scope of a case is also relevant for understanding which type of transnational actors are likely to be involved. In cases aiming for public health–related structural change, transnational influences are likely to come from civil society actors and donors working on human rights and public health issues, while in litigation for individuals' private gain, transnational influences are more likely to come from commercial interests and patients' organizations. Since "aiming for structural change" is difficult to measure directly, we suggest a proxy: identifying whether a case is brought by affected individuals or in the public interest. This distinction must, however, be applied with contextual sensitivity and judgment, since how a case is argued depends on the legal opportunity structure. Individual cases may, for example, be brought with an aim to change the situation for "all" (e.g., a disadvantaged group such as HIV-positive prisoners).

The vertical axis in table 10.1 represents the cost/profit dimension. Commercial interests are assumed to potentially exert influence only where substantial profit is at stake (toward the top of the table). Patients' organizations are assumed to be involved primarily where per-patient costs are high.

The cells illustrate how health rights cases vary along the two dimensions. The dimensions should be thought of as continuums rather than sharply defined categories; thus, the three-by-three division is not an exhaustive typology but simply an attempt to show how some right-to-health cases align with the interests and goals of certain types of transnational actors, rendering it more likely that these actors play a role.

The upper-left and upper-middle cells of table 10.1 represent cases brought for individualized benefit, where per-patient costs are high. These types of cases, particularly litigation for medicines, are what most often draw criticism and concern. Representing a significant part of litigation-induced expenses, they seem to skew resources toward patients who are better-off (see Mæstad et al. in this volume) and toward forms of treatment that should not be prioritized from a public health perspective (Norheim and Gloppen in this volume). They are also perceived to contribute to the increasing medicalization of health and to drain resources away from prevention and primary care.[28] It is thus particularly important to try to understand the driving forces behind the escalation and spread of such cases—including the potential role of international actors.

Before focusing on potential transnational actors, we should, however, take account of domestic incentive dynamics. In these cases, even middle-class patients have much at stake, and individual demand is likely to be considerable where the legal opportunity structure is favorable. In our material, such cases are common to and principal among all the Latin American countries. This could indicate that these countries share similar conditions conducive to the spread of this type of litigation. The country chapters have shown that—compared to India and South Africa—the Latin American countries have legal opportunity structures that are better suited for individual right-to-health litigants (i.e., relatively easy access to the courts, likelihood of favorable decisions, and health system compliance). The simultaneous spread of litigation may thus plausibly be understood as "uncoordinated" local responses to transnational structural changes, such as the development of new medications. However, transnational (and domestic) actors also might actively contribute to the spread of such litigation. Networks of patients' organizations (domestic as well as transnational) may play a role in spreading information and contributing expertise.[29] Commercial actors, particularly transnational (and domestic) pharmaceutical companies, may "push" (directly or via patients' organizations, doctors, etc.) in cases where the profits at stake are high—due to either very high per-patient costs or a high number of potential patients. Below, we make a very preliminary inquiry into pharmaceutical companies' involvement in this type of litigation.

In table 10.1, the cases in the left and middle cells of the middle row concern litigation for individualized benefit where the cost to the individual patient is moderate or low, with little profit at stake for transnational commercial actors (e.g., litigation regarding waiting time, off-patent drugs, or disputes over health-plan coverage).[30] Such cases are particularly common in Colombia, but also occur in the other Latin American countries. They often concern treatment that in principle is provided by the public health system but in practice is lacking or inadequate. They are likely to be demand-driven by individual litigants in response to opportunity structures with a low threshold for access to courts, combined with structural problems in the provision of health care. Although litigants may be assisted by local organizations, significant engagement of transnational actors or commercial interests is unlikely; these cases will not be a focus here.

In the bottom row, the left and middle cells regard access to health services for particularly vulnerable individuals, such as prisoners or members of ethnic or sexual minorities. Such cases are likely to be taken up by national human rights and public health NGOs. Transnational NGOs and donors may play a role, either directly as parties or in inspiring or facilitating litigation (e.g., providing resources or serving as back-stop institutions). This type of case, while in principle interesting to investigate for transnational involvement, has not been our focus.

The cases discussed so far are brought for particular (groups of) patients' individualized benefit. Another category of cases aims to bring about structural changes in the health system (legislation or policy changes). These cases are often framed as public interest cases. We find such cases in most of the countries,[31] but they comprise a much larger share of health rights cases in India and South Africa. Usually, public interest cases are brought by local NGOs or public interest lawyers, but sometimes they are brought directly by transnational organizations, working alone or with local partners. Transnational networks, activist organizations, and donors may also play a more indirect role by inspiring, encouraging, and facilitating litigation. Particularly in areas where there is a strong transnational engagement (e.g., HIV/AIDS and reproductive rights), our hypothesis is that such direct and indirect engagement has played an important role in the global spread of litigation for structural change.

Tracing the Influence of Transnational Actors

Having set forth an analytic typology, we use the remainder of this chapter to explore whether actual litigation processes support the hypotheses outlined above. We have selected cases that represent important aspects of the health litigation phenomenon and where, according to the framework, significant transnational involvement could be expected. Data have been collected through a combination of literature reviews,[32] documentary sources, and interviews with key informants (litigants, donors, and activists) about their experiences with transnational influences.

We start by exploring the way transnational dynamics play out in litigation that seeks to improve the health system in the public interest (right-hand column in table 10.1), beginning with the most direct and open forms of involvement and proceeding to look at more subtle and indirect ways in which transnational actors contribute to "spreading the gospel." A main focus is on HIV/AIDS cases, since these are the first significant health rights cases in many countries, raising the question of what makes them spread beyond borders. We assume that transnational engagement is more important in countries where barriers to court access are steep in terms of the need for case preparation and legal sophistication, compared to contexts where barriers to court access are low, thus limiting the importance of legal expertise and funding (and of collective action generally). South African HIV/AIDS litigation is therefore a particular focus.

In the last part of the chapter, we examine the involvement of transnational actors in cases where profits are high (top-left and middle cells in table 10.1). Some of the relationships subject to analysis here might be (perceived as) legally or ethically problematic, which has made data collection difficult, as certain actors—particularly pharmaceutical companies—have been unwilling to disclose their involvement in litigation, and documentary evidence is scarce.[33] More extensive investigation is needed to reach firm conclusions, but the following exploration indicates some of the transnational dynamics at play in various forms of health litigation and may serve as a basis for further research.

International Influence on Litigation to Transform the Health System in the Public Interest

Sometimes, transnational human rights and public health actors openly undertake, initiate, or facilitate litigation aiming to transform a country's health system for the benefit of vulnerable groups. The best example in our material is the U.S.-based organization Center for Reproductive Rights. CRR focuses on legal and policy change to advance reproductive rights, notably the decriminalization of access to medical services such as abortion and contraceptives.[34] These cases are large in scope, potentially increasing access to health services for broad groups. Initially, CRR's international focus was on transnational litigation in Latin America, filing petitions before the Inter-American Commission on Human Rights after local NGOs had exhausted domestic remedies.[35] More recently, CRR has supported local NGOs in countries such as Nepal and India with cases regarding the decriminalization of abortion.[36]

The Geneva-based Centre on Housing Rights and Evictions (COHRE) has been directly involved in litigation on housing rights in several countries,[37] but for our purposes, it is particularly interesting to note that the organization was a party to the *Mazibuko* case on the right to water in South Africa (see

Cooper in this volume). According to the leading South African researcher in the case, COHRE, after learning about the litigation, offered its assistance: "COHRE was the amicus and provided invaluable input on the international law and comparative examples." She also noted that expertise on water sufficiency was provided by a U.S.-based global expert on the issue; that funding for the case came from the Ford Foundation, Bread for the World (Germany), the Unitarian Universalist Service Committee (United States), and the Norwegian Centre for Human Rights; and that the litigants received "lots of solidarity from researchers, academics, [and] activists. These all had huge value and were a great source of support, expertise, [and] encouragement."[38]

Cases where transnational involvement is direct and visible in court documents are rare. Usually, such engagement and influence is more subtle, ranging from technical or financial assistance to the general promotion of litigation as a strategy (such as when a meeting with the United Nations Special Rapporteur on the Right to Health inspires and encourages Ugandan health rights activists in their litigation efforts).[39] In the following section, we examine transnational influences in HIV/AIDS-related cases. These were among the most significant early cases in every country analyzed in this volume, rendering it particularly interesting to explore to what extent the spread of such litigation can be ascribed to transnational activism.

Litigation for HIV/AIDS Medication

In our analytical framework, HIV/AIDS-medication litigation falls into two categories. Prior to 1997, prices for HIV/AIDS drugs were very high, and litigation was cast in terms of individual access (table 10.1, middle cell in top row). After 1997, drug effectiveness improved, prices dropped, and activists tended to litigate in the public interest (table 10.1, top and middle cells in right column). Our focus is on post-1997 litigation.

With regard to pre-1997 HIV/AIDS-medication litigation, we will note only that in our material, such cases occur in the two countries with the easiest access to courts. In Costa Rica, an unsuccessful case was filed in 1992 by the president of the Association of the Fight Against AIDS.[40] In Colombia, from 1992 onwards, the Constitutional Court started granting access to HIV/AIDS medication.[41] In both countries, interviews suggest that such litigation was initiated by activists, with no indications of ties to commercial actors or donors.[42] The low threshold for access in terms of costs and legal representation also minimizes the need for support or concerted action around litigation. Some indicate that informal networks with similar organizations elsewhere in the region played a role in these early HIV/AIDS cases,[43] but otherwise we have not found evidence to indicate significant transnational influences. It should, however, be noted that representatives of Colombian associations for people living with HIV/AIDS indicate that there have been close links between patients' organizations and pharmaceutical companies, including pharmaceutical companies' financing of meetings of patients' organizations in which experts were contracted to provide advice on legal strategies.[44] When barriers to access are low, such encouragement may have significant effects. Additional research, however, is necessary for understanding the exact nature of the relationship and the extent to which it has directly affected specific litigation processes.

Around 1997, constitutional and human rights claims began to win access to HIV/AIDS medication in a variety of jurisdictions (UNAIDS 2006). The timing is no accident.[45] In July 1996, the discovery of combination antiretroviral therapy providing much more effective treatment was announced at the 11th International AIDS Conference held in Vancouver (Mukherjee 2004). Subsequently, drug prices declined dramatically, partly due to the concerted efforts (including litigation) of transnational and national NGOs.[46]

The Vancouver conference not only raised hopes of effective treatment but also provided opportunities for activists to interact and strategize with one another.[47] In November 1996, eight Argentinean NGOs jointly brought the first successful *amparo* action against their country's Ministry of Health and Social Welfare for its failure to supply medicines to people living with HIV/AIDS (Bianco et al. 1998).[48]

The South African advocates who, in 2002, filed perhaps the most celebrated access-to-treatment case, *Minister of Health and Others v. Treatment Action Campaign and Others*,[49] were also present in Vancouver. On the heels of the conference, the Treatment Action Campaign (TAC) and its partners began to strategize approaches for overcoming governmental barriers to access. Despite widespread support for access to HIV/AIDS treatment, few wanted to sue the African National Congress government. Litigation was an action of last resort, after repeated government intransigence, in the face of overwhelming evidence of the efficacy and cost-effectiveness of nevirapine in preventing mother-to-child transmission of HIV.[50]

For this type of litigation (transformation of the health system in the public interest and/or for vulnerable groups by introducing low-cost interventions), we could expect to see influence from transnational human rights and public health NGOs. However, representatives of TAC and the AIDS Law Project (ALP), one of its partners in the case, deny such influence and explain that while they consulted widely with others, the decision to litigate was homegrown.[51] To be sure, international donors supported the organizations' legal efforts for treatment access—but while these resources were important, they did not provide the initiative or impetus for the litigation.[52] On the other hand, TAC and ALP representatives noted that they are often invited by NGOs in South Africa and abroad to talk about their litigation and have thus themselves turned into transnational actors serving as a resource and model for others.

Donors were reluctant to talk about litigation as a part of their strategies. An exception was the Swedish International Development Cooperation Agency (Sida), which has supported TAC and the ALP's legal efforts against the South African government. Sida representatives explained that openly supporting litigation may be politically costly[53] and that many donors are reluctant to support litigation out of political concerns.[54]

Still, some donors openly encourage litigation. The guidelines developed by the Joint United Nations Programme on HIV/AIDS (UNAIDS) for accessing the Global Fund to Fight AIDS, Tuberculosis and Malaria specifically encourage NGOs to submit proposals to use strategic litigation as a means to create a "supportive environment" or improve the conditions of people living with HIV/AIDS (UNAIDS 2008).[55] A member of a Moldovan consortium receiving a UNAIDS grant intimated that "the idea [to litigate] in the first place belongs to advocacy by UNAIDS along with Soros Foundation-Moldova."[56] A former UNAIDS employee in China also noted that while the institution could not openly encourage litigation, it engaged informally with organizations preparing litigation.[57] Several of the most active organizations involved in strategic litigation regarding HIV/AIDS (and social rights more generally) receive financial support from the same international donors, especially the Ford Foundation, which seeks to advance a social and economic human rights agenda through litigation.[58]

In preliminary conclusion, we note that while the "drivers" strategizing and initiating South African HIV/AIDS litigation were local, the litigation is facilitated by international donors and should be seen in the context of international networks and arenas, including the 1996 International AIDS Conference in Vancouver. The first important case, described above, and the organizations and individuals behind it seem to have influenced litigation elsewhere, inspiring and aiding activists and possibly also influencing the policies and best-practice accounts of transnational actors, such as UNAIDS, who proactively encourage HIV/AIDS-related litigation.

Individual/Group Litigation for Access to High-Cost Treatment

Lawsuits seeking to provide individuals or groups, at public expense, with high-cost treatments that are not authorized by the health system have potentially huge cost implications. Litigation for the same treatments commonly arises around the same time in various jurisdictions, begging questions about transnational driving forces. Commercial interests are particularly strong in cases concerning expensive treatment relevant for a large number of patients (such as new drugs for cancer, diabetes, and rheumatoid arthritis) and in cases that are relevant to small numbers of patients, but where the drugs are extremely expensive (such as orphan drugs for very rare diseases) (table 10.1, left and middle cells in top row).

Pharmaceutical companies are occasionally directly and openly involved in litigation to get their drugs into the public health package or essential drugs list. Eisai, a Japan-based multinational pharmaceutical company involved in the marketing of Aricept, a drug for Alzheimer's, brought a judicial review claim against the British National Institute for Health and Clinical Excellence's decision to restrict access to medications for Alzheimer's.[59] The Alzheimer's Society took part in the judicial review as an "interested party."[60]

In other cases, it is possible to trace a covert or indirect influence from pharmaceutical companies. A well-documented case centered on Tania Gonzales, a ten-year-old Costa Rican girl diagnosed with Gaucher disease, a rare condition caused by a genetic inability to metabolize cellular waste.[61] Genzyme, a U.S.-based drug company, developed Cerezyme, a bioengineered treatment for the disease. Cerezyme is sold at US$160,000 per patient per year, and patients must be on it for life. Genzyme does not negotiate preferential or affordable pricing for low-income countries or individuals, but rather follows "an extremely disciplined 'one price' strategy: find patients; donate the drug at first if necessary, but press constantly to be paid full retail price" (Heuser 2009). A journalist investigating the case uncovered connections between Genzyme and the Constitutional Court litigation. Genzyme does not appear as an official party to the suit, but its imprint can be traced to the company's hiring of a local health-care consultant who brought Tania's case to the national ombudsman, who, in turn—faced with a sick, poor, and dying child—petitioned the Constitutional Court. The Court ordered the government to cover her treatment, resulting in Costa Rica's public health-care system paying full price for Tania's treatment.

In Brazil, there is evidence that a local pharmaceutical company colluded with physicians and lawyers to use litigation to bolster sales of its products.[62] In most cases, however, there are only indirect signs of pharmaceutical companies' influence. What emerges as a pattern is the development of linkages between patients' organizations and the pharmaceutical companies that manufacture treatment regimes, with companies providing financial and other assistance to patients' groups.[63] At the same time, many patients' organizations actively facilitate litigation. Through his interviews with diabetes patients' organizations in Brazil, Octavio L. Motta Ferraz found that they were holding weekly legal clinics in which lawyers provided advice.[64] Furthermore, a recent study from Brazil concluded that

> [in] 67.65% of lawsuits the plaintiffs requested drugs for rheumatoid arthritis. Coincidently (or not), those were exactly the plaintiffs who could not even inform us of the name of the association which helped them with the judicial demand. Although, on one hand, there is no conclusive evidence that such associations are sponsored by the pharmaceutical industry, it is hard to believe, on the other hand, that an independent association not only offers free help to citizens, but also pays all the costs of a lawsuit. (da Silva and Terrazas, forthcoming, 13)

Colombian scholars researching right-to-health litigation have also highlighted the intimate relationship between pharmaceutical companies and patients' organizations.[65] In a study on litigation for cancer drugs in Colombia, they found that fifteen of thirty-nine cancer patients' organizations "offer some kind of 'legal advice' among their basic services to patients. . . . Between 2003 and 2008 cancer was the most litigated—and expensive—condition with a total 16370 Tutelas."[66]

With regard to the rapid and simultaneous growth in Latin American countries of litigation claiming costly patented drugs that the national health system does not cover, our exploration indicates that national and multinational pharmaceutical companies do play a role in stimulating such litigation—but mainly indirectly, through their ties with patients' organizations.

However, the data are still rudimentary, and more research is needed to reach a firm conclusion on the nature and extent of this influence.

Conclusion

Based on our analytical typology systematizing various actors' incentives in relation to different types of right-to-health litigation, we have explored some cases in which transnational influence is most likely.

Our investigation strengthens the perception of litigation as a transnational phenomenon, but at the same time suggests that the answer to the question in this chapter's title is generally no. Transnational agents rarely "drive" litigation. There are cases in which transnational health rights activists litigate openly—on their own or with local activists—to transform health systems, or where pharmaceutical companies litigate to get their drugs into publicly funded health packages, but this is rare. In most cases, the main "drivers" of health rights litigation are domestic to each country—motivated by similar concerns (in response to transnational changes) and responding to local opportunity structures. We have found little to suggest that transnational actors impose or infuse litigation that is "foreign" to the context.

This does not mean that transnational influences and actors are not an important part of this phenomenon. The cases examined here show numerous links with transnational activists, donors, and pharmaceutical companies that play a facilitating or encouraging role. Transnational institutional spaces (including virtual spaces, such as that provided by the ESCR-Net) play a critical role in germinating ideas, with the 1996 International AIDS Conference in Vancouver as a particularly important case in point.

Whether a matter winds up being framed as a constitutional right-to-health case at all—and the extent to which external drivers are involved—depends on the legal opportunity structures. In the Latin American countries in our material, the legal opportunity structures generally encourage individual litigation for access to treatment. At the same time, where the threshold for accessing the courts is exceptionally low, such as in Colombia and Costa Rica, individuals need little or no assistance to litigate. Transnational commercial actors that have a clear pecuniary interest in these cases might thus achieve their aims through very subtle means (if any). There is evidence to suggest a role for patients' organizations in litigation, as well as for pharmaceutical companies (directly and through links with patients' organizations), but further investigation is needed to reach firm conclusions. Further studies could also contribute to a fuller understanding of the nature and extent of transnational collaboration around public interest litigation cases, where the threshold for litigation is high.

NOTES

1. For a discussion of litigants' opportunity structures, see the analytical framework presented in chapter 2. Whether cases are brought to court depends on the legal system, the nature of the health system, and whether there are other, more efficacious avenues for resolving the claim. Factors affecting the legal opportunity structure include which types of cases are accepted—and successful—before the courts; the time and costs involved in litigation; whether individual representation requires a lawyer; and possibilities for representation by an organization or association. Relative chances of success for different types of cases vary between countries—while public interest cases in South Africa have a higher success rate than cases for private gain, the opposite is true in Brazil. More fundamentally, the terms for bringing constitutional cases on the right to health differ between countries and legal systems, meaning, for example, that an individual case identified as a constitutional case in the Colombian context might not qualify as such in India—or would be more feasible if brought under an administrative-law framework (thus not falling into the universe of cases analyzed here) or transformed into a public interest case. This affects the universe of cases and represents a challenge for cross-national comparison. See also chapter 1 for a discussion of dilemmas in defining the universe of cases.
2. Whether health rights litigation is directed against the state, semi-private social security funds, insurance companies, or service providers depends on the organization of the health system, which varies greatly between countries (see the country chapters in this volume). The extent to which cases against (semi-) private institutions are brought under the right to health—and thus included in the current volume—also varies between countries. See *supra* note 1.
3. The degree to which this happens differs between countries. In Costa Rica, where the social security fund must cover the costs for lost cases, it happens routinely. It is also common in Argentina and Brazil, while it is rare in Colombia.
4. Particularly where there are differentiated insurance-based health plans, many disputes arise over the terms of coverage (e.g., types of conditions and treatments or the plan's membership terms).
5. By structural change, we mean legislative or policy changes motivated by a human rights or public health concern. This is sometimes also referred to as "policy change" or change in the "public interest."
6. In Brazil, public interest cases are also brought by the state itself, through the *Ministério Público.*
7. Such as *Viceconte* (1998), ordering production of the vaccine for hemorrhaging fever, and *Mendoza* (2006), regarding the pollution of the Matanza-Riachuelo River Basin. See Bergallo (this volume).
8. See Ferraz (this volume).

9. Important cases include C-355/06. See Yamin et al. (this volume).
10. *Soobramoney v. Minister of Health, KwaZulu-Natal*, 1998 (1) SA 765 (CC), concerning a patient with kidney failure seeking access to dialysis. See Cooper (this volume) and Norheim and Gloppen (this volume).
11. In some cases, economic constraints have led to a retraction of services previously provided.
12. On the concept of right revolutions, see Epp (1998) and Tushnet (2008a).
13. On the rise of global constitutionalism, see, for example, Ackerman (1996). On the involvement of the World Bank, the United States Agency for International Development, and other international organizations and donor agencies in initiating and advising rule-of-law reform around the globe, see Domingo and Sieder (2001) and Carothers (2006).
14. Regional human rights courts and commissions also gained prominence during this period, enriching the transnational human rights environment by issuing rulings on economic, social, and cultural rights and building rights awareness among jurists (Carver 2010; Lord and Stein 2008; Cavallaro and Brewer 2008).
15. Peculiarities in health and legal systems help us understand why, in some contexts, there are more and different forms of litigation (which is not our focus here) and condition how transnational actors might influence litigation dynamics.
16. The following statement by Martha Minow, dean of Harvard Law School, suggests the diffusive power of Court judgments:

    > I have been very struck by the symbolic influence of [U.S. Supreme Court decision] *Brown* in inspiring social movements for school reforms and in inspiring litigation efforts to reform schooling in other countries that don't have our same constitutional provisions. Frankly, the symbol of *Brown* is powerful in this country in inspiring legal action that has nothing to do with schools and nothing to do with race. And in that sense I do believe it's had an enormous symbolic effect. (Miller 2010)

17. World Conference on Human Rights, June 14–25, 1993, Vienna, Austria; United Nations International Conference on Population and Development, September 5–13, 1994, Cairo, Egypt; Fourth World Conference on Women, September 4–15, 1995, Beijing, China; and World Summit for Social Development, March 5–12, 1995, Copenhagen, Denmark. See also Reichenbach and Roseman (2009); Petchesky (2003); Clapham and Robinson (2009).
18. See www.iasociety.org for a list of International AIDS Conferences and their programs; see also Declaration of Commitment on HIV/AIDS, General Resolution of the United Nations General Assembly, U.N. Doc. A/RES/S-26/2 (2001).
19. This includes companies and organizations with local subsidiaries/branches/members whose activities relate to more than one country. It also includes organizations whose main activities are domestic but that influence litigants elsewhere through bilateral relations.
20. The International Network for Economic, Social & Cultural Rights (ESCR-Net) also maintains an online database of relevant case law. See www.escr-net.org; see also the website of the International Federation of Health and Human Rights Organisations, www.ifhhro.org.
21. The latter includes law clinics that assist with case research; networks that brainstorm health litigation strategies and share resources; and national NGOs whose representatives

speak at conferences, publish papers, or otherwise transmit work, methods, and strategies across borders (Grebe 2008, 2009; Gloppen 2005).

22. For example, the cases brought by TAC and the ALP in South Africa (which were involved in ten of the eighteen right-to-health cases surveyed by Cooper in this volume), Centro de Estudios Legales y Sociales in Argentina, and the Lawyer's Collective in India.
23. Patients' organizations may litigate directly or assist their members in bringing cases.
24. Where individuals can litigate at a very low cost (e.g., Colombia and Costa Rica), the issue of funding is less important. Where litigation imposes high costs (in terms of fees, legal expertise, and extensive research, as in South Africa), funding is crucial.
25. For example, the World Bank, UNAIDS, and the World Health Organization.
26. For example, the overseas development agencies of the United States (USAID), Britain (DFID), and Norway (NORAD).
27. For example, the Ford Foundation, Open Society Institute, Bill & Melinda Gates Foundation, and Global Fund to Fight AIDS, Tuberculosis and Malaria.
28. On the relationship between litigation and the medicalization of health, see Biehl (2004, 2007) and Petryna (2007).
29. This includes public health organizations in areas where potential health benefits are large, such as in cases regarding antiretroviral drugs for HIV/AIDS.
30. (Semi-) private health insurance companies and service providers play a role in the public health system in most of these countries, particularly in Argentina and Colombia. Cost-limiting strategies by such companies are likely to be a triggering factor for this type of litigation, but since these are overwhelmingly domestic companies and dynamics, we will leave this issue aside. It is, however, worth mentioning that in some cases—most notably in Colombia—weak regulation of drug prices, combined with arrangements for public refund of litigation-induced costs of treatment not covered by the public health plans, have made such litigation very profitable for health insurance companies.
31. In Costa Rica, individual cases dominate—but here, the combination of a very low threshold for accessing the courts and an almost routine incorporation into the health system of successfully litigated interventions makes individual cases a logical strategy even if the aim is structural change. See also *supra* note 1.
32. We used online search engines to identify articles and books discussing right-to-health litigation from the point of view of litigants, or as a part of a social transformative or marketing strategy. From this literature, we identified NGOs, donors, pharmaceutical companies, and other relevant actors, whom we contacted for more in-depth information. We also interviewed additional key informants and collected information from other members of the research group.
33. No pharmaceutical company was willing to speak with us, even in altruistic terms, about using right-to-health litigation to increase access to life-saving or essential medicines and treatments. Abbott Laboratories referred us to a section on its website that describes the company's programs to expand access to its medications for those who cannot afford it and its efforts to educate and organize patients' groups (www.abbott.com/global/url/content/en_US/40.20.5:5/general_content/General_Content_00479.htm).
34. Author's (Mindy Jane Roseman's) personal experience as previous employee of CRR, supplemented with telephone interview with Ximena Andión (international advocacy director, CRR), August 2010. See also CRR's website, www.reproductiverights.org.
35. In 1998, CRR and its partners filed a petition concerning reproductive rights in Peru before the Inter-American Commission on Human Rights (*MM v. Peru*, Case 12.041,

IACHR, friendly settlement, March 6, 2000), and in 2002, it filed a case against the Mexican government (*Paulina Ramírez v. Mexico*, Case 161.02, IACHR, friendly settlement, March 9, 2007).

36. According to CRR's website, "since 1992, the Center's innovative legal work has fundamentally transformed the landscape of reproductive health and rights worldwide, and has already strengthened laws and policies in more than 50 countries" (www.reproductiverights.org/en/our-issues/safe-healthy-pregnancy/coercive-policies). See, e.g., *Lakshmi Dhikta v. Government of Nepal*, Supreme Court of Nepal, 2007; *Ramakant Rai v. Union of India*, Supreme Court of India, 2008; and *Paulina Ramírez v. Mexico*, *supra* note 35. While CRR's engagement is normally initiated by local demand for assistance, these are controversial cases in which there will usually also be local and transnational resistance. Local NGOs may be accused of importing Western notions of "rights" (whether or not they have relationships with transnational NGOs or donors). There is also increasing evidence of conservative transnational activism on abortion and sexual rights issues (Kaoma 2009).
37. COHRE uses litigation and legal advocacy at the international, regional, and national levels as part of its strategy to advance housing rights, including water and sanitation as preconditions of health. COHRE also produces resources that provide "practitioners, academics and other human rights advocates with information on the latest development of the law of economic, social and cultural rights" (Centre on Housing Rights and Evictions 2009).
38. Jackie Dugard (executive director of the Socio-Economic Rights Institute of South Africa; previously researcher at the Centre for Applied Legal Studies, where she led its work on the *Mazibuko* case), personal communication, May 21, 2010.
39. Personal communication with Ugandan health rights activist, October 21, 2010. The current Special Rapporteur, Anand Grover, is a leading Indian health rights litigator and founder of the Lawyers Collective.
40. The case was filed after Costa Rica's health-care agency had denied a request for HIV/AIDS treatment on the basis that the drug was not on the nation's list of essential medicines, as it was considered too expensive and was not a cure for HIV/AIDS. The Constitutional Court accepted the argument that there were financial limits on the extent of an individual's right to health. The Court ruled against the claimant, denying him state-funded access to the medication (Resolution 280–292). After 1997, the Court started granting *amparos* for antiretrovirals. See Wilson (this volume).
41. These were individual petitions (*tutelas*) arising after denial of treatment (e.g., because an employer stopped contributing to the state social security premium or because the medication was not approved as part of the social security health system). The Court held that, despite the costs to the state, the harm caused by denying treatment violated the right to life (*Alonso Muñoz Ceballos v. Instituto de Seguros Sociales [ISS]*, Sentencia T-484 de 1992; *Diego Serna Gómez v. Hospital Universitario del Valle*, Sentencia T-505 de 1992; *Miguel Angel Ibarguen Rivas v. Instituto de Seguros Sociales [ISS]*, Sentencia T-158 de 1995; *X v. Instituto de Seguros Sociales [ISS]*, Sentencia T-271 de 1995). See also Yamin et al. (this volume).
42. Interviews with officials at the Constitutional Court and Ombuds Office (*Defensoría de los Habitantes*) with experience in health rights cases generally and HIV/AIDS cases in particular, San José, June 2008.
43. Regional networks for people living with HIV/AIDS (such as LACCASO, which is part of the International Council of AIDS Service Organizations) are described as "incubators"

for access-to-antiretroviral-treatment litigation (Tatiana Andia [Department of Economics, Los Andes University, Bogotá] and Everaldo Lamprea [Los Andes Law School, Bogotá], interview, Bergen, July 2010).

44. Andia and Lamprea interview, *supra* note 43. See also Andia and Lamprea (2010).
45. Changes in legal opportunity structures facilitated the rise in right-to-health litigation in the late 1990s, as countries underwent reforms introducing new constitutional rights protections and offering simplified and direct access to courts, and as potential litigants exhibited heightened rights awareness.
46. NGOs such as ACT UP and Health GAP began to shame pharmaceutical companies into lowering their prices and pressure governments on intellectual property and trade issues, enlisting, among other things, the vocabulary of human rights. Lawsuits were filed against Abbott Laboratories in the United States regarding pricing matters, against Gilead Sciences in Brazil and India concerning patents, and against Merck in South Africa regarding licensing. All were settled, resulting in lowered prices. In South Africa, *Hazel Tau v. GlaxoSmithKline, Boehringer Ingelheim*, brought before the Competition Commission in 1998, claimed that excessive pricing of antiretrovirals was causing death. This led to a negotiated settlement in which the pharmaceutical companies allowed for voluntary licensing, provided that the generic manufacturers pay a royalty (see Cooper in this volume). Also of note is that the U.S. government abandoned its practice of siding with pharmaceutical companies against generic manufacturers. Around this time, pressure on the governments of Brazil, Thailand, and the United States resulted in laws ensuring the coverage of antiretroviral medications for those unable to pay (UNAIDS 2006). Eventually, antiretroviral prices fell from approximately US$10,000–15,000 per patient per year (under patented manufacture) to $132 per patient per year (under generic production)
47. Among those present were Venezuelan HIV/AIDS activists who had previously unsuccessfully litigated for HIV/AIDS treatment—but by 1999, the Supreme Court ordered free HIV testing and treatment for all Venezuelan residents (Carrasco 2000).
48. *Asociación Benghalensis y Otros v. Ministerio de Salud y Acción Social – Estado Nacional s/Amparo Ley 16.688*, Supreme Court, June 1, 2000. The organizations were Asociación Benghalensis, Fundación Descida, Fundación para Estudio e Investigación de la Mujer, Fundación RED, Asociación Civil Intilla, Fundación CEDOSEX (Centro de Documentación en Sexualidad), Asociación Civil SIGLA, and Fundación Argentina Pro Ayuda al Niño con SIDA. Subsequently, several cases were brought to ensure the supply of HIV/AIDS medication in accordance with the law. On the early Argentinean HIV/AIDS cases, see Bianco et al. (1998) and UNAIDS (2006).
49. *Minister of Health and Others v. Treatment Action Campaign and Others*, (No. 2) 2002 (5) SA 721 (CC).
50. TAC's decision to file this case has been discussed elsewhere. See Kapczynski and Berger (2009); see also Cooper (this volume).
51. According to Adila Hassim, head of the ALP's litigation and legal services, the decision to litigate was

> a combination of internal deliberations and consultation with other [South African] NGOs. . . . We strategize with . . . a number of partners. TAC is our closest and longest ally. We have a synergistic relationship with them; they are the biggest NGO in the social movement. Along with them, we also work with COSATU [Congress of South African Trade Unions], . . . with health-care workers

> [from] MSF [Médecins Sans Frontières], university-based health centers, [and] rural health advocacy projects." (telephone interview, March 2010)

Nathan Geffen, treasurer at TAC, offered a similar picture of TAC formulating its own litigation issues and strategies, in collaboration with like-minded local NGOs:

> [Litigation is] . . . such an integral part of our strategy and we're very open about it. . . . With the [P]MTCT court case, we tried a lot of negotiation paths and tried to avoid litigation. We then obtained legal advice, and after much strategizing we decided to run the case. But we would also consult with MSF and the Legal Resources Center, the AIDS Law Project, and also COSATU. (telephone interview, March 2010)

Interestingly, MSF, mentioned as a local partner, is a transnational NGO.

52. Among the bilateral donors supporting the work of TAC and the ALP are the Royal Netherlands Embassy, Sida, Ford Foundation, and the Bill & Melinda Gates Foundation.
53. Since bilateral overseas development programs are tailored primarily to support governments, funding NGOs that actively oppose government policies raises potential diplomatic challenges. A Sida representative explained the dilemmas:

> When we started to fund HIV/AIDS in South Africa in 2004 we knew TAC and the AIDS Law Project was going to take the government to court. We knew how political it was and this was an issue for us. We were the first bilateral donors to fund TAC although we've been funding the ALP for years. We took a lot of hammering for it. Mbeki in 2006 made a speech saying people like the Swedes and the Dutch are funding our enemies. (Ria Schoeman [senior HIV/AIDS advisor, Pretoria office], telephone interview, March 2010)

Sida saw litigation as the best option for achieving improved access to HIV/AIDS treatment and decided to support it, despite the political costs:

> We have a mandate from the Swedish government to specifically support projects in human rights and democracy even in situations where it is sensitive and political. It's part of our dialogue. We're not telling them [the host government] to change but we are at least bringing the subject up. (Gunilla Essner [senior program manager, Health Division], telephone interview, March 2010)

A recent Sida report heralded its support for both NGOs, stating that TAC's advocacy is important "for the rule of law and the Constitution and the development of a people's health for all," and that the ALP "engages in public impact litigation to influence the government's legislative and policy decisions in the HIV/AIDS field" (Sida 2007, 19, 20–21). Sida has also supported the Lawyer's Collective and other NGOs in India to challenge anti-sodomy laws (Sida 2009).

54. David Cote (head of strategic litigation unit, Lawyers for Human Rights), personal communication, May 2010.
55. UNAIDS is in a partnership with the Global Fund. See also UNAIDS (2006), a collection of best practices in litigating the rights of people living with HIV/AIDS.

56. "Stigma and discrimination along with human rights issues came out as one of the major impediments in scaling up national response to AIDS in the framework of the Mid-Term Review of the National AIDS Programme and the idea was to involve the NGOs with good experience in human rights in dealing with HIV/AIDS." (Natalia Mardari [litigation program coordinator, Moldovan Institute for Human Rights], personal communication, May 12, 2010)
57. Personal communication, January 14, 2011.
58. For a broader account of the Ford Foundation's activities in this field, see McClymont and Golub (2000). See also Cummings and Trubek (2008) and Frühling (2000). NGOs supported by Ford include the ALP and TAC in South Africa and the Centro de Estudios Legales y Sociales in Argentina.
59. See Alzheimer's Society (2007) and BBC (2010).
60. Costa Rican HIV/AIDS activists have alleged that an agent for Abbott Laboratories has contacted people living with HIV/AIDS who are taking Kaletra, one of its patented drugs, to join a lawsuit opposing the provision of a generic equivalent. Abbott denies both contacting people and funding litigation (Richard Stern [director, Asociación Agua Buena], personal communication, July 4, 2010).
61. Exp. 2003-8377. See Wilson (this volume).
62. The Vitiligo and Psoriasis Association of São Paulo contacted patients and referred them to a cooperating physician who prescribed the company's drug. The company also paid a lawyer to file a lawsuit demanding that the drug be covered by the state. The court, unaware of the collusion, ordered the health department to provide the drug to the patients, and the company then kicked back money to the lawyer and physician (*O Estado de S. Paulo* 2008; see also São Paulo Public Security Department 2008).
63. According to Moynihan et al. (2002), groups lobbying for access to certain drugs sometimes are funded by the manufacturers of those drugs.
64. Octavio L. Motta Ferraz, interview, Bergen, September 2009. Other scholars have also noted cozy relationships between the pharmaceutical industry and health NGOs in Brazil, especially in the industry's funding of patients' associations (Brazilian Ministry of Health 2005). Hoffman and Bentes have observed that

    > these [pharmaceutical companies] are certainly implicated in the generation of health rights litigation, though their influence is, as would be expected, mostly indirect. It is direct only in those relatively rare cases where a lawyer with ties to the industry encourages potential plaintiffs to sue for a specific medicine. Indirectly, however, pharmaceutical companies are able to push litigation for medicines in their portfolio via their ordinary relationship with physicians who prescribe their products or confirm such prescriptions as expert witnesses, as well as via induced media coverage. Even NGOs are not always immune to overtures from the pharmaceutical industry, and some openly admit that they are co-sponsored by private sector health companies. (2008, 114–15)

65. Andia and Lamprea interview, *supra* note 43. They note that companies finance activities such as conferences in which patients meet with experts who promote litigation as an avenue for accessing treatment. Sometimes as part of their corporate social responsibil-

ity strategies, pharmaceutical companies support patients' organizations and offer drug-donation and discount programs. This is also common in other countries, including the United States (see, e.g., Abbott Laboratories: www.abbott.com/global/url/content/en_US/40.20.15:15/general_content/General_Content_00066.htm). For an industry perspective on the importance of "liaising with relevant patient groups," see Gow (2007).

66. Andia and Lamprea (2010), footnotes omitted. They also note an increasingly strained relationship between patients' groups and social movements working for justice in health. While patients' groups and networks, sometimes in (indirect) alliance with the pharmaceutical industry, have effectively litigated for the provision of treatment, emerging social movements are taking on the industry in their push for cheaper drugs. In Colombia, the HIV/AIDS movement fractured over the ethics of taking part in litigation financed by the industry. After the movement's recent break with the industry, "breakaway" HIV/AIDS advocates were more willing to speak of these relations (Andia and Lamprea interview, *supra* note 43).

Chapter 11

Assessing the Impact of Health Rights Litigation: A Comparative Analysis of Argentina, Brazil, Colombia, Costa Rica, India, and South Africa

Ottar Mæstad, Lise Rakner, and Octavio L. Motta Ferraz

The remarkable wave of lawsuits on the right to health during the past two decades calls for a systematic assessment of its impact. To what extent has health rights litigation benefited litigants and the groups they represent? What have been the effects of litigation on health policies and budgets? And how has the overall availability and distribution of health services been affected in the countries where health rights litigation has taken place?

This chapter discusses these questions in light of the findings from the country chapters in this volume. By synthesizing and comparing impact across countries, this chapter seeks to advance our understanding of when litigation is likely to have a positive impact on access to and the distribution of health services, and when the impact is more likely to be negative. As we will see below, differences in impact are closely associated with differences in health and judicial systems. However, while the country case studies have provided a number of valuable insights regarding impact, many questions remain largely unanswered. In order to provide some direction for future research, this chapter also discusses various methodological approaches that may be useful for future assessments of the impact of health rights litigation.

The potential impact of health rights litigation is significant. Medical and technological advances produce ever more sophisticated treatments, often with high associated costs. If courts interpret the right to health to include a right to these advanced treatments, the economic implications may be enormous. An example from Brazil illustrates the point: 1% of the Brazilian population is estimated to suffer from chronic hepatitis C

We would like to thank Daniel Brinks and Siri Gloppen for their useful comments on earlier drafts of this chapter.

(Vieira 2008). This condition can be treated with pegylated interferon, an extremely costly drug. If the state were to provide this medication to 25% of people with the disease, the costs would amount to 64% of the Ministry of Health's current budget.

This example draws our attention to the potential of health rights litigation to reshuffle resource allocations in the health sector in ways that may be both inequitable and inefficient. But health rights litigation also has the potential to do the opposite: to offer a tool for poor and vulnerable groups to claim health services that they are entitled to through national policies but that they do not receive due to various types of implementation failures. For instance, a large share of health rights litigation in Colombia concerns the fulfillment of entitlements established through the national health plan.

This chapter focuses on litigation's impact on access to health services, for both litigants and the general population. Litigants naturally seek to capture a larger share of available resources for their cause. When they succeed, fewer resources become available for other groups and other causes, unless additional money is allocated to cover the expenditures resulting from litigation. This raises three key questions about the impact of health rights litigation: To what extent has litigation enhanced access to health services for litigants and the groups they represent? To what extent has litigants' success eroded service availability for other groups? And has overall access to health services become more or less equitable?

We are also interested in the impact on intermediate outcome variables, including health policies and budgets. Does health litigation overcome political blockages and ensure that authorities are held accountable for their health-related commitments? Or does litigation undermine democratic processes, long-term planning, and rational priority setting in health policy?

An Analytical Framework

Many different types of health rights claims have been brought before the courts. Some litigants have claimed access to a particular medication or treatment, or have sought implementation of a particular health policy. Others have claimed provision of underlying determinants of health (e.g., food, shelter, water, sanitation, safe labor practices, and environmental standards). Claims have been raised against both the state and private actors. Accordingly, the impact of health rights litigation may be felt at many levels and in many dimensions, from changes in access to health services, to higher costs for private companies when forced to improve safety in the working environment, to effects on the international market for pharmaceuticals.

We will not attempt to comprehensively cover every type of case and impact here. Instead, given the focus of the country chapters, we will highlight litigation that has direct implications for health budgets and expenditures—particularly claims regarding public health policies and the provision of health services.

Likewise, we will confine the scope of relevant impacts to the realm of health. Our ultimate concern is the effect of health rights litigation on people's *health outcomes*. However, the large number of other factors that affect people's health and the time lag between interventions and measurable impact will prevent any meaningful measurement of health outcomes in our case. A more modest, though still challenging, aim is to assess how health rights litigation has affected people's *access to health services*. In our analysis, we will take this as our primary dependent variable.

Access to health services is a characteristic of the supply side and should not be confused with actual utilization. Access can be characterized in terms of the availability of services (including their quality), the financial and non-financial costs of accessing services, and the level of information about their availability (see, e.g., Goddard and Smith 2003).

The question of whether litigation can bring about significant social change—and if so, through which political and social mechanisms litigation operates—is debated extensively in the literature, and empirical analyses offer diverging results, ranging from the very negative conclusions drawn by Gerald Rosenberg in *The Hollow Hope: Can Courts Bring About Social Change?* (1991) to the nuanced legal realism of Stuart Scheingold's *Politics of Rights: Lawyers, Public Policy, and Political Change* (2004) to the more positive findings of scholars such as Michael McCann (1994, 2006) and Charles Epp (1998) (see also the discussion of this literature in chapter 1).[1] Building on the theoretical approaches taken by these scholars (which also provide the basis for the general theoretical framework of this book, outlined in chapter 2), our point of departure is that health rights litigation potentially influences access to health services through various channels. A simple visualization is provided in figure 11.1.

First, litigation may have a direct impact on access to health services for litigants and other patients included in a judgment. (If the judgment has general effect, other patients will include "all similarly placed," as is the norm in common-law systems.) The direct impact hinges on both a positive decision and subsequent compliance with the court's order by relevant authorities (the latter is particularly important and challenging to establish with regard to orders of general effect).[2]

Second, litigation may affect access to health services—for both litigants and the population at large—by influencing health policies and budgets. Policy impact may be direct (such as in cases where the court explicitly orders changes in health policies) or indirect (for example, when court decisions providing specific litigants with access to certain health services compel health authorities to change policies accordingly or otherwise alter their priorities and budgets). Policy-level impact does not hinge on a positive judgment from the court. Out-of-court settlements, threatened litigation, or even lost cases may also trigger a response at this level. This may come about if litigants experience an enhanced bargaining position in the "shadow" of litigation; if litigious processes facilitate political mobilization or produce "blaming and shaming" effects or changes in public opinion that alter policy makers' strategic calculi; or if such processes cause policy makers' rights consciousness to change as new issues are perceived as rights violations.[3] Litigation efforts by the Treatment Action Campaign in South Africa speak to the power of negotiations in the shadow of litigation, as well as the mobilizing

Figure 11.1. Framework for analyzing the impact of health litigation

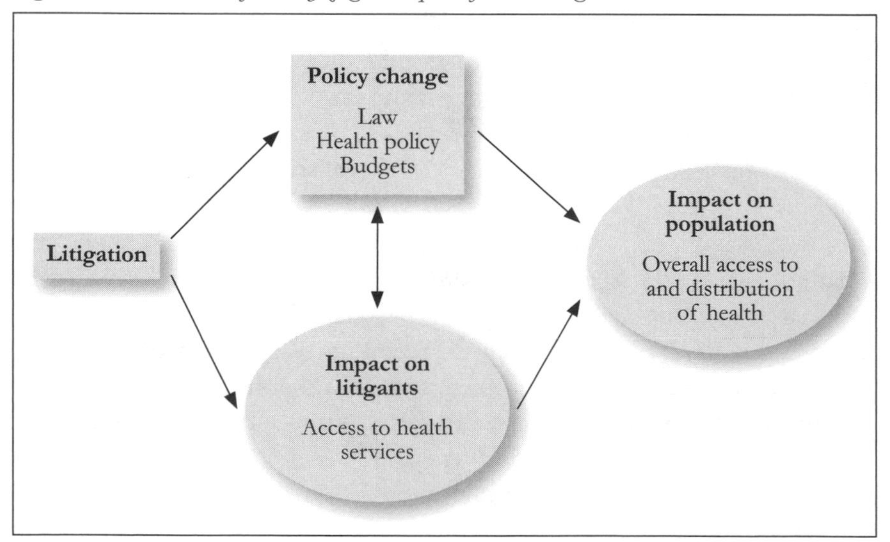

potential of litigation (see, in this volume, Cooper; Norheim and Gloppen; and, for Indian examples, Parmar and Wahi). Another example is offered by the state of São Paulo in Brazil, where a group of litigants lost, on appeal, a case against the state regarding drugs for epilepsy but health authorities nevertheless decided to continue providing the drug, as had been ordered by the first instance judge in an interim decision (see below).

Finally, litigation that increases access to health services for individuals or patient groups (either directly or through affecting policy processes) may have consequences for access to and the distribution of health services for the population as a whole. The nature of population-level impact depends on how the extra costs arising from litigation-induced health services are financed. If the total health budget is increased, or if extra resources are mobilized by reducing inefficiencies in the health sector, litigation does not negatively affect access to health services for nonlitigants. However, and perhaps more likely, when resources are drawn from existing health budgets, nonlitigants are likely to suffer a loss. An important question, then, is whether the reallocation of resources resulting from litigation is causing a more or less equitable distribution of resources.

It is beyond the scope of this chapter to discuss in depth the various approaches to equity in the allocation of health services. Broadly speaking, consequentialist approaches range from utilitarianism, with its focus on aggregate outcomes, to radical egalitarianism, with its exclusive focus on outcomes for the worst-off. Prioritarianism, which can be seen as a middle position, values aggregate outcome at the same time that it attaches special importance to outcomes for the worst-off. In addition, there are nonconsequentialist approaches, which may value, for instance, procedural aspects. Our discussions of equity as it concerns health rights litigation will be guided by a prioritarian approach (see, e.g., Brock 2002).

Some Methodological Issues

Assessing the impact of health rights litigation raises some fundamental methodological issues, for both the study design and the interpretation of results. They all relate to the fundamental issue of establishing the counterfactual: what would have happened to people's access to health services without health rights litigation?

First, litigation is one among a number of strategies through which individuals and social groups can promote their interests. Disentangling the impact of litigation from the impact of these alternative strategies is extremely challenging. Alternative strategies include legislation and political-party mobilization, lobbying by interest groups and social movements, media campaigns, and demonstrations. In some cases, these strategies can be *substitutes* for litigation; if the legal option is not pursued, other channels may produce a similar outcome. In other cases, these alternative channels can *complement* a litigation strategy; they may increase the probability of winning a case in court, or litigation may be a means of generating publicity around an issue that can ultimately be resolved through political channels only. In some cases, the mere threat of litigation may be enough to lead to change (McCann 1994).

These interdependencies among strategies for change make it extremely challenging to identify the precise impact of litigation. One strategy for disentangling the various influences is to trace decision-making processes in order to identify the relative importance of various causal factors. We have not been able to follow this strategy to any great extent. Our focus will therefore be on the nominal impact of litigation—that is, on effects that arise in the wake of actual litigation without regard to possible co-influence of alternative channels. We briefly discuss the effects of possible substitute channels in those rare cases when such data are available, but we make no attempt to assess how litigation or the threat of litigation may strengthen the impact of other channels.

Second, there is the challenge of identifying counterfactual outcomes. The preferred approach is to establish control groups and randomly assign interventions—in this case, health rights litigation—to treatment and control groups (see, e.g., Khandker et al. 2010). This strategy is clearly not feasible here. Nor is it meaningful to make comparisons between countries where people *do* have and *do not* have the option of litigating for their health interests. The number of confounding variables at the national level is simply too high to draw comparisons that could help determine the impact of health rights litigation.

Without relevant control groups, we are basically left with a before/after type of evaluation. An important criticism of this approach is that changes in access to health services may simply be the result of a general evolution over time. The best way to address this criticism is to utilize the ideas of an interrupted time-series analysis (McDowall et al. 1980). An interrupted time series refers to a before/after evaluation that takes a longer historical perspective and incorporates trends over time into the analysis, both before and after an intervention has taken place. In this way, it may be possible to at least partially assess whether changes following litigation were related to litigation or were a result of other processes. In practice, it is often difficult to establish a time-series data set. However, the core idea of this approach—namely, incorporating a longer time horizon into the analysis, including both pre- and post-intervention phases—is nevertheless a useful one that can be adopted by many types of studies on the impact of health rights litigation.

Regarding the validity of our findings for contexts other than those discussed in this book, it is important to bear in mind that litigation cases studied here are the result of decisions made within institutional contexts that themselves affect the anticipated impact of litigation and therefore the decision to litigate in the first place. For instance, the legal system (which encompasses access to courts, legal rules, and legal practices) and the health system (which encompasses access to health services, health-service financing, and priority-setting principles) affect the expected costs and benefits of making a claim in the courts and thus the decision whether or not to litigate. This implies that observed impacts of litigation cannot be easily generalized to different institutional settings.

The country chapters in this volume allow us to compare the impact of litigation across various countries. These comparisons illuminate the heterogeneous impact of litigation across various institutional settings and contribute to our understanding of how litigation may produce different impacts in different contexts. But the difficulty in determining impact at country level in the first place calls for some caution when interpreting the comparative findings.

Direct Impact on Litigants' Access to Health Services

Impact on litigants' access to health services may be direct or indirect (see figure 11.1). Direct impact arises as a result of court orders—for instance, a decision to grant a particular health service. Indirect impact occurs through changes in health policies, which may be triggered directly by court orders or may be a response by health authorities to successful litigation (on the part of the litigants). Later in the chapter, we will discuss indirect impact; in this section, we develop a framework for assessing direct impact, including its magnitude, and discuss empirical findings from the country chapters in light of this framework.

A successful outcome in the court is a necessary condition for a direct impact on litigants' access to health services. A natural starting point for addressing direct impact, therefore, is to list successful health rights litigation cases, count the number of successes, and/or measure the frequency of successes versus failures. Such measures, however, do not provide a lot of information; they may indicate positive effects for the litigants, but they add no information about the magnitude of impact, as one "big" case may have a much larger impact than hundreds of "small" cases.

As a first step toward measuring the magnitude of impact, one might count the *number of people who benefit* directly from court orders. This approach was used by Varun Gauri and Daniel Brinks (2008). The method can be straightforwardly applied to individual court cases but is more problematic when litigation is pursued on behalf of larger groups of people, as the number of affected individuals may be hard to assess. The same difficulties arise in common-law judicial systems, where individual court cases create precedent. For this type of exercise, it is also important to distinguish between *potential* and *actual* beneficiaries. As is clearly documented, for example, in Shylashri Shankar and Pratap Mehta's study from India (2008) and Jonathan Berger's assessment of health rights litigation in South Africa (2008), we should not assume that all court orders are fully complied with by relevant authorities.

Even if we were able to count the exact number of people who actually benefit from health rights litigation, we would have learned little about the substance or magnitude of the gains. To understand this dimension, it is useful to ask some specific questions about how litigants' access to health services has been affected:

- Which additional health services have been ordered?
- What health benefits can these services provide?
- How have the financial and nonfinancial costs of access to health services been affected?

Answering the first question involves *listing the additional services that have been provided* as a consequence of litigation. For instance, which new medications or treatments have been delivered as a result of court orders? The starting point here would be to review successful litigation. In countries where court orders are not always implemented, it is also necessary to assess compliance rates. For individual cases in judicial systems without precedent (civil-law systems), this might require tracking each individual case. For collective cases or cases that have created precedent, data on compliance may be more conveniently obtained from health service providers directly, by inquiring whether the service is available on the terms ordered by the court.

To answer the second question, we must assess the *expected health impact* of the additional services provided. Although actual health impact cannot be measured, estimates of expected health gains may sometimes be possible to obtain. Some new types of medication and treatments come with an estimate of likely health impact in the form of healthy life years or quality-adjusted life years gained. When such figures are combined with data on the number of beneficiaries, it may be possible to estimate the expected health impact for litigants (see Norheim and Gloppen in this volume). Published estimates of burden of disease might also be helpful in making such calculations (see, e.g., Lopez et al. 2006).

Finally, for the third question, it is useful to measure how litigation has affected the monetary and nonmonetary *costs of accessing health services*. This approach can be applied, for instance, when litigation has resulted in reduced drug prices or improved geographical access, including local provision of services that previously were available only abroad.

Empirical Findings

The country chapters indicate that hundreds of thousands of litigants have been successful in court, especially in the four Latin American countries studied in this volume. Although some litigants have struggled with a lack of enforcement, many have benefited directly from court orders (data do not allow us to establish the precise level of enforcement). It is also likely that many other individuals have benefited indirectly from changes in health policies as a result of litigation, but there are not enough data in the country studies to produce precise figures.

In order to estimate the number of beneficiaries, we must first look at the number of cases that have been brought before the courts (see table 11.1). By all standards, Colombia has the highest number of health rights cases: 674,612 *tutelas* were filed between 1999 and 2008. Almost 150,000 cases—nearly 3,300 cases per million—were brought in 2008 alone. Figures for Brazil are less comprehensive, but existing data indicate 40,000 cases per year, which is almost double the amount in per capita terms as the 500 annual health rights cases in Costa Rica. In Argentina, systematic data are not widely available, but according to one estimate, the number of cases exceeded 1,000 in 2007. This places Argentina somewhat below Costa Rica, with 29 annual lawsuits per million. In India, the authors of the country studies found only 218 health-related lawsuits in law reports and academic writings over the last few decades. Even if we were to factor in unreported cases, this number seems unlikely to come anywhere near the absolute (let alone per capita) levels of Brazil and Colombia. South Africa seems to have the lowest absolute volume of litigation among the country cases included in this volume. Nineteen cases decided between 1996 and 2010 were analyzed in the country chapter, implying a per capita volume along the same lines as in India. The low number of South African cases seems to be due partly to the difficulty of accessing the legal system and the enormous resources required by public interest litigators in order to run a case. The table below is an estimate, admittedly tentative,[4] of per capita levels of litigation based on the data provided in the country chapters.

Figures presented in the country chapters indicate that 97–99% of the lawsuits in the Latin American countries are individual cases. In South Africa and India, conversely, collective suits are much more common. At first sight, this might suggest that the magnitude of direct impact (i.e., impact on litigants) should be higher in India and South Africa than in the Latin American countries. However, as explained in the analytical framework above, direct impact is a function not only of the nature of the claimant (individual versus collective) but of a complex set of indicators that includes the scope of collective claims (i.e., the number of individuals affected), the success rates of these claims, and the actual enforcement of successful claims.

The scope of collective claims varies significantly from country to country, ranging from the *TAC–PMTCT* case in South Africa, with millions of

Table 11.1. Number of health rights cases per capita (tentative figures)

Country	Lawsuits *annual figures* (*) *cumulative figures* (**)	Population (millions)	Health litigation per capita (lawsuits per 1,000,000)
Colombia	150,000*	45.6	3,289
Brazil	40,000*	193.7	206
Costa Rica	500*	4.6	109
Argentina	1,159*	40.2	29
South Africa	17**	49.3	0.3
India	218**	1,150	0.2

Source: Country chapters (this volume); World Bank (2010).

people potentially affected, to cases seeking the improvement of individual hospitals, common in Brazil, which potentially affect hundreds or thousands of people over a long period of time.

Success rates also vary from country to country and even from court to court within a country, but are generally high in all countries studied in this volume. They seem to be higher in the Latin American countries than in India and South Africa. In Argentina, the success rate varies between 80% and 90% (Bergallo in this volume); and in Brazil, between 90% in the lower courts to almost 100% in the Supreme Federal Tribunal (Ferraz 2009a). In Colombia, 86% of all health *tutelas* were granted between 2006 and 2008 (Yamin et al. in this volume). In South Africa, where courts have arguably been hesitant to interfere with social policy, the success rate is somewhat lower, around 75% (Cooper in this volume). In India, the success rate is 61% in Supreme Court cases (Parmar and Wahi in this volume).

As already explained, the number of potential beneficiaries and the success rates of claims are not sufficient for gauging direct impact. If successful claims are not enforced, there will be no impact. Compliance with court orders, however, is a challenging variable to measure. Given the practical difficulty of contacting all (or even a representative sample of) successful claimants to establish if they are actually enjoying the health benefit ordered by a court, one must rely on other methods to measure enforcement, which are not always easily available in the countries studied. In Costa Rica, for instance, interviews with public officials, including officials at the Caja (*Caja Costarricense de Seguro Social*, the state institution entrusted with providing health services, including those judicially mandated) confirmed that the Caja normally complies with court orders (see Wilson in this volume). In Brazil, Octavio L. Motta Ferraz has concluded that in the state of São Paulo, at least, compliance seems to be high for individual medication cases. The state of São Paulo has a special pharmacy for dispensing judicially ordered medicines, and lawyers representing claimants confirm that they have not encountered obstacles in the enforcement of judicial decisions. With regard to collective cases, the situation is somewhat different. Public lawyers from the *Ministério Público* have faced enormous difficulties in enforcing structural orders for the improvement of basic sanitation systems, hospitals, and health and educational services for certain groups.[5] In Argentina (*Mendoza*), Colombia (T-760/08), South Africa, and India, a similar enforcement problem seems to affect collective cases. In South Africa's *TAC–PMTCT* case, the court's decision ordering the state to roll out antiretroviral medications was initially met with apathy by certain provinces, forcing the claimants to go back to court to complain (e.g., Mpumalanga Province). Carole Cooper observes that it is much harder to monitor compliance with collective claims that include a large number of potential beneficiaries.

There are plausible explanations for this apparent discrepancy in enforcement between collective (including structural) and individual cases. Individual cases, especially in Latin America, are often argued by private lawyers whose fees can depend on effectively getting the benefit for the client, whereas collective cases are often sponsored by public lawyers who lack the time and resources to follow up on the cases they bring to court. Judges might also order shorter implementation timelines and attach stronger noncompliance sanctions in simpler individual cases than in complex collective and structural ones. In the Latin American countries surveyed, for instance, courts have often resorted to provisional injunctions in individual medication cases, which must be complied with in a matter of hours or days. Forceful punishment strategies for noncompliance have been common: in Argentina, Brazil, and Costa Rica, court orders normally involve fines for noncompliance and even personal responsibility for the leaders of the implementing agencies, with imprisonment as the ultimate threat. In Brazil, the press widely reported a few cases of secretaries of health being sent to jail for failing to comply with court orders; this may have had an effect in discouraging other secretaries from doing the same.[6]

While there is considerable variation in the types of benefits enjoyed by litigants, some patterns stand out. Most litigation in the Latin American countries was brought by individuals demanding some kind of medical treatment (e.g., 72% in Argentina and 97% in Brazil), particularly improved access to medication. This type of litigation surfaced largely around the issue of access to HIV/AIDS medicines and later expanded to a broad range of treatments for other diseases, such as cancer and diabetes. In India and South Africa, a different pattern emerges. Only one-third of the litigation surveyed in the Indian study was brought by individuals (most of which involved monetary damages for medical negligence). In South Africa, most cases (around 80%) were public interest litigation. Public health measures, such as hiring more doctors and building health facilities, have also been the subject of litigation in Latin America and India, but in the overall picture such cases are rare.

A significant portion of individual treatment cases, especially medication cases, seems to involve relatively advanced and often expensive medical treatments that are not included in national health plans or the minimum benefit package covered by insurance schemes. In Brazil, for instance, imported drugs granted by courts and not originally included in the national list of medicines represented a staggering 78.4% of the costs of all right-to-health litigation against the federal government in 2009 (Ferraz in this volume). Costa Rica has also experienced a similar situation regarding court orders for hugely expensive drugs such as Herceptin for breast cancer and Cerezyme for Gaucher disease, neither of which was included in the original coverage package (Wilson in this volume). Even in Colombia, where the majority of cases (54% between 2003 and 2008) involve treatment and services contained in the national health insurance scheme (POS, for its Spanish acronym), expenditures related to services beyond the POS remain significant. Reimbursements of medications not covered by the POS have increased substantially, from Col$1 billion (1997 to 2000 annual average) to Col$1.15 trillion in 2008 (Yamin et al. in this volume).

Little systematic evidence has been produced on the magnitude of the health benefits experienced by litigants. However, Ole Norheim and Siri Gloppen (this volume) estimate that, in 2010 in South Africa, 19,500 HIV infections in children were avoided by the introduction of prevention of mother-to-child transmission (PMTCT) services; they estimate the resulting number of life years saved to be more than one million. As in South Africa and other countries studied here, improved access to HIV/AIDS medication has clearly contributed to prolonging lives and reducing morbidity, while some of the more costly cancer treatments granted through litigation prolong life for no more than weeks or months.

There is almost no evidence on how litigation has affected the monetary and nonmonetary costs of accessing health services. Norheim and Gloppen (this volume) discuss the reduction in drug prices that resulted from a complaint filed against pharmaceutical companies concerning excessive pricing of antiretroviral drugs in South Africa. This case was settled out of court. To our knowledge, no one has investigated how domestic provision of services that previously were available only in other countries has affected individuals' costs of obtaining such services.

Taking all relevant variables into consideration, we tentatively conclude that direct impact on litigants is strongest and most likely to occur in individual litigation for medical treatment, a model that is more prevalent in the four Latin American countries than in India and South Africa. Collective or structural cases, on the other hand, seem to face more obstacles in terms of courts' receptivity and effective enforcement, which diminish their impact on litigants. When sponsors of collective cases have reasonable resources, however, this tendency can be broken, as was the case to some extent with HIV/AIDS litigation in India, Brazil, and South Africa, although in the latter, as observed by Cooper (this volume), enforcement remains problematic.

Finally, it is important to note that a favorable decision and its effective implementation do not necessarily result in a positive impact for the litigant. In some cases, the health benefits of services provided through litigation have been quite dubious. Courts in Brazil have been reported to grant, on occasion, services and medicines with little or no documented effect, such as experimental eye surgery in Cuba and experimental stem-cell treatment in the United States (Ferraz 2009a, this volume). There is also some evidence, though not systematic, that pharmaceutical companies in several of the Latin American countries have lobbied doctors to increase the market for brand-name drugs and other medicines with little or no value added and that courts have often concurred, inadvertently, by granting these drugs via judgments (Collucci and Pinho 2008).

The direct impact on litigants, as we can see, provides us with only a partial picture of how health rights litigation leads to improved protection of the right to health in a given country. Given that health resources are necessarily limited, we cannot automatically conclude that any gain accrued through the courts results in a more equitable allocation of health or health services. We must also consider the overall impact of litigation on that country's health system and its population at large. Therefore, in the following sections, we expand our analysis to the realms of health policy, budgets, and impact on the population as a whole.

Impact on Health Policy

Assessing litigation's impact on health policies is key to understanding to what extent and through which causal pathways it affects both litigants and the general population. An important part of this assessment involves understanding how health authorities and the judiciary view their respective roles and how this contributes to shaping litigation practices. Health rights litigation sometimes leads courts to order new health policies; when this happens, implementation of policy change is a direct outcome of litigation, perhaps in combination with other factors. In other cases, policy change is a by-product of litigation, as when litigation forces policy makers to alter their priorities or their budgets.[7] Assessments of policy change should distinguish between the setting of policies and their actual implementation. We should also look beyond narrow compliance with court orders and map broader structural impact, if any.

Policy-level assessments should include a description of the nature of the policy changes observed (e.g., new or restructured laws, health reforms, restructured national health plans, or new policies at the local or national levels). But in order to establish a causal link between observed policy changes and litigation, we must also assess the extent to which political actors (e.g., political parties, civil society, and government authorities) have made reference to and drawn leverage from health rights litigation, either from the substance of the cases or their budget implications. The analysis should also explore whether there are other relevant factors behind observed policy change and the extent to which these factors are linked to health rights litigation.

Empirical Findings

In a number of cases, litigation has clearly led to changes in health policies. Sometimes these impacts are the indirect result of several individual cases in which health authorities lost and subsequently decided to change policy. In others instances, courts have directly instructed governments to amend their policies.

Examples of the first kind (indirect policy change) include what has emerged as a common pattern in Brazil and Costa Rica: once health authorities lose a certain number of lawsuits concerning a particular drug or treatment, that service is included in the public health plan. This happened, for instance, with antiretroviral drugs for HIV/AIDS in both Brazil and Costa Rica. Other examples from Brazil include medications for rheumatoid arthritis and hepatitis C (see Ferraz in this volume). In these and other cases, even though the decision applies only to the parties to a case, policies are changed due to the aggregate force of a large number of individual cases. This implies that there are many indirect beneficiaries of litigation—that is, individuals with the same health needs as litigants, who were not a party to the litigation but ended up benefiting from the change in health policy. Similar mechanisms have also been operating in Argentina, where litigation and other forms of pressure have resulted in the incorporation, via policy change, of treatment for several conditions into the minimum compulsory package of services, including treatments for multiple sclerosis patients, people with disabilities, obese persons, and couples with infertility (Bergallo in this volume). Colombia has also experienced something similar, although health service providers have continued to ignore their obligation to provide certain treatments, even after being ordered by the courts to do so.[8]

Whereas this kind of indirect policy change is common in the Latin American countries (where the prevalent model is individualized litigation), in India and South Africa (where litigation is generally collective or structural in nature), one finds more examples of health policy changes ordered by the courts directly. South Africa's HIV/AIDS cases, in which courts directly ordered an overhaul of treatment and prevention policies, offer a clear example. With respect to the government's change in policies—from a complete denial of responsibility for providing antiretrovirals in 1999 to a complete rollout of these drugs in 2004—it is impossible to fully disentangle the role of litigation from other forms of civil society pressure (in addition to the country case study, see Norheim and Gloppen in this volume). Cooper (this volume) claims, however, that litigation, together with other strategies, played a significant part. In India, courts have directly ordered the government to adopt measures in several areas suffering from policy gaps: blood banks, drugs and vaccines, emergency care, mental health care, medical negligence, tobacco control laws, and reproductive rights.

The most profound attempt by a court to affect health policies directly seems to be the Colombian Constitutional Court's decision T-760/08, which ordered the government to substantially reform the health system in order to comply with existing laws and regulations. The final impact of this decision is still unknown, but some of its requests, such as the establishment of a universal health plan for children, have been implemented.

It is one thing to identify the types of policy impact and another to gauge the real changes on the ground and the quality of these changes in terms of improving the population's access to health services. To do so, one must, again, determine whether the policy changes have been effectively implemented (or enforced) and then analyze their effect on services and benefits to the population. This last issue depends on where resources to finance litigation orders and policy changes come from (discussed further below). Here, we focus briefly on implementation and enforcement.

Enforcement of policy changes affecting a larger number of people, as already noted, seems more difficult to achieve and monitor than enforcement of individual orders. Parmar and Wahi (this volume) note that despite the incredible activism of the Indian Supreme Court—expressed by the numerous policy change orders it has issued—real outcomes are mixed due to the absence of judicial follow-up or sustained implementation of court orders by all parties involved. Cooper (this volume) makes a similar observation regarding South Africa. Although the country's HIV/AIDS litigation is regarded as a success story, it is difficult to monitor implementation of the new policy, and the coverage of PMTCT services is estimated to vary widely—from 30% to 90%—across the country.

Impact on Health Budgets

Since governments necessarily face limited health resources, expenditures caused by litigation may affect budget allocations for other health services enjoyed by the population. Studying changes in health budgets is therefore a potentially useful way to gauge the impact of litigation on the population's access to health services. Litigation can affect health budgets in various ways, depending on how compliance with court orders is financed:[9] (i) health authorities can raise additional revenues—that is, increase the health budget to accommodate the new expenditure; (ii) they can reallocate resources within the system, reducing the provision of other health services; or (iii) they can reduce waste and other inefficiencies in the health system. These three possibilities are, of course, not mutually exclusive.

Time-series budget data, adjusted for inflation, would allow us to analyze budget trends over time and compare budgets before and after significant judgments or clusters of judgments. Expenditures on particular goods (e.g., medications) may be possible to estimate even without separate budget lines, if accounts are made of the quantities consumed (in some cases, the number of patients may suffice). These data can then be combined with price data obtained from the market in order to estimate the amount of resources spent. Litigation's effect on the resources available for other health services can be estimated only if it is possible to estimate the amount of resources allocated to services that have been affected by litigation. We may then construct a time series of the residual budget (i.e., what is left after the "litigation services" have been paid for). A shift in this time trend at the point when litigation took place would indicate that litigation has had an impact on the budgets allocated for other services. No shift in the time trend would indicate that additional resources have been supplied from external sources to accommodate the increased costs due to litigation. Analysis of budget data can be conducted at the regional, national, and health-facility levels. In addition to budget data, information about the budget *process* may help us further understand the extent to which litigation has actually led to policy changes.

In practice, however, it is not easy to determine litigation's impact on the health budget with any degree of precision. First, there are difficulties with access to relevant data. As highlighted in one of the country chapters in this volume, officials are unsurprisingly hesitant to admit that resources for financing litigation orders are drawn from other areas of the budget, let alone give access to information that identifies which areas have suffered (i.e., who the losers of litigation are). Second, a number of parallel policy changes may be taking place, effectively blurring the relationship between litigation and health budgets. The Brazilian Parliament's refusal to renew the "health tax" is a good example. From one year to another, a significant source of revenue disappeared. If this tax is reintroduced by the newly elected Parliament, as the new president wants, the budget will again change, this time upwards, as a result of a political decision totally unrelated to litigation.

It is not surprising, therefore, that none of the country studies in this volume can precisely identify the connection between budget movements and litigation. Nevertheless, some chapters do manage to raise important (even if fragmentary) information that allows us to draw interesting, albeit tentative, conclusions.

Empirical Findings

Available evidence on the economic implications of health litigation suggests that impact can be sizeable. In São Paulo, the largest state in Brazil, with more than forty million inhabitants, litigation-triggered expenditures for drugs amounted to 25% of the medicines budget and 4.3% of the total health budget in 2008. Figures are less clear from other states, but it is noteworthy that Rio Grande do Sul, which has only one-quarter of the population of São Paulo, has a higher absolute number of reported lawsuits and therefore faces possibly even larger economic implications. At the municipal level, where litigation is also growing, anecdotal evidence suggests that some small municipalities have had their entire health budgets affected by a few expensive cases. Impact is lower at the federal level, with the total costs of litigation amounting to only one-eighth of the costs in São Paulo State, and representing just 1% of the medicines budget.

In Colombia, litigation related to health services not included in the national health plan amounted to US$750 million in 2009—that is, 5.4% of the health budget (Yamin et al. in this volume). The many instances of litigation for services contained in the public health plan also have economic implications, of course, but unfortunately there is a lack of data compiling information across different providers. However, Colombia's increase in litigation has not been accompanied by an increase in the total health expenditure relative to the gross domestic product nor in the share of government health expenditure as a percentage of total health expenditure (Gloppen in this volume).

Aggregate budget implications in other countries are largely unknown, although there are repeated reports of particular cases with enormous financial consequences. One example from Costa Rica is the twenty-two breast cancer patients and nine other patients who were granted extremely expensive drugs—whose costs amounted to 1% of the national medicines budget—by the court. Another example from the same country is the inclusion in the late 1990s of HIV/AIDS medicines in the national health plan, which amounted to 11% of the medicines budget (benefiting a group of just 680 patients). In Costa Rica, total health expenditure as a share of the gross domestic product has been increasing, and government health expenditure as a share of the total health expenditure has increased significantly (Gloppen in this volume). Whether or not these trends can be attributed to litigation is, however, unknown.

As already mentioned, in order to gauge the impact of the extra expenditures created by litigation, we must know where the funds are coming from—in other words, from additional revenue, reduction of waste and inefficiency, or (as we believe is more likely, for reasons explained below) reallocation of existing resources. None of the country chapters, however, are able to present data on how the costs of litigation have been financed. Ferraz, for example, interviewed health officials in the state of São Paulo's Secretariat of Health to try to elicit some information on this issue, but they were reluctant to disclose precise data. This is hardly surprising, given the sensitive nature of such information. If we can clearly see which health benefits and services are being reduced in order to fund benefits and services for litigants, the losers of litigation become clearly identifiable—which, in turn, might create more problems for the government and result in even more litigation. The typical attitude of health officials, therefore, is to complain that litigation is distorting health priorities and diverting resources away from important programs, but without specifically identifying these programs. This leads, in turn, to skeptical responses from litigation activists and judges, who dismiss cost implications as the government's excuse for not respecting the right to health.

In Costa Rica, for instance, judges generally claim that the main impact of litigation has been to reduce inefficiencies in the health sector and that litigation is therefore not necessarily a zero-sum game in terms of availability of health services. The head of the Caja also argued that litigation helped push for efficiency. Evidence from the health-facility level nevertheless suggests that health authorities are sometimes forced to change their priorities and reallocate resources when courts have ordered expensive medications for particular patients.[10] These effects are starker in health systems with highly decentralized financing structures, due to less flexibility in the reallocation of resources.

Without clear and transparent data on how litigation-related expenditures have been financed, however, it is possible only to speculate on litigation's impact on budgets. Governments' arguments that litigation can threaten the financial stability of health systems now seem somewhat exaggerated. At least in the countries studied here, litigation has not yet reached costs of a magnitude that could justify these worries. Where litigation seems to be highest, according to available data, it consumes around 5% of the health budget. It is also possible to conclude that in the Latin American countries, the prevalent model of litigation (individual claims for treatment), coupled with under-enforcement of the significantly less frequent collective or structural lawsuits, has likely increased the share of health budgets allocated to curative care. But again, from a purely economic perspective, the magnitude of such reallocation is not likely to be great.

From an equity perspective (e.g., the distribution of health services among the population as a whole), however, any reallocation of resources within the health budget can have important implications.

Impact on Overall Access to and Distribution of Health Services

Has health rights litigation increased overall (or aggregate) access to health services or simply redistributed resources from nonlitigants to litigants? Has litigation contributed to more or less equality, and, in particular, how has it affected the worst-off? These are key questions for evaluating the equity impacts of health rights litigation and are indeed among the core questions raised in this volume. They cannot be answered by simply analyzing the impacts on litigants, health policies, and budgets; they also require analyses of how nonlitigants are affected.

In order to address these questions, we need to precisely define the meaning of "overall access" to health services and "equality" in the context of health services distribution. As previously noted, the concept of access relates to the types of services that are available, the health benefits they provide, and the costs for individuals in accessing and utilizing them. Overall access to health services can thus increase by enhancing the range of available services, increasing the aggregate health benefits provided by the service package, or reducing the monetary and nonmonetary costs of individuals in accessing and utilizing the services.

Successful litigation for health services will usually broaden the range of available services for some individuals or groups (or reduce the costs of obtaining those services if already available in the private market domestically or abroad). But this in itself is obviously a too-narrow criterion for judging whether the population's access to health services has improved. A more informative way of measuring overall access to health services would be to measure the aggregate potential health benefits of the existing service package. Assuming that the costs of access remain unchanged, a necessary requirement for an improvement in overall access would then be that the aggregate potential health benefits have increased.

One way to evaluate the impact on aggregate potential health benefits is to compare the cost-effectiveness of services provided to litigants with the cost-effectiveness of other services provided by the health system. If litigants are successfully accessing treatments with relatively low cost-effectiveness (implying that health gains are low relative to the resources spent), litigation may reduce the average cost-effectiveness of the service package, implying a lower aggregate health improvement for the population at the existing level of expenditure. An increase in public health budgets, or an improvement in the efficiency of the health system, is then needed to maintain overall access to services. Conversely, if new treatments are relatively cost-effective, overall access might increase even at the existing level of expenditures.[11]

A discussion of "equality" in the context of health services distribution should begin by addressing the fundamental question, equality of what? A common approach is to define equality in the distribution of health services as "equal access for equal need" (Oliver and Mossialos 2004).[12] (While there are several ways to interpret "need," one interpretation is that for every kind of health problem, access to treatment should be independent of socioeconomic status.) This approach should make us inquire (i) whether litigation has enhanced the availability of existing services for groups that previously were excluded from access and (ii) whether new services provided because of litigation are offered equally to all or only to those who litigate—the latter of whom, in several of the countries studied here, are the more advantaged groups in terms of socioeconomic status (see, in this volume, Ferraz; Yamin et al.; Bergallo).

A weakness of the "equal access for equal need" criterion seems to be that it easily leads to a narrow perspective of equity by focusing on equality of access within groups with a particular kind of need. An alternative approach would be to focus on equality in health *outcomes* (Anand et al. 2006). Inequalities in access to health services might then be acceptable, provided the end result is greater equality in health outcomes. Others would go perhaps even further and argue that our ultimate concern should be with a broader notion of welfare that includes, for example, economic resources and freedoms (Sen 2006). In this case, inequality in access to health services would be acceptable, provided it contributes to a more equal distribution of welfare.

Firm conclusions on whether litigation has enhanced overall access to health services and contributed to their equitable distribution cannot be made without knowing how the expenditures resulting from litigation have been financed. As discussed above, such data are currently scarce. In this section, we will discuss possible impacts under alternative assumptions about funding. We believe the most plausible assumption is that, at least in the short and medium term (say, one to two years), litigation will likely be funded not by additional resources but rather by reallocation of existing resources and/or a reduction in waste or inefficiencies. This is so because neither health officials obliged to comply with court orders nor judges have the power to increase health budgets. Such power is normally a prerogative of members of the legislature and relevant regulatory authorities. Therefore, given the short timeframe within which court orders must be complied with—especially individual treatment orders where judges often make use of interim injunctions, to be complied with in a matter of hours or days—health officials do not have the time to await an increase in the health budget. They must find the money within existing budgets.

Empirical Findings

Impact on Aggregate Health Benefits

Norheim and Gloppen (this volume) present the most comprehensive assessment to date of the cost-effectiveness of medicines accessed through litigation in four countries: Brazil, Colombia, Costa Rica, and South Africa. The large majority of the medicines provided through litigation in Brazil, Colombia, and Costa Rica appear to have low—and sometimes extremely low—cost-effectiveness. There are exceptions, though: they show in Colombia, for example, that some cost-effective medicines have been litigated, and in South Africa that the nevirapine treatment for preventing mother-to-child transmission of HIV is highly cost-effective.

Such analyses of cost-effectiveness can be extremely useful when analyzing impact on aggregate health benefits. In general, aggregate health benefits will increase when litigation results in one of the following:

- provision of services that increases the average cost-effectiveness of the service package (since more health can then be bought within the existing resource envelope); or
- provision of services that reduces the average cost-effectiveness of the service package, but at the same time results in budget expansions or efficiency gains sufficiently large to outweigh any initial loss.

Similarly, a loss in aggregate health benefits occurs when litigation results in the provision of services that reduces the average cost-effectiveness of the service package, while at the same time failing to result in budget expansions or efficiency gains sufficiently large to outweigh this loss.

The very low cost-effectiveness of many of the treatments that have been ordered through litigation in several Latin American countries does not prove beyond doubt that litigation has reduced overall access to health services in these countries. The lack of data on how litigation has been funded prevents us from drawing firm conclusions. However, unless significant amounts of extra resources are mobilized, the impact is likely to be negative (assuming that the health benefits discontinued to fund additional services are not in fact less cost-effective). This is a concern since, as we have argued above, resources are likely to be drawn partially from existing budgets, at least in the short run.

The picture is different in South Africa in the particular case of litigation for nevirapine, which led to the provision of a treatment that is very cost-effective compared to almost all other possible interventions. Therefore, this most likely enhanced overall access to health services for the population.

Note that it is always a waste of resources to add treatments with very low cost-effectiveness, even if budgets are increased to avoid a reduction in the aggregate health benefits. Indeed, especially in the middle- and low-income countries surveyed in this volume, there is a host of highly cost-effective health-care measures that are lacking and would bring much higher health benefits than the low cost-effective drugs currently being litigated.

It seems fair to suggest, thus, that Norheim and Gloppen's approach can elicit valuable information on impact and should be used more widely in future research.

Impact on the Distribution of Health Services

Some evidence has also been made available in this volume on how litigation might affect the distribution of health services. Yet, again, a full picture would require information on whether litigation orders have reduced access to other health services, and if so, who the losers are. We have already noticed several times that this type of data is the most difficult to collect. But we can elicit interesting conclusions by looking at the more accessible data on litigants and the benefits they receive.

It is important to note that the countries studied in this book are all low- and middle-income countries with stark socioeconomic inequalities. These inequalities translate into significant health inequalities and unequal access to health services among the population (see chapter 2). Only in Costa Rica has the health system been able to provide services on a reasonably equitable basis to people of all socioeconomic levels. In all other countries, whereas the better-off have fairly high health indicators and access to a reasonable standard of health services through various forms of private health arrangements (e.g., insurance, prepaid plans, and out-of-pocket services), the poor present much worse health indicators and rely more heavily on significantly underfunded public health systems and/or subsidized systems with lower coverage of services. Litigation's impact on the distribution of health services must be understood within this context—that is, one in which large portions of the population are severely disadvantaged in terms of access to health services and attainment of health outcomes. Under such circumstances, a prioritarian approach to equity is likely to emphasize the extent to which litigation has improved access to health services for the worst-off, relative to the better-off.

Equal access for equal need. Let us first consider whether litigation has contributed to "equal access for equal need." Here, it may be useful to distinguish between litigation that seeks to improve access to services that are already provided through the public health system and litigation that seeks the inclusion of additional services in the system. In Colombia, for instance, most litigation has addressed the nonprovision of services already included in the national health plan and already provided to certain sectors of the population. These cases, at least on the face of it, appear to contribute to more equal access for equal need. The need to file *tutelas* again and again for the same type of services shows, however, that litigation has been unable to resolve the issue of equal access on a more permanent basis.

Judgment T-760/08 of the Colombian Constitutional Court ordered the subsidized system to provide the same coverage as the nonsubsidized one—that is, it ordered an increase in coverage so as to equalize benefits for those earning less than twice the minimum wage or working outside the formal sector. The effect of this judgment remains to be evaluated; yet, if fully implemented, it could lead to significantly more "equal access for equal need."

Other examples of litigation (or threats of litigation) apparently improving equal access for equal need include HIV/AIDS litigation in India, which ensured, at least on paper, universal lifetime access to first-line antiretroviral treatment;[13] the Treatment Action Campaign case in South Africa, which arguably contributed to improved PMTCT services to mothers and children throughout the country; and the successful efforts to bring down prices of antiretrovirals in South Africa (see Norheim and Gloppen in this volume; Heywood 2009).

These examples contrast with the more commonly observed pattern in the Latin American countries, where a large share of litigation is brought by individuals in order to access treatments excluded from national health plans. The civil-law system of these countries, which lacks precedent, implies that litigation tends to benefit some (the individual litigants) but not all. This may contribute to more unequal access to particular services. To some extent, these consequences have been alleviated when health authorities have decided to include certain treatments in national health plans after losing a number of court cases (e.g., in Argentina, Brazil, and Costa Rica). However, such extensions of services to the general population do not always happen. In Brazil, health authorities have decided not to include expensive new treatments for diabetes in the national health plan despite numerous cases lost in court, because expenditures would be too high.[14] Here, litigation for new treatments seems to have contributed to less equal access for equal need—at least in the short run.

This conclusion is strengthened by the fact that in countries where advantaged groups enjoy health services outside the public system, the provision of new and costly services within the public system will reduce access to other services more for the poor than for the better-off (provided that new services are partly funded from existing budgets). This conflicts with the principle of equal access for equal need. Moreover, if litigation introduces high-tech services for older populations into a generally deficient and basic public health system, the poor—though they may theoretically enjoy these new services—may fail to reap the benefits, as there would be less money to cover more cost-effective services that would help them live long enough in the first place to benefit from these high-tech services.

As already mentioned, a limitation of the "equal access for equal need" criterion is that it tends to assess equality within a rather narrow perspective by focusing on people who suffer from a single disease. Imagine that greater equality of access for people suffering from breast cancer is achieved by drawing funds away from nutrition programs for severely malnourished children. It is far from obvious that such equality is also equitable and fair. Such paradoxes can be dealt with by focusing on equality of health outcomes rather than on equal access for equal need.

Equality of health outcomes. Data presented in this volume from Argentina, Brazil, and Colombia indicate that individual litigants tend to belong overwhelmingly to the middle class—which enjoys greater access to the courts—and only sporadically to the lower classes. In Brazil, for instance, of all health litigation brought against the federal government, 93.3% originated in the ten states with the highest human development index levels, whereas a meager 6.6% originated in the seventeen least developed states. A similar picture emerged within states and cities, with most claims originating in better-off regions and districts. In Argentina, most cases surveyed came from areas with higher average family income, and most litigants were represented by private lawyers, indicating the litigants' relatively high socioeconomic status. In only one case did the litigant make use of legal aid, and in no cases did the litigant reside in an area where the poorest generally reside. In Colombia, those in the contributory regime (the better-off) file *tutelas* six times more frequently than those in the subsidized regime. There is also some evidence from Brazil and Colombia that not only are the better-off more likely to litigate in the first place but they are also more likely to litigate for the most advanced and expensive medical treatments. In São Paulo, for instance, whereas most claims represented by public attorneys seek affordable health benefits (e.g., geriatric diapers, special food, and ordinary drugs), claims supported by private lawyers, who represent mostly the better-off, focus on expensive new drugs and treatment (Ferraz in this volume).

Given that in these countries, as we have seen, the better-off already enjoy superior health conditions (due, in part, to more access to private health services of considerably higher coverage and quality), these data suggest that litigation in many countries may have contributed to enhancing rather than reducing inequalities in health outcomes.[15] And since health outcomes are typically positively correlated with income as well as other sources of welfare (Commission on Social Determinants of Health 2008), litigation also seems to have enhanced inequalities in welfare.

This pattern is not universally true, however. As already mentioned, the *TAC–PMTCT* case in South Africa is likely to have contributed to a more equal distribution of health outcomes (Norheim and Gloppen in this volume). A study of infants with HIV-positive mothers in rural northern KwaZulu-Natal, for example, found that infant mortality declined from 86 to 37 per 1,000 live births between 2001 and 2006 through the application of both antiretroviral therapy and PMTCT programs, which were arguably introduced at least in part as a response of litigation. The substantial increase in life expectancy for many children who otherwise would have died prematurely due to HIV/AIDS very likely contributed to a more equal distribution of health outcomes. Some cases in India (e.g., the right-to-food case) also have the potential to equalize health outcomes if effectively enforced.

The final distributional consequences of individual lawsuits may be less inequitable than the socioeconomic status of the litigants suggests. There are many examples from Costa Rica, along with Argentina and Brazil, showing how a series of successful individual cases brought about health policy changes extending benefits to the general population. However, the country chapters have not been able to provide systematic data on the extent of such health policy change, nor, of course, on the degree of implementation of such policies.

In sum, the distributive impact of litigation depends on the characteristics of the litigant; the type of claim (e.g., individual versus collective and the object of litigation); the judicial system (e.g., access to courts, civil- or common-law system, and interpretation of the right to health); and the health system (e.g., responsiveness to judicial decisions, funding of litigation-related expenditures, and degree of private supply of health services). Unfortunately, we cannot draw bold conclusions for lack of sufficiently accurate and comprehensive information on several of these variables. Even with the scarce information we have, however, it is possible to draw some important tentative conclusions. In countries where the prevailing model of litigation is individualized lawsuits for curative treatment (e.g., Latin American countries), the better-off seem to enjoy an advantage due to their greater access to lawyers and courts. It is unlikely, under such a model, that litigation will have any significant positive effect on health equality, particularly if the advantaged already have access to comprehensive private health services and health authorities do not respond by universalizing services ordered by the courts. On the other hand, in countries where the prevailing model is collective litigation on behalf of vulnerable groups (e.g., India and South Africa), the potential for a positive impact on health equality is higher. Here, however, enforcement obstacles highlighted in previous sections seem to be more significant.

Conclusion

To delineate the impact of health rights litigation is a difficult endeavor, not only due to data limitations but, more fundamentally, due to the many potential confounding variables that are difficult to identify and measure. Moreover, since the type of litigation that we observe is a product of the institutional settings—including the health and judicial systems—in which it takes place, it is hard to assess what the results of health rights litigation would have been in other institutional settings. Our comparisons across case studies may, however, help in identifying how litigation operates in an intimate interplay with other structural factors to produce social change.

The available evidence portrays a mixed picture. In some cases, litigation has contributed to improved governmental responsiveness and systemic changes that benefit disadvantaged groups, while in other cases litigation has exacerbated existing inequities in health service delivery and reduced the scope for improving the health conditions of the general population. Understanding the characteristics of the health and judicial systems is central to understanding these widely different outcomes. The more worrying outcomes seem to occur where individuals can access courts relatively easily, but where the costs of access still are high enough to prevent the poor from litigating; where the court interprets, without considering cost-effectiveness, the right to health as an absolute right to receive available health services; where there is a civil-law system and health authorities do not universalize access to services ordered by the court; and where services ordered by the court are financed from existing budgets, and advantaged groups receive a substantial share of their health services from private providers.

The long-term impact of litigation may of course differ from the immediate impact, and the litigation wave has probably not yet matured to a stage where its long-term effects can be properly judged. For now, it is worth mentioning that, with regard to those cases that seem to have increased inequities, in a historical perspective, rights have always been first claimed by the middle classes and later extended to the general population. In order for this to happen with health rights litigation as well, successful litigation over time must be accompanied by increased health budgets. Another important parameter is the willingness and ability of health authorities to respond to successful litigation by universalizing access to the services concerned.

NOTES

1. For different positions within the debate over courts' usefulness for achieving social change, see Gottlieb and Schultz (1998), Garth et al. (1998), and Sabel and Simon (2004).
2. Country chapters in this volume demonstrate that compliance cannot be taken for granted, particularly when it goes beyond individual litigants. Among the factors assumed to influence compliance are legal culture, political will, and litigants' support structures for conducting follow-up. See, e.g., Epp (1998).
3. For a discussion of "winning when losing," see, for example, McCann (1998). These processes are also captured by Rodríguez Garavito's concept of "symbolic impact"—that is, impact beyond the material, which may occur, for instance, when a court case changes people's perceptions of what constitutes a rights violation and what is needed to address it. Short-term symbolic impacts may have material impacts in the long run (Rodríguez

Garavito and Rodríguez Franco 2010a). In a similar vein, Scheingold (2004) argues that the symbolic character of rights may have concrete political effects by facilitating political activity—the "myth of rights" may activate political consciousness and facilitate public acceptance of litigants' claims, which, in turn, may have material effects by spurring a realignment of resources and values at the level of public policy. Scheingold thus holds that while litigation is rarely directly empowering on its own, it may contribute to political mobilization by being constitutive of social action.

4. The estimates presented here are in most cases conservative due to lack of comprehensive and accurate data. In Argentina and Brazil, data are available only for certain regions, often the most economically developed and the most populous ones. For instance, cases for Argentina correspond only to those filed with the Federal Civil and Commercial Courts of the City of Buenos Aires. In India, the authors were restricted to cases mentioned in law reports, which are by no means exhaustive. The actual volume of litigation is therefore likely to be higher in most countries.
5. Reynaldo Mappeli (public attorney) and Luiz Duarte (state attorney), interview, São Paulo, August 2010.
6. Maria Cecilia Correa (director of litigation department, Secretariat of Health of São Paulo State) and Ana Luiza Chieffi (pharmacist, Secretariat of Health of São Paulo State), interview, São Paulo, July 2009.
7. There is also the possibility, though less common, that unsuccessful litigation produces health policy changes. This happened in the state of São Paulo with epilepsy drugs. The *Ministério Público* managed to get an interim order forcing the state to provide a specific drug for epilepsy. When the Court of Appeals overturned the order a few years later, the state decided not to discontinue provision of the drug in the public health system (Maria Cecilia Correa [director of litigation department, Secretariat of Health of São Paulo State], interview, São Paulo, August 2010).
8. Not all policy changes stimulated by voluminous repeated litigation are implemented because the relevant authority recognizes an obligation to do so. Some, and perhaps most, of such policy changes are motivated rather by strategic reasons, such as the potential lower cost of changing policy in comparison to responding in court to hundreds or thousands of individual cases with no prospects of success. When the opposite happens, however—when the cost of litigation is lower than that of a policy change—the state often prefers to continue responding to litigation. This is the case, for example, in diabetes litigation in Brazil.
9. We are assuming here, of course, that health authorities comply with court orders. When they do not, as has happened in all countries studied in this volume, there should be no impact on health budgets.
10. Interview with senior official at Hospital Nacional de Niños, San José, June 2008.
11. This "marginalist" approach to evaluating the impact of health rights litigation may in some cases be complemented by surveys that measure overall access to health services before and after major litigation, especially when court orders imply fundamental and profound changes in the health system. Needless to say, such surveys are major undertakings and involve a number of methodological challenges.

12. For a further discussion of the concept of "need," see Culyer (1995).
13. Litigation seeking universal access to second-line treatment is presently pending.
14. Interview with public health official, São Paulo, August 2010.
15. It can be argued that although the rich, on average, have better health than the poor, there may be cases where rich people who litigate for particular life-saving treatments are actually worse off in terms of health outcomes than many of the poor. But even if single cases like this can be identified, it would be inequitable both according to the "equal access for equal need" criterion and a broader welfarist notion of justice to maintain a socioeconomic gradient in the provision of health services.

Chapter 12

Litigating for Medicines: How Can We Assess Impact on Health Outcomes?

Ole Frithjof Norheim and Siri Gloppen

This chapter proposes a methodology for evaluating whether health rights litigation makes health systems more (or less) just. It then uses this methodology to analyze some of the significant forms of litigation emerging from the country studies in the first part of this book in order to explore their impact on priority setting in health.

The chapter explores long-term social outcomes of litigation with regard to the effects on resource allocation between diagnostic groups.[1] A diagnostic group consists of patients with a defined condition, or a defined sub-population with particular risk factors (e.g., women with breast cancer, patients with schizophrenia, healthy people at risk for cardiovascular disease, or children at risk for vertical transmission of HIV). A group's access to a particular medicine or treatment may affect the distribution of health between this group and other groups in need. Health-impact comparisons are typical in the literature concerning priority setting in health and health care.[2] Our aims are twofold: to propose methods to evaluate existing litigation in order to determine its impact on priority setting in health, and to develop a framework to evaluate the long-term social outcomes of court decisions concerning access to medicines. We hope that our proposed methods can offer a framework for future studies in this area.

The first part of the chapter suggests a methodology for assessing and evaluating the potential impact of access-to-medicines litigation, which it then applies to a selection of cases from Brazil, Costa Rica, and Colom-

---

The authors wish to thank Norman Daniels for very constructive comments and Carole Cooper, Octavio L. Motta Ferraz, Camila Gianella, Oscar Parra-Vera, Bruce M. Wilson, and Alicia Ely Yamin for contributing data to this chapter.

bia. The distributional impact of cases claiming access to medicines is significant in light of the escalating number of court cases concerning (often costly) drugs—including in countries with limited resources for health care (Hogerzeil et al. 2006). The country studies indicate that medication cases, of all health rights litigation, dominate in terms of numbers and even more in terms of costs (see, in this volume, Ferraz; Yamin et al.; Wilson). Not only is the number of cases high and rising—as seen most dramatically in Colombia, reaching 145,000 in 2008 alone (Yamin et al. in this volume)—but the success rates are also very high. It is therefore relevant to ask the following questions: When such cases are successful in court, whom do they benefit? Is litigation an avenue that provides marginalized patients with fair access to medicines, or is it a back road for patients seeking access to treatments that from a public health perspective would be assigned low priority?

This analysis of a limited sample of cases can indicate how access-to-medicines litigation affects priority setting in health. It does not, however, say anything about the scale of the impact in terms of the people affected and their health gain. This is particularly important to address in common-law legal systems, where decisions theoretically have an effect on all similar cases and a single case may affect millions of patients. In civil-law countries like Brazil, Costa Rica, and Colombia, most cases concern a specific individual, and judgments normally apply to only the individual at hand. While there are exceptions—both in the form of collective and structural judgments and indirect general effects through judgment-induced policy changes—the volume of court cases in these countries provides a certain indication of the number of people affected by judicial decisions.

The second part of the chapter analyzes South Africa's health rights litigation to suggest how scale can be included in the assessment of the distributional impact of health litigation with generalized effect, as is the norm in a common-law context. We start with a case concerning access to medication, using an analysis parallel to that of the first part of the chapter but adding a methodology for assessing the scope of the impact. We then show how a similar analysis of distributional impact can be conducted for other types of cases, such as those involving expensive treatment (e.g., dialysis). Finally, we look at a different form of health rights litigation—cases aimed at reducing drug prices—to address the impact on priority setting. This last type of case is fought as much "in the shadow of litigation"—that is, outside the courtroom—as in the courtroom, giving rise to other methodological challenges.

Our preliminary analysis shows that litigation's effect on improving access to essential high-priority treatment depends on the nature of the health and legal systems as well as on what is litigated for.

Assessing Social Outcomes

The social outcomes of health rights litigation should be viewed against the background of inequality and inequity in the societies in which the litigation takes place. As chapter 2 shows, the four countries examined in this chapter are all highly unequal middle-income countries. With the exception of Costa Rica, social disparities are reflected in health systems, with marked differences between the privatized health-care system of the middle and upper classes and the publicly provided services available to the poor.

In the context of low- and middle-income countries, where poor people have little or no access to modern medicine, Paul Farmer has noted that "the more effective the treatment, the greater the injustice meted out to those who do not have access to care" (2001, 209). Building on this point, we argue that the social outcomes of health litigation—the implications for distributive justice, for instance—depend not only on whether the litigation provides access to medicines but also on the characteristics of the recipient (is the patient poor, otherwise disadvantaged, or severely ill?) and characteristics of the treatment (how effective is the medicine, how much does it cost, and what are the alternative uses of these resources?). In what follows, we explore social outcomes in terms of impact on the distribution of health. A positive social outcome improves both efficiency and equity in the distribution of health, in line with the two central goals of health policy: to maximally improve the population's health and to distribute that health fairly (Daniels 2008).

Previous work on health equity has been based on measurement of health disparities between social groups defined by characteristics known to be associated with social and health disadvantage. This is known as a bivariate approach to health inequality (Wolfson and Rowe 2001). These analyses have focused on differences in health related to poverty or wealth, using household survey data on assets and consumption to define wealth and calculating differences in health status between various categories, such as wealth quintiles. Studies have also focused on other social factors related to vulnerability, such as sex, education level, ethnicity, and area of residence (Moser et al. 2005; Vapattanawong et al. 2007; Wirth et al. 2008; Reidpath et al. 2009). Such studies have demonstrated important inequities based on wealth and other social group characteristics that are important from a social justice perspective. The few studies assessing social outcomes of health litigation have also used a bivariate approach (see Ferraz in this volume).

A less common approach to the study of impacts on health inequalities uses a different focal variable—the distribution of health itself within a population. This is sometimes called a univariate approach to health inequality (Wolfson and Rowe 2001). Among the relatively few empirical applications of this approach (Gakidou and King 2002; Tang et al. 2007, 2009), none has yet focused on health rights litigation.

From a public health perspective, the univariate approach is relevant because it looks at the distribution of health itself from a population-level perspective by considering population summary measures such as life expectancy at birth and inequality in the age of death (table 12.1). Inequality in the age of death is measured by Gini-health (Norheim et al. 2010).

The two population summary measures are calculated from life tables. Relevant information derived from life tables can be represented graphically, as seen in figure 12.1.

Figure 12.1 uses data from Brazil, Colombia, Costa Rica, and South Africa—as well as Japan for comparison—to illustrate the number of persons dying in each age group, as if a cohort of 100,000 children born in 2006 went through a society with the age-specific mortality pattern as given in the World Health Organization life tables.[3] Developed countries (such as Japan) with high life expectancy typically have a mortality pattern in which age at death is concentrated in the older age groups. Inequality in life-length (Gini-health) is low. Low- and middle-income countries tend to have more deaths in lower age groups (compare Brazil with Japan). Of particular interest is South Africa, where, largely due to high HIV/AIDS prevalence, we see a shift in the curve toward the left, meaning that a substantial proportion of the population is at risk of leading a short life. South Africa thus has greater

Table 12.1. Life expectancy and inequality in age of death (Gini-health) in a selection of countries

Country	Life expectancy, both sexes	Gini-health
South Africa	53.5	0.26
Brazil	73.3	0.14
Colombia	75.5	0.13
Costa Rica	78.4	0.11
Japan	82.8	0.09

Source: World Health Organization (2008).

inequality in life-length (higher Gini-health)—some die before reaching five years of age; some die between twenty-five and fifty years of age; and some reach a full or normal life span.

Against this backdrop, the analysis in this chapter is informed by the perspective that distributive justice concerns more than income and wealth: inequality in the age of death (health distribution) is also relevant.[4] From a public health perspective, high priority should be assigned to health services that have a large impact on life expectancy (improving average health) and target those who will live the shortest life (reducing overall health inequality) (Norheim and Asada 2009; Norheim 2010).[5]

To the best of our knowledge, no studies have evaluated the public health implications of successful health rights litigation in terms of equity and efficiency in the distribution of health. In their study of health and education litigation in India, Indonesia, and South Africa, Varun Gauri and Daniel Brinks (2008) provide rough estimates of the number of people affected, but not *who* is affected or *how* they are affected (magnitude of the impact).

Figure 12.1. Number of deaths per age group (per 1,000 people) in a selection of countries

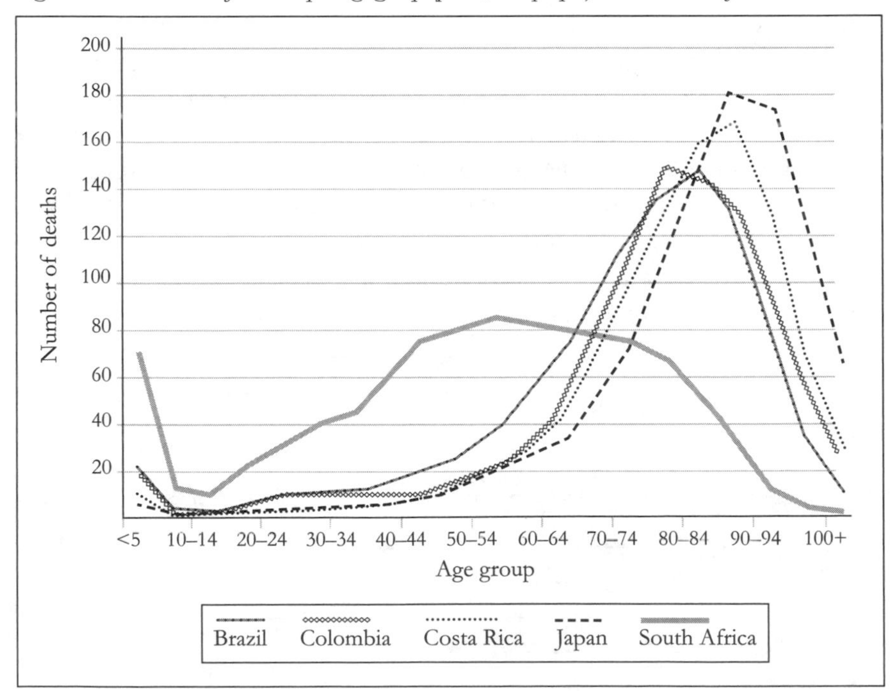

Source: World Health Organization (2008).

This chapter explores methods for assessing the health equity impact of litigation. Methodological development is central; the following three sections explain our classification system for typical access-to-medicine cases from Brazil, Colombia, Costa Rica, and South Africa. Thereafter, our selection of cases, though not representative, provides an indication as to whether and when litigation for medications has improved access to essential high-priority services.

Material and Methods

For each of the Latin American countries—Brazil, Colombia, and Costa Rica—we assembled a database of cases for the year 2008. From each database, which contained anywhere from one hundred to thousands of cases, we selected only those cases concerning access to medicines. We then randomly selected approximately fifty successful cases from each country and extracted a brief description of the case and the medication involved.[6]

Second, we searched for published cost-effectiveness studies and reports that have evaluated these medicines according to the methods of health technology assessment (HTA) (Drummond et al. 2008; Banta 2009). We used PubMed (a database for medical publications) for the identification of published academic studies and the website of the National Institute for Health and Clinical Excellence in the United Kingdom as a starting point for relevant and up-to-date publicly available HTA reports.

Third, from the identified studies and reports, we extracted priority-relevant medical evidence concerning health outcomes and costs. Priority-relevant evidence is information necessary to evaluate the effectiveness of a given medication, the medication's overall costs, and the severity of the condition for a typical patient in need of such medication. In addition, we extracted information concerning the quality of evidence concerning health outcomes and costs. After extracting the evidence for the medications in question, we evaluated each medicine according to predefined criteria for priority classification.

Finally, we summarized the evidence for each criterion and combined it into an overall assessment, classifying each medicine into one of four priority groups ranked in order of importance from a standard public health or priority-setting perspective. High-priority medicines were those with a potential to affect life expectancy and reduce overall inequality in health. Using this method, we evaluated existing litigation for its potential impact on priority setting in health. A large proportion of cases falling into the high-priority category would imply that litigation improves access to high-priority or essential medicines for the litigants in question. A small proportion of such cases would indicate that litigation is less likely to be in accordance with public health views on the kinds of drugs that should be given high priority.

A System for Priority Classification of Cases

Most authors concerned with health policy, priority setting, and social justice agree that just health systems should seek to further two goals: efficiency and fairness in the distribution of health and health care (Williams 1988, 1996, 1997; Daniels 1994, 2008; Murray and Lopez 1996; Nord 1999; Nord et al. 1999). Although people disagree about how much weight to grant each concern, there are certain criteria that almost all theories of resource allocation in health care would recognize (Ham 1995; Norheim 1996, 2000; Ham and Locock 1998; Ham and Coulter 2000). This set of accepted criteria states that the priority of a given condition and its intervention should be assessed in terms of (i) the severity of disease if given standard care or left untreated; (ii) the effectiveness of the intervention; (iii) the cost-effectiveness of the intervention; and (iv) the quality of evidence for items i–iii. In other words, this information is formulated by examining the characteristics of the patient,[7] the condition, and the health intervention in question.

From this set of accepted fairness criteria from the public health and priority-setting literature, we developed a framework for priority classification:

- priority group I = high priority
- priority group II = medium priority
- priority group III = low priority
- priority group IV = experimental interventions[8]

Threshold Criteria for Classification of Cases

An intervention for a given condition was assigned high priority when the following conditions were met: the untreated condition is severe (poor prognosis, measured as health gap in terms of lost life years or loss of quality of life); the intervention is highly effective (improved prognosis compared to standard treatment in terms of life years or quality of life); and the intervention is reasonably cost-effective. In addition, effectiveness and cost-effectiveness should be *documented* in high-quality studies (preferably randomized clinical trials) (Guyatt et al. 2008). For the detailed framework, see table 12.2.

The measure of effectiveness used in most HTA reports and cost-effectiveness studies is the quality-adjusted life year (QALY). As indicated in table 12.2, we grade clinical effectiveness in terms of QALYs. Our threshold of 1 QALY for very effective (grade I) is not particularly restrictive.

For studies where severity of disease was not reported, we extracted relevant information and indirectly estimated the health gap by using QALY gain in the absence of treatment (or with standard treatment) with the help of life tables for the relevant country. For example, if a forty-year-old patient from Costa Rica with terminal breast cancer had a prognosis of 1 QALY, her health gap was calculated as life expectancy at age forty (= 42.2) minus 1 QALY (= 41.2). We use this as an indicator of her severity of disease. Here, we regard a condition as very severe (grade I) if the loss is more than 5 QALYs, severe (grade II) if the loss is between 1 and 5 QALYs, and not severe (grade III) if the loss is less than 1 QALY. Ideally, these thresholds should be discussed and

Table 12.2. Criteria for priority classification

Criterion	Information needed	Measure[a]	Grading
Effectiveness of intervention	Mortality Morbidity	QALY gain[b]	I. > 1 QALY II. < 1 & > 0.5 QALY III. < 0.5 QALY
Severity of disease	Mortality Morbidity	QALY loss[c]	I. > 5 QALY loss II. > 1 QALY loss < 5 QALY loss III. < 1 QALY loss
Cost-effectiveness of intervention	Total and incremental cost-effectiveness	Cost per QALY gained	I. Cost-effective: < GDP per capita II. Intermediate: > GDP per capita < 3 x GDP per capita III. Not cost-effective: > 3 x GDP per capita
Quality of evidence	Type of studies documenting treatment effects	Evidence grading systems[d]	I. Meta-analysis or randomized clinical trial II. Observational, noncomparative studies III. Single case reports

[a] Quality-adjusted life years (QALYs).

[b] Compared to standard intervention.

[c] Compared to normal healthy life expectancy.

[d] Such as the AGREE instrument or others.

determined in health-policy deliberations; but in the absence of agreement on thresholds, we believe that these are not unreasonable.

To grade cost-effectiveness, we used data from the World Bank (2009) on gross domestic product (GDP) per capita for 2008 for the relevant countries in U.S. dollars (adjusted for purchasing power parity):

- Brazil: US$9,520
- Colombia: US$8,130
- Costa Rica: US$10,370
- South Africa: US$9,340

Again, there is no unanimously accepted standard, but the World Health Organization and others have suggested that an intervention be classified as highly cost-effective if cost per QALY is less than GDP per capita; intermediate if cost per QALY lies between 1 x GDP per capita and 3 x GDP per capita; and not cost-effective if cost per QALY is above 3 x GDP per capita (Hutubessy et al. 2003; Evans et al. 2005; Jamison et al. 2006). According to this rule of thumb, all interventions costing more than approximately US$30,000 per QALY gained would be judged as not cost-effective in the countries examined here. The underlying ethical rationale for considering cost-effectiveness is that there may be unmet needs in the system for which there are more cost-effective interventions and that health is more efficiently distributed if priority is given to the most cost-effective interventions first. These thresholds seem to have originated in the United Kingdom as an extrapolation from existing cases endorsed or rejected by the National Institute for Health and Clinical Excellence; the justification for these thresholds is not discussed in the existing literature.

As a general rule, a condition and its medication must satisfy all criteria cumulatively; that is, to qualify for priority group I, the condition must be severe enough and the treatment effective and cost-effective enough. To qualify for priority group II, all criteria must be II or higher. This will qualify all clearly high-priority medicines (all grade I) and disqualify all clearly low-priority medicines (all grade III). However, acknowledging that priority setting may allow—indeed, require—balancing the criteria against each other, we have marked "debatable" priority groups with the "#" symbol. For example, a drug targeting a condition whose severity is grade I, and in which the drug's effectiveness is grade II or above and its cost-effectiveness is grade III, will—since all criteria must be cumulatively satisfied—qualify only for priority group III. However, in this case it may be argued that severity should be assigned such a high weight that the overall priority classification would be one level higher. We thus classify this condition/medicine pair as priority group III#.

We acknowledge that any system of priority classification is bound to be controversial. Despite some agreement on priority criteria, reasonable people may disagree on classification. However, our method has the advantage of being based on publicly available evidence and explicit criteria grounded in theories of fair priority setting in health.

Examples of Cases Classified

In this section, we present five successful cases each for Brazil (São Paulo City), Costa Rica, and Colombia that are seen as typical (but not representative). We also present three cases from South Africa. For each country's analysis, we include two tables. The first table summarizes evidence for each criterion for each case. The second table synthesizes this information into an overall assessment of each medicine, which classifies each drug into one of the four priority groups discussed above.

Brazil

Brazil has experienced an enormous volume of health litigation concerning medicines. We provide five illustrative cases.

None of these medications has a clinical effectiveness above 1 QALY. The new cancer drug bevacizumab will, on average, yield a gain of 0.85 QALYs for a patient with rectal cancer with metastases (for which the drug is indicated). Severity of the disease in terms of QALY loss is very high. However, the drug is costly, and cost-effectiveness is more than US$50,000 per QALY gained—far above the 3 x GDP per capita criterion for cost-effectiveness. The evidence base is from randomized clinical trials and high-quality HTAs. The overall priority classification for this condition/medication is group III, or low priority.

All of the Brazilian cases presented here can be described as providing small or marginal health benefits for very severe conditions (except for osteoporosis) at a high opportunity cost for the health-care system. We judge four of the five cases to be clearly low priority, while bevacizumab for rectal carcinoma is classified as "debatable" (III#) because the condition is very severe and the effectiveness is grade II or better. Although we do not claim that this set of examples is representative for Brazil or even São Paulo, preliminary analyses of a larger sample indicate a similar trend.[9]

Table 12.3. Evidence table, five cases, Brazil (São Paulo)

Medication	Condition	Effectiveness (individual QALY gain)	Severity of disease (QALY loss)	Cost (US$) per QALY	Quality of evidence[a]	References
Bevacizumab (Avastin)	Adeno-carcinoma in rectum, metastases in liver and lungs	0.85	18.43	51,120	2 RCT	Tappenden et al. (2007)
Rivastigmine (Exelon)	Alzheimer's	0.14	>1 and < 5[b]	92,910	1 RCT	Loveman et al. (2006)
Teriparatide (Forteo)	Osteoporosis	0.1	0.2	255,095	2 RCT	Liu et al. (2006)
Infliximab (Remicade)	Rheumatoid arthritis	0.22	5.6	61,940	Several RCTs	Chen et al. (2006); Kobelt et al. (2003)
Insulin-glargine (Lantus)	Diabetes (type I)	0.067	>5[b]	19,343	1 RCT	Grima et al. (2007)

[a] RCT: randomized clinical trial.
[b] Authors' estimate.

Table 12.4. Priority table, five cases, Brazil (São Paulo)

Medication	Condition	Effectiveness	Severity	Cost-effective-ness	Strength of evidence	Priority group[a]
Bevacizumab (Avastin)	Adenocarci-noma in rectum, metastases in liver and lungs	II	I	III	I	III#
Rivastigmine (Exelon)	Alzheimer's	III	II	III	I	III
Teriparatide (Forteo)	Osteoporosis	III	III	III	I	III
Infliximab (Remicade)	Rheumatoid arthritis	III	I	III	I	III
Insulin-glargine (Lantus)	Diabetes (type I)	III	I	II	II	III

[a] I = high priority; II = medium priority; III = low priority; IV = experimental treatment.

Costa Rica

The Costa Rican cases show a slightly different pattern. Of particular interest is the breast cancer drug trastuzumab. Clinical effectiveness is estimated to be more than 1 QALY gained, and severity of disease is much more than 5 QALYs lost. With cost-effectiveness at about US$20,000 per QALY, it is in the intermediate range for Costa Rica.

Two of the Costa Rican cases fall into priority group III. Besides trastuzumab, another drug, rituximab (for lymphoma), is classified in priority group II. Sildenafil (for pulmonary hypertension) is classified as experimental treatment (priority group IV), lacking evidence of clinical effectiveness from a randomized clinical trial (a small open-label trial showed limited effectiveness).

As in the Brazilian examples, Costa Rican litigants are provided access to high-cost drugs with comparatively low effectiveness (priority group III). But we also find cases regarding medication of medium priority (group II), such as trastuzumab (for breast cancer), which the Costa Rican health authorities subsequently included in the health plan so that litigation is no longer

Table 12.5. Evidence table, five cases, Costa Rica

Medication	Condition	Effectiveness (individual QALY gain)	Severity of disease (QALY loss)	Cost (US$) per QALY	Quality of evidence[a]	References
Imatinib (Glivec)	Leukemia	< 1 QALY	>5[b]	74,314	RCT	Garside et al. (2002); Reed et al. (2008)
Clopidogrel (Plavix)	Heart disease	0.1	11.89	15,400	RCT	Schleinitz and Heidenreich (2005)
Rituximab (MabThera)	Lymphoma (Hodgkin's disease)	0.82	> 5[b]	17,271	RCT	Knight et al. (2004)
Trastuzumab (Herceptin)	Breast cancer	1.54	10.45	19,913	RCT	Liberato et al. (2007)
Sildenafil (Viagra)	Pulmonary hypertension	0.2	> 5[b]	N/A	Small open-label trial only	No HTA/ cost-effectiveness assessment study found

[a] RCT: randomized clinical trial.
[b] Authors' estimate.

needed to access the drug. We classify three of the five cases as "debatable" (II# or III#) because their conditions are very severe and their medications' effectiveness is grade II or better.

Colombia

In Colombia, we see yet another mix of cases. Alongside cases involving costly "last-chance" therapies for very severe conditions are cases that feature standard medications that are, or should be, considered essential services.

Tamoxifen for breast cancer and prednisolone for rheumatoid arthritis are off-patent, relatively inexpensive medicines that are on Colombia's essential medicines list and considered standard therapy in all middle-income countries. Although HTAs and cost-effectiveness analyses are lacking for these drugs (they tend to be performed for new drugs only), we have classified these cases as priority group I (high priority).

Such litigation seems to respond to systemic problems. As the chapter on Colombia in this volume explains, deficiencies in Colombia's system of service delivery may explain why these drugs were not provided in the first place (Yamin and Parra-Vera 2009). In addition, we classify two of the other cases as "debatable" (II# or III#) because their respective medical conditions are very severe and their drugs' effectiveness is grade II or better. Thus, in the examples provided for Colombia, litigation has proven to be successful not just in low-priority cases, but in high-priority ones as well; further analysis is needed.

Table 12.6. Priority table, five cases, Costa Rica

Medication	Condition	Effectiveness	Severity	Cost-effectiveness	Strength of evidence	Priority group[a]
Imatinib (Glivec)	Leukemia	I	I	III	I	III#
Clopidogrel (Plavix)	Heart disease	III	I	II	I	III
Rituximab (MabThera)	Lymphoma (Hodgkin's disease)	II	I	II	I	II#
Trastuzumab (Herceptin)	Breast cancer	I	I	II	I	II#
Sildenafil (Viagra)	Pulmonary hypertension	III	I	N/A	III	IV

[a] I = high priority; II = medium priority; III = low priority; IV = experimental treatment.

In sum, the priority classification system applied to three Latin American cases allows us to distinguish medications that should be assigned high, medium, low, or no priority, according to available evidence and fairly standard fairness criteria from the public health and priority-setting literature. Further studies of a representative set of cases are needed to evaluate whether health litigation contributes to a more or—as now seems more likely—less

Table 12.7. Evidence table, five cases, Colombia

Medication	Condition	Effectiveness (individual QALY gain)	Severity of disease (QALY loss)	Cost (US$) per QALY	Quality of evidence[a]	References
Donepezil (Aricept)	Alzheimer's	0.08	> 1 and < 5[b]	130,400	RCT	Loveman et al. (2006)
Etanercept (Enbrel)	Psoriatic arthritis	1.4	> 5[b]	42,968	RCT	Bravo Vergel et al. (2007)
Peginterferon alfa (Peg-Intron)	Hepatitis C	0.49	> 5	12,352	RCT	Shepherd et al. (2000)
Tamoxifen (Tamoxifen)	Breast cancer	> 1	> 5	< GDP per capita	. . .	. . .
Prednisolone (Prednisolone)	Rheumatoid arthritis	> 1	> 5	< GDP per capita	. . .	. . .

[a] RCT: randomized clinical trial.
[b] Authors' estimate.

Table 12.8. Priority table, five cases, Colombia

Medication	Condition	Effectiveness	Severity	Cost-effectiveness	Strength of evidence	Priority group[a]
Donepezil (Aricept)	Alzheimer's	III	III	III	I	III
Etanercept (Enbrel)	Psoriatic arthritis	I	I	III	I	III#
Peginterferon alfa (Peg-Intron)	Hepatitis C	II	I	II	I	II#
Tamoxifen (Tamoxifen)	Breast cancer	I	I	I	. . .	I
Prednisolone (Prednisolone)	Rheumatoid arthritis	I	I	I	. . .	I

[a] I = high priority; II = medium priority; III = low priority; IV = experimental treatment.

fair distribution of health in these countries. Like the current analysis, such studies should be based on a framework that draws on widely agreed principles of fair distribution and assigns high priority to health services that have a large impact on life expectancy (thus improving average health). In addition, more comprehensive analyses should assign priority to interventions targeting those with least lifetime health measured in terms of quality of life and premature mortality (thus reducing overall health inequality). If a majority of cases won through the courts leads to greater access only to new and expensive medications with marginal benefits, the impact is likely to be regressive when measured against a standard of fair distribution of health.

In the following section, we assess a set of health rights cases from South Africa in order to better grasp the significance of litigation in a common-law context, where rulings have general effect. Under these circumstances, we suggest how priority classification can be supplemented with other methods for evaluating the scale of impact. In addition to applying this methodology to medication cases, we suggest how a similar methodology may be used for cases regarding access to treatment. We also offer an approach for assessing the priority-setting effect of litigation processes aimed at bringing down drug prices.

South Africa

The countries discussed so far all belong to a civil-law tradition, where court decisions normally do not have general effect. While there are exceptions and cases may, in practice, set precedent or indirectly change policy, the situation is very different from countries with a common-law tradition, such as South Africa, where rulings normally have effect for all similarly situated persons. Hence, while South African courts hear far fewer health rights cases than Latin American courts, the impact of each case is potentially great.

Prevention of Mother-to-Child Transmission of HIV

In August 2001, the Treatment Action Campaign (TAC), a social movement advocating for improved policies and treatment for people living with HIV/AIDS, brought a suit against the South African government challenging its very limited policy for preventing HIV-positive mothers from passing the virus on to their children at birth (prevention of mother-to-child transmission, or PMTCT). Treatment with nevirapine was restricted to two public hospitals in each province involved in a pilot study of the drug's safety and efficacy. TAC argued that these restrictions on the drug's availability violated the constitutional right to health (Heywood 2009). The government claimed that the drug's price was a barrier to rolling out treatment, but by the time the case was heard, South Africa had been offered a five-years' supply of nevirapine free of charge (see next section on the campaigns against pharmaceutical companies concerning excessive drug prices).

In July 2002, the Constitutional Court issued a decision[10] ordering the government to remove restrictions preventing nevirapine from being made available to everyone in need and to take "reasonable measures to extend the testing and counselling facilities . . . to facilitate and expedite the use of nevirapine" (Annas 2003; Cooper in this volume).

Is it possible to estimate the potential social outcome of this judgment? We start by classifying nevirapine for children at risk of vertical transmission of HIV according to the priority classification system (tables 12.9 and 12.10).

According to available evidence at the time of the ruling, nevirapine clearly falls into priority group I as a very high-priority intervention (table 12.10).[11] It was documented to be effective and to be targeting a risk group facing a severe QALY loss. Cost-effectiveness was estimated to be US$11–45

Table 12.9. Evidence table for nevirapine, South Africa

Medication	Condition	Effectiveness (individual QALY gain)	Severity of disease (QALY loss)	Cost (US$) per QALY	Quality of evidence[a]	References
Nevirapine	Risk of vertical transmission of HIV	> 1	> 5	11–45	Several RCTs and CEAs	Guay et al. (1999); Marseille et al. (2000); Stringer et al. (2000)

[a] RCT: randomized clinical trial; CEA: cost-effectiveness assessment.

Table 12.10. Priority table for nevirapine, South Africa

Medication	Condition	Effectiveness	Severity	Cost-effectiveness	Strength of evidence	Priority group[a]
Nevirapine	Risk of vertical transmission of HIV	I	I	I	I	I

[a] I = high priority; II = medium priority; III = low priority; IV = experimental treatment.

per QALY gained, which is very good compared to almost all other possible interventions. Nevirapine improved life expectancy and reduced inequalities in age of death. Its efficacy was documented in several randomized clinical trials.

Since rollout of treatment depends on the availability of testing and counseling facilities, the judgment did not even in theory extend access to all in need; rather, it only potentially improved coverage. Implementation was slow, and would likely have been even slower in some provinces had it not been for the TAC's monitoring and threatened legal actions (Heywood 2009; Cooper in this volume). How can we estimate the number of lives and life years saved by the introduction of nevirapine for PMTCT in South Africa? We believe the following method can provide a fairly good picture.

We extracted data from published reports and studies on unmet need and coverage for PMTCT drugs in South Africa for 2002, 2005, and 2007 (WHO/UNAIDS/UNICEF 2007), and on the effectiveness, or absolute risk reduction, of nevirapine (Guay et al. 1999; Marseille et al. 2000; Stringer et al. 2000). We then used the data as input in a simple spreadsheet and calculated the following:

- *The annual number of patients with met need* (HIV-positive pregnant women and children treated). This was calculated by multiplying unmet need (estimated number of HIV-positive pregnant women and their babies) with reported coverage rates. We assumed coverage in 2002 to be 5%.
- *The number of children avoiding HIV infection.* This was calculated by multiplying met need with absolute risk reduction (risk without PMTCT care minus risk with PMTCT care).
- *The number of life years saved.* This was calculated by multiplying the number of children avoiding HIV infection with life expectancy at birth (derived from the latest life table available).

Table 12.11 shows that if coverage for 2002 was 5%, an estimated 1,625 children avoided HIV infection. By 2005, coverage had increased to 30%, and the number of children avoiding infection increased to 9,750. In 2010, this number reached 19,500. The estimated number of life years saved in 2010, at 60% coverage, was approximately one million. Full coverage would save 1.6 million life years per year.

There are uncertainties around these numbers. Estimated need and reported coverage are sometimes inaccurate (see Cooper in this volume); additionally, in the absence of available data on unmet need, we applied the

2005 estimate to 2002 and 2010, assuming unmet need to be constant. Furthermore, risk reduction is based on a few randomized clinical trials studying the effect of nevirapine alone, whereas treatment policies are now modified so that PMTCT programs include other treatment regimens (combination therapies) as well as feeding advice. Increased coverage for pediatric antiretroviral therapy provision is also not taken into account. The number of life years gained is calculated by using the life-table method. This is an appropriate method because life tables incorporate background mortality from other risk factors. However, we ignored the impact of PMTCT care itself on life expectancy within the whole population.

Despite these caveats, it is beyond question that South Africa's introduction of a PMTCT policy had a significant direct impact on mortality for children at risk and a clear positive impact on the distribution of health. Increased survival for children who otherwise would have died prematurely from HIV-related illnesses improves life expectancy substantially in that patient group. It also reduces inequality in the age of death, since children saved would have otherwise lived for about two years in the absence of antiretroviral therapy. If we see this as a redistribution of life years lost (see figure 12.1), the reduction of early deaths will shift the left part of the curve to the right, thus reducing inequality in age of death as measured by the Gini-health index. The cost of provision is relatively low and very cost-effective compared to most other interventions. Compared to most of the Latin American drug cases discussed above, PMTCT medications demonstrate a far stronger impact on both inequality and efficiency. Hence, there are compelling and overlapping reasons to define nevirapine as essential

Table 12.11. Estimated numbers of lives and life years gained from PMTCT care per year

Year	Coverage	Unmet need (number of HIV-infected pregnant women, 2005)[a]	Risk without PMTCT care	Risk with PMTCT care	Number of children avoiding HIV infection	Life years saved
2002	0.05	250,000	0.25	0.12	1,625	83,363
2005	0.30[b]	250,000	0.25	0.12	9,750	500,175
2010	0.60[c]	250,000	0.25	0.12	19,500	1,000,350
Full coverage	1.00	250,000	0.25	0.12	32,500	1,667,250

[a] In the absence of available data, we assume a constant number of unmet needs based on data for 2005.
[b] WHO/UNAIDS/UNICEF (2007).
[c] South African Ministry of Health (2010).

and belonging to the class of high-priority interventions that unquestionably should be provided according to the right to health.

But even if we can calculate the effect of the PMTCT policy in terms of life years saved and impact on inequality, it is unclear what proportion of the estimated effects can be attributed to litigation and the Constitutional Court ruling.[12] Some have argued that by the time the case arrived at the Constitutional Court, it had already been won in the streets (Roux 2004). Litigation was only one part of TAC's mobilization process, which also included out-of (and in)-court mobilization, campaigns to bring down drug prices, advocacy, the lobbying of politicians and bureaucrats, and, later, the threat of follow-up litigation (Heywood 2005, 2009; Cooper in this volume). From the theoretical perspective informing this book, the independent effect of the litigation *process* is not surprising or a problem for the analysis of the impact of litigation. Even lost cases may potentially affect policy by creating momentum for change.

For our purposes, the challenge is determining what would have happened had there been no litigation at all. Would the government have taken initiative independently? Or would other domestic and international pressures on the government to implement a PMTCT policy have succeeded? It is likely that at some stage—even without litigation—a PMTCT policy would have been put in place. The interesting and difficult question is *when* this would have happened—and how many lives would have been lost in the meantime.

The government's foot-dragging on HIV/AIDS policies were linked to former president Mbeki's personal skepticism (see Cooper in this volume). Without domestic mobilization, the inactivity might well have continued throughout Mbeki's entire presidency. However, given the pilot projects already in place, a gradual extension of the program would have been likely even without a favorable judgment (on the other hand, the pilot sites were established in the context of threatened legislation and may, as Cooper argues in this volume, be seen as a response to the emerging legal mobilization).

All things considered, TAC's mobilization around the issue undoubtedly contributed to a faster process and a higher implementation rate than would have otherwise been the case. While it is difficult to precisely assess the importance of litigation in the overall strategy, we can infer that litigation added visibility and force. It is thus reasonable to conclude that the Constitutional Court's judgment made a significant difference in terms of the timing of the rollout.

Negotiating for Generic Medication and Price Reductions in the Shadow of Litigation

Pursuing the argument that litigation processes involve more than activities inside the courtroom, we now turn to a set of cases that were never formally decided in a court of law but nevertheless created a push for policy change. In the shadow of ongoing or threatened litigation, litigants may increase their bargaining power and/or gain privileged access to decision makers. This is particularly significant when the process is lengthy and costly (financially and/or politically).

If litigation is part of a broader, long-term mobilization strategy, what goes on outside the courtroom, in its "shadows," may be more important than what happens in court—and indeed may be the real motive for legal action.[13] This is relevant in the *TAC–PMTCT* case discussed above, but even more pronounced with regard to TAC's various efforts to reduce prices on antiretroviral drugs.

One of these efforts took place in 1999, when forty-one multinational pharmaceutical companies took the South African government to court over the amended Medicines Act, which provided for generic substitution of off-patent medicines and for compulsory licensing and parallel importation of patented medicines.[14] TAC, viewing excessive pricing of essential antiretroviral medications as a primary obstacle to realizing the right to health of South Africa's poor, joined the case as amicus curiae on the government's side. The case unleashed both global concern and local mobilization, including a TAC-led march of five thousand people to the Constitutional Court. In April 2000, the pharmaceutical companies withdrew the case. This case did not, however, spark decisive changes in HIV/AIDS policies or the price or availability of antiretroviral treatment.

The government continued to claim high costs as the primary barrier to the use of antiretrovirals and other medications for treating people living with HIV/AIDS. In July 2001, TAC thus challenged Pfizer's patenting and pricing of Diflucan (fluconazole), an antifungal medicine that prevents painful symptoms and complications experienced by people living with HIV/AIDS. At over R100 per tablet, the drug was unaffordable. In defiance of the law, TAC openly imported a generic from Thailand and threatened legal action. In response, Pfizer announced a donation program estimated at US$50 million (South African Department of Health 2000).

In September 2002, TAC filed a complaint with South Africa's Competition Commission against pharmaceutical companies GlaxoSmithKline and

Boehringer Ingelheim alleging excessive pricing of four essential antiretroviral drugs. The complaint argued that profiteering from essential medicines violated fundamental rights under the South African Constitution, particularly the rights to life, dignity, equality, and access to health services. In a December 2003 out-of-court settlement, the companies agreed to issue voluntary licenses to generic drug manufacturers, which would increase supply and reduce prices (AIDS Law Project 2003). This implied huge cost savings for the government in advance of the launch of its national antiretroviral treatment program in early 2004 (Treatment Action Campaign 2003).

Finally, in 2007, TAC filed yet another complaint with the Competition Commission against Merck Sharp & Dohme in response to the company's refusal to license the antiretroviral drug efavirenz on reasonable terms. The June 2008 settlement led to price reductions.

In other cases, "the mere threat of legal action by TAC and the AIDS Law Project was enough to bring about a reduction in the price of several essential medicines for HIV-related opportunistic infections, including Amphotericin B" (Berger 2008; Heywood 2009).

Price reductions and estimated impact on lives saved. Is it possible to estimate the impact on lives and the life years saved from these price reductions? A rough estimate can be calculated by using published data on the costs of antiretrovirals, taken from a cost-effectiveness study providing information on cost per life year gained according to public-sector prices for 2003 compared with anticipated tender prices (based on 2005 contracts between the South African Department of Health and international pharmaceutical companies) (Badri et al. 2006). In 2003, the total treatment cost per patient year was estimated at US$1,342. Tender prices would have reduced this to US$793. The corresponding cost per life year gained was US$1,622 at public-sector prices and US$675 at tender prices. In 2006, 833,653 patients were on antiretrovirals (South African Ministry of Health 2010). Using the study's estimate of an 83% survival rate among those treated, this means that 691,932 life years were saved in 2006. The estimated total costs are US$661 million. At 2003 public-sector prices, investing US$661 million would save only 407,575 life years. Therefore, it can be argued that the price reductions in 2006 saved an additional 284,357 life years.

Can TAC's legal mobilization be credited with the entire price reduction? We cannot rule out the possibility of price reductions in the absence of the legal mobilization. Competition might have reduced prices somewhat, although the effect is usually small for patent-protected medicines. It is unlikely that substantial reductions in antiretroviral drug prices would have occurred at the time without the efforts of TAC and its affiliates, and the effective use of legal strategies seems central to the organization's success. Framing excessive profits on essential drugs as matter of human rights and constitutional rights provided leverage and transformed the issue from a political one into a legal one. Claims were directed at both pharmaceutical companies and the government, which it saw as constitutionally obliged to address the unaffordability of medicines. South Africa's government had the means to do so through the Medicines Act (which provides for generic substitution, compulsory licensing, and parallel import) but was reluctant due to pressure from pharmaceutical companies and the U.S. government (Heywood 2009). TAC's campaigns increased the political costs of not acting, both for the pharmaceutical companies and for the government.

When assessing the relative importance of TAC's legal mobilization in these cases, the international dimension complicates the picture. The fight for cheaper drugs and generic licensing was part of a global battle that was extremely active in the early 2000s. International nongovernmental organizations such as Médecins Sans Frontières, Oxfam International, and Health GAP campaigned alongside TAC to expose the pharmaceutical industry's excessive pricing. And generic competition via antiretroviral production in Brazil and Thailand added to the pressure.

While TAC did not operate in a vacuum, South Africa is home to more people suffering from HIV/AIDS than is any other country, and TAC is an important actor in both a global and a national perspective. TAC and the developments in South Africa arguably affected international developments as much as the other way around. While the organization's legal mobilization effort was not the only factor that caused antiretroviral drug prices to drop, it provided an important initial impetus and sustained pressure to ensure implementation. Like the *TAC–PMTCT* case, it arguably would have taken longer for prices to drop without TAC's activism. Other factors could have eventually led to a similar result, but it seems unlikely that much would have happened in South Africa under the Mbeki administration.

Litigating for Dialysis Treatment in South Africa

The first right-to-health case came before the South African Constitutional Court in November 1997.[15] While it did not concern medication, it is an individual access-to-treatment case that can be analyzed along the same lines as the Latin American cases discussed above.

Thiagraj Soobramoney suffered from chronic renal failure and had additional medical problems that made him ineligible for a kidney transplant. His life depended on dialysis, which he had financed privately until he ran out of funds. The public hospital refused him treatment because his condition did not meet the criteria: given the hospital's limited resources, only patients who could be cured or were eligible for a kidney transplant qualified for dialysis. Soobramoney then brought a constitutional application for access to dialysis treatment. The case was argued on the basis of the right to emergency health services. The Constitutional Court found that chronic renal failure requiring regular dialysis did not qualify as an "emergency." Under the right to health (secs. 27[1] and [2] of the Constitution), access to (nonemergency) health services is dependent on available resources. The Court found the hospital's standards reasonable and fairly applied, and dismissed the appeal.

Was this a reasonable decision from the perspective of fair priority setting in health? Again, we apply the priority classification system to assess what priority group this treatment would fall into, given the resources available in South Africa (table 12.12).

Dialysis probably would have given Soobramoney more than one extra year of life; hence, we judge clinical effectiveness as grade I. The disease was severe (grade I); without treatment, he would die within weeks. Cost-effectiveness is grade III. Dialysis is one of the least cost-effective treatments available in the health-care system: one study from Thailand estimated the cost-effectiveness of hemodialysis to be US$63,000 per QALY gained (Teerawattananon et al. 2007), much more than three times the 1997 GDP per capita for South Africa. Priority setting involves comparative effectiveness analysis: compared to nevirapine with higher QALY loss, higher effectiveness, and a far better cost-effectiveness ratio, dialysis is ranked lower in terms of priority setting. All things considered, the case falls into priority group III#.

Table 12.12. Priority classification for dialysis for end-stage renal disease

Medication	Condition	Effectiveness	Severity	Cost-effectiveness	Strength of evidence	Priority group[a]
Dialysis	End-stage renal disease	I	I	III	I	III#

[a] I = high priority; II = medium priority; III = low priority; IV = experimental treatment.

Based on our priority classification and from the perspective of fair priority setting in health, the South African Constitutional Court made the right decisions in both the nevirapine case and the dialysis case. It is interesting to note that in *Soobramoney,* the Court's reasoning resembled that of the priority-setting literature: it took into account other similarly situated patients and alternative uses of the resources. Such reasoning is almost totally absent in the Latin American countries, where individual cases are common. This may stem from the South African judges' awareness that their decision would create precedence, unlike what is the norm in civil-law systems. It is significant that the first health rights case in South Africa so clearly signaled that the Court would not take on a gate-keeping role for individuals seeking treatment but would rather police the reasonableness of the procedures developed for this purpose. Had the case gone the other way, the situation in South Africa might have been more similar to that of the other countries discussed in this chapter, in which a large portion of litigation concerns access to expensive medical treatment with comparatively small health benefits.

Discussion: Methodological Considerations

We have reviewed here five successful access-to-medicines cases each from Brazil, Costa Rica, and Colombia (all from 2008). For South Africa, we reviewed two access-to-treatment cases: one individual case (*Soobramoney*), and one public interest case aiming to increase access to nevirapine in order to prevent vertical transmission of HIV; we also examined TAC's use of the "shadow of litigation" to pressure for lower antiretroviral medication prices. After considering available evidence, we classified the cases according to standard fairness criteria from the public health and priority-setting literature. Most, but not all, of the cases were classified as low priority, providing "marginal" health benefits for severe conditions at a very high cost for the health-care system.

How robust is our system for priority classification? There is some agreement on priority criteria, and the method is based on available evidence and explicit criteria grounded in theories of fair priority setting. However, reasonable people may disagree on classification. Our system is crude and there might be room for a more fine-tuned system of classification. We try to make the system more flexible by allowing for balancing of different concerns. For example, psoriatic arthritis is very severe (grade I) but the treatment (etanercept) is only grade III in terms of cost-effectiveness. A possible reasoned judgment could be to adjust the cost-effectiveness threshold so that overall the case is classified as priority group II (we marked it III#). However, there is no agreement on how much the cost-effectiveness threshold should be adjusted if the intervention targets a very severe condition where the QALY loss is particularly great (Rawlins and Culyer 2004). In health policy, such a trade-off would probably be made; but for the purposes of this study, it seems premature to build exact priority weights into our framework when there is no general agreement on their use.

The thresholds are adopted to make analysis possible, and we acknowledge that others may disagree. In practice, deliberative procedures are needed to identify high-priority services that should be protected by a right to health (Gruskin and Daniels 2008). In each country, thresholds and trade-offs must be made explicit through public policy decisions. It would also be possible to have the priority classification system itself examined and revised by a broader, fair deliberative process.

Our method does not capture all aspects relevant for the evaluation of equity; we focus on the fair and efficient distribution of potential health outcomes. Our method does not assess fair outcomes or fair access to treatment in terms of socioeconomic status, gender, or other grounds related to nondiscrimination. Furthermore, we evaluate the conditions and medicines for average patients. Particular characteristics of patients may vary, but our data did not allow for a fine-tuned examination of each patient's history and circumstances. Finally, the case selection from the Latin American countries is not representative of the wide range of cases decided by these courts. Further studies are underway in which larger, more representative sets of cases will be analyzed according to the methods described in this chapter.

Conclusion

Does litigation claiming access to medication on the basis of the right to health make health systems more or less just? This chapter reflects on possible methods for evaluating and comparing impacts of litigation outcomes, including an indirect priority-classification method based on evidence from health technology assessment reports and cost-effectiveness analyses, as well as more direct methods based on actual data on improvements of coverage rates.

Effects of health rights litigation depend on many factors: the health system, structural inequities in welfare and health, the nature of the legal institutions, and, of course, what is litigated for. In Latin America, individual access-to-medicines claims dominate. Our preliminary analysis of medicine cases indicates that resources are often allocated to fund costly treatments that provide only marginal health benefits for severe conditions. The rulings as such usually do not have effect beyond the individual case (but the indirect effects may be substantial when they influence policy). Common-law countries with rules of precedence and provisions for public interest litigation, such as South Africa (and India), have more legal claims aiming directly at policy change in the provision of treatment. This chapter argues that while these cases are few in number, they may have significant positive effects in terms of justice in health.

NOTES

1. Resource allocation is only one aspect of social outcome. Other chapters in this book explore different aspects, such as budgetary implications and distributional effects between social groups.
2. For an overview, see Brock and Wikler (2006) and Daniels (2008).
3. For the methodology used in the World Health Organization life tables to estimate the probability of dying among different age groups, see www.who.int/healthinfo/statistics/mortality_life_tables/en.
4. Quality-of-life improvements, while important, are not incorporated into these data.
5. We acknowledge that some authors argue that life years gained for the very young may have less value (Persad et al., 2009).
6. This methodology is described in more detail in ongoing studies from Brazil, Colombia, and Costa Rica (works in progress by Ferraz et al. [forthcoming], Gianella et al. [forthcoming], and Wilson et al. [forthcoming], respectively).
7. We can also identify a set of unacceptable criteria for priority setting that no policy document or established theory of distributive justice has accepted (personal characteristics such as race, ethnicity, religion, sex, social status, sexual orientation, and physical or mental disability). These are criteria that people affected by such decisions would have good reason to reject and are considered normatively irrelevant from the perspective of distributive justice. Age and responsibility for choice of lifestyle are contested criteria.
8. Interventions judged as experimental according to (lack of) evidence by a trustworthy health technology assessment agency.
9. Ongoing study from Brazil (São Paulo) by Ferraz et al. (forthcoming).
10. *Minister of Health and Others v. Treatment Action Campaign and Others*, South African Constitutional Court, (No. 2) 2002 (5) SA 721 (CC).
11. Later evidence has indicated increased risk of side effects from single-drug therapy, and new policy recommendations include triple therapy with standard antiretrovirals.

12. For discussions of attribution problems, see Mæstad et al. (this volume).
13. For discussions of "winning while losing," see McCann (1994, 1998, 2006). See also the theoretical framework in Gloppen (this volume) and Mæstad et al. (this volume, n. 3).
14. *Pharmaceutical Manufacturers Assoc. of South Africa (PMA) v. President of the RSA*, High Court of South Africa (Transvaal Division), Case No. 4183/98.
15. *Soobramoney v. Minister of Health, KwaZulu-Natal*, 1998 (1) SA 765 (CC).

CONCLUSION

Chapter 13

Power, Suffering, and Courts: Reflections on Promoting Health Rights through Judicialization

Alicia Ely Yamin

"Within countries, the differences in life chances are dramatic and are seen worldwide. The poorest of the poor have high levels of illness and premature mortality. But poor health is not confined to those worst off. In countries at all levels of income, health and illness follow a social gradient: the lower the socioeconomic position, the worse the health. It does not have to be this way and it is not right that it should be like this. Where systematic differences in health are judged to be avoidable by reasonable action they are, quite simply, unfair. . . . Putting right these inequities—the huge and remediable differences in health . . . —is a matter of social justice. . . . Social injustice is killing people on a grand scale."

— Commission on Social Determinants of Health (2008)

"Of all the forms of inequality, injustice in health care is the most shocking and inhumane."

— Martin Luther King, Jr.

In this volume, and in the underlying research project, we start with the premise that health is a matter of fundamental social justice. Further, we do not question whether a right to health, which includes not just health care but also underlying preconditions of health, exists or whether health should be conceptualized as a human right. As the introduction states, and as most of the chapters make implicit, we take those points of departure for granted. However, it is worth stating explicitly that to conceptualize health as a right

I am deeply grateful to Siri Gloppen and Camila Gianella for their helpful insights in both conversations and comments on this chapter and, as always, I am appreciative of Adriana Benedict's help in preparing the final text for publication.

is to understand that it is of special importance and, in turn, that health and health care are more than just another commodity to be allocated by the market (Daniels 2008; Sen 2004). Throughout the volume, we see that courts have rejected the notion that access to care should be determined by the price mechanism or that mobilization of resources is a legitimate prerequisite for obtaining necessary services and medications. As a 2010 judgment from the Delhi High Court stated forcefully,

> when it comes to the question of public health, no woman, more so a pregnant woman, should be denied the facility of treatment at any stage, irrespective of her social and economic background. This is the primary function in the public health services. This is where the inalienable right to health which is so inherent to the right to life gets enforced.[1]

Furthermore, we do not revisit abstract debates as to *whether* economic, social, and cultural rights (ESC rights), including health, can or should *ever* be justiciable. Empirically, as the case studies in this volume demonstrate, this question has been forcefully answered (Langford 2008; Gauri and Brinks 2008; Barak-Ertez and Gross 2007). As a normative matter, we also accept as a given that the increasingly widespread "rights-based approaches to health" cannot be reduced exclusively to programming tools; without some ability to vindicate legal entitlements through judicial enforcement, the right to health is ultimately hollow. We are, rather, concerned with questions of implementation and impact in the real, and flawed, democracies that exist in the world today.

Nevertheless, in attempting to understand from a socio-legal perspective *when* and *how* judicialization can be a means of achieving greater social justice in health, both empirical and fundamental normative questions reassert themselves. We have set out to explore the following questions, among others: What are the consequences of right-to-health litigation for equity within health systems, in specific contexts? Under what circumstances can litigation serve to hold governments accountable for their commitments toward vulnerable groups whose right to health is at risk? And, on the other hand, when does litigation increase inequalities in health by providing a tool for more privileged groups to access expensive treatment and a larger share of health-care spending? In responding to these questions, the authors in this volume necessarily craft explicit or implicit normative assessments regarding the boundaries of the constitutional competence of courts as they enforce health rights, as well as practical evaluations of courts' institutional competence, or decision-making capacity, in the health domain.

While some authors condemn judicial intervention as distorting budgets and others are far more optimistic, the overall evidence suggests that health rights litigation is neither a dangerously infectious trend to be urgently contained nor a panacea for health inequity.[2] Indeed, collectively, the stories told here argue strongly that we should resist the temptation to seek astringent clarity or eschew sweeping conclusions about the phenomenon of right-to-health litigation around the world.

For one thing, the role of courts and the possibilities for effecting social change through courts are inextricably embedded in social contexts. Each of the case studies in this volume tells a story with its own cast of characters, themes, and plot—and even high drama. There is also an inevitably subjective element to the telling of these stories, which is worth making explicit. The book's analytical framework provides consistency regarding the variables that we have considered, and the conclusions drawn are supported by the most extensive empirical investigation that has been done in a comparative work to date. Nevertheless, methodologies for assessing equity impacts, from litigants' profiles to economic costs, are evolving and subject to refinement. Just as importantly, each of us has approached this project with our own disciplinary and ideological biases—and our own lived experiences of how social change happens in a specific social context—leading us to highlight certain facts over others or to interpret information in a particular way.

For example, the propriety of judicial intervention is at least to some degree inherently related to how one assesses the capacity of the political branches of government to maintain health systems that respond rationally to the population's needs. Colombia illustrates just how contentious this assessment can be. On the one hand, Colombia's health system has been applauded by international institutions for increasing coverage and reducing out-of-pocket payments (Glassman et al. 2009; World Health Organization 2010c). Yet, when judging dimensions of access to care that go beyond coverage—as well as accountability, oversight, and systemic equity—the system looks entirely different. Indeed, in Colombia, both the Human Rights Ombuds Office (*Defensoría del Pueblo*) and the Attorney General's Office in conjunction with Dejusticia had separately found the health system to reflect such a widespread and flagrant violation of rights that they had urged the Constitutional Court to declare the system to be in an "unconstitutional state of affairs," before the Court issued its T-760/08 decision (Defensoría del

Pueblo 2007; Procuraduría General de la Nación and Dejusticia 2008; see also Yamin et al. in this volume).

Similarly, across a number of the Latin American countries, cases involve both the enforcement of care to which patients are entitled under the system and the granting of additional treatments (often expensive medications) in accordance with constitutional guarantees. While some authors in this book emphasize the "quality-skimping" dimensions of the former, and the failures of regulation it implies, others focus more on the costs incurred by the unbudgeted care. Even slightly distinct emphases result in different portraits of the nature and effects of judicialization.

Furthermore, fundamental questions relating to issues such as the relative weakness of courts as political actors, the degree to which courts reflect prevalent normative attitudes, the extent to which litigation is dialectically related to institutional governance issues, and even the criteria for judging justice in health are all contested questions (Langford 2008), including among the authors in this volume. However, far from presenting a weakness, the multidisciplinary nature of our project and the differing perspectives that we bring to bear create a valuable dialogue within the volume that highlights the inherent complexity of this subject. Some of these unappeasable ambiguities also reflect the larger dialogues occurring within countries deeply affected by this phenomenon and, increasingly, at the international level.

It also bears reiterating here that our conclusions regarding the effects of health rights litigation depend on the variables selected for measurement. That is, what constitutes litigation relating to health rights? In this study, we chose to focus on claims based on a constitutional right to health or related right(s)—such as the right to life—and to adopt the definition of the right to health established by the United Nations Committee on Economic, Social and Cultural Rights in its General Comment 14, which includes both health care and the underlying determinants of health, such as water and sanitation.[3] As the introduction asserts, this is not unproblematic, and others would question this circumscription of cases, pointing out that administrative law, private actions against providers, and malpractice cases are also highly relevant in many contexts.

Our definition of the universe of cases can be justified not only as necessary to create consistency in comparisons across countries but also because the use of a rights discourse is itself constitutive of experience, and that is a central dimension of what we seek to explore here. The enforcement of a claim—an entitlement to health facilities, goods, and services as an asset of citizenship—itself has an effect on a claimant's individual sense of identity, as well as on the broader social meaning of health and, ultimately, our understanding of health systems. In many of the chapters, authors follow how and when social demands are translated into legal claims and, in turn, at times into public debates about health as an entitlement of citizenship and not merely a consumer good (see, in this volume, e.g., Cooper; Parmar and Wahi; Yamin et al.). Nonetheless, there is inevitably some latitude and variation among the kinds of cases covered in each country. For example, in the South Africa chapter, it would have been absurd for Carole Cooper not to include a discussion of *Hazel Tau*, a pivotal competition case, which, although settled, resulted in price reductions for several critical antiretroviral medications.

In this chapter, given these variables and uncertainties, I face the daunting challenge of interpreting what we have seen thus far, across these varying contexts, as well as positing reflections on the circumstances under which health rights litigation advances the right to health in society and makes health-care systems more just. With all of the inevitable qualifications, I first construct an overall narrative of health rights litigation, highlighting what I see to be differences among the countries as well as some universal trends. I then return to some of the fundamental questions raised by this volume regarding how we assess the equity impacts of health rights litigation. In offering my own views (which do not necessarily reflect those of the other authors), I emphasize that in assessing the effects of judicialization, the following considerations, among others, should be taken into account: impacts evolve over time and assessments are related to complex normative and empirical assumptions; equity in health involves more than income; true evaluations of contributions to justice in health require assessments of judicial interventions regarding social determinants; how the right to health is construed, together with the authority of physicians to make fact-related judgments upon which rights are enforced, affects possibilities for justice in health; and finally, assessing what counts as impact is inextricably related to conceptions of judicial power. I note throughout that the collected studies sometimes raise as many questions as they answer, both normatively and empirically. I conclude by suggesting some potential avenues for further research and advocacy and arguing for the importance of situating judicial enforcement within broader efforts to achieve justice in health, including comprehensive and democratic priority setting.

An Overview of Health Rights Litigation

Beginnings: HIV/AIDS, New Constitutions

In general, the global phenomenon of health rights litigation emerged in the 1990s with the achievement of effective antiretroviral therapy for the treatment of HIV/AIDS.[4] India is an exception to this in some ways, as the Supreme Court issued a prominent decision as early as 1980 ordering a municipality to comply with statutory duties regarding water and sanitation.[5] In India and elsewhere, there were other strands of early health rights litigation relating to workplace safety issues; health policies concerning public employees; prisoners' rights; reproductive and sexual rights; and claims to underlying determinants of health, especially by marginalized communities, such as indigenous peoples. However, the framing of these other kinds of cases tended to share one or more characteristics with HIV/AIDS cases in that (i) the right to life was expansively interpreted to include aspects of the right to health, (ii) there were clear duty bearers as well as duties being invoked, and/or (iii) issues of discrimination or regulatory failure were involved.

Even if litigation began earlier and included other aspects, it is fair to say that the trajectory of right-to-health litigation globally, as well as within the countries under study, was undoubtedly shaped by cases centering on HIV/AIDS medications, precisely because these cases presented a clear-cut argument for justiciability. First, HIV/AIDS cases implicated the right to life, which was clearly protected as a fundamental right even when the right to health was not. For example, in Costa Rica in 1992, the Constitutional Chamber of the Supreme Court refused to grant a case that was brought for antiretrovirals. Five years later, as Bruce M. Wilson describes in his chapter, an almost identical case was brought. However, by 1997, the Constitutional Chamber, citing such sources as the *Morbidity and Mortality Weekly Report*, was convinced that recently developed antiretroviral combination therapies were indeed effective in turning what had been a death sentence into a chronic disease.[6] The Court unanimously reversed itself and ordered the provision of antiretrovirals, stating, "What good are the rest of the rights and guarantees, the institutions and programs, the advantages and benefits of our system of liberties, if a person cannot count on the right to life and health assured?"[7]

In the 1990s, HIV/AIDS cases simultaneously brought attention to what was perceived as a potentially major epidemiological threat and issues relating to the treatment of marginalized and excluded populations. The life-expectancy charts presented by Siri Gloppen and Mindy Jane Roseman in the introduction show the starkest threat by far in South Africa. Yet, the sense of HIV being different or unprecedented in its status as a major public health problem is played out in many of the early judgments relating to antiretrovirals across multiple contexts.[8] Also, the stigma and discrimination faced by affected populations meant that these cases often involved arguments regarding discrimination, which courts were familiar with addressing (Toebes 1999).

Further, contrary to many of the classical arguments against the justiciability of ESC rights, these antiretroviral cases presented a clearly defined obligation (provision of a certain medication or combination of medications), a clear duty bearer (the ministry of health or equivalent institution), and a clear remedy (Toebes 1999). There was no need to sort out diffuse responsibility or to grapple with complex chains of causality: without these medications, the plaintiffs would die; with the medications, as some courts explicitly noted, there was the "Lazarus effect" whereby the patient could resume a "normal and productive life."[9] And it was within the scope of the ministry of health's functions to provide the plaintiffs with these miraculous drugs.

However, it is not enough to point to the advent of effective antiretrovirals, as courts' role in securing treatment for HIV/AIDS has been highly variable. For example, some countries that saw important early HIV/AIDS medications cases, such as Venezuela, have not experienced the same boom in health rights litigation that other countries have.[10] In the countries under study, we find a confluence of additional factors that led to burgeoning waves of litigation.

In Argentina, Brazil, Colombia, and South Africa, the 1980s and early 1990s ushered in new, emancipatory constitutions with robust enumerations of ESC rights, in addition to important structural reforms. In India, beginning in the 1970s, important judge-initiated reforms strengthened the role of the courts in a constitution that Jawaharlal Nehru had envisioned as a socially transformative document (Galanter and Krishnan 2004). In South Africa and Colombia, newly created constitutional courts took on iconic significance as actors using the law—which in the past was popularly understood as entrenching oppression in South Africa and, at a minimum, condoning horrific inequity in Colombia—to advance greater social justice in their respective societies.

Across these countries, reforms that made for favorable legal opportunity structures included, for example, the establishment of a high court (or chamber of the high court in the case of Costa Rica) as a specialized tribunal overseeing a new "constitutional jurisdiction"; the loosening and, in some cases, almost complete abolition of standing requirements;[11] and a notable move away from legal formalism. In some countries, the speed with which health cases could be resolved was also crucial to making litigation appealing; for example, the *tutela* mechanism in Colombia required claims to be resolved in under ten days; in Brazil, interim orders could be used to resolve constitutional health rights petitions in as little as forty-eight to seventy-two hours.

Neoliberalism, Structural Adjustment, and Clashing Conceptions of Rights

At the same time, the political organs of many of the governments under study were deeply influenced by neoliberal economic policies emanating from the so-called Washington Consensus. In the 1980s and 1990s, Washington-based institutions, including the International Monetary Fund, World Bank, and U.S. Treasury Department, developed a series of policies that they deemed necessary for the recovery of Latin American and other governments from the economic crises of the 1980s.[12] Many countries were forced to implement structural adjustment programs that included currency devaluation, managed balance of payments, reduction of government services through public spending cuts and privatization of public enterprises, steps to reduce inflation, wage suppression, privatization, lower tariffs on imports, increased free trade, and deregulation.

No domain was more affected by these neoliberal policies than health (Schoepf et al. 2000). Structural adjustment programs reduced the availability and accessibility of health services through cuts in health spending and increased reliance on user fees; at the same time, they reduced household income, which in turn left people less able to pay for health services. Health-sector reforms implemented during this time emphasized privatization of services and allocation through market mechanisms, coupled with targeting for the very poor (McGregor 2001). According to the World Health Organization (2010c),

> Studies have shown that SAPs [structural adjustment program] policies have slowed down improvements in, or worsened, the health status of people in countries implementing them. The results reported include worse nutritional status of children, increased incidence of infectious diseases, and higher infant and maternal mortality rates.

Further, the World Trade Organization's Agreement on Trade-Related Aspects of Intellectual Property Rights (1994), negotiated in the 1986–94 Uruguay Round, introduced intellectual property rules into the multilateral trading system, which also deeply affected access to medications and, in turn, the possibilities for people in the global South to enjoy their right to health.

In many countries in the global South, the political branches of government were forced to swallow the bitter medicine of structural adjustment even when, as in the case of South Africa, it openly conflicted with their ideologies. In others, such as Argentina and Colombia, governments seemed to embrace it with zeal, together with its implied neoliberal vision of modernity (de Currea Lugo 2003). However, high courts—if not the entire judiciaries—were well-placed to act as bulwarks against the hegemonic onslaught of neoliberalism, and they appear to have done so to greater or lesser extents, at least regarding health.[13] Some degree of judicial independence and both respect for the rule of law and a tradition of judicial review was present in all of the countries studied here—with the arguable exception of Argentina under the Menem administration—and seems to be critical to enabling courts to play robust roles in the enforcement of programmatic rights, including the right to health, in the context of neoliberalism or any other pervasive ideology. For example, Sharanjeet Parmar and Namita Wahi cite commentators who argue that the Indian Supreme Court, and perhaps in particular Justices P. N. Bhagwati and Y. V. Chandrachud, who had earlier ruled that fundamental rights could be suspended through Indira Gandhi's emergency decrees, went out of their way to lead the public interest litigation movement and demonstrate independence concerning the enforcement of ESC rights, including the right to health.[14]

Beyond any individual motivations, there was clearly an important clash of worldviews and conceptions of rights. Together with other scholars, I have argued elsewhere that neoliberalism's push toward commodification, commercialization, and privatization undermines both the concept and enjoyment of a right to health, in addition to other ESC rights (O'Connell 2007; Gross 2007; Scott and Macklem 1992; Yamin 2008). Neoliberal economic paradigms are closely linked with narrow liberal—i.e., libertarian—conceptions of rights, which construe rights as negative shields against governmental interference and leave little space for positive claims on the government (Yamin 2008). In contrast, the erosion of the distinctions between classes of rights lies at the heart of much of the ESC rights jurisprudence from the 1990s, including both national- and international-level jurisprudence relating to the right to health.[15]

In international law, a series of general comments from the Committee on Economic, Social and Cultural Rights made clear that all rights—civil and political, as well as economic, social, and cultural—give rise to three dimensions of state obligations: to respect (to refrain from interfering with the enjoyment of a right); to protect (to safeguard the enjoyment of the right from third-party interference); and to fulfill (to take steps to provide the underlying conditions necessary for the enjoyment of a right).[16] Across these countries in the 1990s (and in India before), even when not directly influenced by international law, we see courts abandoning formalistic distinctions between negative and positive rights, and, in turn, fundamental rights (e.g., the right to life) and directive principles (e.g., the right to health in many constitutions). For example, the Constitutional Court of Colombia noted in a 1999 opinion unifying its jurisprudence on the right to health that justiciability is a fluid concept, more aptly applied to dimensions than to categories of rights.[17] According to the Court, broad notions underlying ESC rights

> tend to become transmuted into individual rights to the extent that elements are in place that permit an individual or groups of individuals to demand that the State comply with a specific obligation, thereby consolidating the generalized duty of assistance with the concrete reality for a specific person or group of persons.[18]

Democratic Failure; Judicial Roles and Competencies

The sometimes stark philosophical and ideological differences between the neoliberal policies often being executed by the executive branch and the conceptions of rights and society being promoted by the courts do not fully explain the phenomenon of health rights litigation. Rather, appealing legal opportunity structures, resulting from liberalized standing and low thresholds for bringing cases, were coupled with closed political avenues for reform across most of the countries under study. South Africa presents perhaps the clearest example in that former president Mbeki's AIDS denialism precluded an adequate political response to the country's HIV/AIDS epidemic. In turn, the courts seemed to be the only channel for redress in the face of both the multinational pharmaceutical industry's intellectual property practices and the government's recalcitrance (as in the groundbreaking *PMA* and *TAC–PMTCT* cases, respectively, described in Cooper in this volume). Reading the *TAC–PMTCT* case, one gets a visceral sense of the Constitutional Court's literally *right*eous indignation at the patent unreasonableness of confining prevention of mother-to-child transmission treatment to eighteen pilot sites and not developing a national plan of action.[19]

In general, the cases collected here speak to governmental failures to design public policies aimed at resolving pressing health-related problems. Throughout this volume, we see how steep inequities in wealth and power that marginalize vast swathes of the population are often combined with entrenched corruption, lack of institutional capacity, and deeply autocratic traditions in ways that undermine the possibilities for responsive, democratic decision making regarding health, as well as other social issues. From the right-to-food case in India to *TAC–PMTCT* in South Africa to *Mendoza* in Argentina to T-760/08 in Colombia, we find judiciaries reacting to patterns that express governmental indifference to massive human suffering.

In some cases, the democratic failure is perceived to be more chronic than in others. In South Africa, for example, the Constitutional Court's deference regarding the "reasonableness" of governmental action in the *Soobramoney* and *Mazibuko* cases indicates a very different perception of genuine democratic possibilities than in the *TAC–PMTCT* case. In *Soobramoney*, the Court specifically stated that "a court will be slow to interfere with *rational* decisions *taken in good faith* by the political organs and medical authorities whose responsibility it is to deal with such matters."[20] It is worth noting that the Court's perception of the actions of political organs in both *Soobramoney* and *Mazibuko* was open to question. As Cooper writes, the Court's "coyness with regard to budgetary issues and resource allocation sits uneasily with the Court's decisions in civil and political rights cases, which have had significant budgetary implications" (212). Indeed, both decisions have been heavily criticized for abdicating meaningful judicial review and hollowing out the reasonableness standard (O'Connell forthcoming; Ngwena and Cook 2005, 137–8).

The T-760/08 judgment in Colombia lies perhaps at the opposite end of the spectrum. In this decision, the Constitutional Court took it upon itself to order the systematic restructuring of Colombia's health system because, despite previous legislation calling for, among other things, universal coverage and unification of the differentiated benefits schemes, the executive branch had for years neglected to take any deliberate steps in that direction—and, at the same time, there was no push for accountability for that failure from the legislature. However, as we assert in the case of Colombia, even in this bold decision the Court did not dictate solutions to the political organs of government. Rather, it attempted to catalyze a broader democratic debate about both the scope of the right to health and the reform of the health-care system (see Yamin et al. in this volume).

In turn, even in the Latin American contexts featuring high numbers of individual cases, it is too simplistic and at times even fallacious to characterize the phenomenon of litigation as a juxtaposition between ad hoc individualism by the courts and a democratic decision-making process—or even merely a comprehensive and rational calculus—on the part of the political branches of government. It is certainly true that where the judicial concession of care does not entail consideration of the implications of universalizing that benefit, it raises serious concerns about both formal and substantive equality. However, the conditions necessary for such rational deliberation on the part of the political organs of government have often not been present. In fact, to the extent that there are established governmental health schemes in these countries, these schemes were generally set by bureaucrats based on partial information and without robust political deliberation on guiding principles, and were then amended in piecemeal fashion over the years.[21] Peruvian health economist Juan Arroyo refers to these processes in Latin America as "silent reforms" precisely because they were largely effected through decrees, behind closed doors, and without public debate or participation in the process (Arroyo 2000).

Indeed, the overall picture painted in this volume expands on, if not challenges, dominant understandings of the role of the judiciary, which are based largely on U.S. constitutionalism, such as the writings of John Hart Ely (1980). In his chapter, Roberto Gargarella notes the potential for judiciaries to facilitate democratic deliberation and dialogic justice by, among other things, bringing neglected voices into public fora, unblocking channels for resolving difficult or marginalized issues, defining boundaries of political decisions, and reorganizing structural dimensions of social problems. Elsewhere, Keith Syrett (2007) has argued that as we engage in substantial ethical disputes over the allocation of priorities in health care, it is particularly important that legitimate lawmaking in this field stem from public deliberation, and that, in turn, judiciaries are in a position to facilitate reasoned decisions about such issues in democracies.

The structuring of dialogic remedies is inextricably related not only to constitutional competence but also to institutional capacity issues. Lon Fuller (1978, 353) famously argued that courts were ill-suited to addressing "polycentric," or spiderweb-like, situations, where multiple repercussions ensue from any one decision. Fuller asserted that the existence of polycentricity is not clear-cut, but that the question is whether "the polycentric elements have become so significant and predominant that the proper limits of adjudication have been reached" (1978, 397–9). Nevertheless, from the right-to-food case in India to the T-760/08 case (and the earlier T-025/04 case relating to internally displaced persons) in Colombia, courts have structured remedies in order to generate improved decision-making processes about issues that are intractably polycentric and inevitably relate to resource-allocation questions. Even the Supreme Federal Tribunal in Brazil—long reticent in this regard—has recently begun to entertain a different role in structuring remedies to foster dialogue regarding health rights, instead of merely finding violations (see Ferraz in this volume).

Variations across Contexts; Factors to Consider in Health Systems, Legal Systems, Judgments, and Implementation

When telling the collective story, distinctions are critical. To understand why litigation takes different forms in different countries, it is important to look at both differences between health systems—particularly the way they adapt to changes—and differences between legal systems and contexts. There are obvious distinctions between India and South Africa, as the two common-law countries that also have the weakest health systems, on the one hand, and the Latin American countries on the other. Litigants' opportunity structures also affect the scale and nature of the cases. While the success rates for individual cases are very high in all the Latin American countries, incentives for individuals to litigate are much weaker in South Africa, for example, where courts are generally less likely to grant cases concerning individual access to treatment as constitutional matters (although there are separate considerations for labor and administrative cases regarding health). Similarly, only one-third of the litigation reviewed in the India chapter was brought by individuals, the majority of which involved medical negligence damages.

However, even within Latin America, Brazil's health system offers far greater possibilities for public participation than Argentina's or Colombia's (see, in this volume, Ferraz; Bergallo; Yamin et al.). Moreover, the Brazilian government notably took dramatic proactive steps to oppose the World Trade Organization with respect to the licensing and production of generic medications, and has regulated the pharmaceutical industry to a far greater extent than has the Colombian government to date.

The analyses in this volume show how such differences in health systems can create different incentives for litigation, as well as different effects.

For example, characteristics of the Colombian health system are central to understanding why the volume of litigation has been greater in Colombia than anywhere else (see table 11.1 in Mæstad et al.). First, lack of compliance by insurance companies and providers has led to high numbers of claims merely to secure access to benefits to which people are entitled under the obligatory insurance plan (POS, for its Spanish acronym). Second, unlike cases where successful litigation is quickly and routinely incorporated into public health schemes, thus removing incentives to litigate for these interventions (e.g., Costa Rica and São Paulo, Brazil), the results of successful litigation for health services that fall outside the Colombian POS have not been rapidly reflected by changes in the scheme—and when benefits have been incorporated, the providers again have failed to comply systematically. Since often each new patient has needed to litigate in order to gain access to the services, the same interventions have produced litigation for years (this is also to some extent the case in Argentina, as captured in Paola Bergallo's analysis of routinization). Third, how the costs of litigation are borne is also important; for example, the fact that the Solidarity and Guarantee Fund in Colombia (FOSYGA, for its Spanish acronym) has historically reimbursed costs from medications not included in the POS at higher-than-market rates has created special incentives for insurance companies, both with regard to encouraging litigation for non-POS drugs and not lobbying for including successfully litigated drugs in the POS (see Yamin et al. in this volume).

These distinctions also have implications for litigation's effects in terms of distribution and costs. However, the distinctions are not only contextually specific but also complex. For example, where successfully litigated interventions are routinely incorporated into public health schemes, the costs incurred though litigation are potentially much greater. This may not always be the case, though, as incorporation into the general health scheme places health authorities in a better negotiating position and tends to drive down per-unit prices. Also, litigation cannot be isolated from the (de)regulation of pharmaceuticals; experts argue, for example, that the costs of litigation in Colombia would have been drastically reduced with effective regulation of pharmaceutical pricing.[22]

Arguably, routine incorporation would tend to be more equitable in terms of distribution, regardless of who litigates the case, because the benefits would in principle be available to all. On the other hand, in a highly unequal society, successful litigation by the middle class for expensive medications or interventions that their private insurance does not cover could push health spending away from services that are of greater importance for the poorer quintiles of the population and toward less effective use of health-care resources (see Norheim and Gloppen in this volume).

It is also clear from these analyses that a low threshold for accessing the courts may not necessarily be positive from the perspective of enhancing equitable health systems because individuals tend to exploit opportunities within the health system. As Octavio L. Motta Ferraz argues in the chapter on Brazil, where the threshold is low and the remedies effective, courts tend to be predominantly a channel for individuals, which in turn appears at least to some extent to benefit the middle classes rather than the poorest sectors of society, and cases tend to concern medications rather than underlying preconditions. Where the threshold is higher, such as in India and South Africa, collective action may be likelier and public interest litigation may be more apt to contribute to more systemic reforms, which may be more pro-poor.

However, in order to be pro-poor in fact, structural judgments require implementation. As Cooper reports for South Africa, implementation of the *TAC–PMTCT* judgment has been patchy, with estimates ranging from 30% to over 90% (see, e.g., Chopra et al. 2009). Cooper writes, "Even the Department of Health in its 2008–9 annual report stated that it could not say how many HIV-positive women and babies were taking ARVs as its data collection system was not in place—six years after the *TAC–PMTCT* judgment" (220–21).

The *TAC–PMTCT* case is not unusual. Indeed, in South Africa, nonimplementation (at least in the short term) is arguably the norm; in India, the vast breach between judicial exuberance and implementation has been a constant critique (Muralidhar 2008; Shankar and Mehta 2008); and even in Colombia, there is at best a mixed record of implementation of structural orders.

There are countless variables that influence the effective implementation of structural orders, including, for example, the nature of the protected population and the duty bearer(s); the rights recognized and the extent to which their protection requires increased resources; the nature of the process and public participation ordered by the court; whether the court establishes a specific period for compliance and how actively it supervises both the deadlines it sets and the inclusiveness of the process; the court's allies in pressuring for dialogue and implementation, including social movements and members of the political branches of government; and of course the social context in which the order is made.

Moreover, it is not always the case that structural judgments are pro-poor in their conception. A number of scholars have pointed to the Indian middle class's appropriation of the public interest litigation mechanism. For instance, the 1998 Indian Supreme Court decision in the Delhi clean-air case drove out small industry and moto-rickshaws but had little impact on private cars owned by the middle and upper classes.[23] Indeed, substantial public interest litigation in India has been filed to criminalize begging—an agenda put forward by middle-class Indians apparently embarrassed by the extreme poverty in their midst (O'Connell, forthcoming).[24] Even when relying on the logic of rights, the transformation of a system or structural situation need not be progressive.[25] In fact, some scholars see evidence of trends toward growing conservatism across a number of jurisdictions, including India, South Africa, and even Colombia, which suggest less concern for equality and marginalized populations and less capacity to challenge prevailing neoliberal ideologies with respect to ESC rights more broadly.[26]

Expansion of Health Rights Litigation and Evolution up to the Present; the Variable Role of Social Movements, Patients' Groups, and Transnational Actors

It was inevitable that early successes in HIV/AIDS litigation would lead to health rights litigation in other areas. The combination of continual advances in biomedical treatments, especially medications; the exploding importance of the Internet and social networks in sharing litigation strategies around the world; and rapid normative developments regarding health and other ESC rights in international law, coupled with locally driven diffusion of experiences, created conditions ripe for the flowering of health rights litigation, albeit in different patterns, in the countries under study.

Early litigation regarding HIV/AIDS medications resulted in the incorporation of antiretrovirals into national health plans and medicines lists. As noted above, this occurred more quickly in some countries than in others. For example, in Costa Rica, although the aforementioned 1997 case did not strictly have precedential value, from 1997 onward, antiretrovirals were uniformly ordered by the courts, and subsequently health policy was changed to include access to the Caja to supply and pay for the necessary medications. In Argentina, by contrast, litigation to secure antiretrovirals had to become what Bergallo calls "routinized"—that is, a necessary step to secure access, which took years—before they were incorporated into the obligatory medical plan (PMO, for its Spanish acronym).

It is important to note distinguishing characteristics of the HIV/AIDS litigation, which suggest that lessons drawn from that extraordinary story will not necessarily translate to other realms of health rights litigation in terms of the actors involved and the implications for equity. For example, strong social movements around HIV/AIDS—from India to South Africa, Brazil to Argentina—effectively used contextual events and maximized opportunities that arose, emboldening socially marginalized groups to understand their claims as underpinned by demands for justice rather than charity. Litigation did not so much displace social struggle—rather, it became an integral tool of social struggle across a number of widely varying contexts.

An entire volume could be devoted to the relationship between social movements and health rights litigation, and the space here does not afford the topic its due. However, it is important to underscore in this narrow regard that although we see substantial differences across these contexts in terms of the role played by social movements, and indeed how social movements are defined in different contexts, the HIV/AIDS movements played critical roles in all of these countries. In comparison with the positive people's groups in India or the coalition of groups that makes up the Treatment Action Campaign in South Africa, the HIV/AIDS movement in Colombia is a beleaguered and oppressed group. Yet it has played and continues to play an important role in debates about health as a human right.[27] The role of social movements relates also to the likelihood of implementation of judgments, which as Ferraz notes is higher for HIV/AIDS cases than others in Brazil, as well as to the kinds of suits brought and the political stance adopted.

One of the fundamental characteristics of the social movements mobilizing around HIV/AIDS, made up in large measure by people living with HIV/AIDS (PLWAs) at both the national and international levels, was that these movements challenged the power of pharmaceutical companies to use pricing practices to limit access to life-saving medications. As Lisa Forman (2009, 37) writes,

> the AIDS medicine experience and the seminal corporate litigation in South Africa in 2001 [in the PMA case] in particular, point to the transformative potential of the right to health to raise the priority of public health needs in trade-related intellectual property rights, and to advance access to critical health interventions in resource-poor settings.

This has not proven to be the case regarding other types of medications.

Although certain PLWA groups appear to have formed alliances at times with pharmaceutical companies in countries such as Colombia and Costa Rica, such linkages seem to have evolved quite differently from those between pharmaceutical companies and other patient groups. As Roseman and Gloppen propose in this volume, the anecdotal evidence that we have with respect to, for example, cancer patients or people who suffer from certain rare or neglected diseases that require expensive treatment (such as Gaucher disease) suggests that pharmaceutical companies are actively promoting litigation in different countries for two reasons: to expand markets for their patented medications and to foster litigation for patented rather than generic medications included in national schemes. The admittedly scant evidence we have to date suggests that patients' organizations may have little capacity to set an independent agenda (see also Heuser 2009).

Although the implications of a phenomenon that began with HIV/AIDS litigation are not yet clear in many other domains of health rights litigation, it is indisputably true that the success of HIV/AIDS communities in harnessing rights strategies, including litigation, is now being increasingly questioned as to whether such strategies are actually crowding out monies for other more desperately needy people (see Ferraz in this volume). In a provocative 2009 article, William Easterly argues not only that "rights advocacy . . . favours some aspects of health relative to others" but also that "those who are HIV-positive advocate effectively for their right to treatment, while those who will get Aids in the future cannot organise a lobby for a 'right to prevention.'"[28] He concludes that "the lesson is that, while we can never be certain, the 'right to health' may have cost more lives than it saved." The next section addresses the concerns of Easterly and others, setting out some considerations with regard to assessing what has been and might be accomplished through litigation in terms of justice in health.

Selected Considerations in Assessing the Impacts of Litigation on Justice in Health

Evolution over Time; Normative and Empirical Questions Regarding Equity

This volume presents a snapshot of the state of health rights litigation in selected countries. However, in analyzing the impacts on equity of this litigation, we need to consider how it evolves over time, both within individual countries and as a global phenomenon. In Colombia, for example, the T-760/08 judgment appears to have had certain clear effects, such as the equalization of children's health schemes, a marked increase in oversight and investigations by regulatory authorities, and a sharply reduced number of *tutelas* (though a concomitant increase in Scientific Technical Committee non-POS benefits) (Supersalud 2010). It also appears to have contributed to a major investigation into corruption in the health sector and to opening the debate on systemic reform. However, it is simply too soon to say what will be the ultimate effect of the T-760/08 judgment (see Yamin et al. in this volume). Yet how long must we wait to determine the "ultimate effect"? Scholars continue to debate the impacts of *Brown v. Board of Education* in the United States almost sixty years later. As time goes by, other factors intervene, such as political reforms and changes in government, making causal attribution virtually impossible in many cases (Rosenberg 1991).

The guideposts for assessing equity in health also shift with time. For example, Ole Frithjof Norheim and Siri Gloppen in their chapter argue that antiretrovirals are cost-effective—as well as clinically effective and an antidote to a severe illness—and therefore should be high priority in all of the health systems under study, given their available resources. But antiretrovirals were not always cost-effective, and arguably rights-based approaches were directly related to achieving revised pricing policies. Thus, the priority of medications and treatments shifts over time. Indeed, perhaps one of the lessons to be drawn here is that the parameters in this field are extremely dynamic, as well as subject to exogenous forces.

In our snapshot, the Latin American cases (and the Argentine, Brazilian, and Colombian cases in particular) seem to show that health rights litigation in those countries, which largely relates to access to individual treatments, benefits the middle class more than the very poorest quintiles of society. This is not surprising, as the middle class generally enjoys greater access to justice and has more education and rights awareness than do the poor.[29] However, an appraisal of how deleterious this middle-class appropriation is for health equity depends on both our understanding of equity and an assessment of the phenomenon over time (Temkin 1993). Let us assume that after ten to fifteen years of substantial litigation, the worst-off are not faring better in relation to the rest of the population. At the same time, there are more individual instances of access to "comprehensive care" (however defined) by the middle class than was the case before litigation. Is equity undermined or improved? The response depends in part on the normative question about the aspect of inequality that most troubles us. Are we concerned about the distance between the worst-off and the best-off? The most destitute and the mean? The distance between the average, or even slightly below-average, and the very wealthy? Abstract prioritarian concepts of the "haves" and "have-nots" mask deep differences in the social realities of these countries.

The response also depends on empirical information. On the one hand, these middle-class claimants who achieve coverage could be obtaining very expensive low-priority services, and, as a result, affirmatively exacerbating the situation of the worse-off, if monies that could be spent on preventive services that would benefit this population's health in other ways (water, sanitation, etc.) are directed toward providing coverage for the better-off. This is the assertion that has been made by some health economists about the Colombian situation, and is the inference that Ferraz draws in his chapter on Brazil. In this case, substantive inequalities would certainly be greater as a result of the litigation, and the effects would worsen over time, with resulting resource allocations that would clearly run afoul of a rights-based approach to health. As the Committee on Economic, Social and Cultural Rights has stated,

> Inappropriate health resource allocation can lead to discrimination that may not be overt. For example, investments should not disproportionately favour expensive curative health services which are often accessible only to a small, privileged fraction of the population, rather than primary and preventive health care benefiting a far larger part of the population.[30]

At this time, however, we lack sufficient evidence to show that this is what is happening in practice. As Ottar Mæstad, Lise Rakner, and Octavio L. Motta Ferraz write in their chapter, there is a "potential of health rights litigation to reshuffle resource allocations in the health sector in ways that may be both inequitable and inefficient. . . . In practice, however, it is not easy to determine litigation's impact on the health budget with any degree of precision" (274, 290). Although we do have evidence that judicially awarded treatments can be low priority, based on various criteria set out by Norheim and Gloppen, we simply do not have robust evidence to conclude that the funds for paying for litigated care are systematically coming at the expense of important preventative public health measures or the infrastructure of the health system itself. Moreover, it would be extremely difficult to draw causal inferences, as shifts in political priorities and the design of the health system may affect spending as much or far more.[31]

On the other hand, it would also be a fallacy to assume that litigation would yield such reforms in the health system that eventually almost everyone would get "comprehensive access," even to costly medications. The Colombian case suggests that when litigation reaches a certain threshold—where there are potentially significant economic impacts (approximately 5.4% of the health budget in that case), as well as other systemic effects—there may be pressures for the entire system to undergo reform.[32] In turn, such triggered reform may or may not improve equity overall.

Indeed, there is strong reason to believe that middle-class appropriation of health rights will not automatically trickle down to the poorest quintiles, as has happened with some other rights historically, because health rights differ in important ways. We need not reflexively accept the mantra of resource scarcity to acknowledge that some limits are an inevitability in the field of health and health care. All health-care systems engage in some form of rationing, whether explicit or implicit (Daniels and Sabin 2002; Daniels 2008; Syrett 2007; Buchanan 2009). This is not the simplistic argument that ESC rights cost money while civil and political rights do not; that is clearly not the case. However, as discussed below, the nature of health care—with its constant technological innovations and treatment expansions, and limitless demands that do not necessarily align with needs—is in real respects different from political participation or due process, for example.

Inevitabilities of Rationing; Equity Considerations beyond Income

As discussed above, in many of these contexts, the health system faces a serious problem of legitimacy. Profiteering and corruption have led to public doubt as to whether limits on health-care resources are necessary. For example, as Wilson reports regarding the Caja in Costa Rica, there is a pervasive notion that inefficiencies interfere with meeting health needs fairly. In Colombia, the press frequently covers allegations of corruption and collusion by insurance companies and the general failure of the governmental oversight body to address it (*Semana* 2011; León 2011). A 2011 scandal recorded corruption by officials in the Ministry of Social Protection and certain insurance companies that has cost the health system more than Col$4.5 trillion between 2008 and 2010. The pillaging, which will perhaps prove to be as much as the government's estimated cost of unifying the contributory and subsidized regimes of the POS in accordance with T-760/08, was so monumental in scope and involved such enormously inflated prices for reimbursements from FOSYGA, among other things, that it gave the lie to arguments blaming the courts for the system's financial troubles (*El Tiempo* 2011).

Similarly, in India, a 2011 report from the *Lancet* on Karnataka noted that an estimated nearly 25% of the health budget is lost due to corruption:

> For example, 18% of the drug-procurement budget went on nimesulide, a non-essential drug. . . . From childbirth to post mortems, informal payments often occur for all services in government hospitals and most often, it is the poorest people who are most at harm because of power imbalances. (Sudarshan and Prashanth 2011)

In the context of indifferent, if not predatory, governments and wholly opaque policy-setting processes, it is not surprising that governmental arguments about "lack of available resources" are met with skepticism on the part of judges and refusals to make plaintiffs bear the price of such inefficiencies and corruption. It is also not surprising that these gross avoidable inefficiencies, coupled with the unavoidable inefficiencies associated with clinical uncertainty, make it difficult to determine the exact nature of litigation's impact on the health-care system (Arrow 1963; Daniels and Sabin 2002).

Nevertheless, even systems that have universal coverage and maintain strong solidarity values grapple with setting limits. As Norman Daniels and James Sabin write, "avoiding the problem of setting limits fairly thus risks adding unfair limit setting to a system that is already unfair in other ways" (2002, 22).

Once the need for setting limits is accepted, the question is how to allocate resources fairly. In the health realm, an enormously complicating element in determining whether courts are creating more justice or less is that social class is not the only factor to consider. Amartya Sen (1973) has argued that income is the wrong space altogether in which to adjudge equality. For Sen, what really matters are people's capabilities to enjoy certain basic functions, which are affected by discriminatory laws, social norms, institutional arrangements, and physical and mental conditions. Under human rights law, special concern is applied to marginalized and vulnerable populations, such as indigenous persons, pregnant women and children, and disabled persons.

Norheim and Gloppen discuss other dimensions of equity in healthcare priority setting, including criteria relating to severity of illness and capacity to benefit. Yet, as they concede, the manner in which these factors are weighed when setting priorities in specific health systems inexorably reflects ethical judgments, not the mechanical application of technical evidence. Indeed, as Daniels and Sabin note with respect to limit setting in health care,

> our task would be much simpler if people could agree on principles of distributive justice that would determine how to set fair limits to health care. If societies agreed on such principles, it would be possible to check decisions about health care limits against them . . . [and] disagreements about the fairness of actual limit setting decisions would either be about how to interpret the distributive principles or the facts of the situation. (2002, 2)

Many philosophers have tried to set out such principles (Singer 2010; Segall 2010). However, Daniels and Sabin conclude that "unfortunately no democratic society we are aware of has achieved consensus on such distributive principles for health care" (2002, 2).

Procedural Justice and Judicial Roles; Challenges to Democratic Deliberation in Health

Consistent with a human rights framework, which values voice and participation, fundamental disagreements over limit-setting principles require deliberative procedures to achieve justice in health care. Daniels and Sabin (2002) have proposed four necessary conditions to ensure "accountability for reasonableness":

- *Publicity.* Decisions regarding direct and indirect limits to meeting health needs, and the rationales for these decisions, must be publicly accessible.
- *Relevance.* The rationales for limit-setting decisions should aim to provide a reasonable explanation of how criteria will help to effectively meet the varied health needs of a defined population under reasonable resource constraints.
- *Revision/appeals.* There must be mechanisms for challenge and dispute resolution regarding limit-setting decisions in atypical cases and in the light of new evidence or arguments.

- *Enforcement/regulation.* There must be either voluntary or public regulation of the process to ensure that the first three conditions are met.

Multiple authors in this volume support the argument that these conditions "connect decisions to a broader educative and deliberative democratic process" (Daniels and Sabin 2002; Daniels 2008; see also, in this volume, Yamin et al.; Gargarella; Norheim and Gloppen). Syrett asserts that given the particular tendencies in the health policy domain of opaque decision making based on ostensibly technical criteria, coupled with continual problems of political legitimacy, courts can play an especially important role in this domain by "giving effect to the educative function which Daniels and Sabin identify as a necessary precondition to a process of deliberation upon issues of rationing" (2007, 233). Syrett argues that courts can do so "by requiring open articulation of rationales for limit-setting decisions within the courtroom and, in consequence, by providing stimulus for further debate upon such matters within the political branches of government and broader civil society" (ibid.).

Nonetheless, the same factors that Arrow (1963) famously showed to cause market failure in the health sector—moral hazard, decisions under conditions of uncertainty, and asymmetrical information—are also likely to cause partial democratic failure when debate is stimulated in the broader society. For example, providers often determine not just supply but also demand for health services. Provider-induced demand may distort perceptions of the true "need" for health services, and these distortions are likely to affect different areas of health and populations differentially (Yamin and Norheim, forthcoming). Also, as Norheim and Gloppen's chapter discusses, there is often scientific uncertainty about the effects of any given intervention. This scientific uncertainty is compounded by asymmetric information between providers or "experts" and patients, which contributes to mistaken public perceptions that can sometimes lead to legal demands for unproven therapies or very costly therapies with marginal benefits. These issues in the health context, coupled with steep power disparities in society, make democratic decision making particularly challenging (see Yamin et al. in this volume).

Justice in Health Beyond Health Care

Göran Dahlgren and Margaret Whitehead (1991) famously asserted that inequalities in health constitute inequities when they are unnecessary, unreasonable, or unfair. As pointed out above, determining which inequalities are unnecessary, unreasonable, or unfair is an extraordinarily complex matter in the health domain. However, it is clear that if we are concerned about inequalities in health, we must look beyond health care, and indeed beyond basic preconditions such as water and sanitation.

That social policies and structures profoundly affect a broad range of health outcomes has been abundantly demonstrated in an ever-growing literature in social epidemiology, as well as work in social medicine and medical sociology (Commission on Social Determinants of Health 2008; Berkman and Kawachi 2000; Marmot and Wilkinson 1999; Tajer 2003; Dahlgren and Whitehead 1991). In particular, the burgeoning field of social epidemiology has brought attention to the overarching importance of social determinants to population health—relating patterns of disease with the way society is organized in terms of, for example, class and racial inequalities and employment, educational, and housing patterns (Kawachi and Kennedy 2002; Berkman and Kawachi 2000; Marmot and Wilkinson 1999). Social determinants go far beyond health care or the health sector to the conditions that we grow, live, and work in (Commission on Social Determinants of Health 2008). All of the contexts under study show patterns of enormous social inequality; indeed, some of these countries, such as Brazil, Colombia, and South Africa, are among the most unequal countries in the world.

The Committee on Economic, Social and Cultural Rights has also explicitly stated that patterns of health and ill-health are shaped by discrimination, poverty, and exclusion and that health can be influenced by "both biological and socio-cultural factors."[33] Further, other international and regional human rights treaties and declarations have delineated measures that states should take to protect and promote health; these measures require states to address these broader factors, which link health not only to social determinants of health (e.g., education, housing, and work) but also to questions of democratic openness and accountable government.[34]

If we were to seriously consider how to meet health needs fairly and to fully understand the role of judiciaries in doing so, we would need to look at much broader records of judicial enforcement and implementation, which address these wider patterns of inequality. The South African Constitutional Court, for example, has issued significant opinions on squatters' rights; in *Grootboom*, the Court called explicitly for government policy in this regard to take account of the worst-off in society.[35] Yet the Court's call for broader policy changes regarding housing rights has met with very disappointing implementation.[36] For its part, the Brazilian Supreme Federal Tribunal has been extremely conservative—indeed, hostile—regarding land rights claims brought by social movements, failing to provide protections for even the most marginalized of indigenous groups in Brazil.

The way that courts behave has everything to do with what is at stake, as well as their capacity—and will—to question the entrenched powers that be. In Brazil, for example, the framing of health rights as individual access to medications—where the Supreme Federal Tribunal grants 90% to 100% of plaintiffs' claims—may not threaten real sites of power, while land issues surely do (Ferraz 2009a). Similarly, scholars have argued that the Indian Supreme Court has been reluctant to award rights relating to land, which might interfere with economic development issues that are critical to the government.

At the same time that we must acknowledge that the enjoyment of the right to health is interdependent on and indivisible from the enjoyment of other ESC rights, as well as to a broad spectrum of civil and political rights, it is important to distinguish between a rights-based understanding of the determinants of health and the delineation of the content of the right to health, for which courts hold governments and other actors accountable.

The Relationship between a Right to Health and Justice in Health; the Concept of a "Life of Dignity"

Given the inherently contested nature of justice in health and the explosion of health rights litigation over the past fifteen to twenty years, there is remarkably little literature interpreting the normative foundations of the right to health. Not surprisingly, in judicial opinions, contrasts can be found between deontological philosophical traditions, such as those of Immanuel Kant and John Rawls, and the utilitarian assumptions and arguments presented by governments. However, judicial reasoning can be eclectic and frequently makes use of consequentialist considerations, including safety and efficacy of a certain treatment.

For the most part, whether enforcing the right to health as inherently of fundamental value or as instrumental to the right to life, courts have historically interpreted the scope of the right in some relation to the concept of "a life of dignity." In international law, too, General Comment 14 states in article 1 that "every human being is entitled to the enjoyment of the highest attainable standard of health conducive to living a life in dignity." From the perspective of positive international law, though, there is no need to choose among competing theories of why health is of special moral importance, rather than just another commodity to be allocated according to market mechanisms. Indeed, international advocacy around economic and social rights has struggled to overcome old debates about "natural rights" and for ESC rights, including the right to health, to be considered enforceable positive norms alongside civil and political rights.[37]

Nevertheless, when judiciaries interpret the right to health, its normative foundations take on a central importance. Just as with competing notions regarding the special importance of freedom of expression or other civil rights, so too are there different sets of philosophical reasons for protecting the right to health—from protecting a normal range of opportunities to avoiding suffering to preserving people's capabilities—which create different contours for enforceability (Daniels 2008; Ruger 2010; Singer 1995).

A life of dignity is often expressed in terms of Rawls's notion of carrying out a life plan. For example, the Argentine Supreme Court has noted that "the right to health is intimately related to the rights to life and autonomy, as a gravely ill individual is not in condition to freely select his own life plan."[38]

Yet, courts rarely address the nature of health per se. For example, for many health policy makers and philosophers alike, health is a limit concept, understood as "normal" functioning, or the absence of pathology. However, under some international instruments, health is defined in accordance with the World Health Organization Constitution as a "complete state of physical, mental and social wellbeing," a concept with no apparent limits.[39] Thus, a number of Latin American courts appear to have no qualms in enforcing entitlements to so-called enhancements—ranging from post-mastectomy breast replacements to growth hormone treatment for children of borderline short stature—which are not directly related to normal functioning, but have been construed as essential to a life of dignity.

It is fair to say that, in general, courts are expert at adjudging whether laws and policies disproportionately interfere with protected interests or further a compelling interest. The answer to these questions, in turn, tends to help answer the larger questions about the meaning and scope of the right at hand. Yet, both the connection to the right to life—often framed by courts as the "*inviolable* right to life"[40]—and the dignity to which the enjoyment of the right to health is deemed essential do not easily lend themselves to priority setting.

In these respects, the definition of the right appears to set out an absolute demand, not subject to the ambiguities of resource availability or progressive realization. For example, international advocacy around rights to pain medication and palliative care has focused on the connections between the right to health and the "absolute and non-derogable nature" of proscriptions against torture and cruel, inhuman, and degrading treatment (Lohman et al. 2010). Thus, for instance, Human Rights Watch has denounced the fact that "fewer than 4% of the roughly one million terminal cancer patients in India who suffer severe pain every year were able to receive adequate treatment" (Amon 2010).

Beyond the narrowest questions of excruciating pain, though, in the realm of health, the conditions necessary for a life of dignity do not constitute an absolute and universal idea but rather are necessarily "dependent on historical, cultural and even individual contexts" (Bohrequez Monsalve and Aguirre Roman 2009, 40). Therefore, what is considered essential for a life of dignity can vary greatly from one country to another, depending on income levels and biomedical advances, as well as cultural values. For example, courts in Latin America have ordered Viagra as essential to a life with dignity, while fertility treatments for women are generally not covered. In fact, in vitro fertilization is illegal in Costa Rica. As Mary Ann Glendon (1999, 3) writes, "it is not clear how far dignity can be counted on as an anchor for rights amid competing visions of human dignity in the pursuit of a good life."

In some cases, such as Israel (not considered here) and Colombia, courts have adopted what amounts to a "minimum core content" approach, which was rejected by the South African Constitutional Court. But here, too, there is little clarity on the borders of a minimum core. The Colombian Constitutional Court goes to lengths in T-760/08 to distinguish the right's "essential nucleus" from the actual POS, which is to be updated and defined through public participation. However, criteria for delimiting the essential nucleus are not well defined and are tied to an elusive notion of "minimum vital interests."

Further, health is not the only pillar of a life of dignity or minimum vital interest. In India, the Supreme Court has interpreted the right to life to include a wide array of other rights, including housing and education (see Parmar and Wahi in this volume). In Argentina and Colombia, the influence of Catholicism, where papal encyclicals have historically emphasized a right to subsistence with dignity, undoubtedly has played an important role; also influential has been the development of German constitutional jurisprudence and legislative practice around concepts such as the "subsistence minimum," of which access to health care may be one element.

If we accept that there are competing visions of a life of dignity even within one society, and that health is only one element in a life of dignity or component of minimum subsistence, the nature of health rights changes from uncompromising absolutes to products of social negotiation. In turn, clarifying the normative foundations and conceptions of health will be critical in order for courts to provide a framework for facilitating appropriate decision-making processes relating to constantly evolving claims of what we owe each other in regard to health and health care.

"Medical Necessity" and the Role of Physicians

The extent to which a health claim requires constitutional protection turns on facts and fact-related judgments. Therefore, closely linked to the question of what is necessary for a life of dignity or a minimum-threshold level of health is the issue of how decisions are made and who makes them. Courts in Latin America, which deal with thousands and tens of thousands of individual cases, seem largely to have turned to attending physicians to determine "medical necessity" in the case of threats to health. The courts, whether enforcing expansive rights to health or the right to life, imbue physicians with tremendous authority. Moreover, many of the Latin American courts seem to assume, whether genuinely or out of expediency, that physicians (i) act in the best interests of the patient, irrespective of other potential incentives the physicians may face, and (ii) are in a position to assess the patient's best interests, unlike inefficient government bureaucracies or avaricious third-party payers, depending on the country.

Given the contexts described above, the desire to enable physicians to make decisions based on "medical reasons" is understandable. However, neither of these assumptions appears to be well founded. Abundant evidence from different countries suggests that physicians are as vulnerable to structural incentives as any other profession and that they are rarely best situated to evaluate the latest evidence on medications' clinical and cost-effectiveness (Dong et al. 1999; Haynes et al. 2002; Lizardo et al. 2004; Oliveri et al. 2004; Radyowijati and Haak 2004). Indeed, reliance on the discretion of physicians introduces yet another arbitrary element into decision making regarding which patients are awarded benefits and which are not.

Moreover, this view of physicians' ethical duties and aptitudes is strikingly outdated, and its implicit paternalism is arguably at odds with the implications of a right to health. The physician's role has changed enormously since the time when sole practitioners made house calls, carrying with them in their little black bags the sum total of their tools. Physicians in many of the urban (though, sadly, not often the rural) contexts in Latin America, India, and South Africa are part of a larger configuration of professionals and institutions, such as laboratories and hospitals, that collectively bring to bear an array of tools to diagnose and treat patients.

It would seem more reasonable to view physicians' ethical duties not as reflecting some transcendent duty to obtain every possible treatment that the physicians, in their wisdom, determine necessary but rather in terms of a set of necessarily evolving and socially negotiated norms regarding stewardship of resources, advocacy of population health, protection of autonomy, and the like (Daniels 2008). However, for the physicians' individual authority to be reduced, a broader priority-setting process—with democratic legitimacy—likely must be put into place.

Power, Empowerment, and the Courts; What Counts as Impact

As noted above, questions of timeframe and access to reliable empirical data make it a daunting challenge to assess the impact of litigation in any one context, let alone across multiple contexts. First, the impact of litigation does not necessarily hinge on winning a case. As Mæstad, Rakner, and Ferraz write in their chapter, "out-of-court settlements, threatened litigation, or even lost cases may also trigger a response at this level" (276). Second, in some cases, one judgment directly influences other cases, which do lead to direct material effects—such as *Grootboom*, where implementation was a failure, influencing the *TAC–PMTCT* case. However, it is difficult to systematically take those impacts into account.

More broadly, there is the question of how to compare the thousands of individual cases in Latin America with precedent-setting judgments in India or South Africa. In *Courting Social Justice*, Varun Gauri and Daniel Brinks propose a formula to assess the impact of health and education litigation across civil- and common-law jurisdictions:

> Impact = $(N_{ind}*DE_i) + (100N_{col}*DE_c) + (N_{IE}*I)$ where N_{ind} is the number of individual cases, and DE_i is the direct effect of those cases, calculated as the proportion of individual cases that favored the plaintiff and in which the judicial order is implemented. N_{col} is the number of collective cases, which we multiply by 100, an arbitrary number meant to denote the average num-

> ber of individuals potentially directly affected by each collective case in that policy area. DE_c is the direct effect of these collective cases calculated as the product of the percentage of collective cases decisions that favor the claimants and the estimated proportion of the ordered relief that is actually carried out. N_{IE} is a measure of . . . the indirect effects of litigation in each area, primarily through legislative changes produced in response to successful (or even unsuccessful) legal strategies. Finally, I (for implementation) is the estimated proportion of those benefits that actually reached the beneficiaries. (2008, 326)

While useful in permitting a comparison across contexts, this formula, as Gauri and Brinks readily admit, is far from perfect. Principally, there is substantial "uncertainty absorption" in the estimation of the numbers—for example, of where relief is carried out. Uncertainty absorption "takes place when inferences are drawn from a body of evidence, and the inferences instead of the evidence itself, are then communicated" (Davis et al. 2010, 8 [citing March and Simon 1958, 165]). As a result of removing the premises behind the numbers, estimates of impact appear more robust than they actually are. Further, converting particularistic knowledge about the interactions of courts and other political actors into readily comparable numerical representations "strips meaning and context from the phenomenon" (Davis et al. 2010, 4) and reveals little about the power dynamics involved in courts' interventions in this arena.

In this volume, Mæstad, Rakner, and Ferraz reach far more tentative conclusions regarding impact, suggesting analysis of different sorts of effects: direct impact on litigants' access to health services, impact on health policy, impact on health budgets, impact on overall access to and distribution of health services, and impact on the distribution of health services. But they, too, focus exclusively on material impacts of litigation, and largely in economic terms.

By contrast, other scholars have pointed to the importance of "symbolic" impacts in addition to material or instrumental impacts (Rodríguez Garavito and Rodríguez Franco 2010b). Symbolic effects can relate to both the redefinition of the issue and the transformation of public opinion about the problem. For example, the Colombia chapter discusses how health care has begun to be construed as a right and public good rather than merely a consumer commodity after the T-760/08 decision (see Yamin et al. in this volume).

Assessments of what kinds of impact count are inextricably tied to understandings of judicial power. Traditionally, judicial capacity has been viewed in terms of what Cesar Rodríguez Garavito and Diana Rodríguez Franco (2010b) call a neorealist notion of power. Essentially, in such a view, power is exercised when the court imposes its will. The court's judgment forces the defendant to act or desist from acting in a way that it would not otherwise. Thus, the ministry of health can be forced to provide a certain medication or a given policy can be changed. Courts' power in this view can be tabulated in terms of "successes" and "defeats."

However, as many of the chapters in this volume make implicit, judicial interventions can operate on a second dimension of power as well. At issue here is that "a set of predominant values, beliefs and rituals, and institutional procedures ('rules of the game') . . . operate systematically and consistently to the benefit of certain persons and groups at the expenses of others" (Lukes 2005, 21 [citing Bachrach and Baratz 1970, 43–44]). Thus, as Gargarella suggests in this volume, and other scholars have argued elsewhere, if the rules of the political game systematically preclude certain issues from arising in the decision-making arena, courts can play a role in "ensuring democratic attention to important interests that might otherwise be neglected in ordinary debate" (Sunstein 2001a, 221–2).

Yet, there should be some link between symbolic impact and material impact; the politics of recognition, in Nancy Fraser's terms, cannot replace the politics of redistribution (Fraser 1997, 11). And even if courts are equipped to play a broader and more facilitative role, they remain relatively weak actors. As Syrett says, "especially when one or more of the political branches are uncooperative, there are limits to the catalytic impact which adjudication may have" (2007, 228). Although this is not a new insight (and indeed was made as early as *The Federalist Papers*), in the complex health domain, courts are especially dependent on the political organs of government for both the will and capacity to allocate appropriate resources, issue effective regulations, and engage in sustained oversight (Hamilton et al. 1788).

The British sociologist Steven Lukes distinguishes a third dimension of power from the second discourse-opening dimension. This third facet of power occurs before preferences and interests can even be identified, which affects both patterns of who litigates and what claims are litigated. As we know, the fact that certain oppressed populations are less likely to have complaints based on their everyday experience is not to say that their health needs are being met. Indeed, as Lukes has written, it is

> the most insidious exercise of power to prevent people, to whatever degree, from having grievances by shaping their perceptions, cognitions, and preferences in such a way that they accept their role in the existing order of things, either because they see no alternative to it, or because they see it as natural and unchangeable, or because they value it as divinely ordained and beneficial. (2005, 28)

Litigation, in conjunction with other social action, can play a role in creating new expectations among people who are not direct beneficiaries of judgments. For example, in the case of HIV/AIDS litigation, which was embedded in social movements, not only did the discourse change in terms of governmental responsibility in many of these countries, but PLWAs in many cases appear to have shifted their understandings of their own situations (Forman 2009). At the same time, it would be naive not to acknowledge that judicialization can legitimate the power of the beneficiaries of the status quo by reinforcing distinctions between those who are empowered to articulate social demands as rights and those who are not.

However, in either case, this understanding of impact is related to but distinct from merely looking at who obtains the material benefits, and is linked to the definition of right to health litigation that we have chosen. This political understanding of empowerment calls for further analysis of the extent to which courts, in conjunction with other actors in specific contexts, can play a role in creating among the most marginalized a consciousness of being subjects of rights, both health and other rights.

Concluding Reflections and Agendas for Future Research and Activities

Health is perhaps the most radical of subjects for human rights because, more than any other topic, it challenges the boundaries of what is "natural." There can be no right to be healthy; some features of ill-health are beyond human control. But much of population health is indeed subject to social control through laws, policies, and programs that influence exposures and mitigate effects—and the boundaries for technological interventions are constantly evolving. It is in this ever-shifting context that the very notion of a *right to health* becomes intimately tied to how we understand our own suffering and that of others. As stated above, to the extent that people see themselves as rights bearers and see distributions of disease not in terms of misfortune but injustice, there may be a significant shift in self-identity, social meaning, and empowerment. Whether and to what extent the facilitation of this empowerment through judicialization destabilizes dynamics of exclusion based on different grounds and opens space for political action—or further entrenches certain privileges—has long been a subject of debate, and is increasingly contested regarding right-to-health litigation in particular.

This volume delivers no sweeping, unequivocal answers. Rather, it offers dialogue among the authors whose voices are collected here and presents factors to consider regarding the organization of health and legal systems, the nature of litigants and claims, and the responses of governments to judgments, as well as the way courts function as political actors embedded in specific contexts. As a result, the overall narrative of health rights litigation that I have described is perhaps more mosaic than narrative, filled with inconvenient incongruities within each country and across the larger picture.

A number of the authors featured here do make the reasonably modest, but significant, claim that courts have an important role to play in facilitating public dialogue and structuring inquiries into the justifiability of government conduct on health-related issues—ranging from the cleanup of the polluted Riachuelo River in Argentina to the development and implementation of HIV/AIDS policies in various countries to the reform and organization of a health system in Colombia.

In the cases discussed here, the judicial promotion of deliberative democracy is based to greater and lesser extents on dissatisfaction with standard forms of representative democracy and on some belief in the capacity of deliberation to promote improved decisional outcomes from existing institutions (Syrett 2007, 110). As we have seen, there are special challenges to doing so in the health realm, and judicial interventions are certainly not always successful.

Nevertheless, a useful future research agenda could entail exploring the contours of an appropriate judicial role in establishing the legitimacy of limit-setting decisions in the health realm. Across these country contexts, we have seen evidence of how health systems communicate and enforce values and norms, through, for example, the use of explicit versus implicit rationing, the provision of differentiated or universal entitlements, the treatment of both patients and providers within the system, the manner in which services are financed and the extent of social solidarity in resource allocation for health, and the degree of transparency and accessibility of pertinent information. The analyses collected here suggest that courts have a role to play in ensuring that these decisions are taken in accordance with certain fundamental principles, such as formal and substantive equality, and meaningful participation.

Currently, however, few judiciaries are equipped to play an effective role as they might. Both health policy makers and economists, as well as judges in a number of countries where these issues are urgent, could benefit from objective information and dialogue on such issues as allocative criteria and processes for priority setting, substantive and formal equality, effective participation, normative foundations of the right to health, questions regarding medical necessity and who decides, different conceptions and metrics of equity in health, and factors relating to the implementation of structural judgments. Cross-fertilization among judiciaries would also be extremely beneficial, both within and across regions.

Second, we also clearly need additional empirical studies that further develop methodologies for assessing the equity impacts of litigation on health, within and across country contexts. Comparative studies that focus exclusively on jurisprudence are limited in their usefulness for assessing courts' potential to play a role in meaningful social change. Better data and refined methodologies are required for obtaining and assessing litigant profiles, evaluating the nature of claims presented and success rates, calculating costs, and examining not only the direct and indirect material effects but also the symbolic impacts of judgments over time.

Third, throughout the volume, it is clear that courts do not function in isolation, and indeed depend on allies for both formal compliance and broader implementation. Yet the roles that these different actors play remain quite vague. Beyond the HIV/AIDS groups, we know little about many of the social movements involved in health rights litigation. We know even less about transnational actors, such as pharmaceutical companies, which appear to deliberately obscure their protagonism in some of this litigation. We need more information about whether these commercial actors, which have objective interests at stake, are playing a prominent role in the spread of cases for certain expensive medications or for nongeneric medications. At the same time, it would be useful to better understand the dynamics behind the rise of similar cases in different countries seeking to transform the health system in the public interest, including but not limited to HIV/AIDS litigation, and the role of transnational actors that have an explicitly rights-based or public health agenda.

Fourth, many of the dynamics that have yet to be explored in depth fall into the seams and interstices of the judicial and implementation processes. We know very little about the anthropological aspects of bringing and deciding claims in these different country contexts, including the self-understanding of both rights claimants and judges. For example, how *in practice* does the translation of grief into a grievance regarding the right to health really change diverse petitioners' senses of self identity? And how might that sense of *right* differ across contexts or when it underpins one's demands for food versus clean water versus a costly cancer drug? On the other side of the coin, we have only anecdotal evidence as to how judges respond to right-to-health claims. Aeyal Gross (2007) has suggested that the individual case presentation may elicit a more typically "feminine" (in Carol Gilligan's terms) compassionate response. Others, including judges themselves, have criticized their fellow judges for not taking into account the universal effects of their actions.[41] However, except insofar as what we can glean from the judgments themselves, we do not have a good understanding of how judges are reacting to these cases, emotionally as well as analytically, including how they take into account arguments regarding costs (Rakner and Mæstad 2010).

Finally, the overall story of judicialization of health rights needs to be situated in a larger account of the matrix of the history and political economy of health, not only in the national contexts under study but also at the international level. Global forces beyond the nation-state create the conditions that drive much of the access-to-treatment litigation. For example, international intellectual property regimes set the rules of the game for many of these countries' governments; similarly, globally driven models of health reform, ranging from pay-for-performance to privatization of services, can undermine the right to health at national and local levels. Examining the country level alone obscures the power dynamics in the global order and the upstream decisions that often determine patterns of health and access to care, types of litigation, and the ideological context for judicial assessments of governmental efforts.

Beyond directly health-related policies, there is a long shadow of misery emanating from the steadfast global march toward neoliberal economic growth. Indeed, almost three-quarters of people living on less than a dollar a day live in middle-income countries today, which is a vastly different scenario than when the phenomenon of health rights litigation began. In India, for example, even as the country has shown economic growth of 8–9% per year, close to half of its children remain malnourished, and expenditures on health are a significant source of poverty (Sen 2011; see also Parmar and Wahi in this volume). As noted earlier, the brutal social inequalities in virtually all of the countries under study are striking.

In these contexts, the real question for health rights—and social policy more broadly—revolves not around absolute resources but around incorporating equity considerations into decision-making processes and institutional design at all levels (i.e., local, national, and international). It is not so much a question of remedying specific violations as changing decision-making processes to incorporate prospectively an equity lens, which goes beyond health specifically to also contemplate other social determinants, from fiscal to labor to land policy. However, global and national "pathologies of power," in Paul Farmer's words, are inevitably also reflected within health systems (2003). Residents of all societies have a stake in the fairness and legitimacy of their health systems, just as they do in their criminal justice systems, for both moral and pragmatic reasons. Indeed, a notion of the right to health calls on us to adopt an understanding of the health system as a core social institution, akin to a fair justice system or a democratic political system (Freedman 2005; Hunt and Backman 2008; Yamin 2008, 2010). As Lynn Freedman writes, "Health systems are part of the very fabric of social and civic life. A new respect for the role of health systems in creating or reinforcing poverty and, conversely, in building a democratic society should be the foundation for policies" (2005, 21). In turn, over the next decade, we should develop a far better understanding of to what extent and in what contexts courts are able to contribute meaningfully to processes for incremental institutional reform, as well as to bolder transformations in both the organization and conceptualization of health systems.

NOTES

1. The Court continued,

> There cannot be a situation where a pregnant woman who is in need of care and assistance is turned away from a Government health facility only on the ground that she has not been able to demonstrate her BPL status or her "eligibility". . . . Instead of making it easier for poor persons to avail of the benefits, the efforts at present seem to be to insist upon documentation to prove their status as "poor"

and "disadvantaged". This onerous burden on them to prove that they are the persons in need of urgent medical assistance constitutes a major barrier to their availing of the services. (Laxmi Mandal v. NCT Delhi and Others, W.P. [C] Nos. 8853 of 2008 and 10700 of 2009 at 40 of 51)

The Delhi High Court is not a court considered in this volume.

2. Note that the editors of *Courting Social Justice* come to similarly qualified and nuanced conclusions in their study of litigation on the rights to health and education.
3. United Nations Committee on Economic, Social and Cultural Rights, General Comment 14, U.N. Doc. E/C.12/2000/4 (2000).
4. India is in some ways an exception to this statement, as Parmar and Wahi report that early health rights litigation concerned medical reimbursement claims by public employees, as well as medical negligence and workplace safety cases.
5. *Municipal Council, Ratlam v. Vardhichand and Others*, 1980 Cri LJ 1075. Litigation in Colombia began in the early 1990s, strictly before the advent of effective combination therapy.
6. *García Alvarez v. Caja Costarricense de Seguro Social*, Judgment 5934, Exp. 5778-V-97 No. 5934-97 (1997).
7. Ibid., sec. III.
8. For example, *García Alvarez v. Caja Costarricense de Seguro Social, supra* note 6; Agrg. No Recurso Extraordinário No. 271.286-8, Rio Grande do Sul, November 24, 2000.
9. *García Alvarez v. Caja Costarricense de Seguro Social, supra* note 6.
10. *Cortez et al. v. Instituto Venezolano de Seguros Sociales*, Supreme Court of Venezuela, Constitutional Chamber, Exp. 00-0995 (2002) (retrogression in providing antiretroviral treatment impermissible when antiretrovirals are commonly available on the market).
11. There is, however, significant variation among the countries, with still substantial barriers to accessing the courts in South Africa, for instance.
12. Note that some countries implemented structural adjustment programs earlier than others, but I am referring here to the general period between the 1980s and the mid- to late 1990s.
13. As noted below, other domains (such as land rights) are a very different matter.
14. See discussion in Parmar and Wahi of this speculation around the judges' reaction to their participation in the decision *A. D. M Jabalpur v. Shiva Kant Shukla*, (1976) 2 SCC 521 AIR 1976 SC 1207.
15. India is again in some ways an exception, as conservative trends in public interest litigation began to emerge in the mid- to late 1990s.
16. For one of the first elaborations of the tripartite obligations of states to respect, protect, and fulfill rights, see Report on the Right to Adequate Food as a Human Right, U.N. Doc. E/CN.4/SUB.2/1987/2 (1987). See General Comment 14, *supra* note 3, for the respect, protect, and fulfill framework concerning the right to health.
17. Sentencia Su-819 de 1999.
18. Ibid.
19. *Minister of Health v. Treatment Action Campaign*, 2002 (10) BCLR 1075 (CC) (public health evidence on efficacy and safety point to provision of nevirapine for prevention of mother-to-child-transmission of HIV).

20. *Soobramoney v. Minister of Health, Kwa-Zulu Natal*, 1998 (1) SA 765 (CC), para. 29, emphasis added.
21. As mentioned below, the SUS in Brazil is an exception to this in some respects, as it affords significant public participation.
22. Oscar Andia (Director, Colombian Medical Federation) and Tatiana Andia (Department of Economics, Los Andes University, Bogotá), interview, Bogotá, May 2010. See also *El Tiempo* (2011).
23. *M. C. Mehta v. Union of India*, (1998) 6 SCC 63.
24. See also Harsh Mandrick (Commissioner, Supreme Court of India), remarks at International Workshop on Implementation of Judicial Enforcement of ESC Rights, Bogotá, May 5, 2010; Varun Gauri, remarks at International Workshop on Implementation of Judicial Enforcement of ESC Rights, Bogotá, May 5, 2010.
25. For a different context in which this has proven true with respect to health rights, see, for example, *Chaoulli v. Quebec* (Attorney General), 2005 SCC 35, [2005] 1 S.C.R. 791.
26. See, e.g., O'Connell (forthcoming); General Comment 14, *supra* note 3, art. 19.
27. Further, the interaction between judiciaries and social movements proves tremendously varied.
28. Easterly goes on: "The results can be seen in the 2009 report of the President's Emergency Plan for Aids Relief (Pepfar), one of the largest foreign aid programmes in American history. Only 22 per cent of its budget goes towards prevention, compared with 48 per cent towards treatment" (2009).
29. It is consistent with the findings of *Courting Social Justice* (Gauri and Brinks 2008) regarding Brazil as well.
30. General Comment 14, *supra* note 3, art. 19.
31. Gauri and Brinks (2008) come to similar conclusions in *Courting Social Justice*.
32. Note, however, that the litigation itself cannot be assumed to be the direct cause of the system's financial problems; it should rather be understood symptomatically, as a fever indicates a serious underlying condition.
33. General Comment 14, *supra* note 3, arts. 9, 19, 20, 21.
34. Beijing Declaration and Platform for Action, Fourth World Conference on Women, September 15, 1995, U.N. Doc. A/CONF.177/20 & Add.1 (1995), para. 91; Additional Protocol to the American Convention on Human Rights in the Area of Economic, Social and Cultural Rights, "Protocol of San Salvador," O.A.S. Treaty Series No. 69 (1988), entered into force November 16, 1999, reprinted in Basic Documents Pertaining to Human Rights in the Inter-American System, OEA/Ser.L.V/II.82 doc.6 rev.1 at 67 (1992); Report of the International Conference on Population and Development, September 5–13, 1994, U.N. Doc. A/CONF.171/13 (1995).
35. *Grootboom and Others v. Oostenberg Municipality and Others*, (6826/99) [1999] ZAWCHC 1.
36. Ibid.; *Residents of Joe Slovo Community, Western Cape v. Thebelisha Homes and Others*, (CCT 22/08) [2011] ZACC 8.
37. The long-standing campaign for adoption and entry into force of an optional protocol to the International Covenant on Economic, Social and Cultural Rights typifies this advocacy.

38. *Asociacion Benghalensis y Otros v. Estado Nacional,* June 6, 2000, para X.
39. Constitution of the World Health Organization, 1946.
40. Agravo Regimental Em Petição No. 1246-1, Santa Catarina, Supreme Federal Tribunal of Brazil, February 13, 1997.
41. Rodrigo Uprimny, aclaración de voto, Constitutional Court of Colombia, Sentencia T-654 de 2004.

References

Abramovich, V. 2009. El rol de la justicia en la articulación de políticas y derechos sociales. In *La revisión judicial de las políticas sociales: Estudio de casos*, ed. V. Abramovich and L. Pautassi, 1–89. Buenos Aires: Editores del Puerto.

Abramovich, V., and L. Pautassi. 2008. Judicial activism in the Argentine health system: Recent trends. *Health and Human Rights: An International Journal* 10 (2): 53–65.

Ackerman, B. 1991. *We the people: Foundations.* Cambridge, MA: Harvard Univ. Press.

———. 1996. The rise of world constitutionalism. Yale Law School: Occasional Papers. Paper 4. http://digitalcommons.law.yale.edu/ylsop_papers/4.

Agence France Press. 2010. Protestas en Colombia contra medidas para evitar el colapso de servicios de salud. February.

AIDS Law Project. 2003. *The price of life: Hazel Tau and Others v GlaxoSmithKline and Boehringer Ingelheim; A report on the excessive pricing complaint to South Africa's Competition Commission.* http://www.aidslex.org/site_documents/T012E.pdf.

———. 2006. *Annual review.*

———. 2007. *18-month review: January 2006 to June 2007.*

———. 2008. *18-month review: July 2007 to December 2008.*

———. 2010. *Final review: January 2009 to March 2010.*

Alonso, G. V. 2007. *Capacidades estatales, instituciones y política social.* Buenos Aires: Prometeo Libros.

Alzheimer's Society. 2007. Judicial review update. July 3. http://www.alzheimers.org.uk/site/scripts/news_article.php?newsID=91.

Amon, J. 2010. Abusing patients: Health providers' complicity in torture and cruel, inhuman and degrading treatment. In *Human Rights Watch world report 2010.* New York: Human Rights Watch.

Anand, S., F. Peter, and A. Sen, eds. 2006. *Public health, ethics, and equity.* Oxford: Oxford Univ. Press.

Andersen, E. A. 2005. *Out of the closets and into the courts: Legal opportunity structure and gay rights litigation.* Ann Arbor, MI: Univ. of Michigan Press.

Andia, T. 2009. CNPM emite circular intrascendente mientras sistema de salud colombiano marcha hacia el colapso financiero. *Boletin Informatica y Salud* 35. http://www.med-informatica.net/BIS/WebMail_24a30ago09.htm.

———. 2010. Acuerdo 8 de 2009 de la cres no modifica listado de medicamentos incluidos en el pos. *Boletín Informática y Salud* 20. http://www.med-informatica.net/BIS/BisBcm01de2010_29dic09a03ene10.htm.

Andia, T., and E. Lamprea. 2010. Local maladies, global remedies: Rethinking right to health duties. Draft paper presented at the Bergen Summer Research School, Bergen, June 28.

Annas, G. J. 2003. The right to health and the nevirapine case in South Africa. *New England Journal of Medicine* 348 (8): 750–54.

Ansolabehere, K. 2009. Oportunidades y decisiones: La judicialización del aborto en perspectiva comparada. In *Derechos y sexualidades: Seminario en Latinoamérica de teoría constitucional y política.* Buenos Aires: Editorial Libreria.

Argentine Ministry of Health. 2008. *Regiones sanitarias de la Ciudad de Buenos Aires: Herramientas para la actualización de la vigilancia y el análisis de situación de salud.*

Ariza, L. 2005. La prisión ideal: Intervención judicial y reforma del sistema penitenciario en Colombia. In *Hacia un nuevo derecho constitucional,* ed. D. Bonilla and M. Iturralde, 283–328. Bogotá: Universidad de Los Andes.

Armijo, G. 2003. La tutela supraconstitucional de los derechos humanos en Costa Rica. *Revista Ius et Praxis* 9 (1): 39–62.

Arrow, K. 1963. Uncertainty and the welfare economics of medical care. *American Economic Review* 53 (5): 941–73.

Arroyo, J. 2000. *Salud: La reforma silenciosa.* Lima: Universidad Peruana Cayetano Heredia.

Ashtekar, S. 2008. The National Rural Health Mission: A stocktaking. *Economic and Political Weekly*, September 13.

Atkinson, D. 2007. Taking to the streets: Has developmental local government failed in South Africa? In *State of the nation: South Africa 2007*, ed. S. Buhlungu, J. Daniel, R. Southall, and J. Lutchman, 53–77. Cape Town: Human Sciences Research Council Press.

Ávalos, Á. 1997. CCSS no da fármacos: 300 enfermos de sida carecen de medicinas. *La Nación*, April 16. http://www.nacion.com/ln_ee/1997/abril/16/sida.html.

———. 2001. Enfermos reclaman medicinas. *La Nación*, November 5. http://wvw.nacion.com/ln_ee/2001/noviembre/05/pais8.html.

———. 2004. CCSS obligada a reactivar el plan de transplantes de hígado. *La Nación*, 5A.

———. 2005. Costosa oleada de amparos. *La Nación*, June 6. http://wvw.nacion.com/ln_ee/2005/junio/06/pais7.html.

———. 2008. Sala IV ordena vacunar contra neumococo y rotavirus. *La Nación*, October 22. http://wvw.nacion.com/ln_ee/2008/octubre/22/pais1746428.html.

Ávalos, Á., and W. Méndez. 1999. Caja y Sala IV chocan por medicinas. *La Nación*, November 29. http://www.nacion.com/ln_ee/1999/noviembre/29/pais1.html.

Avert. 2009. HIV and AIDS in Latin America. http://www.avert.org/aidslatinamerica.htm.

Azarkevich, E. 2007. La obesidad ya es considerada una enfermedad en Misiones. *Clarín*, September 14. http://edant.clarin.com/diario/2007/09/14/sociedad/s-03701.htm.

Bachrach, P., and M. S. Baratz. 1970. *Power and poverty: Theory and practice.* New York: Oxford Univ. Press.

Baderin, M., and R. McCorquodale. 2007. *Economic, social, and cultural rights in action.* Oxford: Oxford Univ. Press

Badri, M., G. Maartens, S. Mandalia, et al. 2006. Cost-effectiveness of highly active antiretroviral therapy in South Africa. *PLoS Medicine* 3 (1): e4.

Bajpai, N., and S. Goyal. 2004. Primary health care in India: Coverage and quality issues. Center on Globalization and Sustainable Development Working Paper No. 15.

Bakan, J., and D. Schneiderman, eds. 1992. *Social justice and the Constitution: Perspectives on the social union for Canada.* Ottawa: Carleton Univ. Press.

Balakrishnan, K. G. 2008. The role of foreign precedents in a country's legal system. Lecture delivered at Northwestern University, October 28.

Balkin, J., and R. Siegel. 2009. *The Constitution in 2020.* Oxford: Oxford Univ. Press.

Banta, D. 2009. What is technology assessment? *International Journal of Technology Assessment in Health Care* 25 (suppl. 1): 7–9.

Barak-Ertez, D., and A. Gross, eds. 2007. *Exploring social rights: Between theory and practice.* Oxford: Hart Publishing.

Báscolo, E. 2008. Características institucionales del sistema de salud en Argentina y limitaciones de la capacidad del estado para garantizar el derecho a la salud de la población. In *Las capacidades del estado y las demandas ciudadanas: Condiciones políticas para la igualdad de derechos*, ed. I. Cheresky, 95–132. Buenos Aires: UNDP.

Báscolo, E., and G. Blejer. 2009. *Primer boletín económico de la dirección de economía de la salud.* Buenos Aires: Ministerio de Salud de la Nación.

Baxi, U. 1988. Taking suffering seriously: Social action litigation before the Supreme Court of India. In *Law and poverty: Critical essays*, ed. U. Baxi, 387–415. Bombay: N. M. Tripathi.

BBC. 2010. Groups hail Alzheimer's drug U-turn by health watchdog. October 7. http://www.bbc.co.uk/news/health-11486367.

Bell, D. A. 2004. *Silent covenants: Brown v. Board of Education and the unfulfilled hopes for racial reform.* New York: Oxford Univ. Press.

Belmartino, S. 2005. *La atención médica argentina en el siglo XX: Instituciones y procesos.* Buenos Aires: Siglo XXI Argentina.

Berger, J. 2008. Litigating for social justice in post-apartheid South Africa: A focus on health and education. In *Courting social justice: Judicial enforcement of social and economic rights in the developing world*, ed. V. Gauri and D. Brinks, 38–99. Cambridge: Cambridge Univ. Press.

Berkman, L., and I. Kawachi, eds. 2000. Social epidemiology. Oxford: Oxford Univ. Press.

de Bertodano, I. 2003. The Costa Rican health system: Low cost, high value. *Bulletin of the World Health Organization* 81 (8): 626–27.

Bianco, M., M. I. Re, L. Pagani, and E. Barone. 1998. Human rights and access to treatment for HIV/AIDS in Argentina. Case study developed under the LACCASO's human rights project and in collaboration with UN AIDS office. http://www.aidslex.org/site_documents/T044E.pdf.

Biehl, J. 2004. The activist state: Global pharmaceuticals, AIDS, and citizenship in Brazil. *Social Text* 22 (3): 105–32.

———. 2007. Pharmaceuticalization: AIDS treatment and global health politics. *Anthropological Quarterly* 80 (4): 1083–1126.

Bilchitz, D. 2003. Towards a reasonable approach to the minimum core: Laying the foundation for future socio-economic rights jurisprudence. *South African Journal on Human Rights* 19:1–26.

———. 2005. Health. In *Constitutional law of South Africa*, ed. S. Woolman et al., 56A:1–47. 2nd ed. Cape Town: Juta.

Bishop, M., and J. Brickhill. 2009. Constitutional law. *Juta's Quarterly Review of South African Law* 4.

Blood Index. 2007. Regulatory requirements of blood and/or its components including blood products in India. http://www.bloodindex.org/rules.php.

Bohman, J. 1996. *Public deliberation: Pluralism, complexity, and democracy*. Cambridge, MA: MIT Press.

Bohrequez Monsalve, V., and J. Aguirre Roman. 2009. Tensions of human dignity: Conceptualization and application to international human rights law. *Sur: International Journal on Human Rights* 11 (6): 39–59.

Borges, D. L. 2007. Uma analise das acoes judiciais para o fornecimento de medicamentos no ambito do SUS: O caso do Estado do Rio de Janeiro no ano de 2005. MPhil thesis, Fundação Oswaldo Cruz. http://bvssp.icict.fiocruz.br/lildbi/docsonline/3/3/1233-borgesd-clm.pdf.

Bork, R. 1979. The impossibility of finding welfare rights in the Constitution. *Washington University Law Quarterly* 695–701.

———. 1990. *The tempting of America*. New York: Free Press.

Bossert, T. 2000. *Methodological guidelines for enhancing the political feasibility of health reform in Latin America*. Boston: Harvard School of Public Health.

Bravo Vergel, Y., N. S. Hawkins, K. Claxton, et al. 2007. The cost-effectiveness of etanercept and infliximab for the treatment of patients with psoriatic arthritis. *Rheumatology* 46:1729–35.

Brazilian Ministry of Health. 2005. *O remédio via justiça: Um estudo sobre o acesso a novos medicamentos e exames em HIV/AIDS no Brasil por meio de ações judiciais*.

Brazilian National School of Public Health. 2008. Judicialização do acesso a medicamentos no Brasil em debate. http://www.ensp.fiocruz.br/portal-ensp/informe/materia/index.php?origem=9&matid=11953.

Brewer-Carías, A. R. 2009. *Constitutional protection of human rights in Latin America: A comparative study of amparo proceedings*. New York: Cambridge Univ. Press.

Briceño, I. 2009. Ex secretario de salud de Córdoba reconoció sus nexos con los paramilitares. *Radio Santa Fé*, September 10. http://www.radiosantafe.com/2009/09/10/ex-secretario-de-salud-de-cordoba-reconocio-sus-nexos-con-los-paramilitares.

Brinks, D. M., and V. Gauri. 2008. A new policy landscape: Legalizing social and economic rights in the developing world. In *Courting social justice: Judicial enforcement of social and economic rights in the developing world*, ed. V. Gauri and D. Brinks, 303–52. Cambridge: Cambridge Univ. Press.

Brock, D. 2002. Priority to the worse off in health-care resource prioritization. In *Medicine and social justice*, ed. R. Rhodes, M. Battin, and A. Silvers, 362–72. Oxford: Oxford Univ. Press.

Brock, D., and D. Wikler. 2006. Ethical issues in resource allocation, research, and new products development. In *Disease control priorities in developing countries*, ed. D. Jamison, J. Breman, A. Measham, et al. New York: Oxford Univ. Press and the World Bank.

Buchanan, A. 2009. *Justice and health care: Selected esssays.* Oxford: Oxford Univ. Press.

Budlender, G. 2006. Amicus curiae. In *Constitutional law of South Africa*, ed. S. Woolman et al., 8:1–17. 2nd ed. Cape Town: Juta.

Byrne, I. 2007. Making the right to health a reality: Legal strategies for effective implementation. *Law and Society Trust* (Sri Lanka) 17 (232): n.p.

Cambio. 2008. Unificación del sistema de salud costará cerca de 6,5 billones de pesos. August 27. http://www.cambio.com.co/economiacambio/791/ARTICULO-WEB-NOTA_INTERIOR_CAMBIO-4470311.html.

———. 2009. Ataques, amenazas y asesinatos a pacientes: Entre las amenazas que enfrenta personal de salud. May 23. http://www.cambio.com.co/paiscambio/830/ARTICULO-WEB-NOTA_INTERIOR_CAMBIO-5289253.html.

Cameron, E. 2006. Legal and human rights responses to the HIV/AIDS epidemic. *Stellenbosch Law Review* 17 (1): 47–90.

Camps, S. 2010. Fertilización: Fallos a favor y en contra de prepagas. *Clarín*, February 10. http://edant.clarin.com/diario/2010/02/10/sociedad/s-02137233.htm.

Canon, B. C., and C. A. Johnson. 1998. *Judicial policies: Implementation and impact.* 2nd ed. Washington, DC: CQ Press.

Carothers, T., ed. 2006. *Promoting the rule of law abroad: The problem of knowledge.* Washington, DC: Carnegie Endowment for International Peace.

Carrasco, E. 2000. Access to treatment as a right to life and health. *Canadian HIV/AIDS Policy and Law Review* 5 (4): 102–3.

Carver, R. 2010. A new answer to an old question: National human rights institutions and the domestication of international law. *Human Rights Law Review* 10 (1): 1–32.

Cavallaro, J., and S. Brewer. 2008. Reevaluating regional human rights litigation in the twenty-first century: The case of the Inter-American Court. *American Journal of International Law* 102 (4): 768–827.

Center for Reproductive Rights. 2008. *Maternal mortality in India: Using international and constitutional law to promote accountability and change.* New York: Center for Reproductive Rights.

Central Intelligence Agency. 2010. The world factbook. http://www.cia.gov/library/publications/the-world-factbook.

Centre on Housing Rights and Evictions. 2003. *Litigating economic, social and cultural rights: Achievements, challenges and strategies.* Geneva: Centre on Housing Rights and Evictions.

———. 2009. *Leading cases on economic, social and cultural rights: Summaries.* Geneva: Centre on Housing Rights and Evictions.

Centro de Estudios Legales y Sociales. 2008. *La lucha por el derecho.* Buenos Aires: Siglo XXI Argentina.

Centro de Información Judicial. 2010. Obligan a una obra social a cubrir un by-pass gástrico a una asociada. 22 February. http://www.cij.gov.ar/nota-3483-Obligan-a-obra-social-cubrir-un-by-pass-gastrico-a-una-afiliada.html.

Cepeda, M. J. 2004. Judicial activism in a violent context: The origin, role and impact of the Colombian Constitutional Court. *Washington University Global Studies Law Review* 3 (special issue): 529–700.

Cercone, J., and J. Pacheco Jiménez. 2008. Costa Rica: "Good practice" in expanding health care coverage; Lessons from reforms in low- and middle-income countries. In *Good practices in health financing lessons from reforms in low- and middle-income countries*, ed. P. Gottret, G. J. Schieber, and H. R. Waters, 183–226. Washington, DC: World Bank.

Chaskalson, M., G. Marcus, and M. Bishop. 2007. Constitutional litigation. In *Constitutional law of South Africa*, ed. S. Woolman et al., 3:1–31. 2nd ed. Cape Town: Juta.

Chaves Matamoros, A. 2008. Política de medicamentos Caja Costarricense de Seguro Social. Paper presented at a workshop on health rights in Costa Rica, Estado de la Nación, San José, June 24.

Chen, Y-F., P. Jobanputra, P. Barton, et al. 2006. A systematic review of the effectiveness of adalimumab, etanercept and infliximab for the treatment of rheumatoid arthritis in adults and an economic evaluation of their cost-effectiveness. *Health Technology Assessment* 10 (42): 1–266.

Chieffi, A., and R. Barata. 2009. Judicialização da política pública de assistência farmacêutica e eqüidade [Judicialization of public health policy for distribution of medicines]. *Cadernos de Saúde Pública* 25 (8): 1839–49.

Chopra, M., E. Daviaud, R. Pattinson, and S. Fonn. 2009. Saving the lives of South Africa's mothers, babies and children: Can the health system deliver? *The Lancet* 374 (9692): 835–46.

Clapham, A., and M. Robinson, eds. 2009. *Realizing the right to health.* Zurich: Rueffer and Rub.

Clarín. 2006. Fallo sobre by-pass gástrico. June 17. http://edant.clarin.com/diario/2006/06/17/sociedad/s-05802.htm.

———. 2010. Fertilidad asistida gratuita en Río Negro. June 5. http://www.clarin.com/sociedad/salud/Fertilidad-asistida-gratuita-Rio Negro_0_274772583.html.

Clark, M. 2002. Health sector reform in Costa Rica: Reinforcing a public system. Paper prepared for the Woodrow Wilson Center Workshops on the Politics of Education and Health Reforms, Washington, DC, April.

Cohen, J. 1989. The economic basis of a deliberative democracy. *Social Philosophy and Policy* 6 (2): 25–50.

Coleman, C., L. Nee, and L. Rubinowitz. 2005. Social movements and social-change litigation: Synergy in the Montgomery bus protest. *Law and Social Inquiry* 30 (4): 663–737.

Collucci, C. 2009. Triplicam as ações judiciais para obter medicamentos. *Folha de S. Paulo*, January 9.

Collucci, C., and M. Pinho. 2008. Ministério critica "epidemia" de ações por remédio. *Folha de S. Paulo*, May 8.

Colombian Ministry of Finance and Public Credit, ed. 2008. *Presupuesto general de la nación, seguridad y confianza para el desarrollo social: Mensaje presidencial.* http://www.minhacienda.gov.co/portal/page/portal/MinHacienda/haciendapublica/presupuesto/programacion/proyecto/2008/Mensaje%20Presidencial%20230%20PM.pdf.

Colombian Ministry of Social Protection. 2005. *Boletín estadístico sectorial.* http://www.minproteccionsocial.gov.co/VBeContent/Estadistica/Boletin_Estadistico_2005/1_2%20%20AFILIACI%C3%93N%20A%20SALUD.pdf.

———. 2010. Gobierno nacional alista reforma a la salud. *Boletin de Prensa No. 254.* http://www.minproteccionsocial.gov.co/comunicadosPrensa/Paginas/GobiernoNacionalalistareformaalasalud.aspx.

Comisión de Seguimiento a la Política Pública sobre el Desplazamiento Forzado. 2010. *Estado de avance de la realización del derecho a la participación efectiva de la población desplazada.* Bogotá: Comisión de Seguimiento a la Política Pública sobre el Desplazamiento Forzado.

Commission on Social Determinants of Health. 2008. *Closing the gap in a generation: Health equity through action on the social determinants of health.* Geneva: WHO. http://www.who.int/social_determinants/final_report/en.

Coovadia, H., R. Jewkes, P. Barron, D. Sanders, and D. McIntyre. 2009. Health and the health system of South Africa: Historical roots of current public health challenges. *The Lancet* 374 (9692): 817–34.

Correa, J. 2009. En riesgo salud de 3 millones de pobres por destinación de presupuesto a compras no incluidas en el POS. *Portafolio*, June 10. http://www.portafolio.com.co/economia/economiahoy/ARTICULO-WEB-NOTA_INTERIOR_PORTA-5409214.html.

Correio Braziliense. 2009. Tião Viana defende projeto que desobriga SUS de fornecer medicamentos sem registro na ANVISA. September 25.

Corte Suprema de Justicia, Sala Constitucional. 1999. Reseña histórica. On file with the author.

———. 2008. *Base de datos del Centro de Documentación de la Corte Suprema de Justicia.* San José, Costa Rica.

———. 2010a. La Sala Constitucional en números. http://www.poder-judicial.go.cr/salaconstitucional/estadisticas.htm.

———. 2010b. Seguimiento de sentencias. http://www.poder-judicial.go.cr/salaconstitucional/documentos/Cuadros%20seguimiento%20al%2031_05_2010.pdf.

Cortés, C. 2009. El Plan Obligatorio de Salud: Antes no; Ahora, tampoco. *La Silla Vacía*, October 1. http://www.lasillavacia.com/historia/4554.

———. 2010. El peso de los medicamentos en la emergencia social. *La Silla Vacía*, February 11. http://www.lasillavacia.com/historia/6657.

Costa, L. A. 2009. Experiência da Bahia no enfrentamento das ações judiciais por medicamentos. Workshop presentation at Fundação Oswaldo Cruz, Rio de Janeiro. http://www4.ensp.fiocruz.br/biblioteca/home/exibedetalhesBiblioteca.cfm?id=6241&tipo=B.

Courtis, C. 2008a. Argentina. In *Social rights jurisprudence: Emerging trends in international and comparative law*, ed. M. Langford, 163–81. New York: Cambridge Univ. Press.

———. 2008b. *Courts and the legal enforcement of economic, social and cultural rights: Comparative experiences of justiciability*. Geneva: International Commission of Jurists.

Coutsoudis, A., K. Pillay, L. Kuhn, E. Spooner, and W. Tsai. 2001. Method of feeding and transmission of HIV-1 from mothers to children by 15 months of age: Prospective cohort study from Durban, South Africa. *AIDS* 15 (3): 379–87.

Cruz Castro, F. 2007. Costa Rica's constitutional jurisprudence, its political importance and international human rights law: Examination of some decisions. *Duquesne Law Review* 45 (3): 557–76.

———. 2009. Magistrados defienden votos de la Sala IV que condenan a la Caja. *Radio Reloj* broadcast, June 3.

Culyer, A. J. 1995. Need: The idea won't do—but we still need it. *Social Science and Medicine* 40 (6): 727–30.

Cummings, S., and L. G. Trubek. 2008. Globalizing public interest law. *UCLA Journal of International Law and Foreign Affairs* 13 (1): 1–54.

de Currea-Lugo, V. 2003. *El derecho a la salud en Colombia: Diez años de frustraciones*. Bogotá: Textos de Aquí y Ahora.

———. 2006. La encrujijada del derecho a la salud en América Latina. In *Los derechos económicos, sociales y culturales en América Latina: Del invento a la herramienta*, ed. A. E. Yamin, 215–34. Mexico City: Plaza y Valdés Editores.

Cutler, A. D., and A. Lleras-Muney. 2006. The determinants of mortality. *Journal of Economic Perspectives* 20 (3): 97–120.

Dahlgren, G., and M. Whitehead. 1991. *Policies and strategies to promote social equity in health*. Stockholm: Institute for Futures Studies.

Damsky, I. A. 2006. La construcción del derecho a la salud en Argentina a partir de la internalización de los ordenamientos jurídicos. In *Estudios de homenaje a Marcia Muñoz de Alba Medrano*, ed. D. Cienfuegos Salgado and M. C. Macías Vázquez, 161–205. Mexico: UNAM.

Danchin, P. 2010. A human right to water? The South African Constitutional Court's decision in the Mazibuko case. *EJIL: Talk! Blog of the European Journal of International Law* (blog), January 13. http://www.ejiltalk.org/a-human-right-to-water-the-south-african-constitutional-court's-decision-in-the-mazibuko-case.htm.

Daniels, N. 1994. Principles for national health care reform. *Hastings Center Report* 24 (3): 8–9.

———. 2008. *Just health: Meeting health needs fairly*. New York: Cambridge Univ. Press.

Daniels, N., and J. Sabin. 2002. *Setting limits fairly: Can we learn to share medical resources?* Oxford: Oxford Univ. Press.

Das Gupta, J. 2001. India's federal design and multicultural national construction. In *The success of India's democracy*, ed. A. Kohli, 49–77. Cambridge: Cambridge Univ. Press.

Das Gupta, M. 2005. Public health in India: Dangerous neglect. *Economic and Political Weekly*, December.

Davis, D. 2006. Adjudicating the socio-economic rights in the South African Constitution: Towards "deference lite"? *South African Journal on Human Rights* 22: 301–27.

Davis, K. E., B. Kingsbury, and S. E. Merry. 2010. Indicators as a technology of global governance. IILJ Working Paper 2010/2, Global Administrative Law Series.

Deccan Herald. 2010. MCI buried, new panel takes charge. May 15. http://www.deccanherald.com/content/69686/mci-buried-panel-takes-charge.html.

Defensoría del Pueblo. 2007. *La tutela y el derecho a la salud: Período 2003–2005*. Bogotá: Defensoría del Pueblo.

———. 2009. *La tutela y el derecho a la salud: Período 2006–2008*. Bogotá: Defensoría del Pueblo.

———. 2010. *La tutela y el derecho a la salud 2009*. Bogotá: Defensoría del Pueblo.

Desai, M., and K. B. Mahabal. 2007. *Health care case law in India*. Mumbai: Centre for Inquiry in Health and Allied Themes and India Centre for Human Rights & Law.

Dixon, R. 2007. Creating dialogue about socio-economic rights. *International Journal of Constitutional Law* 5 (3): 391–418.

Domingo, P., and R. Sieder. 2001. *Rule of law in Latin America: The international promotion of judicial reform*. London: Institute of Latin American Studies.

Dong, H., L. Bogg, C. Rehnberg, and V. Diwan. 1999. Association between health insurance and antibiotics prescribing in four counties in rural China. *Health Policy* 48 (1): 29–45.

Doryan Garron, E. 2008. Data presented as a PowerPoint by executive president of the Caja Costarricense de Seguros Sociales, San José, June.

Drummond, M. F., J. S. Schwartz, B. Jönsson, et al. 2008. Key principles for the improved conduct of health technology assessments for resource allocation decisions. *International Journal of Technology Assessment in Health Care* 24 (3): 244–58.

Dugard, J. 2010. Losing Mazibuko: (Re) considering the campaign following judicial defeat. Paper presented at Law's Locations: Textures of Legality in Developing and Transitional Societies Conference, Univ. of Wisconsin Law School, April 23–25.

Dugard, J., and T. Roux. 2006. The record of the South African Constitutional Court in providing an institutional voice for the poor: 1995–2004. In *Courts and social transformation in new democracies: An institutional voice for the poor?*, ed. R. Gargarella, P. Domingo, and T. Roux, 107–26. Aldershot: Ashgate.

Duggal, R. 2006. Is the trend in health changing? *Economic and Political Weekly*, April.

Dworkin, R. 1996. *Freedom's law: The moral reading of the American Constitution.* Cambridge, MA: Harvard Univ. Press.

Easterbrook, F. 1992. Abstraction and authority. *University of Chicago Law Review* 59:349–69.

Easterly, W. 2009. Human rights are the wrong basis for healthcare. *Financial Times*, October 12.

Economic and Political Weekly. 2010. Evaluation of the Health Mission. January.

Economic Research Foundation. 2006. Government health expenditure in India: A benchmark study. Report sponsored by the MacArthur Foundation, India.

Eddy, D. M. 1990. Anatomy of a decision. *Journal of the American Medical Association* 263 (3): 441–3.

Edelman, P. 1988. The next century of our Constitution: Rethinking our duty to the poor. *Hastings Law Journal* 39 (1): 1–61.

Eijkman, Q. 2006a. "Around here I am the law!" Strengthening police officers' compliance with the rule of law in Costa Rica. Paper presented at Police Human Rights Strategies Symposium, Univ. of Utrecht. On file with the author.

———. 2006b. To be held accountable: Police accountability in Costa Rica. *Police Practice & Research* 7 (5): 411–30.

———. 2011. Policia hallo nuevas evidencias en caso de corrupcion de la salud. May 2. http://www.eltiempo.com/justicia/escandalo-de-corrupcion-en-el-ministerio-de-la-proteccion-social_9254840-4.

El Espectador. 2010. Miles de personas protestan en varias ciudades contra la emergencia social. February 6. http://www.elespectador.com/noticias/salud/articulo186238-miles-de-personas-protestan-varias-ciudades-contra-emergencia-social.

El Tiempo. 2006. Alcalde de Riohacha busca acogerse a los beneficios de ley de justicia y paz. January 31.

———. 2009. El próximo año podrían desaparecer nueve EPS; Fosyga les debe más de $900.000 millones. November 12. http://www.portafolio.com.co/economia/pais/ARTICULO-WEB-NOTA_INTERIOR_PORTA-6567527.html.

———. 2010a. Iglesia pide que sean ajustados los decretos de la Emergencia Social. February 8. http://www.eltiempo.com/archivo/documento/CMS-7146108.

———. 2010b. Ministro Palacio no convenció en foro de la Javeriana sobre Emergencia Social. February 12. http://www.eltiempo.com/archivo/documento/CMS-7184867.

———. 2011. Policía halló nuevas evidencias en caso de corrupción de la salud. May 2. http://www.eltiempo.com/justicia/escandalo-de-corrupcion-en-el-ministerio-de-la-proteccion-social_9254840-4.

Ellmann, S. 2010. Metering the right to water in South Africa. *Not Without Hesitation* (blog), June 30. http://nowwithouthesituation.blogspot.com/2010/06/metering-right-to-water-in-south-africa.html.

Elster, J., ed. 1998. *Deliberative democracy*. Cambridge: Cambridge Univ. Press.

Ely, J. H. 1980. *Democracy and distrust: A theory of judicial review*. Cambridge, MA: Harvard Univ. Press.

Emanuel, E. J., and L. L. Emanuel. 1996. What is accountability in health care? *Annals of Internal Medicine* 124 (2): 229–39.

Epp, C. 1998. *The rights revolution: Lawyers, activists, and supreme courts in comparative perspective*. Chicago: Univ. of Chicago Press.

Epstein, R. 1997. Takings, exclusivity and speech. *The University of Chicago Law Review* 64 (1): 21–56.

Espeland, W. N., and M. L. Stevens. 2008. A sociology of quantification. *European Journal of Sociology* 49 (3): 401–36.

Evans, D. B., T. Adam, T. Tan-Torres Edejer, S. S. Lim, A. Cassels, and T. G. Evans. 2005. Time to reassess strategies for improving health in developing countries. *British Medical Journal* 331 (7525): 1133–36.

Fabre, C. 2000. *Social rights under the constitution: Government and the decent life*. Oxford: Oxford Univ. Press.

Farmer, P. 2001. The major infectious diseases in the world: To treat or not to treat? *New England Journal of Medicine* 345:208–10.

———. 2003. *Pathologies of power: Health, human rights, and the new war on the poor*. Berkeley: Univ. of California Press.

Federación Médica Colombiana. 2010. Análisis y documentos sobre la crisis del sector salud y los decretos de emergencia social. *Boletín Federación Médica Colombiana*. http://www.med-informatica.net/EmergenciaSocial2010.htm.

Feeley, M. M., and E. L. Rubin. 2000. *Judicial policy making and the modern state: How the courts reformed America's prisons*. Cambridge: Cambridge Univ. Press.

Ferraz, O. L. M. 2009a. The right to health in the courts of Brazil: Worsening health inequities? *Health and Human Rights: An International Journal* 11 (2): 33–45.

———. 2009b. Right to health litigation in Brazil: An overview of the research. Social Science Research Network. http://papers.ssrn.com/sol3/papers.cfm?abstract_id=1426011.

Ferraz, O. L. M., and O. F. Norheim. Forthcoming. Impact on health outcomes of litigation for medicines in Brazil. Draft on file with the author.

Ferraz, O. L. M., and F. Vieira. 2009. Direito à saúde, recursos escassos e equidade: Os riscos da interpretação judicial dominante. *Dados: Revista de Ciências Sociais* 52 (1): 223–51.

Fisher, W., and C. Rigamonti. 2005. The South Africa AIDS controversy: A case study in patent law and policy. Harvard Law School. http://cyber.law.harvard.edu/people/tfisher/South%20Africa.pdf.

Fiss, O. 2003. *The law as it could be.* New York: New York Univ. Press.

Folha de S. Paulo. 2010. Gastos com processos é de R$83 mi em 2009. July 24.

Folha On Line. 2009. Maioria dos brasileiros é contra criação de nova CPMF, diz pesquisa. September 8. http://www1.folha.uol.com.br/folha/dinheiro/ult91u620841.shtml.

Fordhan, K. 2008. This is MINE: No, this is OURS; Holding "Big Pharma" to account. December 1. http://www.yorku.ca/robarts/projects/gradpapers/pdf/Forhan.pdf.

Forman, L. 2005. Ensuring reasonable health: Health rights; The judiciary and South African HIV/AIDS policy. *Journal of Law, Medicine & Ethics* 33 (4): 711–24.

———. 2009. "Rights" and wrongs: What utility for the right to health in reforming trade rules on medicines? *Health and Human Rights: An International Journal* 10 (2): 37–52.

Fraser, N. 1992. Rethinking the public sphere: A contribution to the critique of actually existing democracy. In *Habermas and the public sphere*, ed. C. Calhoun, 109–42. Cambridge, MA: MIT Press.

———. 1997. *Justice interruptus: Critical reflections on the "postsocialist" condition.* New York: Routledge.

Freedman, L. 2005. Achieving the MDGs: Health systems as core social institutions. *Development* 48:19–24.

Freedom House. 2009. Combined average ratings: Independent countries, 2008. http://www.freedomhouse.org/template.cfm?page=410&year=2008.

Friedman, A. 2007. Costs. In *Constitutional law of South Africa*, ed. S. Woolman, 6:1–20. 2nd ed. Cape Town: Juta.

Frühling, H. 2000. From dictatorship to democracy: Law and social change in the Andean Region and the Southern Cone of South America. In *Many roads to justice: The law-related work of Ford Foundation grantees around the world*, ed. M. McClymont and S. Golub, 55–87. New York: The Ford Foundation.

Fuller, L. 1978. The forms and limits of adjudication. *Harvard Law Review* 92 (2): 353–409.

Gakidou, E., and G. King. 2002. Measuring total health inequality: Adding individual variation to group-level differences. *International Journal for Equity in Health* 1 (3). doi:10.1186/1475-9276-1-3.

Galanter, M. 1974. Why the "haves" come out ahead: Speculations on the limits of legal change. *Law & Society Review* 9 (1): 95–160.

Galanter, M., and J. K. Krishnan. 2004. "Bread for the poor": Access to justice and the rights of the needy in India. *Hastings Law Journal* 55 (4): 789–834.

García Jaramillo, L. 2008. Recepción de postulados deliberativistas en la jurisprudencia constitucional. *Revista Argentina de Teoría Jurídica* 8 (2). http://www.utdt.edu//ver_contenido.php?id_contenido=2450&id_item_menu=3555.

García Villegas, M. 1993. *La eficacia simbólica del derecho: Examen de situaciones Colombianas.* Bogotá: Universidad de los Andes.

Gargarella, R. 2005. *Los fundamentos legales de la desigualdad: El constitucionalismo en América (1776–1860).* Buenos Aires: Siglo XXI.

———. 2006a. Should deliberative democrats defend the judicial enforcement of social rights? In *Deliberative democracy and its discontents*, ed. S. Besson and J. L. Martí, 233–52. Aldershot: Ashgate.

———. 2006b. Theories of democracy, the judiciary and social rights. In *Courts and social transformation in new democracies: An institutional voice for the poor?*, ed. R. Gargarella, P. Domingo, and T. Roux, 13–34. Aldershot: Ashgate.

Gargarella, R., P. Domingo, and T. Roux. 2006. *Courts and social transformation in new democracies: An institutional voice for the poor?* Aldershot: Ashgate.

Garside, R., A. Round, K. Dalziel, K. Stein, and P. Royle. 2002. The effectiveness and cost-effectiveness of imatinib for chronic myeloid leukaemia: A systematic review. *Health Technology Assessment* 6 (33): 1–162.

Garth, B., F. Levine, and A. Sarat. 1998. *How does law matter?* Evanston, IL: Northwestern Univ. Press.

Gauri, V., and D. Brinks, eds. 2008. *Courting social justice: Judicial enforcement of social and economic rights in the developing world.* Cambridge: Cambridge Univ. Press.

George, A. L., and A. Bennett. 2005. *Case studies and theory development in the social sciences.* Cambridge, MA: MIT Press.

Gerring, J. 2004. What is a case study and what is it good for? *American Political Science Review* 98 (2): 341–54.

Gianella, C., O. F. Norheim, A. E. Yamin, and O. Parra-Vera. Forthcoming. Impact on health outcomes of litigation for medicines in Colombia. Draft on file with the author.

Gianella-Malca, C., O. Parra-Vera, A. E. Yamin, and M. Torres-Tovar. 2009. ¿Deliberación democrática o mercadeo social? Los dilemas de la definición pública en salud en el contexto del seguimiento de la Sentencia T-760 de 2008. *Health and Human Rights: An International Journal* 11 (1): Perspectives. http://hhrjournal.org/blog/perspectives/deliberacion-democratica.

Glassman, A. 2007. After a decade: Health insurance in Colombia Law 100 of 1993. Paper presented at the Global Health Council Conference, Health Systems 20/20 Auxiliary Session, Washington, DC.

Glassman, A., M. L. Escobar, A. Giuffrida, and U. Giedion, eds. 2009. *From few to many: Ten years of health insurance expansion in Colombia.* Washington, DC: Inter-American Development Bank and The Brookings Institution.

Glendon, M. A. 1999. Foundations of human rights: The unfinished business. *American Journal of Jurisprudence* 44:1–14.

Glenn, H. P. 2000. *Legal traditions of the world: Sustainable diversity in law.* 3rd ed. Oxford: Oxford Univ. Press.

Gloppen, S. 2005. Public interest litigation, social rights and social policy. Paper presented at New Frontiers of Social Policy Conference, Arusha, December 12–15.

———. 2006. Courts and social transformation: An analytical framework. In *Courts and social transformation in new democracies: An institutional voice for the poor?*, ed. R. Gargarella, P. Domingo, and T. Roux, 153–68. Aldershot: Ashgate.

———. 2008a. Litigation as a strategy to hold governments accountable for implementing the right to health. *Health and Human Rights: An International Journal* 10 (2): 21–36.

———. 2008b. Public interest litigation, social rights, and social policy. In *Inclusive states: Social policy and structural inequalities*, ed. A. A. Dani and A. De Haan, 343–68. Washington, DC: World Bank.

———. 2009. Legal enforcement of social rights: Enabling conditions and impact assessment. *Erasmus Law Review* 2 (4): 465–80.

Gloppen, S., B. M. Wilson, R. Gargarella, E. Skaar, and M. Kinander. 2010. *Courts and power in Latin America and Africa.* New York: Palgrave Macmillan.

Goddard, M., and P. Smith. 2003. Equity and access to health services: Theory and evidence from the UK. *Social Science and Medicine* 53 (9): 1149–62.

Gottlieb, S. E., and D. Schultz, eds. 1998. *Leveraging the law: Using courts to achieve social change.* New York: Peter Lang.

Gow, I. 2007. Challenges of orphan drug development. Presentation by the director of scientific affairs, Nexus Oncology, May 1. http://www.nexusoncology.com/presentations/Orphan%20May07.pdf

Goyer, K. C., Y. Salojee, M. Richter, and C. Hardy. 2004. *HIV/AIDS in prison, treatment, intervention and reform: A submission to the Jali Commission.* Johannesburg: AIDS Law Project and Treatment Action Campaign.

Grebe, E. 2008. Transnational networks of influence in South African AIDS treatment activism. Centre for Social Science Research Working Paper 222. http://www.cssr.uct.ac.za/publications/working-paper/2008/222.

———. 2009. Leaders, networks and coalitions in the AIDS response: A comparison of Uganda and South Africa. Centre for Social Science Research Working Paper 241. http://www.cssr.uct.ac.za/publications/working-paper/2009/241.

Grima, D. T., M. F. Thompson, and L. Sauriol. 2007. Modelling cost effectiveness of insulin glargine for the treatment of type 1 and 2 diabetes in Canada. *Pharmacoeconomics* 25 (3): 253–66.

Gross, A. 2007. The right to health in the era of privatisation and globalisation: National and international perspectives. In *Exploring social rights: Between theory and practice*, ed. D. Barak-Erez and A. Gross, 289–339. Oxford: Hart Publishing.

Gruskin, S., and N. Daniels. 2008. Process is the point: Justice and human rights; Priority setting and fair deliberative process. *American Journal of Public Health* 98 (9): 1573–77.

Guay, L. A., P. Musoke, T. Fleming, et al. 1999. Intrapartum and neonatal single-dose nevirapine compared with zidovudine for prevention of mother-to-child transmission of HIV-1 in Kampala, Uganda: HIVNET 012 randomised trial. *The Lancet* 354 (9181): 795–802.

Gutiérrez Gutiérrez, C. J. 1999. La Constitución cincuenta años después. In *Temas clave de la Constitución Política,* ed. C. J. Gutiérrez Gutiérrez et al., 25–52. San José, Costa Rica: Editorial Investigaciones Jurídicas.

Gutman, A., and D. Thompson. 1996. *Democracy and disagreement.* Cambridge, MA: Harvard Univ. Press.

Guyatt, G. H., A. D. Oxman, R. Kunz, G. E. Vist, Y. Falck-Ytter, and H. J. Schünemann. 2008. What is "quality of evidence" and why is it important to clinicians? *British Medical Journal* 336 (7651): 995–98.

Ham, C. 1995. Synthesis: What can we learn from international experience? *British Medical Bulletin* 51 (4): 819–30.

Ham, C., and A. Coulter. 2000. Where are we now? In *The global challenge of health care rationing*, ed. A. Coulter and C. Ham, 233–50. London: Open Univ. Press.

Ham, C., and L. Locock. 1998. *International approaches to priority setting in health care: An annotated listing of official and semi-official publications, with a selection of key academic references.* Birmingham: Univ. of Birmingham.

Hamilton, A., J. Madison, and J. Jay. [1788] 1961. *The federalist papers.* Ed. C. Rossiter. New York: New American Library.

Hammer, J., Y. Aiyar, and S. Samji. 2007. Understanding government failure in public health services. *Economic and Political Weekly*, October 6.

Hassim, A., M. Heywood, and J. Berger, eds. 2007. *Health and democracy: A guide* to *human rights, health, law and policy in post-apartheid South Africa.* Cape Town: SiberInk.

Haynes, R. B., P. J. Devereaux, and G. H. Guyatt. 2002. Physicians' and patients' choices in evidence based practice. *British Medical Journal* 324 (7350):1350.

Hertogh, M., and S. Halliday, eds. 2004. *Judicial review and bureaucratic impact: International and interdisciplinary perspectives.* Cambridge: Cambridge Univ. Press.

Heuser, S. 2009. One girl's hope, a nation's dilemma. *Boston Globe*, June 14.

Heywood, M. 2001. Debunking "Conglomo-talk": A case study of the amicus curiae as an instrument for advocacy, investigation and mobilisation. *Law, Democracy and Development* 5 (2): 133–63.
———. 2003. Preventing mother-to-child HIV transmission in South Africa: Background, strategies and outcomes of the Treatment Action Campaign case against the Minister of Health. *South African Journal on Human Rights* 19:278–315.
———. 2005. Shaping, making and breaking the law in the campaign for a national HIV/AIDS treatment plan. In *Democratising development: The politics of socio-economic rights in South Africa*, ed. P. Jones and K. Stokke, 181–212. Leiden: Brill Academic Publishers.
———. 2009. South Africa's Treatment Action Campaign: Combining law and social mobilisation to realise the right to health. *Journal of Human Rights Practice* 1 (1): 14–36.

Hirschl, R. 2004. *Towards juristocracy: The origins and consequences of the new constitutionalism.* Cambridge, MA: Harvard Univ. Press.

Hoffman, F., and F. Bentes. 2008. Accountability for social and economic rights in Brazil. In *Courting social justice: Judicial enforcement of social and economic rights in the developing world,* ed. V. Gauri and D. Brinks, 100–145. Cambridge: Cambridge Univ. Press.

Hogerzeil, H. V., M. Samson, J. V. Casanovas, and L. Rahmani-Ocora. 2006. Is access to essential medicines as part of the fulfilment of the right to health enforceable through the courts? *The Lancet* 368 (9532): 305–11.

Holmes, S. 1993. Precommitment and the paradox of democracy. In *Constitutionalism and democracy*, ed. J. Elster and R. Slagstad, 195–240. Cambridge, MA: Cambridge Univ. Press.

Hunt, P., and G. Backman. 2008. Health systems and the right to the highest attainable standard of health. *Health and Human Rights: An International Journal* 10 (1): 81–92.

Hutubessy, R., D. Chisholm, and T. Tan-Torres Edejer. 2003. Generalized cost-effectiveness analysis for national-level priority-setting in the health sector. *Cost Effectiveness and Resource Allocation* 1 (8): 1–29.

Indian Ministry of Health and Family Welfare. 2005. Manual for family planning insurance scheme. December. http://mohfw.nic.in/index1.php?lang=1&level=2&sublinkid=540&lid=530.

Indian National Human Rights Commission. 2006. Report presented at the 11th Annual Meeting of the Asia Pacific Forum, Suva, Fiji Islands. http://www.asiapacificforum.net/about/annual-meetings/11th-fiji-islands-2006/downloads/apf-members/india.pdf.

Instituto de Estudios Políticos y Relaciones Internacionales, ed. 2006. *Nuestra guerra sin nombre: Transformaciones del conflicto en Colombia.* Bogotá: Norma and Universidad Nacional de Colombia.

Irshad, M., Y. N. Singh, and S.K. Acharya. 1992. HBV status in professional blood donors in north India. *Tropical Gastroenterology* 13 (3): 112–14.

Jamison, D. T., J. G. Breman, A. R. Measham, et al. 2006. *Disease control priorities in developing countries*, 2nd ed. New York: Oxford Univ. Press and the World Bank.

Jaramillo, I. 2010. La emergencia social en salud: ¿Error o jugada maestra? http://www.med-informatica.net/OBSERVAMED/ReformaSistemaSalud/EmergenciaSocial2010/EmergenciaSocial_CometariosIJP.pdf.

Joint Monitoring Programme for Water Supply and Sanitation. 2010a. *Estimates for the use of improved sanitation facilities: Colombia*. Geneva: UNICEF/WHO.

———. 2010b. *Estimates for the use of improved drinking-water sources: Colombia*. Geneva: UNICEF/WHO.

Kalmanovitz, S. 2000. Los efectos económicos de la Corte Constitucional. Working Paper, Banco de la República, Bogotá.

Kaoma, K. 2009. *Globalizing the culture wars: U.S. conservatives, African churches, & homophobia*. Somerville, MA: Political Research Associates. http://www.publiceye.org/publications/globalizing-the-culture-wars/pdf/africa-full-report.pdf.

Kapczynski, A., and J. Berger. 2009. The story of the TAC case: The potential and limits of socio-economic rights litigation in South Africa. In *Human rights advocacy stories*, ed. D. Hurwitz and M. Satterthwaite, 43–79. New York: Foundation Press.

Kapindu, R. 2009. Pulling back the frontiers of constitutional deference: Mazibuko & others v. City of Johannesburg & others and its implications. Paper presented at a SAIFAC colloquium, Johannesburg, October 11.

Kapoor D., R. Saxena, B. Sood, and S. K. Sarin. 2000. Blood transfusion practices in India: Results of a national survey. *Indian Journal of Gastroenterology* 19 (2): 51–2.

Katz, J. M. 1993. *El sector salud en la República Argentina: Su estructura y comportamiento*. Buenos Aires: Fondo de Cultura Económica.

Kawachi, I., and B. Kennedy. 2002. *The health of nations: Why inequality is harmful to your health*. New York: The New Press.

Khandker, S. R., G. B. Koolwal, and H. A. Samad. 2010. *Handbook on impact evaluation: Quantitative methods and practices*. Washington, DC: The World Bank.

King, G., R. O. Keohane, and S. Verba. 1994. *Designing social inquiry: Scientific inference in qualitative research*. Princeton, NJ: Princeton Univ. Press.

Klein, R. 1993. Dimensions of rationing: Who should do what? *British Medical Journal* 307 (6899): 309–11.

Knight, C., D. Hind, N. Brewer, and V. Abbott. 2004. Rituximab (MabThera) for aggressive non-Hodgkin's lymphoma: Systematic review and economic evaluation. *Health Technology Assessment* 8 (37): 1–82.

Kobelt, G., L. Jönsson, A. Young, and K. Eberhardt. 2003. The cost-effectiveness of infliximab (Remicade) in the treatment of rheumatoid arthritis in Sweden and the United Kingdom based on the ATTRACT study. *Rheumatology* 42:326–35.

Kramer, L. 2005. *The people themselves: Popular constitutionalism and judicial review.* Oxford: Oxford Univ. Press.
Krishnan, V. 2010. Private hospitals dodge "poor" clause, doors still shut to underprivileged. *Indian Express*, August 2.
Kugler, M., and H. Rosenthal. 2000. Checks and balances: An assessment of the institutional separation of political powers in Colombia. Working Paper No. 9, Department of Economics and Econometrics, Univ. of Southampton.
Kumar, A., K. Shiva, L. C. Chen, et al. 2011. Financing health care for all: Challenges and opportunities. *The Lancet* 377 (9766): 668–79.
La Libertad. 2009. Quince EPS en la mira del gobierno nacional. June 9.
La Mesa por la Vida y la Salud de las Mujeres. 2009. *Un derecho para las mujeres: La despenalización parcial del aborto en Colombia.* Bogotá: La Mesa por la Vida y la Salud de las Mujeres.
La Nación (Argentina). 2006a. El bypass gástrico y el efecto Maradona. September 5. http://www.lanacion.com.ar/nota.asp?nota_id=837880.
———. 2006b. La obesidad, atendida por ley. November 29.
———. 2007. Una obra social deberá pagar un tratamiento de fecundación. December 4. http://www.lanacion.com.ar/nota.asp?nota_id=967941.
La Nación (Costa Rica). 1999. Cuestión de números. http://wvw.nacion.com/ln_ee/1999/noviembre/29/sida.gif.
———. 2006. Sala IV obliga a CCSS a dar costosos tratamientos. November 19. http://wvw.nacion.com/ln_ee/2006/noviembre/19/pais883648.html.
Langford, M., ed. 2008. *Social rights jurisprudence: Emerging trends in international and comparative law.* New York: Cambridge Univ. Press.
Laurell, A. C. 2000. Globalización y reforma de estado. In *Saúde, equidade e gênero: Um desafio as políticas públicas*, ed. A. M. Costa, E. Merchan-Hamann, and D. Tajer, 35–60. Brasilia: Universidad de Brasilia.
Law Reform Commission. 2006. 201st report on emergency medical care to victims of accidents and during emergency medical condition and women under labour.
Leary, V. A. 1994. The right to health in international human rights law. *Health and Human Rights: An International Journal* 1 (1): 24–56.
León, J. 2011. El "Consenso de Acemi": Al acuerdo de las EPS para negar servicios de salud. *La Silla Vacia*, May 1. http://www.lasillavacia.com/historia/el-consenso-de-acemi-el-acuerdo-de-las-eps-para-negar-servicios-de-salud-23528.
Liberato, N. L., M. Marchetti, and G. Barosi. 2007. Cost effectiveness of adjuvant trastuzumab in human epidermal growth factor receptor 2–positive breast cancer. *Journal of Clinical Oncology* 25:625–33.
Liebenberg, S. 1998. Socio-economic rights. In *Constitutional law of South Africa*, ed. M. Chaskalson et al., 41:1–56. Cape Town: Juta.
———. 2010. *Socio-economic rights: Adjudication under a transformative constitution.* Cape Town: Juta.

Lisulo, A. S. 2003. Costa Rica: Health policies. Background paper prepared for the World Bank. http://www-wds.worldbank.org/external/default/WDSContentServer/IW3P/IB/2004/02/27/000265513_20040227161925/Rendered/PDF/28007.pdf.

Liu, H., K. Michaud, S. Nayak, D. B. Karpf, D. K. Owens, and A. M. Garber. 2006. The cost-effectiveness of therapy with teriparatide and alendronate in women with severe osteoporosis. *Archives of Internal Medicine* 166:1209–17.

Lizardo, I. A., M. L. Acosta M., Y. A. Pimental R., et al. 2004. Determinación de conocimiento sobre la medicina basada en la evidencia de los médicos/as del hospital Dr. Francisco E. Moscoso Puello. *Revista Médica Dominicana* 65:242–3.

Lloyd-Sherlock, P. 2005. Health sector reform in Argentina: A cautionary tale. *Social Science and Medicine* 60:1893–1903.

Lohman, D., R. Schleifer, and J. J. Amon. 2010. Access to pain treatment as a human right. *BMC Medicine* 8 (1): 8–16.

Lopez, A. D., C. D. Mathers, M. Ezzati, D. T. Jamison, and C. J. L. Murray, eds. 2006. *Global burden of disease and risk factors*. Washington, DC: The World Bank.

López Medina, D. 2008. "Sistema de salud" y "derecho a la salud": Historia de su interrelación en la jurisprudencia constitucional. Paper presented at the Contexto Económico y Jurisprudencial del Sistema de Salud, Bogotá, June 25.

Lord, J. E., and M. A. Stein. 2008. The domestic incorporation of human rights law and the United Nations Convention on the Rights of Persons with Disabilities. *Washington Law Review* 83 (4): 449–79.

Loveman, E., C. Green, J. Kirby, et al. 2006. The clinical and cost-effectiveness of donepezil, rivastigmine, galantamine and memantine for Alzheimer's disease. *Health Technology Assessment* 10 (1): 1–160.

Lukes, S. 2005. *Power: A radical view.* 2nd ed. London: Macmillan Press.

Maharatna, A. 2002. India's family planning programme: An unpleasant essay. *Economic and Political Weekly*, September.

March, J. G., and H. A. Simon. 1958. *Organizations.* New York: Wiley.

Marmot, M., and R. Wilkinson, eds. 1999. *Social determinants of health.* Oxford: Oxford Univ. Press.

Marseille, E., J. G. Kahn, F. Mmiro, et al. 2000. The cost effectiveness of a single-dose nevirapine regimen to mother and infant to reduce vertical HIV-1 transmission in sub-Saharan Africa. *Annals of the New York Academy of Sciences* 918:53–56.

Martínez Guevara, G. 2008. *Anthoc ante el genocidio y la liquidación.* Bogotá: ANTHOC.

Maurino, G., E. Nino, and M. Sigal. 2005. *Las acciones colectivas.* Buenos Aires: Lexis Nexis.

Mbali, M. 2005. *The Treatment Action Campaign and the history of rights-based, patient-driven HIV/AIDS activism in South Africa.* Durban: Centre for Civil Society.

McCann, M. W. 1994. *Rights at work: Pay equity reform and the politics of legal mobilization.* Chicago: Univ. of Chicago Press.

———. 1998. Gaining without winning: Legal advocacy and the politics of pay equity. Unpublished manuscript, Univ. of Washington.

———. 2006. Law and social movements: Contemporary perspectives. *Annual Review of Law and Social Science* 2:17–38.

McClymont, M., and S. Golub, eds. 2000. *Many roads to justice: The law-related work of Ford Foundation grantees around the world.* New York: The Ford Foundation.

McDowall, D., R. McCleary, E. Meidinger, and R. A. Hay. 1980. *Interrupted time series analysis.* Beverly Hills, CA: Sage Publications.

McGregor, S. 2001. Neoliberalism and health care. *International Journal of Consumer Studies* 25 (2): 82-9.

McGuire, J. W. 2010. *Wealth, health, and democracy in East Asia and Latin America.* New York: Cambridge Univ. Press.

McKneally, M. F., B. M. Dickens, E. M. Meslin, and P. A. Singer. 1997. Bioethics for clinicians: Resource allocation. *Canadian Medical Association Journal* 157:163–7.

McLean, K. 2010. *Constitutional deference, courts and socio-economic rights in South Africa.* Pretoria: Univ. of Pretoria Press.

Medical Council of India Notification. 2002. *Gazette of India*, pt. III, sec. 4. http://www.issuesinmedicalethics.org/103do066.html.

Merry, S. E. 2006. *Human rights and gender violence: Translating international law into local justice.* Chicago: Univ. of Chicago Press.

Mesa de Seguimiento al Auto 006 de 2009 Desplazamiento y Discapacidad. 2010. *Informe de seguimiento.* Bogotá: Mesa de seguimiento al Auto 006 de 2009 Desplazamiento y Discapacidad.

Messeder, A., C. Osorio-de-Castro, and V. Luiza. 2005. Mandados judiciais como ferramenta para garantia do acesso a medicamentos no setor público: A experiência do Estado do Rio de Janeiro, Brasil [Can court injunctions guarantee access to medicines in the public sector? The experience in the state of Rio de Janeiro, Brazil]. *Cadernos de Saúde Pública* 21 (2): 525–34.

Meydani, A., and S. Mizrahi. 2006. The politics and strategies of defending human rights: The Israeli case. *Israel Law Review* 39 (1): 39–56.

Meyer, D. S. 2004. Protest and political opportunities. *Annual Review of Sociology* 30:125–45.

Meyer, J. W., J. Boli, G. M. Thomas, and F. O. Ramirez. 1997. World society and the nation-state. *American Journal of Sociology* (103) 1: 144–81.

Miller, E. 2010. Ask the author: Interview with Martha Minow, part I. *SCOTUSblog* (blog), July 28. http://www.scotusblog.com/2010/07/ask-the-author-interview-with-martha-minow-part-i.

Moellendorf, D. 1998. Reasoning about resources: Soobramoney and the future of socio-economic rights claims. *South African Journal on Human Rights* 14:327–33.

Moser, K. A., D. A. Leon, and D. R. Gwatkin. 2005. How does progress towards the child mortality millennium development goal affect inequalities between the poorest and least poor? Analysis of Demographic and Health Survey data. *British Medical Journal* 331 (7526): 1180–82.

Moynihan, R., I. Heath, and D. Henry. 2002. Selling sickness: The pharmaceutical industry and disease mongering. *British Medical Journal* 324 (7342): 886–91.

Mukherjee, J. S. 2004. The International AIDS Conferences from Vancouver to Bangkok: How far have we come in eight years? *Pan American Journal of Public Health* 16 (2): 75–77.

Muralidhar, S. 1997–98. India: Public interest litigation survey 1997–1998. *Annual Survey of Indian Law* 33–34 (525). http://www.ielrc.org/content/a9802.pdf.

———. 2002. Implementation of court orders in the area of economic, social and cultural rights: An overview of the experience of the Indian judiciary. International Environmental Law Research Centre Working Paper.

———. 2006. The right to water: An overview of the Indian legal regime. In *The human right to water*, ed. E. Riedel and P. Rothen, 65–81. Berlin: Berliner Wissenschafts-Verlag.

———. 2008. India: The expectations and challenges of judicial enforcement of social rights. In *Social rights jurisprudence: Emerging trends in international and comparative law*, ed. M. Langford, 102–24. New York: Cambridge Univ. Press.

Murillo Víquez, J. 1994. *La sala constitucional: Una revolución político-jurídica en Costa Rica.* San José, Costa Rica: Editorial Guayacán.

Murray, C. J., and A. D. Lopez. 1996. Evidence-based health policy: Lessons from the Global Burden of Disease Study. *Science* 274 (5288): 740–43.

Naraj, G., G. D. Puri, D. Arun, V. Chakravarty, J. Aveek, and P. Chari. 2003. Assessment of intraoperative blood transfusion practice during elective non-cardiac surgery in an Indian tertiary care hospital. *British Journal of Anaesthesia* 91 (4): 586–89.

Naundorf, B. 2008. Enfrentamento das demandas judiciais na assistência farmacêutica: A experiência do Estado do Rio Grande do Sul. Workshop presentation at Fundação Oswaldo Cruz, Rio de Janeiro. http://www4.ensp.fiocruz.br/biblioteca/home/exibedetalhesBiblioteca.cfm?id=6240&tipo=B.

Navia, P., and J. Ríos-Figueroa. 2005. The constitutional adjudication mosaic of Latin America. *Comparative Political Studies* 38 (2): 189–217.

Ndirangu, J., R. Bland, and M. Newell. 2009. A decline in early life mortality in a high HIV prevalence rural area of South Africa: Associated with implementation of PMTCT and/or ART programmes? Paper presented at the 5th International AIDS Society Conference on HIV Treatment, Pathogenesis and Prevention, Cape Town, July 19–22.

New, B. 1996. The rationing agenda in the NHS. *British Medical Journal* 312 (7046): 1593–1601.

Ngwena, C., and R. Cook. 2005. Rights concerning health. In *Socio-economic rights in South Africa*, ed. D. Brand and C. Heyns, 107–51. Pretoria: Pretoria Univ. Law Press.

Nino, C. S. 1996. *The constitution of deliberative democracy*. New Haven: Yale Univ. Press.

Nord, E. 1999. *Cost-value analysis in health care*. Cambridge: Cambridge Univ. Press.

Nord, E., J. L. Pinto, J. Richardson, P. Menzel, and P. Ubel. 1999. Incorporating societal concerns for fairness in numerical valuations of health programmes. *Health Economics* 8 (1): 25–39.

Norheim, O. F. 1996. Limiting access to health care: A contractualist approach to fair rationing. PhD diss., University of Oslo.

———. 2000. Increasing demand for accountability: Is there a professional response? In *The global challenge of health care rationing*, ed. A. Coulter and C. Ham, 222–32. London: Open Univ. Press.

———. 2010. Priority to the young or to those with least lifetime health? *American Journal of Bioethics* 10 (4): 60–61.

Norheim, O. F., and Y. Asada. 2009. The ideal of equal health revisited: Definitions and measures of inequity in health should be better integrated with theories of distributive justice. *International Journal for Equity in Health* 8 (40).

Norheim, O. F., M. Johri, and Y. Asada. 2010. Child mortality, the Millennium Development Goal 4 and its impact on inequality in health in sub-Saharan Africa. Abstract printed in the proceedings of the 8th International Conference on Priority Setting in Health Care, Boston.

Norheim, O. F., and B. M. Wilson. 2010. Health rights litigation and access to medicines in Costa Rica: Priority classification of successful cases from the Constitutional Chamber of the Supreme Court. Paper presented at the Law and Society Association Meeting, Chicago, May.

Nundy, M. n.d. *Primary health care in India: Review of policy, plan and committee reports*. New Delhi: Centre of Social Medicine and Community Health, Jawaharlal Nehru University. http://www.whoindia.org/LinkFiles/Commision_on_Macroeconomic_and_Health_Primary_Health_Care_in_India_Review_of_Policy_Plan_and_Committee_Reports.pdf.

Nussbaum, M., and A. Sen. 1993. *The quality of life*. Oxford: Oxford Univ. Press.

Nygren-Krug, H. 2002. *25 questions and answers on health and human rights*. Geneva: WHO. http://whqlibdoc.who.int/hq/2002/9241545690.pdf.

O Estado de S. Paulo. 2008. Fraude pode ter desviado R$ 200 mi da Saúde em SP. September 2.

O'Connell, P. 2007. On reconciling irreconcilables: Neo-liberal globalisation and human rights. *Human Rights Law Review* 7 (3): 483–509.

———. Forthcoming. The death of socio-economic rights. *Modern Law Review*.

Oliver, A., and E. Mossialos. 2004. Equity of access to health care: Outlining the foundations for action. *Journal of Epidemiology and Community Health* 58:655–58.

Oliveri, R. S., C. Gluud, and P. A. Wille-Jorgensen. 2004. Hospital doctors' self-rated skills in and use of evidence-based medicine: A questionnaire survey. *Journal of Evaluation in Clinical Practice* 10 (2): 219–26.

Ossa, P. 2004. Por enésima vez, el régimen subsidiado en la palestra pública. *El Pulso*. http://www.periodicoelpulso.com/html/jun04/general/general-03.htm.
Oviedo, E. 2009. Sala IV ordena vacunar a ancianos contra neumococo. *La Nación*, June 23. http://www.nacion.com/ln_ee/2009/junio/23/pais2005122.html.
Pacheco, C. I. 2009. Luego de 15 años de la Ley 100 de 1993: El derecho fundamental de la salud para todos los Colombianos. *Le Monde Diplomatique* 78.
Padmini, J. 2003. MCI drafts investigation guidelines for professional misconduct. *Healthcare Management Express*, February.
Pan American Health Organization. 2007. *Health in the Americas*. Washington, DC: PAHO.
———. 2010. PAHO basic health indicator data base. http://www.paho.org/English/DD/AIS/cp_188.htm.
Park, R. 2002. The international drug industry: What the future holds for South Africa's HIV/AIDS patients. *Minnesota Journal of Global Trade* 11:125–54.
Pepe, V. L. E., M. Ventura, J. M. B. Sant'ana, et al. 2010. Caracterização de demandas judiciais de fornecimento de medicamentos "essenciais" no Estado do Rio de Janeiro, Brasil [Characterization of lawsuits for the supply of "essential" medicines in the State of Rio de Janeiro, Brazil]. *Cadernos de Saúde Pública* 26 (3): 461–71.
Pereira, J., R. Santos, J. Nascimento Jr., and E. Schenkel. 2010. Análise das demandas judiciais para o fornecimento de medicamentos pela Secretaria de Estado da Saúde de Santa Catarina nos anos de 2003 e 2004 [Situation of lawsuits concerning the access to medical products brought against the Health Department of Santa Catarina State, Brazil, during the years 2003 and 2004]. *Revista Ciência & Saúde Coletiva* 15 (3): 3551–60.
Pérez Salazar, M. 2003. Razones y sinrazones de un debate: La crítica económica de la jurisprudencia constitucional colombiana. *Revista Derecho del Estado* 14:57–95.
Persad, G., A. Werteheimer, and E. J. Emanuel. 2009. Principles for allocation of scarce medical interventions. *The Lancet* 373 (9661): 423–31.
Petchesky, R. P. 2003. *Global prescriptions: Gendering health and human rights*. London: Zed Books.
Petryna, A. 2007. Clinical trials offshored: On private sector science and public health. *BioSocieties* 2:21–40.
Pharmainfo.net. 2009. List of drugs banned for marketing in India. October 24. http://www.pharmainfo.net/drgunasakaran1/list-drugs-banned-marketing-india.
Picado, G., E. Acuña, and J. Santacruz. 2003. *Gasto y financiamiento de la salud en Costa Rica: Situación actual, tendencias y retos*. San José, Costa Rica: Ministerio de Salud.
Pieterse, M. 2006a. The potential of socio-economic rights litigation for the achievement of social justice: Considering the example of access to medical care in South African Prisons. *Journal of African Law* 50 (2): 118–31.

———. 2006b. Resuscitating socio-economic rights: Constitutional entitlements to health care services. *South African Journal on Human Rights* 22:473–502.

Pinto, D., and M. I. Castellanos. 2004. Caracterización de los recobros por tutela y medicamentos no incluidos en los planes obligatorios de salud. *Revista Gerencia y Políticas de Salud* 56:40–61.

Plaza, B., A. B. Barona, and N. Hearst. 2001. Managed competition for the poor or poorly managed competition: Lessons from the Colombian health reform experience. *Health and Policy Planning* 16 (suppl. 2): 44–51.

Portafolio. 2009. Cuestionan a SaludCoop por uso de recursos. July 7. http://www.eltiempo.com/archivo/documento/MAM-3515481.

———. 2010. Se agudiza la polémica por la crisis de la salud en el país. June 12. http://www.portafolio.com.co/economia/economiahoy/se-agudiza-la-polemica-por-la-crisis-de-la-salud_7749405-3.

Procuraduría General de la Nación. 2010. PGN se pronuncia ante Comisión Interamericana de Derechos Humanos y reitera su compromiso en defensa de los derechos de las mujeres. *Procuraduría General de la Nación Boletin 236*. http://www.procuraduria.gov.co/html/noticias_2010/noticias_236.htm.

Procuraduría General de la Nación and Dejusticia (Centro de Estudios de Derecho, Justicia y Sociedad). 2008. *El derecho a la salud en perspectiva de derechos humanos y el sistema de inspección, vigilancia y control del estado Colombiano en materia de quejas en salud.* Bogotá: Procuraduría General de la Nación/Dejusticia.

Radio Santa Fé. 2010. Gobierno Santos creará el Ministerio del Trabajo. June 29. http://www.radiosantafe.com/2010/06/29/gobierno-santos-creara-el-ministerio-del-trabajo.

Radyowijati, A., and H. Haak. 2004. *Improving antibiotic use in low-income countries: An overview of evidence on determinants.* Geneva: WHO.

Rajagopal, B. 2007. Pro-human rights but anti-poor? A critical evaluation of the Supreme Court of India from a social movement perspective. *Human Rights Review* 18 (3): 157–87.

Rakner, L., and O. Mæstad. 2010. The cost of health rights litigation: The consideration of the courts. On file with the author.

Ravallion, M., S. Chen, and P. Sangraula. 2008. Dollar a day revisited. World Bank Policy Research Working Paper No. 4620. http://ssrn.com/abstract=1149123.

Rawlins, M. D., and A. J. Culyer. 2004. National Institute for Clinical Excellence and its value judgments. *British Medical Journal* 329 (7459): 224–26.

Reddy, K. S., and P. C. Gupta, eds. 2004. *Report on tobacco control in India.* http://www.whoindia.org/LinkFiles/Tobacco_Free_Initiative_Executive_Summary.pdf.

Reed, S. D., K. J. Anstrom, Y. Li, and K. A. Schulman. 2008. Updated estimates of survival and cost effectiveness for imatinib versus interferon-alpha plus low-dose cytarabine for newly diagnosed chronic-phase chronic myeloid leukaemia. *Pharmacoeconomics* 26 (5): 435–46.

Reichenbach, L., and M. J. Roseman, eds. 2009. *Reproductive health and human rights: The way forward.* Philadelphia: Univ. of Pennsylvania Press.

Reidpath, D. D., C. M. Morel, J. W. Mecaskey, and P. Allotey. 2009. The Millennium Development Goals fail poor children: The case for equity-adjusted measures. *PLoS Medicine* 6 (4): e1000062.

Risse, T., S. C. Ropp, and K. Sikkink, eds. 1999. *The power of human rights: International norms and domestic change.* Cambridge: Cambridge Univ. Press.

Roach, K. 2008. The right to legal aid in social rights litigation. In *Social rights jurisprudence: Emerging trends in international and comparative law*, ed. M. Langford, 59–71. New York: Cambridge Univ. Press.

Roach, K., and G. Budlender. 2005. Mandatory relief and supervisory jurisdiction: When is it appropriate, just and equitable? *South African Law Journal* 122:325–51.

Rodríguez, O., and S. Morales. 2010. Health rights dataset, 2006–2010. On file with the author.

Rodríguez Cordero, J. C. 2002. *Entre curules & estrados: La consulta preceptiva de las reformas constitucionales en Costa Rica.* San José, Costa Rica: Investigaciones Jurídicas.

Rodríguez Garavito, C. 2010. Assessing the impact and promoting the implementation of structural judgments: A comparative case study of ESCR rulings in Colombia. ESCR-Net. http://www.escr-net.org/usr_doc/Rodriguez_-_Colombia.pdf.

Rodríguez Garavito, C., and D. Rodríguez Franco. 2010a. *Cortes y cambio social: Cómo la Corte Constitucional transformó el desplazamiento forzado en Colombia.* Bogotá: Dejusticia.

———. 2010b. *Corte de cuentas: Cómo la Corte Constitucional transformó el desplazamiento forzado en Colombia.* Bogotá: Dejusticia.

Rodríguez Herrera, A. 2005. *La reforma de salud en Costa Rica.* Santiago de Chile: United Nations.

Romero, L. C. 2008. *Judicialização das políticas de assistência farmacêutica: O caso do Distrito Federal.* Brasilia: Senado Federal.

Rosenberg, G. N. 1991. *The hollow hope: Can courts bring about social change?* Chicago: Univ. of Chicago Press.

Rosero-Bixby, L. 2004. Evaluación del impacto de la reforma del sector salud en Costa Rica *Revista Panamericana de Salud Pública* 15 (2): 94–103.

———. 2008. The exceptionally high life expectancy of Costa Rican nonagenarians. *Demography* 45 (3): 673–91.

Roux, T. 2002. Understanding Grootboom: A response to Cass R. Sunstein. *Constitutional Forum* 12:41–51.

———. 2004. Legitimating transformation: Political resource allocation in the South African Constitutional Court. In *Democratization and the judiciary: The accountability function of courts in new democracies*, ed. S. Gloppen, R. Gargarella, and E. Skaar. London: Frank Cass.

———. 2006. Democracy. In *Constitutional law of South Africa*, ed. S. Woolman et al., 10:1–77. 2nd ed. Cape Town: Juta.

Rueda, M. I. 2006. ¿Qué tan cierto es que el paramilitarismo se tomó la salud en Colombia? *Semana*, November 18. http://www.semana.com/noticias-nacion/tan-cierto-paramilitarismo-tomo-salud-colombia/98304.aspx.

Ruger, J. P. 2010. *Health and social justice*. Oxford: Oxford Univ. Press.

Sabel, C., and W. Simon. 2004. Destabilization rights: How public law litigation succeeds. *Harvard Law Review* 117:1015–101.

Sánchez, E., and A. Vargas. 2009. Bolsas emergentes: ¿Una nueva burbuja? *Reporte Macroeconómico* 20.

Sánchez Lara, K., R. Sosa Sanchez, D. Green Renner, and D. Motola Kuba. 2007. Importancia de la medicina basada en evidencias en la práctica clínica cotidiana. *Médica Sur* 14 (1): 9–13.

Santa María, M., and G. Perry. 2008. El fallo de la Corte sobre salud: La trinidad imposible. *Economía y Política: Análisis de la Coyuntura Legislativa* 46 (October).

Sant'ana, J. M. B. 2009. Essencialidade e assistência farmacêutica: Um estudo exploratório das demandas judiciais individuais para acesso a medicamentos no estado do Rio de Janeiro. MPhil thesis, Fundação Oswaldo Cruz.

Santos, C. M. 2007. Transnational legal activism and the state: Reflections on cases against Brazil in the Inter-American Commission on Human Rights. *Sur: International Journal on Human Rights* 4 (7): 29–59.

São Paulo Public Security Department. 2008. Polícia prende quadrilha que fraudava Estado em ações judiciais de remédios. September 1. http://www.ssp.sp.gov.br/noticia/lenoticia.aspx?id=4009.

Sarat, A., and S. A. Scheingold, eds. 1998. *Cause lawyering: Political commitments and professional responsibilities*. New York: Oxford Univ. Press.

Sathe, S. P. 2002. *Judicial activism in India: Transgressing borders and enforcing limits*. New Delhi: Oxford Univ. Press.

Savedoff, W. D. 2000. *Reaching the poor through demand subsidies: The Colombian health reform*. Washington, DC: Inter-American Development Bank.

Scheingold, S. A. 2004. *The politics of rights: Lawyers, public policy, and political change*. 2nd ed. Ann Arbor: Univ. of Michigan Press. First published in 1974.

Scheingold, S. A., and A. Sarat. 2004. *Something to believe in: Politics, professionalism, and cause lawyering*. Stanford, CA: Stanford Univ. Press.

Schleinitz, M. D., and P. A. Heidenreich. 2005. A cost-effectiveness analysis of combination antiplatelet therapy for high-risk acute coronary syndromes: Clopidogrel plus aspirin versus aspirin alone. *Annals of Internal Medicine* 142:251–59.

Schoepf, B. G., C. Schoepf, and J. V. Millen. 2000. Theoretical therapies, remote remedies: SAPs and the political ecology of poverty and health in Africa.

In *Dying for growth: Global inequality and the health of the poor*, ed. J. Y. Kim, J. V. Millen, A. Irwin, and J. Gershman, 91–126. Monroe, ME: Common Courage Press.

Schultz, D. A., ed. 1998. *Leveraging the law: Using the courts to achieve social change*. New York: Peter Lang.

Scioscioli, S. 2005. Acceso a la justicia para todos. *Encrucijadas* 39:64–66.

Scott, S., and P. Alston. 2000. Adjudicating constitutional priorities in a transnational context: A comment on Soobramoney's legacy and Grootboom's promise. *South African Journal on Human Rights* 16:206–68.

Scott, C., and P. Macklem. 1992. Constitutional ropes of sand or justiciable guarantees? Social rights in a new South African Constitution. *University of Pennsylvania Law Review* 141 (1): 1–148.

Seekings, J., and N. Nattrass. 2006. *Class, race, and inequality in South Africa*. Durban: UKZN Press.

Segall, S. 2010. *Health, luck and justice*. Princeton: Princeton Univ. Press.

Semana. 2010. Un derecho que se convirtió en debate. August 26. http://www.semana.com/noticias-nacion/derecho-convirtio-debate/143581.aspx.

———. 2011. "El sistema de salud está montado para convertir en ganancia lo que es un derecho": Jorge Robledo. April 25. http://www.semana.com/nacion/sistema-salud-esta-montado-para-convertir-ganancia-derecho-jorge-robledo/155654-3.aspx.

Sen, A. 1973. *On economic equality*. New York: Norton.

———. 2004. Elements of a theory of human rights. *Philosophy and Public Affairs* 32 (4): 315–56.

———. 2006. Why health equity? In *Public health, ethics, and equity*, ed. S. Anand, F. Peter, and A. Sen, 21–33. Oxford: Oxford Univ. Press.

———. 2011. Learning from others. *The Lancet* 377 (9779): 200–201.

Shankar, J. 2009. India's growth rate fails to reverse infant mortality. Bloomberg, October 5.

Shankar, S., and P. B. Mehta. 2008. Courts and socioeconomic rights in India. In *Courting social justice: Judicial enforcement of social and economic rights in the developing world*, ed. V. Gauri and D. Brinks, 146–82. Cambridge: Cambridge Univ. Press.

Shepherd, J., N. Waugh, and P. Hewitson. 2000. Combination therapy (interferon alfa and ribavirin) in the treatment of chronic hepatitis C: A rapid and systematic review. *Health Technology Assessment* 4 (33): 1–67.

Sida. 2007. *Sida country report 2006: South Africa*. Pretoria: Sida.

———. 2009. Major breakthrough for gay rights. September 24. On file with the author.

Sieder, R., A. Angell, and L. Schjolden, eds. 2005. *The judicialization of politics in Latin America*. London: ISA and Palgrave Macmillan.

da Silva, A. V., and F. V. Terrazas. Forthcoming. Claiming the right to health in Brazilian courts: The exclusion of the already excluded. *Law and Social Inquiry.* http://www.ssrn.com/abstract=1133620.

Silverstein, G. 2009. *Law's allure: How law shapes, constrains, saves, and kills politics.* New York: Cambridge Univ. Press.

Singer, P. 1995. *How are we to live?: Ethics in an age of self-interest.* Buffalo, NY: Prometheus Books.

———. 2010. *Rethinking life and death: The collapse of our traditional ethics.* New York: St Martin's Press.

Singer, P., D. K. Martin, M. Giacomini, and L. Purdy. 2000. Priority setting for new technologies in medicine: Qualitative case study. *British Medical Journal* 321 (7272): 1316-18.

Sinha, A. 2009. In defence of the National Rural Health Mission. *Economic and Political Weekly*, April.

Sinha, K. 2010. Urban Health Mission shelved for now. *Times of India*, February 12.

Sloth-Nielsen, J. 2005. Children. In *South African constitutional law: The Bill of Rights*, ed. M. Cheadle, D. Davis, and N. Haysom, 23:1–32. 2nd ed. Durban: LexisNexis Butterworths.

Smulovitz, C. 2010. Judicialization in Argentina: Legal culture or opportunities and support structures? In *Cultures of legality: Judicialization and political activism in Latin America*, ed. J. Couso, A. Huneeus, and R. Sieder, 234–53. New York: Cambridge Univ. Press.

Solano Carrera, L. F. 2007. Derecho fundamental a la salud. *Gaceta Médica de Costa Rica* 9 (2): 141–50.

South African Department of Correctional Services. 2008. *Annual report for the 2007/08 financial year.*

———. 2009. *Annual report for the 2008/09 financial year.*

South African Department of Health. 1997. *White paper for the transformation of the health system in South Africa.* http://www.info.gov.za/whitepapers/1997/health.htm.

———. 2000. South African Ministry of Health and Pfizer initiate diflucan partnership program. Press release, December 1.

———. 2009. *Annual report 2008/09.*

South African Institute of Race Relations. 2008. *South Africa survey 2007/8.* Johannesburg: SAIRR.

———. 2010. *Fast facts*, February.

South African Ministry of Health. 2010. *Country progress report on the Declaration of Commitment on HIV/AIDS: 2010 report.*

South African National Treasury. 2002. *Estimates of national expenditure.*

———. 2003. *Intergovernmental fiscal review.*

———. 2004a. *Estimates of national expenditure.*

———. 2004b. *Intergovernmental fiscal review.*
———. 2006. *Intergovernmental fiscal review.*
———. 2009. *Intergovernmental fiscal review.*
South African Office of the Judicial Inspectorate. 2002. *Annual report.*
Spedo, S. M., O. Y. Tanaka, and N. R. Pinto. 2009. O desafio da descentralização do Sistema Único de Saúde em município de grande porte: o caso de São Paulo, Brasil [The challenge of decentralization of the Unified National Health System in large cities: The case of São Paulo, Brazil]. *Cadernos de Saúde Pública* 25 (8): 1781–90.
Steiner, H. J., P. Alston, and R. Goodman. 2008. *International human rights in context: Law, politics, and morals.* 3rd ed. Oxford: Oxford Univ. Press.
Stern, R. 2010. Costa Rica: Abbott against hetero with PLWA caught in the middle. Press release, Agua Buena Human Rights Association. San José.
Stringer, J. S., D. J. Rouse, S. H. Vermund, R. L. Goldenberg, M. Sinkala, and A. A. Stinnett. 2000. Cost-effective use of nevirapine to prevent vertical HIV transmission in sub-Saharan Africa. *Journal of Acquired Immune Deficiency Syndromes* 24 (4): 369–77.
Sudarshan, H., and N. S. Prashanth. 2011. Good governance in health care: The Karnataka experience. *The Lancet* 377 (9768): 790–92.
Sunstein, C. 1985. Interest groups in American public law. *Stanford Law Review* 38 (1): 29–56.
———. 1994a. The anticaste principle. *Michigan Law Review* 92: 2410–55.
———. 1994b. *The partial Constitution.* Cambridge, MA: Harvard Univ. Press.
———. 2001a. *Designing democracy: What constitutions do.* Oxford: Oxford Univ. Press.
———. 2001b. Social and economic rights? Lessons from South Africa. Univ. of Chicago, Public Law Working Paper No. 12; Univ. of Chicago Law & Economics, Olin Working Paper No. 124. http://www.ssrn.com/abstract=269657.
———. 2004. *The second bill of rights: FDR's unfinished revolution and why we need it more than ever.* New York: Basic Books.
Supersalud. 2010. Superintendencia Nacional de Salud. http://www.supersalud.gov.co/supersalud/LinkClick.aspx?fileticket=fs5oG8JjNJw%3d&tabid=59.
Syrett, K. 2007. *Law, legitimacy, and the rationing of health care: A contextual and comparative perspective.* Cambridge: Cambridge Univ. Press.
Tajer, D. 2003. Latin American social medicine: Roots, development during the 1990s and current challenges. *American Journal of Public Health* 93:2023–27.
Tang, K. K., D. Petrie, and D. S. Rao. 2007. Measuring health inequalities between genders and age groups with realization of potential life years (RePLY). *Bulletin of the World Health Organization* 85:681–87.
———. 2009. Measuring health inequality with realization of potential life years (RePLY). *Health Economics* 18 (suppl. 1): S55–75.

Tappenden, P., R. Jones, S. Paisley, and C. Carroll. 2007. Systematic review and economic evaluation of bevacizumab and cetuximab for the treatment of metastatic colorectal cancer. *Health Technology Assessment* 11 (12): 1–128.

Teerawattananon, Y., M. Mugford, and V. Tangcharoensathien. 2007. Economic evaluation of palliative management versus peritoneal dialysis and hemodialysis for end-stage renal disease: Evidence for coverage decisions in Thailand. *Value in Health* 10 (1): 61–72.

Temkin, L. 1993. *Inequality*. Oxford: Oxford Univ. Press.

Terra.com. 2009. Sentencias de Sala Constitucional de Costa Rica serán transcritas a braille. http://noticias.terra.com/articulos/act1634911/Sentencias_de_Sala_Constitucional_de_Costa_Rica_seran_transcritas_a_braille.

Terreblanche, S. 2002. *A history of inequality in South Africa, 1652–2000*. Pietermaritzburg: Univ. of Natal Press.

Thayer, J. 1908. The origin and scope of the American doctrine of constitutional law. In *Legal essays*, J. Thayer, 1–41. Boston: The Boston Book Company.

Thomas, G., and S. Krishnan. 2010. Effective public-private partnership in healthcare: Apollo as a cautionary tale. *Indian Journal of Medical Ethics* 7 (1): 2–4. http://www.issuesinmedicalethics.org/181ed2.html.

Tinoco-Mora, Z. 2005. Selección de medicamentos en la CCSS comité central de Farmacoterapia. *Fármacos* 18:1–2.

Toebes, B. 1999. *The right to health as a human right in international law*. Antwerp: Intersentia.

Torres, R. 2004. *Mitos y realidades de las obras sociales*. Buenos Aires: Isalud.

Treatment Action Campaign. 2003. Competition agreements secure access to life-saving affordable medicines. http://www.tac.org.za/newsletter/2003/ns10_12_2003.htm.

Treatment Action Campaign and AIDS Law Project. 2003. TAC/ALP Fact Sheet: Settlement agreements reached in Hazel Tau and Others v. Glaxosmithkline (GSK) and Boehringer Ingelheim (BI). *TAC Newsletter*, December 10. http://www.tac.org.za/newsletter/2003/ns10_12_2003.htm.

The Tribune. 2009. Apollo Hospital gets notice for charging money from the poor. November 29. http://www.tribuneindia.com/2009/20091130/delhi.htm#8.

Tushnet, M. 2008a. The rights revolution in the twentieth century. In *The Cambridge history of law in America*, vol. 3, ed. M. Grossberg and C. Tomlins, 377–402. Cambridge: Cambridge Univ. Press.

———. 2008b. *Weak courts, strong rights: Judicial review and social welfare rights in comparative constitutional law*. Princeton: Princeton Univ. Press.

UNAIDS. 2006. *Report on the global AIDS epidemic*. Geneva: UNAIDS.

———. 2008. Technical guidance for Round 8 Global Fund HIV Proposals. Working document, April 2. http://www.who.int/hiv/pub/toolkits/Stigma%20reduction.pdf

Undurraga, V., and R. Cook. 2009. Constitutional incorporation of international and comparative human rights law: The Colombian Constitutional

Court decision C-355/2006. In *Constituting equality: Gender equality and comparative constitutional law*, ed. S. H. Williams, 215–47. New York: Cambridge Univ. Press.

United Nations Children's Fund. 2006. *Progress for children: A report card on nutrition.* New York: UNICEF.

———. 2008a. The state of the world's children 2008. http://www.unicef.org/sowc08/statistics/tables.php.

———. 2008b. Statistics for India. http://www.unicef.org/infobycountry/india_statistics.html.

United Nations Development Programme. 2003. *Informe sobre desarrollo humano: Los objetivos de desarrollo del milenio; Un pacto entre las naciones para eliminar la pobreza.* New York: UNDP.

———. 2009. *Human development report 2009.* New York: UNDP.

Uprimny, R., and M. García Villegas. 2006. The Constitutional Court and social emancipation in Colombia. In *Democratizing democracy: Beyond the liberal democratic canon*, ed. B. de Sousa Santos, 66–100. London: Verso.

Uprimny, R., and D. Rodríguez Franco. 2008. Aciertos e insuficiencias de la Sentencia T-760 de 2008: Implicaciones para el derecho a la salud en Colombia. *Observatorio de la Seguridad Social* 7 (18): 12–16.

Uvin, P. 2004. *Human rights and development.* Bloomfield, CT: Kumarian Press.

Van Bueren, G. 2005. Health. In *South African constitutional law: The Bill of Rights*, ed. M. Cheadle, D. Davis, and N. Haysom, 22:1–18. 2nd ed. Durban: LexisNexis Butterworths.

Vanhala, Z. 2006. Fighting discrimination through litigation in the UK: The social model of disability and the EU anti-discrimination directive. *Disability and Society* 21 (5): 551–65.

Vapattanawong, P., M. C. Hogan, P. Hanvoravongchai, et al. 2007. Reductions in child mortality levels and inequalities in Thailand: Analysis of two censuses. *The Lancet* 369 (9564): 850–55.

Vargas López, K. 2007. El derecho a la protección de la salud en el sistema de salud público costarricense—el caso de los medicamentos. Tesis por licenciada en derecho, Univ. Costa Rica.

Vernick, J. S., L. Rutkow, and S. P. Teret. 2007. Public health benefits of recent litigation against the tobacco industry. *Journal of the American Medical Association* 298:88–89.

Vieira, F. S. 2008. Right to health litigation: A discussion on the observance of the principles of Brazil's health system. *Revista de Saúde Pública* 42 (2): 1–5.

Vieira, F. S., and P. Zucchi. 2007. Distorções causadas pelas ações judiciais à política de medicamentos no Brasil [Distortions to national drug policy caused by lawsuits in Brazil]. *Revista de Saúde Pública* 41 (2): 214–22.

Vile, M. J. C. 1967. *Constitutionalism and the separation of powers.* Oxford: Clarendon Press.

———. 1991. The separation of powers. In *The Blackwell encyclopedia of the American Revolution*, ed. J. Greene and J. R. Pole, 676–81. Cambridge, MA: Basil Blackwell.

Waldron, J. 1994. Vagueness in law and language: Some philosophical issues. *California Law Review* 82 (3): 509–40.

———. 2002. Is the rule of law an essentially contested concept? *Law and Philosophy* 21:137–64.

———. 2009. Refining the question about judges' moral capacity. *International Journal of Constitutional Law* 7: 69–82.

WHO/UNAIDS/UNICEF. 2007. *Towards universal access: Scaling up priority HIV/AIDS interventions in the health sector; Progress report, April 2007*. Geneva: WHO/UNAIDS/UNICEF.

Williams, A. 1988. Ethics and efficiency in the provision of health care. In *Philosophy and Medical Welfare*, ed. M. Bell and S. Mendus, 111–26. Cambridge: Cambridge Univ. Press.

———. 1996. QALYS and ethics: A health economist's perspective. *Social Science & Medicine* 43 (12): 1795–1804.

———. 1997. Intergenerational equity: An exploration of the "fair innings" argument. *Health Economics* 6 (2): 117–32.

Wilson, B. M. 1998. *Costa Rica: Politics, economics, and democracy*. Boulder, CO: Lynne Rienner.

———. 2005. Changing dynamics: The political impact of Costa Rica's Constitutional Court. In *The judicialization of politics in Latin America*, ed. R. Sieder, L. Schjolden, and A. Angell, 47–66 . London: ISA/Palgrave Macmillan.

———. 2007. Claiming individual rights through a Constitutional Court: The example of gays in Costa Rica. *International Journal of Constitutional Law* 5 (2): 242–57.

———. 2009. Rights revolutions in unlikely places: Costa Rica and Colombia. *Journal of Politics in Latin America* 1 (2): 59–85.

———. 2010. Enforcing rights and exercising an accountability function: Costa Rica's Constitutional Court. In *Courts in Latin America*, ed. G. Helmke and J. Rios-Figueroa, 55–80. New York: Cambridge Univ. Press.

Wilson, B. M., and O. F. Norheim. Forthcoming. Impact on health outcomes of litigation for medicines in Costa Rica. Draft on file with the author.

Wilson, B. M., and J. C. Rodríguez Cordero. 2006. Legal opportunity structures and social movements: The effects of institutional change on Costa Rican politics. *Comparative Political Studies* 39 (3): 325–51.

Wirth, M., E. Sacks, E. Delamonica, A. Storeygard, A. Minujin, and D. Balk. 2008. "Delivering" on the MDGs? Equity and maternal health in Ghana, Ethiopia and Kenya. *East African Journal of Public Health* 5 (3): 133–41.

Wolfson, M., and G. Rowe. 2001. On measuring inequalities in health. *Bulletin of the World Health Organization* 79:553–60.

World Bank. 2008. New data show 1.4 billion live on less than $1.25 a day, but progress against poverty remains strong. Press release, World Bank. Washington, DC. http://go.worldbank.org/DQKD6WV4T0.

———. 2009. World development indicators. http://data.worldbank.org/indicator.

———. 2010. *World development report: Development and climate change.* Washington, DC: World Bank.

World Health Organization. 2000. *The world health report 2000: Health systems; Improving performance.* Geneva: WHO.

———. 2007. *Maternal Mortality in 2005: Estimates developed by WHO, UNICEF, UNFPA and The World Bank.* Geneva: WHO. http://www.who.int/whosis/mme_2005.pdf.

———. 2008. WHO life tables for member states. http://www.who.int/healthinfo/statistics/mortality_life_tables/en.

———. 2009a. *Report of the WHO Commission on Social Determinants of Health.* Geneva: WHO.

———. 2009b. *The world health report 2009.* Geneva: WHO.

———. 2009c. *World health statistics 2009.* Geneva: WHO.

———. 2010a. National health accounts. http://www.who.int/nha/country/en/index.html.

———. 2010b. National health accounts report for India. March. http://www.who.int/nha/country/ind.pdf.

———. 2010c. Structural adjustment programmes. http://www.who.int/trade/glossary/story084/en/index.html.

World Trade Organization. 1994. Annex 1C: Agreement on trade-related aspects of intellectual property rights. The Uruguay Round Agreements. Marrakesh, April 15. http://www.wto.org/english/docs_e/legal_e/legal_e.htm.

Yamin, A. E. 2000. Protecting and promoting the right to health in Latin America: Selected experiences from the field. *Health and Human Rights: An International Journal* 5 (1): 116–48.

———. 2008. Will we take suffering seriously? Reflections on what applying a human rights framework to health means and why we should care. *Health and Human Rights: An International Journal* 10 (1): 45–63.

———. 2009. Suffering and powerlessness. *Health and Human Rights: An International Journal* 11 (1): 5–22.

———. 2010. Toward transformative accountability: A proposal for rights-based approaches to fulfilling maternal health obligations. *Sur: International Journal on Human Rights* 7 (12): 95–122.

Yamin, A. E., and O. F. Norheim. Forthcoming. Taking equality seriously: Applying human rights frameworks to priority setting in health. In *Equality and socio-economic rights in international law and perspective*, ed. M. Langford. Cambridge: Cambridge Univ. Press.

Yamin, A. E., and O. Parra-Vera. 2009. How do courts set health policy? The case of the Colombian Constitutional Court. *PLoS Medicine* 6 (2): e1000032.

———. 2010. Judicial protection of the right to health in Colombia: From social demands to individual claims to public debates. *Hastings International and Comparative Law Review* 33 (2): 101–29.

Ybarra, G. 2008. El Congreso aprobó la ley de obesidad. *La Nación*, August 14. http://www.lanacion.com.ar/nota.asp?nota_id=1039518.

Zamora Zamora, C. 2007. Los recursos de amparo y recursos de inconstitucionalidad contra la Caja Costarricense de Seguro Social de 1989 a 2005. *Gaceta Médica de Costa Rica* 9 (2): 130–34.

Contributors

Paola Bergallo is a professor at the Universidad de San Andrés in Buenos Aires. She has also taught law at the Universidad de Palermo and Universidad de Buenos Aires. She has worked as a researcher and consultant for the Centro de Estudios de Estado y Sociedad, Center for Reproductive Rights, United Nations Population Fund, and Pan American Health Organization on projects relating to gender and law, women, human rights, and sexual and reproductive rights. Bergallo is a founding member of *Red Alas*, a Latin American network of law professors. She holds an LLB from the Universidad de Buenos Aires, an LLM from Columbia University, and an MLS from Stanford University, where she is currently an SJD candidate.

Carole Cooper is an advocate at the Johannesburg Bar in South Africa. Until recently, she was an associate professor of law at the Centre for Applied Legal Studies, a human rights research and litigation body, where she served periods as both acting director and deputy director. She has written extensively on equality and discrimination issues and was one of the authors of *Bench Book for Equality Courts in South Africa.* Cooper was also part of the legal team that drafted South Africa's new Labour Relations Act. She was the recipient of a British Council Fellowship, which she fulfilled at the University of Warwick. She holds postgraduate degrees from the University of Sussex and the School of Oriental and African Studies at London University.

Octavio L. Motta Ferraz is an assistant professor at the University of Warwick School of Law. He has served as a senior research officer to the United Nations Special Rapporteur on the Right to Health and has published several articles and a book in the field of health law and human rights. He contributes regularly to Brazil's main daily newspaper, *Folha de S. Paulo*. Ferraz holds an LLB and MPhil from the University of São Paulo; an MA from King's College in London, where he was the recipient of the Benjamin Geijsen prize; and a PhD from University College in London, where he was awarded a Graduate Research Scholarship.

Roberto Gargarella is a senior researcher at the Chr. Michelsen Institute and a researcher at Argentina's National Scientific and Technical Research Council (CONICET). During the first semester of 2010, he was a visiting scholar at Harvard University. Gargarella has written or edited over twenty books published in Argentina, Colombia, Spain, the United States, and the United Kingdom. His latest book is *The Legal Foundations of Inequality: Constitutionalism in the Americas, 1776–1860.* He holds degrees in law and sociology from the University of Buenos Aires and a JD and LLM from the University of Chicago. He pursued post-doctoral studies at the University of Oxford.

Camila Gianella is a PhD candidate at the University of Bergen and fellow at the Chr. Michelsen Institute. She has worked as researcher and consultant for projects on maternal mortality, sexual and reproductive rights, the right to health, HIV/AIDS, tuberculosis, and mental health and transitional justice. She holds a degree in psychology from the Pontifical University of Peru, as well as an MS from the Institute of Tropical Medicine and International Health at Charité Medical School in Berlin.

Siri Gloppen is a professor of comparative politics at the University of Bergen, research director at the Chr. Michelsen Institute (CMI), and a former visiting fellow at Harvard Law School. She established CMI's "Courts in Transition" research program, which for the past decade has investigated courts' role in new and fragile democracies. Gloppen heads the comparative research project "Right to Health through Litigation? Can Court-Enforced Health Rights Improve Health Policy?," which forms the basis of the present volume. Her publications span legal mobilization and courts' role in social transformation, constitution making and constitutionalism, democratization, judicial independence and courts' accountability function, courts and elections, and transitional justice and reconciliation. Her primary empirical focus is on Southern and East Africa.

Ottar Mæstad is an economist currently serving as director of the Chr. Michelsen Institute (CMI). He also runs CMI's research program on global health and development. His research interests include health systems and health policy, with a particular emphasis on human resources for health, governance in the health sector, health and economic development, and the economics and ethics of priority setting in health. He has also worked extensively on issues related to climate policy, energy, and international trade and development.

Ole Frithjof Norheim is a professor of medical ethics in the Department of Public Health at the University of Bergen and a physician in the Department of Internal Medicine at Haukeland University Hospital. He led the research project "The Ethics of Priority Setting in Global Health (2005–2010)," sponsored by a Young Investigators Award from the Norwegian Research Council. From 2006 to 2008, Norheim was chair of the board of the International Society on Priorities in Health Care. His main research interests include theories of distributive justice, fair priority setting in global health, and the measurement of inequality.

Sharanjeet Parmar is an international human rights lawyer with twelve years' experience working on transitional justice, the rights of women and children, and public interest litigation in Africa and India. She currently heads the International Center for Transitional Justice's office in the Democratic Republic of Congo. Prior to that, she taught at Harvard Law School's Human Rights Program, where her work included litigation support to ensuring access to affordable treatment under the right to health in India. Parmar has served as a prosecuting war-crimes attorney with the Special Court for Sierra Leone, director of the Access to Justice Program for Global Rights, and a human rights lawyer with the Lawyers Collective.

Oscar Parra-Vera is a senior staff attorney at the Inter-American Court of Human Rights. Prior to joining the Court, he was a Rómulo Gallegos Fellow and consultant for indicators on social rights at the Inter-American Commission on Human Rights. He has served as a researcher at the Ombudsman's Office of Colombia and the Colombian Commission of Jurists. Parra-Vera has also served as a clerk for the Constitutional Court of Colombia and as a consultant for the Inter-American Institute of Human Rights and the University of Chile's Center for Human Rights. He holds an LLB and LLM from the National University of Colombia.

Lise Rakner is department head and professor of comparative politics at the University of Bergen and a senior researcher at the Chr. Michelsen Institute. Her research focuses on democratization and human rights, economic reform, taxation, institutional change, and international aid. Empirically, her work has primarily centered on Africa. She has published articles on democratic development, economic reform, and party systems in various international journals, including *Development and Change*, *Comparative Political Studies*, *International Political Science Review*, *Party Politics*, *Democratization*, and *Journal of Modern African Studies*.

Mindy Jane Roseman is the academic director of the Human Rights Program, and a lecturer on law, at Harvard Law School. Before joining the Human Rights Program, she was an instructor in the Department of Global Health and Population at the Harvard School of Public Health and a senior research officer at the François-Xavier Bagnoud Center for Health and Human Rights, also part of the Harvard School of Public Health. She also served as a staff attorney at the Center for Reproductive Rights, where she directed its program on Central and Eastern Europe. Roseman holds a doctorate in modern European history, with a focus on the history of reproductive health, from Columbia University.

Namita Wahi is an SJD candidate at Harvard Law School. Her current research is on the right to property and economic development in India. Previously, she worked at Davis Polk & Wardwell in New York, where she litigated commercial law and public interest asylum and criminal defense cases. Wahi has worked extensively with public interest organizations in India, including PRS Legislative Research and the Fisheries Management Resource Centre. She clerked with Justice R. C. Lahoti, former Chief Justice of the Supreme Court of India. She holds an LLM from Harvard Law School and BA and LLB (Hons) degrees from the National Law School of India University, Bangalore.

Bruce M. Wilson is professor of political science at the University of Central Florida and associated senior researcher at the Chr. Michelsen Institute. He has published numerous journal articles on Latin American politics and the role and impact of superior courts. His books include *Costa Rica: Politics, Economics, and Democracy* (1998) and *Courts and Power in Latin America and Africa* (co-authored, 2010). He has also published widely on the Scholarship of Teaching and Learning. He holds a PhD from Washington University.

Alicia Ely Yamin is director of the Program on the Health Rights of Women and Children at the François-Xavier Bagnoud Center for Health and Human Rights at the Harvard School of Public Health, as well as adjunct lecturer on health policy and management at the School. She is also an associated senior researcher at the Chr. Michelsen Institute. From 2007 to 2011, Yamin was the Joseph H. Flom Fellow on Global Health and Human Rights at Harvard Law School. Prior to that, she served as director of research and investigations at Physicians for Human Rights. For twenty years, Yamin has conducted human rights documentation and advocacy with international and local organizations. She has published dozens of scholarly articles and several books relating to health and human rights. Yamin holds degrees from Harvard College, Harvard Law School, and the Harvard School of Public Health.

Index

Page numbers in italics refer to figures and tables.

Index of Cases and Laws

Page numbers in italics refer to figures and tables.